THE LEGEND HUNTER

Historical novels by Romain Wilhelmsen

Buckskin and Satin
The Curse of Destiny

THE LEGEND HUNTER

ONE MAN IN HIS TIME, A MEMOIR

Romain Wilhelmsen

SUNSTONE
PRESS

SANTA FE

Cover photograph by Powell of Pasadena

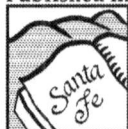

Sunstone books may be purchased for educational, business, or sales promotional use. For information please write: Special Markets Department, Sunstone Press, P.O. Box 2321, Santa Fe, New Mexico 87504-2321.

Library of Congress Cataloging-in-Publication Data:

Wilhelmsen, Romain, 1924–
    The legend hunter: one man in his time, a memoir / Romain Wilhelmsen.—1st ed.
        p. cm.
    ISBN: 0-86534-363-2 (hardcover)   —ISBN: 0-86534-364-0 (pbk)
        1. Wilhelmsen, Romain, 1924– 2. Novelists, American—20th century—Biography.
    3. Motion picture producers and directors—United States—Biography. 4. Adventure and
    adventurers—United States—Biography. I. Title.

PS3573 .I4345Z468 2003
813' .54—dc21   2003042517

Published in   SUNSTONE PRESS
                    Post Office Box 2321
                    Santa Fe, NM 87504-2321 / USA
                    (505) 988-4418 / *orders only* (800) 243-5644
                    FAX (505) 988-1025
                    www.sunstonepress.com

PROLOGUE

"Up there," Santiago pointed as he cantered his mule alongside of my horse. "Up there on the rim of the mesa. You can see it. Those aren't outcroppings. They are walls. Big ones."

He handed me his powerful binoculars. I focused in on the large plateau that rose majestically out of the scrubby vegetation of these high Peruvian Andes Mountains. The sight that filled the eyepiece startled me. I brushed the grit from my eyes and stared at a row of ramparts that jutted upward from the ridge. I could make out doorways, apertures, staircases, and passageways. They were obviously old, very old. We had located the lost pre-Inca city of Huasachga.

✧✧✧

I could see that the revolver he was pointing at me was not of large caliber. Nevertheless, I remembered what Jack Bryan had told me about handguns: "Don't matter how small a gun is; it can do to your body terrible things."

It seemed all of a sudden that all had become quiet. Only the chirping and cawing of birds broke the silence in this little grove of trees in the Cordillera Central highlands of Colombia.

The bandit had already hurt me, badly I thought, and I was angry. No more, I reasoned; he'll probably kill me anyway. "*Miré*," one of the men called out in Spanish as he laid his shotgun down and waved my passport with the 400 United States dollars clipped to it. "Look here." The man with the revolver turned, and I fumbled for the .380 Baretta automatic that was hidden in a holster in the small of my back.

"There she is," brother Fritz excitedly pointed his hand toward the little Pacific Ocean port of Salaverry, Peru. "The last commercially operated square-rigged sailing ship in the world. She's been following the wind for nigh onto a century. Let's get aboard."

I had never really realized how large one of those 19th century tall ships could be. This one was over 300 feet long, and its four masts reached way up into the sky. She was a barque: three masts were hung with square sails, the mizzen was fore-and-aft. She was big all right. Her cargo consisted of tons of bird droppings. We would be enjoying that cargo for the next two months . . . to say nothing of a mutiny.

Sergio set his shovel aside and pulled the Coleman lantern closer to his dig. He needed the extra light because it was very dark in this cave in Mexico's northern Sierra Madre Mountains. Our archaeological technique was on a par with two toddlers playing in a sandbox. He grasped the object in front of him and gave a mighty tug. It broke loose from the detritus of this hole in the mountains and rolled over at his feet. The dust settled and we both stared down upon an iron breastplate. There was a helmet next to it. These and other objects that we had suddenly exposed to the mid-20th century had been carried here by a group of Spanish conquistadors over 400 years ago.

A moment before my lecture was about to begin, the house lights of the Racine Opera House were being dimmed. The curtain was still down. I rushed from the lavatory to the center of the stage which was dimly lit by a single work light. "Dan," I called to my friend, "my zipper is stuck and I can't get it up." He joined me in center stage where I stood in my full tuxedo with a patch of white underpants peeking out of the fly. He arranged his reading glasses and took a look. "Just a minute," he said as he knelt down on the floor in front of me and gazed intently at the obstreperous talon. "Here's the problem," he exalted as he stuck his hand through the fly and grabbed on.

The Racine Opera House was a union house, and when the curtain man reads on his stage direction that 8:00 P.M. is "Curtain Time," up goes the curtain . . . no matter what.

The curtain went up, and the spotlights came on.

I have never been invited back to the Racine Opera House.

The man had to be in his late seventies. Yet he stood erect and had a look in his black eyes that would wither an honest man. I met him on the long bamboo porch of his compound along a tributary of the Napo River in the Amazon jungle of Peru. No matter where he walked on that veranda, he was always within reach of at least one 10-guage automatic shotgun. He took no chances. He was wanted for crimes that amounted to a holocaust forty years before World War II. The government of the United Kingdom had long ago signed a warrant for his arrest for unspeakable crimes against humanity. And the countries of Brazil, Peru, and Colombia still had his name on their dockets of unfinished business.

He extended his arm, and I took the hand of Miguel Loayza.

❖❖❖

I sat on a bench in a small smelly river launch. Alongside of me was a stunning Brazilian woman. All the more unique because she was a true blond in a land of brunettes. "There," she said in a mixture of Portuguese and Spanish. "There is your Fortaleza Principe de Beira. We must do this quickly before the Pacas Novas Indians know we are here." The young lady directed my gaze upward, and I made out the dark form of a wall. To me it seemed to rise to an abnormal height. It was made of smoothly dressed red blocks of stone. The neatness of the wall was broken by the barrel of a dark and fat cannon that protruded from it. All else was obscured by vines and vegetation that seemed to bind the place together.

❖❖❖

Ernesto cautiously lowered himself into the trench that we had dug into the mound. I stood above and watched from the top of the ancient man-made adobe pyramid in the Sechura Desert of northern Peru. Ernesto had protected his mouth and nose with a gauze mask. He needed it. A lot of dirt had been stirred up. The twenty-four human skulls that he had uncovered all grinned at one another from the ledges upon which they had been placed perhaps sixteen centuries before. Somewhere still below us in this ancient crypt the main burial site yet remained to be found. Undoubtedly a prince of the Mochica Empire was interred with all of his personal treasures and those of the twenty decapitated guardians above him. Ernesto handed up to me one of the many little clay pots that shared the shelves with the skulls. The jar was heavy, surprisingly so. Along with sand, I could see yellow, gold. It contained gold. Earrings, bracelets, beads, and other treasure.

❖❖❖

"Will you do it for your country? For the security of the United States?" Mr. Olds looked intently into my eyes. "Will you work for the CIA?"

I answered him, "Yes."

✧✧✧

We stared speechless into the little dugout canoe. I looked down at the severed head of our motorist and companion. His eyes were half open. The head rolled from side to side in a slosh of blood at the bottom of the canoe. Ferdie seemed to be looking up at me, pleading. Dumped into the little dugout with his head were his arms and legs. The torso was missing. The butchery had taken place not long before, perhaps this morning before sunrise. Jim became violently sick. Hermann Becker checked the loads in his shotgun.

✧✧✧

National Geographic Society
Washington D.C.

Dear Mr. Wilhelmsen:

I find it hard to believe that in this day and age one can stroll out into the desert of South America and uncover the remains of a city and burial site that we of the *National Geographic Society* and others know nothing of. Nor do I believe that there is such a prehistoric city such as you claim you found 12,000 feet up in the Andes Mountains of Peru. You are probably referring to the pre-Inca city of Huamachuga that we here at the Society are quite familiar with...

Signed,
Andrew H. Brown

Wrong, Mr. Brown, dead wrong. Thirty years after you dictated the above, your *Society* went to work on the first discovered mound at Sipan in northern Peru.

There are still such things out there in Peru and Mexico and Africa that have yet to be discovered.

I want to tell you about them.

Come along with me for a look-see.

8

1 — I BEGIN

Hermann Becker checked the loads of his automatic shotgun. He crouched as low as he could behind the gunwale of our thirty-foot Monteira. "Mr. Wilhelmsen, Mr. Andersen," he whispered as he motioned palm down for us to remain back and beneath the thatched shelter of the little river launch. "Do not be afraid to shoot," he cautioned in his very German accented English. "They will kill you on sight if they get close enough." He peered intensely at the nearly impenetrable green wall of jungle that flanked us on either side of the Yavari River. The long barreled .38 caliber revolver in my hand felt insignificant as I cocked it. Again I looked toward my friend, even more so than the unseen menace in the Amazon jungle all around us. I had confidence in him, and I knew that he had faced other such dangerous situations in his very colorful and adventurous career.

Indeed Hermann Becker had come a long way from the French Livarot-Vimoutres Road where on July 15, 1944, he had rushed to his fallen commander's side and eased him out of the smoking and bullet-ridden *Mercedes*. As one of the several drivers for the legendary Field Marshal Erwin Rommel, he had experienced events that made history in the modern world of World War II. Now, not fifteen years later, he faced an implausible, but quite real, stone-age war on the borders of Peru and Brazil.

I dared look again at the little dugout canoe that bobbed up and down loosely tied to our launch. The motorist was there. His severed head rolled from side to side in a pool of blood at the bottom of the canoe. His eyes were half open, and he seemed to be looking at me, pleading. His dismembered arms and legs rocked about as the flat-bottom boat dipped and swayed with the current, and occasionally they struck his face. The torso was missing. The butchery had just taken place, perhaps this morning before sunrise. Blood still oozed from the detached head and limbs.

Three times Hermann fired his scattergun into the foliage on our left. He was answered by the howls of the monkeys, the peep-peeps of the coatis, and the caw-caws of toucan birds. And then the jungle became silent again.

"Scheisse," Hermann hissed. "Ya, they know we are here now and that we are ready for them, that we are armed." He slid three shells into the smoking shotgun.

Jim Andersen called out, and his voice seemed unnaturally loud, "Do you hear it? Up there behind us." He pointed to the part of the blue sky that we could see between the canopy of forest that surrounded us. There was a foreign noise for this place: the "thump, thump, thump," of a helicopter as it swung fairly low over the tree tops and followed the flow of the Yavari River.

All of us ignored the immediate threat of the Indians. We stood up in our boats and waved. I'm sure that every living creature within sound of that ugly metal bird was doing as we were, looking up at this modern marvel as it dipped and swayed south of us, came down for a closer look, and then pounded on north towards the city of Iquitos on the Amazon.

We had plenty of time to read the markings on the fuselage: "U. S. Marines." And we could see plainly the men who were in it and the two men who were stretched out on the skids. They waved to us and were gone.

Andersen let fly an expletive. "You'd at least think they'd come down and speak with us . . . better yet, pull us out of here. Who knows . . . "

Becker broke in. "No. No, Mr. Andersen. Those American airmen are flying out the wounded. They have been called in from the Lima American Legation. They cannot stop to pick up a bunch of tropical tramps who shouldn't be here. Those men have been hurt. At least we can still maneuver. I told you I would get you out of here, and I will. And we cannot leave this man" —he indicated the remains in the dugout—to the creatures of the forest." He added, "Besides, I am responsible for this launch. It belongs to the Iquitos Board of Education, and I've got to return it." He brushed past Jim and me, settled down beside the ancient Achemides outboard engine, and pulled the throttle up to a dangerous r.p.m. The vessel shuttered and surged ahead.

Way up in the sky, we made out the silhouettes of two B-26 planes. They bore the colors of the Peruvian Air Force, and they were heading south to where the helicopter had just come. "They are going to bomb the Indians and keep them back until all of the soldiers and engineers can be brought out." Hermann spoke with expertise of a professional soldier. "I believe the Mayarunas might think twice now of coming after us. If this motor holds together another hour, we should be out of their territory."

As he spoke this, he suddenly spotted a slender ten-inch shaft quivering in one of the wooden posts that held up the thatched roof. It was a foot from Jim's shoulder. "Mr. Andersen," he shouted, "was this here a little while ago?"

Jim shook his head in disbelief. He had no answer.

The German pulled it out and sniffed the dark stain that covered two inches of the point. "That's poison, Mr. Andersen," he shouted above the noise of the outboard, "fresh poison."

"Curare?" I spoke up.

"Not at all," he answered. "Probably much stronger. They don't shoot curare darts at people. This is something stronger." We drove on in silence.

An exploratory group of thirty civilian engineers and eight Army engineers had been pinned down by an estimated five hundred Mayaruna Indians. The engineers had been scouting out the possibility of building a road that would connect the large Peruvian city of Iquitos to the small Army post of Requena some one hundred miles to the south.

A press release from the *Los Angeles Times* pretty well told the story.

> ". . . The forest where thirty civilians and eight Army engineers were besieged last week was in the farthest inland reaches of the Amazon jungle in northeastern Peru . . . the engineers had gone into the rain forest area five weeks ago to survey for a 75-mile road to be built from the Peruvian city of Requena to the Brazilian border. They came upon an Indian camp. The Indians attacked with poisoned arrows and rifles, killing one and wounding two. The survey party radioed for help. Peruvian Air Force planes strafed the thick jungle around the hill, fired rockets, dropped bombs and napalm. But the Indians continued to attack. The Indians were believed to be Mayarunas, whom Lima officials described as "wild, naked savages still living in the Stone Age." A gunboat was dispatched down the Yavari River from Iquitos."

My two companions, a motorist, and I had come to this area by pure chance. We had motored down the Amazon and up the Yavari from Iquitos with the intention of locating the primitive, but friendly, Cocomas Indians, and filming their lifestyle for United States television. Our Peruvian motorist had taken our small dugout canoe and had gone ahead hoping to contact the Indians and to alert them that we would be arriving in the larger launch. He did not want the riverboat with its loud engine to frighten them. Ferdie failed to return, but the next morning we spotted the little canoe hung up in river vegetation. The young man had not met up with the Cocomas; instead, the deadly Mayarunas had pounced upon him.

Now it was our sad duty to take him back to his mother, and Hermann Becker would give her his forty dollars in wages.

I wondered at the tragedy of this adventure: the loss of a good man's life for a few moments of entertainment on television. I know that Jim Andersen cried, after first becoming violently sick at seeing the remains of the man we only knew by the name of Ferdinand or 'Ferdie.' Becker, on the other hand, had kept his deep emotions hidden beneath his

German logic and stoicism. After all, he had known the motorist before and had arranged for his hire. I could only think of how this all had come about, and how four men were on this lonely river so far away from Pasadena, California.

❖❖❖

In 1938 *Harper Brothers* published a 415-page book, *Enchanted Vagabonds*. The book was filled with photos of a 16,001-mile kayak trip from San Diego, California, to the Panama Canal. The adventure included the Pacific West Coast of Mexico, continued along Central America's tropical beaches, and had a side trip to remote Cocos Treasure Island. Dana and Ginger Lamb had found their solution to the dreary Depression years, had lived off the land and sea, and had made publishing history doing it. The book went to eighteen editions.

When I was fifteen years old in Michigan, I first came across that book in the Grosse Pointe Public Library. The year was 1939, and I still treasure my copy of it. *Enchanted Vagabonds* became for me a symbol of faraway places, adventure, romance, of escape from the day-to-day drudge of Depression-life, and of the possibility of a vast golden treasure somewhere in an exotic land. I read that book several times while attending *St. Ambrose High School* in Detroit, *St. Joseph's College* in Indiana, and the *Pasadena Playhouse School of the Theatre* in California. I had the book in my bags during the 1945-46 theatrical season on Broadway. In Manhattan, I discovered that my heart was really not in the profession I had chosen and for a while I had studied, that of acting. The book of adventure in distant lands was still with me as a salesman working out of San Francisco and later in southern California. I added to my library other such narratives of travel and adventure. And eventually I met Dana and Ginger Lamb in Corona Del Mar, California, where they lived. We became and remained close friends until their death. We even traveled together on several strange adventures. Ours was a close but flawed friendship.

❖❖❖

Tramp steamers have one strike against them if appearances mean anything; this one seemed to have two. The *S. S. Karl Grammerstorf* was a hobo of the seas; she bummed around from port to port, from continent to continent, seeking a cargo. Any cargo. Often she was empty and rode high in the water. I had boarded her in New York City. Insurance and other laws had prohibited me from traveling as a passenger, so I had been signed on as a 2nd engineer. The cost: $150, New York to Barranquilla, Colombia. I was the only non-working man on the ship, and I was surrounded by a crew of Germans. Our cargo was a hold half full of empty fifty-gallon barrels destined for the oil fields of Colombia, South America.

The day was May 20, 1953, when a stubby little tug pushed us out of New York Harbor. We drifted by the Statue of Liberty, and it and home were soon lost in a wet fog. Behind me were friends and family, a theatrical career that had not gotten off the ground, a very sad attempt at business as a salesman, and a failed ten-month romance with a young lady who preferred the stage to my unsettled future (and who did eventually catch the Big Apple brass ring). All behind me now. Like the obsolete "Tramp," I was on my own. I was twenty-nine years old.

I carried with me a sheaf of notes loaded with all the information of fifteen years of study on the lost treasures and mysterious areas of South America. I was certainly old enough at that time to realize that reading about a fabled Inca treasure was quite different than finding one. So, in my large duffle bag I also carried a 16mm *Bell and Howell* movie camera with forty rolls of film with which to record, if not find, one or more of these treasures. The new boy on the block, television, was just then beginning to capture the imagination of the American public. A couple of theatrical friends had given me the know-how on the use of the camera and how to produce motion pictures that might be bought up by the networks. With me also was an open-end journal in which I hoped to describe all of these adventures (I am now referring to it as I write this narrative). The future looked promising, but eight hundred dollars in American Express checks did not seem like much to finance the dreams I carried with me.

My brother was to meet me in a couple of months down south in Lima, Peru. He had finagled a berth on an ancient square-rigged barque sailing the Pacific to the guano nitrate islands of Peru. The ship was seventy-five years old, and was probably the last commercially run tall ship of its kind still carrying cargo. I was encouraged about the possibilities of making a film of the ship. Another idea was to focus on southern Colombia. Deep in the Andean Cordillera Central highlands, a valley had been found containing scores of stone statues. Some were over twelve feet tall, and all of them displayed a savage and malevolent demonic face. They are a mystery because no remains of a civilization had been found nearby. Additionally, I might film Lake Guatavita, close to Bogotá, the source of the legend of El Dorado. Ecuador, too, had its mysteries, including the fabulous golden horde of the Inca Atahualpa that was hidden from the conquistadors deep in the almost impenetrable Llarangantis Mountains. And, finally, Peru was the country that historians claimed was nothing but one big treasure map.

The challenge was there. Although the voyage on the 'Tramp' only took a week, it nearly ended on the first day out. A great howl was heard all over the ship. I hastened from my cabin and saw the captain and his first mate shouting invectives and shaking their fists at another vessel that had nearly rammed us and had caused quite a scramble in the pilot-house. I clicked a photo of that ship as it disappeared behind a huge swell and then continued its lonely voyage through the otherwise totally empty sea. (I would have fun with that picture seven years later.)

The moment of danger brought the rather stiff German officers of the ship and me somewhat closer together. We loosened up at the dinner table where we all ate together. I listened to their sad tales of World War II. They had all served in the German Navy, and a couple of them had sailed in U-boats. I enjoyed them and I believe they enjoyed me.

I have mentioned that our ship had two strikes against her. The second strike was her tired engines. On the seventh day out, as we passed a mountain peak off Darien in the Gulf of Uraba, Colombia, one of the engines broke down. Looking back I am now surprised that this mishap hadn't occurred sooner. Those same pistons had been pumping up and down since before the war; there had never been enough money to replace them. However, my newfound German friends had experienced this inconvenience before, many times. Unruffled, they shut down all motors, disconnected several couplings, closed up three of the furnaces in the 'black gang' room, and restarted the rest. Indeed, the tramp was a lady; on half power, we chugged the final hours of our voyage with no more incidences. I spent the time leaning over the starboard bulkhead and gazing at the sight of the awesome green jungle that seemed to spill out into the Caribbean Sea. Closer and closer we came to land as the *Grammerstorf* maneuvered her way into the muddy ground swells of the Magdalena caused by that river's disgorging the product of over one thousand miles of flotsam and jetsam from the Andes Mountains and the cloud forests of tropical Colombia.

My adventures were about to begin. The anchors were let loose. They clattered down alongside the hull and splashed into water. The engines suddenly became silent except for the one motor that always—most always—was kept running. The throbbing ceased, and we now wallowed in the grand swells of one of the major rivers in the world. A pilot boat was awaiting us and a helmsman came aboard.

A quarter of a mile off the port bow the superstructure and bow of an ill-fated Swedish steamer protruded from the sea; a month before she had gone aground and sank when an over zealous pilot had attempted to dock her at night.

Now, that same pilot pulled out a cigarette and lounged nonchalantly against the compass while he awaited the whistle from below to complete his job. A couple miles away the derricks and wharves of Barranquilla broke the monotony of the intensely green shoreline.

I nervously walked by the German officers, who were busying themselves preparing for the Colombian bureaucratic customs charade, and went into my cabin. I locked the door and sat down. I surveyed my belongings. There was my huge duffle bag, a U. S. Army Air Corps B-4 suit bag and the small cache of American Express checks. I tucked those into my money belt. I had one other possession besides my camera gear. I touched it with my fingers and then returned it to its proper holster that was securely taped to my left inner thigh beneath my trousers. The weapon was an eight-inch long barreled automatic German *Luger* pistol—well-oiled, fully loaded, big, heavy, and terribly illegal.

The bosun blew his whistle. The pistons began to thump. The scenery through my porthole changed as we moved. A light breeze stirred the air, and we were on our way again. I left my cabin and walked on deck.

The port of Barranquilla is situated several miles up the Magdalena River. As a result, ships must make their way past an enormously long man-made mole that juts out into the Caribbean. Then, after an hour or so, the heavy ocean-going steamers find themselves along side dugout canoes, rafts, floating vegetation, barges, perhaps a Colombian gunboat, and even more unusual, a breed of picturesque river boats. They were extinct on the American scene. Even in Colombia, these vessels were dinosaurs in 1953. They were everywhere, gallant old floating palaces. Many had actually seen service on the Mississippi in the gambling trade of the nineteenth century. These paddleboats had been condemned years ago in the States and were now earning their keep on the Magdalena River. Some had three and even four decks piled upon each other like the balconies of a Virginia mansion. They had beautifully carved railings and banisters and curved staircases. Completing the Mark Twain-look, each boat had two slender smokestacks sticking up into the sky from either side of the pilothouse. Flags fluttered from the bows and in the stern huge round paddles did their best to propel these relics of a bygone era through the current of the stream.

The warm and friendly personality of these ships was contrasted by the concrete wharves and docks of Barranquilla that now emerged with all the cold impersonal detachment of the industrial age. Corrugated sheds and cement warehouses lined up along the waterfront and immediately replaced the intense green brush of a moment ago. The lazy tropical tableau of the last century was replaced by the nervous activity of the present.

The *Grammerstorf* lost momentum and slowly drifted to a standstill. With a sure hand, belying the Swedish wreck down stream, the Colombian pilot maneuvered the freighter so that all forward motion ceased and she gently thumped against the wooden wharf and reclined there, held fast by the current of the river.

Ropes were flung ashore and caught. Shouts and cries went up and down the length of the ship. A whistle blew somewhere. A group of officials dressed in immaculately white suits emerged from a shed. Several heavily armed soldiers marched up and took their positions by the ship. Our wooden walkway was lowered and clattered down upon Colombian soil.

I had arrived in South America. The first sight to greet me in Colombia was a four-foot rattlesnake. This unfortunate reptile had come down stream with the tide inside a rotten log. When the log stopped and was hauled upon the pier to be used as firewood in a boiler engine, the snake naturally came out. He seemed to receive the same treatment I was soon to get that day. As he timidly stuck his head out into the tropical sun of Barranquilla—much as I was then doing from my cabin door—he was confronted by some twenty-odd individuals ranging from stevedore to official. Each had plans for this unannounced intruder. One was for throwing him into the river to see if he could swim, another was for stuffing him into a porthole of the *Grammerstorf*, and then I understand there was talk of putting him in the drawer of the desk of the port authority. But in the end he was hacked to pieces by a razor-sharp machete.

Although this little drama had all taken place in only a few minutes, I had gathered a certain affinity for that snake and was sorry to see him go. True, this is the fate of all such reptiles, but I had more or less identified my situation with this uninvited guest. Both of us had arrived at this port at the same time, and I'm sure the snake didn't like the place any more than I did.

My captain hustled by and cautioned me not to go ashore until my papers had cleared. He was loaded down with bottles of French cognac and cartons of American cigarettes. These were to be distributed to the many officials, their brothers, their passing friends, and I'm sure a few interlopers now swarming over the *Grammerstorf*. I had been given to understand by the German skipper that such is the proper procedure in all Latin American ports. Especially in the case of a tramp steamer. Cognac, cigarettes, cigars, seals, and stamps go hand-in-hand in these ports, and the European master plunged into the confused ritual of Latin America Customs that sometimes is referred to as "legal banditry."

I went into the main salon and presented my passport and visa to the gentleman who seemed to be in charge of the white-dressed group of officials. There were a dozen of them seated about a large round table. All were perspiring profusely from liquor and the humidity. None, it seemed, was content with the quantities given him, but each official also wanted to show the captain his appreciation for his cognac by savoring his private stock.

My papers went the rounds, each man reading all the fine print. Finally, a rather obese fellow produced a rubber stamp and went about the official business of allowing me entrance into his country. The whole procedure was held up momentarily when his portable inkpad was found to be dry. This problem was quickly rectified by pouring the contents of the captain's ink well into it. As a result, my passport and my visa took on the look of a blotter. This condition wasn't helped any by the demand of all present to sign what became an imposing document.

I was then told to sit down and take careful heed. "The Magdalena River," the big fellow began in fast lusty Spanish, "is in a state of martial law." He spoke for about five minutes unimpressed with the fact that I couldn't understand a word he was saying. When he had finished, the German skipper, his first mate, and I got our heads together and translated the conversation. We were aided by a tall good-looking Colombian in a well-pressed white suit. We arrived at the following conclusion: There was then, May of 1953, a civil war being waged in the hinterlands and backwoods of Colombia. This conflict, though receiving little publicity in other countries, was, nevertheless, quite a nasty and deadly one. The revolutionists, "in reality bandits" as the fat man called them, were attempting to strangle shipping on the Magdalena River, which is the overland lifeline of the country. This violent struggle was the reason paddleboats could be seen idle at the docks of Barranquilla. The result of all this parlay was: If I cared to reach the capital Bogotá, I would have to do so by airplane.

Having delivered his imposing speech, the gentleman put the finishing touches to his ambitious signature and returned my papers to me. It was understood, of course, that I must in no circumstances attempt the trip upstream. Since I was a gringo, the officials presumed I could well afford the airfare. Hence, I now had the freedom of their country. The fat man turned his back to me and went about the rest of his official duties, duties which were rapidly taking on the color of a beer bust.

The news that a river trip was being barred to me didn't sit well. The cost of air-freight for my equipment alone would be over sixty dollars, to say nothing of the actual price of the ticket. I was being faced with the prospect of spending fifteen to twenty percent of my travel money just to get started. Apparently, I wasn't doing too well on my first encounter with foreign authority. Still to come was the ticklish business of passing through Customs; I had heard that an overzealous officer might demand that a foreigner completely disrobe.

"*Momentito, señor*." The tall man in the white tropical suit gently took me by the arm and led me to a quiet corner by the port bow. He spoke precisely and slowly to allow me time to translate his Spanish into my Spanish. "You have things that you want sent up the river the captain has told me. Is that not so?" I nodded. "I am told that you have motion picture equipment, and that you intend to make pictures of my country." It was more of a question than a statement.

"For television," I limply responded.

"Do you take pictures of both the good and the bad?"

"Anything of interest to the American public."

He frowned, "I see you are new to my country. These Customs men here do not represent the real Colombiano. They are, many of them, pawns and yes-men for the big companies. They do not want you to see the sad conditions of the countryside. They want you to by-pass all of that and fly to Bogotá where it is beautiful and where the wealth of the peasants is all being gathered and squandered by the rich." He paused and looked out over the wharves and the huge oil storage containers upon which dirty and stained men were working.

I digested what I could of his little homily. I thought, "Could this man be on the other side? Could he be a revolutionist, an agitator, a visionary, or even a Communist?"

Quite off-handedly he continued. "*Señor*, I can get you on a riverboat that is going through rebel country." He emphasized the last several words.

"And the Customs?" I asked.

"No trouble at all, amigo gringo."

I shook his hand and turned towards the cabin for my bags. He put his arm around my shoulders, as all good amigos do, and if anything, gently guided me forward.

I gathered my belongings and was about to step onto the gangway when the German captain came up, and speaking rapidly in German-English to confuse the tall Colombian, pleaded with me to remain aboard his ship. He did not like the political situation, he had his doubts regarding my new acquaintance, and knowing my determination to take the low river road instead of the high road—the Magdalena instead of the *Avianca* Airline—he worried about letting me leave the safety of his ship for the uncertainty of a Latin American revolution. "Come with us, stay on the *Grammerstorf.* Soon we'll go through the Panama Canal and you can enter South America at Guayaquil, Ecuador."

The captain was sincere, and I thanked him. He turned away and then came back. "Mr. Wilhelmsen, in South America always carry a roll of toilet paper with you." Then he went back to work.

I descended the gangway and stepped upon Colombian soil. A couple of young-sters—that hearty breed of street urchins that seemed to dominate the city scene in Latin America—were commandeered to carry my baggage, and we walked through the crowd of sweating stevedores to the Customs Building or *Aduana.* Here my two bags were dumped, rather roughly I thought upon a wooden table. This table and several others like it seemed to be the only furniture in the place.

My movie camera I kept securely tucked away in an old Army knapsack slung around my back. We went into an adjoining room and confronted an official. He seemed much impressed with his position in life. He looked me over.

I am sure I presented a rather interesting picture. Twenty-nine years old, a hundred and eighty-five pounds, six foot one and a half inches in height, blue eyes, and topped off with a genuine Panama hat. The bag hung over my shoulder and the butt of my pistol occasionally pushing out the rear of my trousers giving sort of a wagging-tail effect did little to detract from my well-pressed tropical Palm Beach suit. I handed my credentials across the desk. The official impressed me by not taking them.

I stood in front of him like a non-com awaiting orders from his captain. The man was a fat little fellow, and I could see he was going to give me a hard time. One, two, three minutes went by and he still shuffled papers about his desk refusing to look at me. Then my newfound friend went into action. He leaned over and looked the rascal straight in the eye and began a most vituperative tirade. For several minutes he let the bewildered Customs man have it. The fat man sat back and took every word directed at him. His broad features indicated that he had quite a bit of Indian in him. He provided quite a contrast to the thin aristocratic looking man who was now reading him the riot act.

The uncomfortable bureaucrat quickly signed my visa and placed the proper seals on my bags. "*Vámanos,*" my friend said, and we went out into the midday sun. His driver and car were conveniently awaiting us. We threw in the luggage and piled in ourselves.

Barranquilla with its 160,000 people was quite new for a Latin American city. The pink and white buildings were for the most part only a couple of decades old. The town lacked the colonial dignity and romance of cities elsewhere in the tropics. Developed in the twentieth century as an oil shipping port, Barranquilla had rapidly replaced old Cartagena as the country's major harbor. But like many things in Latin America, once completed, the face of the city had been allowed to rest, and beneath the intense yellow sun and humidity it was slowly disintegrating. I missed the solidity and timelessness that Spain once built into her cities.

Driving along at a nervous pace, now abruptly braking, now lurching forward, I had some little time to gather my thoughts. The motives of the silent man sitting next to me were not at all clear. He hadn't asked for money and this bothered me. He seemed pleased that I wanted to travel up stream, and he was going outside the law to get me there. Perhaps he thought I was a newspaperman wanting to contact the rebels. If so, he would be doing me a favor. All was very strange, as strange as the heart of the city through which we now drove.

We stopped at a busy corner and got out. The man led me to a door, and we went into an office. Through a large front window, the hustle and bustle of Barranquilla could be seen but not heard. I made out several signs and felt relieved to see that I was in a tourist agency's office. Perhaps my guide was on the legit after all. Several people were scattered about the room behind desks, typing or phoning. Three acknowledged our entrance, and I gathered that I was with their superior.

Although still wondering why—with a professional travel agent—I wasn't being directed to the more lucrative commission-paying airport, I nevertheless began to relax about the situation.

"*Primero, el vapor, y entonces el cambio.* First the boat and then the money exchange." He got to work on the telephone.

After some thirty minutes during which the Colombian seemed to call everybody in town, he finally announced that all was arranged, and we went outside again into the sun. Back in his car and off at a racy pace, scattering about indignant pedestrians in our wake, we circled the block and stopped at a *ferreteria* or hardware store. He went in, haggled a bit with the proprietor, and came out accomplishing nothing. This was repeated at several stores, and I soon found out that my friend, far from trying to give me the business, was looking for a favorable exchange for my American dollars. Finally, a drugstore gave me 210 *pesos* for $70 in traveler's checks. I gathered we'd done all right.

Then over to the steamship agency where 66 of my *pesos*, or $22, were handled over for a first class ticket on the paddleboat "*Jesucita*" scheduled to leave Barranquilla late this very day and—God and bandits willing—scheduled to unload a cargo of toilets in La Dorada some time next week. From there I was told a train would take me up to Bogotá, a ten-hour trip. I got back into the car and waited for my friend who had just completed a telephone call from a public phone booth. He quickly joined me, and we made our way through the late afternoon traffic back toward the waterfront. We began to pass boat after boat idly tied up to ugly pilings in the now darkening water. They were mute testimony of the situation further up stream.

We stopped and got out. Gloomily rising out of the rapidly thickening twilight, an ancient riverboat yawned down upon me like some haunted mansion of the past. Its two smokestacks painted orange did little to brighten the gunmetal hull and decks. The vessel was tied to several stumps sticking out of the ooze and water that sucked at it with its very motion. A gangplank, maybe two feet wide, joined it with the muddy shore. Coming over this one avenue, a group of dark brawny sweating laborers gradually filled the first deck with cargo and logs to be used in the boiler which was now beginning to hiss like a gigantic reptile. This deck was completely open and was joined to another directly above it by a wide stairway flanked by two ornate handrails. The second deck was surrounded by an interesting banister and was shaded by torn canvas curtains. All was covered by a roof which, in turn, held the pilothouse. The sun was about gone, but I noticed above the pilot-house, silhouetted against the sky, the round barrel of a machine gun. In the stern, a huge paddlewheel was slowly beginning to turn. Secured to the square bow was a large flat barge loaded with a cargo of gleaming white toilet bowls.

I turned to my friend. "*Diez dolares, amigo*," he said in a businesslike tone. "*Diez dolares, por favor.*" I pulled out my wallet and signed a ten-dollar traveler's check and gave it to him.

"*Gracias*," he said. "*Buenaventura.* Have a good trip, and do not be afraid of the rebels. If you encounter them, tell them that you are filming them for the United States to tell the world about them." He turned abruptly and walked back to his car. I picked up my bags and went aboard. Somebody directed me to the upper deck. A woman took my ticket and showed me to a small cabin on the starboard side. I opened the door and thrust my bags inside.

Soon electric lights began to go on all over the boat, and I stepped to the railing and looked down at the scene below me. Cables were being released and ropes cast off. With a tremendous wheeze and chug the giant paddle on our stern began to churn the water. We began to move. Hasty hands hauled in the gangplank.

Suddenly, there was a commotion on the shore. The stevedores and idlers moved apart. A well-built man was running from a shed to the boat. He carried a small, brown bag in his hand. He leaped aboard and stood there panting as our last connection with Barranquilla was broken. He disappeared into the shadows of the lower deck, and I saw that he wore a full black moustache and was devilishly handsome. The lights were on now and I read again from my ticket which I still held in my hand. In clear Spanish it said," We are not responsible for any accident while upon this vessel."

The *Jesucita* swung out into the mainstream and began her trip up the Magdalena River.

2 — THE RIVER

A trip up the Magdalena was unpredictable. The steamer booklet said that any where from a week to a month was needed for a run to La Dorada and cautioned the traveler not to become impatient. This attitude is frowned on in Colombia and it doesn't do much good anyway.

For my $22 I received a room: a small cabin about eight feet by six feet with a cot-like bunk consisting of flat boards covered with an anemic two-inch mat vaguely resembling a deflated mattress, and a wash basin. Food! How shall I describe it? Pots of rice copiously salted with stones (this may be the reason so many people about me exhibited molar after molar of solid gold); stringy and tough meat just recently hacked off of some unfortunate bovine character who made his last home on the barge in front of us; sickeningly sweet coffee (where was all the good Colombian coffee?), and as an entrée, stuffed, mashed, diced, broiled . . . for all my pleadings I never did get one honest-to-goodness, old-fashioned fresh banana.

Besides the crew and the cow, we carried some twenty-odd Colombian passengers, a cargo of toilets gleaming white on the barge ahead of us, several crates of yo-yos (a yo-yo craze was just hitting South America), a couple of used automobiles, a red fire hydrant, and a brassiere salesman.

This gentleman advertised his product by decorating the *Jesucita* with gay little deceivers during our first night out. When I emerged from my cell the next morning, I was gently slapped in the face by one of these blowing reminders of the finer things in life. As a sideline this enterprising fellow dealt in plumbing supplies. He had quite a nice display of pipes, joints, and lingerie gathered in the center of the large hall separating the starboard rooms from the port rooms. He saw his first mistake—my first name is often taken to be that of a woman—and grumbling through a shaggy mustache he undid the strap on my door and moved them to the next one. Subsequent events proved that this next cabin belonged to a priest.

Of course, I was the only gringo on board: the rest of the passengers, representing odd walks of life, were all Colombians who for one reason or another wanted to go up stream. Some were going the full length; others would be left along the way. All were worried about reports of hostilities several days away, and all made sure to avoid the color red. It seems that the political party now in power had chosen the color blue as their symbol, while the revolutionaries went by red.

I first took the captain to be German because of his immaculate neatness, Nordic looks, and fair complexion. But, later when he opened his mouth and showed gold or no teeth, I knew him to be Colombian. He was a portly gentleman who loved to eat, mingle with his more important passengers, and pass the time of day lounging in a deck chair sipping soft drinks. Occasionally, he would go up to the pilothouse for a word or two with the pilot, and it was obvious that he knew his business.

The crew was a motley group of characters working for room, board, and a few cents a day. They all slept below in hammocks on the first deck along with the passengers. They cooked their own meals over small fires and on the whole enjoyed themselves a great deal more than first class society.

The most important person on board, other than the captain, was the pilot who, though a young man, had spent years learning his profession. He needed an eagle eye and a steady hand. The riverbed is constantly changing and it took a concentrated effort to keep these old boats from going aground. Whenever one went aground, which was quite often, all of us passengers would immediately climb up to the pilothouse and give our opinions on how to go about moving the ship.

For the most part, these first days aboard passed quietly and pleasantly. The scenery on either side of us was lush with green vegetation. Most of it was jungle dotted here and there by small *fincas* or farms. Occasionally, we would stop for firewood or to take on a steer to replenish the larder.

Once we picked up an old Italian trader by the name of Festullo, who showed me a small bag of gold dust. He had a post somewhere out in the mountains, and he would trade Indians civilized gimmicks for their gold. He begged me to join him. He was lonely and he showed me how a small fortune could be secured. Also, he told me, the tiger hunting was quite good in that area.

Sanitation conditions weren't quite up to par. For all the toilets on the barge ahead of us there was none on the *Jesucita*. In the stern directly over the paddlewheel there were several small rooms constructed of corrugated tin. Through a pipe hanging from the ceiling one could shower himself with a thin stream of river water (I usually came out dirtier than when I went in). The water was drained off by a hole on the floor through which the paddlewheel could be seen thrashing about. This hole also served as a toilet and one had to be on his toes to avoid a possible ricochet from below. Once, while pulling away from a small jungle oil camp, a long pipe jutting out into the stream snagged the west wall of one of these privies and pulled it off just in time to give us a look at the astonished occupant inside.

✧✧✧

Pedro Carmago had the look that in Hollywood would have won him the role of a dashing Mexican bandit; about six feet tall with a rugged build, he might have been twenty-six years old. He wore one of those casual mustaches that are so popular in Latin America, and he was the man I had seen board the *Jesucita* under rather odd circumstances just as we left Barranquilla. Although booked in the third class or steerage deck, it didn't take him long to find his way up to a vacant cabin on the first class deck.

I met Carmago on the second day of our voyage. Lunch had just been cleared away, and my table of six including a nurse, the Italian trader, the priest, the brassiere salesman, and a soldier going up stream to join his regiment, were washing down the last of our barbecued bananas with sugary coffee—and I was washing that down with beer—when he appeared from below and sat down.

The toothpicks had been passed around, and I was entertaining all with my attempts at Spanish. "You are an American," he said with a twinkle. "How far do you go?"

He spoke a very bad brand of English, about on a par with my attempts at his language. But, nevertheless, I was glad to hear him. Here, at least, was someone I could talk with and maybe get a clear statement on what lay ahead. He told me that he was going up stream to Bogotá to look for work, just what kind he didn't say. "*Posiblemente, el gringo quisera un guia, un amigo.* Perhaps the gringo would like a guide, a friend." I asked him if he knew where the ancient gold lake of Guatavita was, and could he take me there? He did and although he had never been there himself, he was sure he could make arrangements for the trip. If I so wanted, he would accompany me.

Now, here was a break I wanted. I was lonely entering a foreign country and traveling alone through an underdeveloped area. Being unable to speak the language of the people made my trip all the more lonely.

I warmed to Pedro immediately and we spent the whole day exploring the boat, buying each other beers out of the small icebox in the stern, teasing the brassiere salesman, taking pictures, discussing the female help, making general nuisances of ourselves while several cows were herded on board, and ending the day by attending Benediction in an old church in the town of El Banco.

At this dimly lit place we unloaded a crate of yo-yos and took on some heavy machinery that had been left there by a riverboat not willing to risk the trip farther up stream. This task was completed by a huge concrete wharf composed of several large stone steps leading down to the river, not at all unlike the base of a Mexican pyramid. Several planks were thrown out to join dock and barge, and the heavy steel dynamos were manhandled onto the ship in the finest display of efficient confusion that I have ever seen.

The whole scene reeked with atmosphere. Above was a bright tropical moon surrounded by brilliant stars. Dimly across the shimmering river, the darker outline of the jungle against the sky gave the impression that in all the world only the river and the little town here on its west shore were real. And as such my attention and existence was narrowed down to this little outpost of humanity. As though realizing its importance in the Universe, El Banco spoke in hushed tones and dared show only a few sputtering lights. For an American recently come from the land of skyscrapers, this was unforgettable and I enjoyed its every nuance. Not lost to me was the romance of the place, the small fruit stands, the pineapple vendors, the ugly old hags croaking out bargains to our crew members, a cabaret, and the candle lit church on a hill in the background where an occasional chant could still be heard.

This was the mystery of the tropics, repulsive and fascinating, exotic and commonplace, exciting and quiet, painful and healing. A paradox in living.

Pedro and I had stopped to listen to a blind guitarist plucking out melody after melody on his patched up instrument, when our captain stepped ashore. He was arm-in-arm with the pilot of a vessel now getting up steam to return to Barranquilla. We moved over to listen to their conversation. Pedro was keenly interested in news of the revolution.

The two men spoke quietly together silhouetted against a lantern on a woodpile. My friend translated as best he could for me. It seems that this other paddleboat had left El Banco early in the day for Gamarra. Several hours upstream the smoking remains of a small ship had been found. She probably belonged to the Naveira Line. That riverboat, it appears, had gone aground as so often happens on the Magdalena, and while the pilot and crew were backing her off and seeking out a deeper channel, the revolutionaries attacked. They waded out into the shallow waters on horseback and foot, and swarmed over the helpless ship. Huge holes were chopped into the hull, and within minutes she had settled into the riverbed. Then after robbing all on board, the whole vessel was put to the torch and everyone murdered.

This story had been an easy one to reconstruct for the ship was still smoking when rescue came and it was this pilot who demanded that his captain take off the bodies and return with them. Afraid to go farther, the ship was now turning back entrusting much of its cargo to us. We also learned that seven other paddleboats, a couple of them big ones, had fallen in this manner during the last month.

Early the next morning I was awakened by the thrashing of our paddlewheel. We had laid up the night in El Banco while a military escort was gathered for us. Now the *Jesucita* boasted a full compliment of four soldiers and with Belgium rifles. The spirits of the passengers aboard were considerably raised so that, rather than casting a morbid pall over all, the sight of the unfortunate gutted boat leaning crazily out from the muddy riverbed evoked all sorts of comment and discussion. The captain raced the vessel on and, as we passed the immediate danger zone, the four soldiers made a great display of their efficiency and importance.

The scenery along the river began to change now. Where before the dense jungle growth had been dotted occasionally by small vital little *fincas* or farms, these now began to disappear from the scene. Those that we saw were deserted or burned down. The last year had seen heavy fighting in the area. A sneaky sort of war in which a farmer might awake in the morning to find his home surrounded by desperate and hungry men. He would wait to be killed, his farm burned and his stock run off. And all done in the interests of the Revolution. In actuality as I later found out, most of these roving bands belonged to no political party. They just took to the hills looking for booty.

As a result of these depredations no man knew where he stood; atrocity followed atrocity. Both rebel and government troops would strike back whenever they felt wronged, and the countryside through which the Magdalena flowed ran red with blood. At Barrancabermeja an American oil worker told me of a whole village that had been massacred by bandits because one of their members had been trapped there by federal troops. Later in Bogotá I heard a story from a lumberman that would chill the heartiest man's blood. Soldiers had marched into his plantation, gathered up his employees, and because many of them had no identification papers, they had been shot in the head one by one. More than one hundred of their bodies had been strung up in trees to serve as a lesson to the rebels. My informant had protested and now has a mouthful of broken teeth to show for his pains. The soldier slugged him with a rifle butt, and then set fire to his holdings. By stamping out the means of livelihood, the government hoped to starve out the enemy. And so the whole area trembled in fear while family after family packed up its belongings and fled to the cities.

I remember reading an American article in June of 1953 telling of the "bloodless revolution" then taking place in Colombia. Yet in Colombia, those times were referred to, and still are, as *"La Violencia"*—the time of the violence.

For a while it looked like we might make the trip without incident. Seven days we traveled unmolested. Past the dirty little port of Gamarro, the large oil center of Barrancabermeja where there's quite an American colony, Puerto Berrio where there's a movie theater, and on to the small Army outpost of Nare.

Late afternoon, perhaps an hour or two after leaving the above-mentioned refuge, June the first, 1953, nobody screamed, nobody shouted.

We just gathered on the portside of the *Jesucita* and watched a body float by. Face down, he had recently been murdered, slashed to pieces by machetes. Blood was still flowing through his ripped-up shirt. He swirled by, was caught momentarily in the little eddies of water created by our paddlewheel, and then drifted on like a piece of wood. He struck the shoreline several times, bounced back, and then was swept away by the river.

I looked at Pedro. He was scanning the jungle on either side of the narrowing river. He saw them first. One by one, men appeared along the riverbank. They were on horses and mules. Some were big, most were small. They were dark and incredibly shabby. Most carried rifles, all carried machetes: They were shouting in loud voices to one another. There may have been thirty of them altogether; there appeared to be two leaders. These two men spurred their horses on and motioned the others to follow.

The *Jesucita* might have been traveling four miles an hour. The horsemen had no trouble paralleling us. A shout went up, and I saw that some nine or ten more of these bandits had appeared on the other shoreline.

The captain only had one choice. He had to stick to the river and avoid any and all sand bars. If stuck, our ship would be lost. While we could probably outdistance the horsemen should they attempt to wade and swim out to us, we wouldn't have a chance if ever we bogged down in the riverbed.

Crewmembers were sent running to positions on the prows of the barge. They began casting their sounding weights into the stream. Shouts went the length of the vessel and were conveyed to the pilot. He stood at his wheel with his feet firmly spread apart: His head he pushed forward probing into the very depths of the waters.

For an hour the *Jesucita* gallantly made headway. The passengers looked out into the jungles where occasionally one of the bandits would appear and then be lost in the darkening forest.

Strangely enough, I was elated. I felt little fear. If worse came to worse that machine gun perched on the top of the pilothouse would certainly be a deterrent to those ragged bushmen. There I was, not one week in South America, and I had before me a scene right out of a Hollywood movie. I slipped into my cabin, screwed my movie camera onto its wooden tripod, and then set up on deck awaiting the big show.

An hour went by and it began to look as though we might tire the anxious group of marauders trailing us. The captain came down from the pilothouse. He was full of grease and his face was very white.

"*No hay bueno, la ametralladora.* The machine gun is no good," he said. "*Falta una parte*, a part is missing."

He came over to me. "*Tiene una pistola?* Do you have a gun?"

"*Si*," I told him. He looked at me and went up forward.

I forgot all about my camera.

Nobody, I'm sure, really expected it to happen. But when it did, the *Jesucita* suddenly ground to a stop. We were all shaken a bit, but this was the sort of thing we had come to expect in the past. Consequently, for a moment, the true implication of the situation didn't register. Then the yells began, not only on board, but from the nearby jungle.

The bandits began to appear from the brush with a howl. They waited for a moment to assemble and then plunged into the river. Our captain raced by me and literally leaped into the pilothouse. I felt his hand on the wheel. Slowly, at first, and then faster and faster as the force of the river current caught the *Jesucita* broadside. A minute hadn't elapsed before we began to drift back down stream, barge and boat stretching out across the Magdalena.

Those bandits who were approaching us from the left suddenly found themselves confronted by the huge barge whipping down on them. The iron hull caught the foremost and sent him sprawling into the river. We had completely turned about and reversed our original course.

The horsemen coming in from the right bank now had to contend with the gigantic river paddle. Not a shot was fired. As desperate as they were, the bandits would not waste any of their ammunition on a ship that was rapidly leaving them in the downstream current of the Magdalena. About an hour later we sighted the welcome lights of the little army post of Nare. The speed of the river had doubled our progress on the journey back, and we were now safe for the night.

Where the River Nare joins the Magdalena a small outpost had recently been established. It consisted of a wooden fence circling an area comparable to a city block. Inside were several wooden bungalows and barrack-like shacks housing a small group of officers and perhaps some fifty troopers. The barricades were topped off by barbed wire and in the evening darkness the whole looked not at all unlike pictures I have seen of forts used by the United States Army during the Indian Wars of the nineteenth century.

The Colombian government has seen fit to maintain this fortification because, here, the country is the wildest and the bandits and the revolutionaries the boldest. Better than a hundred miles of wilderness separated the town of Puerto Berrio and La Dorada. Only one settlement broke the isolation of the river. It was a village of plaster-like mud huts, several stores, and the ruins of an old church which might date back to colonial times. Maybe five hundred people called this place home with another couple of hundred occasionally visiting it from outlying plantations. All look to the fort on the outskirts of town for protection.

The *Jesucita* quickly tied up to the logs anchored to the earth for that purpose, and a dozen soldiers marched aboard. They were in full battle regalia, dirty green fatigues, puttees, and tremendous Sam Brown belts crisscrossing their shoulders from which a bayonet and hand grenades hung. Each carried a rifle. All needed a shave.

The captain conferred with an officer, and then let it be known that it would be safe to remain on board for the night. A gunboat was being radioed to escort us in the morning. In the meantime, we were cautioned to stay close to the boat and to the fort.

Although it was quite dark, the few lights of the village made travel possible. I went ashore. After browsing about a bit, poking into the fort, looking into a small outdoor shrine, following a couple of lovers, watching a game of barracks dice, and peeking into the local brothel, I spotted Pedro striding down the dirt path from town with our fellow traveler, the priest, Padre Raimondo Tarabusi. I hailed them, and we sauntered back to the village cabaret.

We went into the dimly lit cantina and ordered a beer from the proprietor who was adjusting a gasoline lamp. Selecting a table commanding a view of the door, we sat down and I asked Pedro to explain to me the cause of the political unrest then plaguing Colombia.

Father Raimondo answered my question. His English was much better than Pedro's, and much better than my Spanish.

The political group then in power, the conservatists, felt that Colombia was much better off being ruled by the larger wealthier families, the elder statesmen, the Church, and the scholars. They pointed out that during the twentieth century the country had improved immeasurably, that the groups mentioned were skilled in national and international economics and politics, and that the masses of illiterate must not have too great a say in their management. In time, as the gradual scheme of things was allowed to run its natural course, those people of the backwoods—the majority—now educated and aware of their responsibilities would be able to intelligently represent themselves and so gradually enter and dominate affairs. But, at the moment, they were only being misled by power-minded individualists.

In contrast to this form of rule, the radical party pointed out that this evolution from peon to statesman was going much too slowly, that in many cases neophytes who had arrived at political prominence were being held down and pushed back with no consideration given their proposals. They felt that too much money was being spent in the cities where the comparatively well-to-do people enjoyed it, while the rural areas—in reality, the backbone of the nation—were neglected. In short, they wanted the pace of social revolution to be stepped up a bit. They wanted a piece of the action.

Father Raimondo admitted that both arguments were a bit too extreme and that both parties have been exposed to corruption. As a result, deadly rivalries had sprung up and all that was bad in either party found its way to the Magdalena River Basin, the economical lifeline of the country.

The priest then pointed out a young *mozo*, or local stevedore, who was carrying two weather-beaten satchels. "There," he continued, "is all that I have to my name. I will be joining another man, Brother Antonio Salvador tomorrow morning. We will then travel into this so-called rebel country and attempt to bring some peace to the region. The government's guns certainly aren't doing it. Perhaps, the cross will be more effective."

Pedro and I said little more that evening as we watched the young priest make his way to one of the small clapboard houses of the river community. It was distinguished by a cross that was attached to its roof.

❖❖❖

With a Colombian gunboat as an escort, the next two days passed uneventfully. The larger steamer, *Atlantico*, joined up with us, and our three ships presented quite a caravan.

At one point, I lost a dollar to a man who boarded the *Jesucita* begging for the fare upstream. It seems he was escaping the ire of an angry dominating wife, so perhaps the money was well spent. At another junction we picked up a prostitute. She nearly fell into the stream making the transfer from dugout canoe to riverboat in enormously high heels, but when she finally did arrive and set up court on the deck of our boat, quite a lively time ensued. She was dressed in the tightest satin dress she could possibly pour herself into, and proceeded to tease all present with her rather accentuated figure. Members of the crew were quite taken by this vision of city life and began plying her with beer from our diminishing stock. She paid for a cabin in second class, and did quite a bit of business. In the end, she drank too much and had her purse stolen.

At one point, we spotted a group of alligators, but they were too far off to shoot. The river once teamed with these saurian characters, but most have now gone the way of sportsmen's rifles.

The bugs that swarm over any stationary object were very active. My nocturnal toilet wasn't complete until I had evicted several odd dozen from my bed every evening. One night a mama bug gave birth, and I had the devil's own time proving to these new little fellows that they were trespassing on private property. I believe they are called "*jején*."

There was a lady on board whose habit of smoking cigars belied her fairly modern clothes. She saw great possibilities in a marital match between el gringo and her fourteen-year-old niece. He might not have thought too ill of the idea except that the niece needed a shave and needed it badly. As it turned out the ship's pilot moved in and a bristling romance was underway when I last saw the couple.

A commotion beneath some of the heavy machinery on the barge exploded into curses and shrieks the morning we reached La Dorada. A couple of ancient ladies were discovered in their hiding places where they had been stowed away for the last several hundred miles. The captain preferred not to press charges.

Our ultimate destination, the town of La Dorada, had a splendid hotel, or so the *Colombian Guide to Hotels* claimed. Just why anyone would want to stay in this place on the river when the capital city of Bogotá was in easy reach was never made quite clear to me. And besides the hotel was not a splendid hotel.

The dock was lined with soldiers and for a while I speculated on the advisability of dropping my pistol into the stream and being done with it. Everybody was being subjected to the most rigid inspection. Guns had been leaked into the backcountry, and the government was out to stop it. The American consul could do me little good in this part of Colombia should my weapon be found. However, the dilemma was easily remedied by the pilot who volunteered to smuggle the gun in himself. As a crewmember, he wasn't suspect, and the whole crime was carried off smoothly. No sooner ashore than we were leaped upon by that army of little urchins with whom I was to wage an unsuccessful war for the rest of my stay in South America. For a nominal sum, this brigade of ragamuffins would move my bags from boat to bus. Arguing was useless—nobody could have heard me anyway—so I let the whole gang unceremoniously haul away my goods.

At this time, I became acquainted with the Latin American idea of schedule. "If the gentlemen don't come immediately, they will miss their bus."

So, naturally, I bounded ashore like a New York commuter. Pedro, on the other hand, once through inspection, just moseyed along. I was sure I was going to lose him.

The bus—and here may I doff my hat to that sad regiment of determined travelers who constantly, day after day, month after month, in the 1950s and 1960s, expose their poor pain-racked bodies to South American buses—was parked conveniently in front of a cantina a couple blocks from the waterfront. This contraption, possibly condemned from the North American scene during the thirties, was painted yellow and was not unlike an old school bus. Scheduled to depart at 8:00 a.m. and to arrive in Bogotá by 6:00, I thought I was indeed lucky to have made the connection. It was just now turning 8:00. The next couple of hours were spent waiting for this great exodus and fighting off the little people who all seemed to have stock in my baggage. Finally, with great shouting, kissing, and tender displays of filial devotion, we sped off in the direction of the Andes Mountains.

This trip sounded like a good deal—$2 for ten hours of travel. But what was gained in money was lost in blood. Within an hour, I was willing to call it a day. The bus was filled to the brim with people, mostly Indians in fairly colorful outfits. Pedro sat across the aisle from me, and I was unhappy to see a huge woman toss her produce filled bags into the vacant seat alongside of me and then follow them herself. It seemed my lot, henceforth, while in the tropics, to have obese Indian ladies choose me for their seat partners. Besides the chickens and dogs, a goat somehow managed passage. The atmosphere was a bit close.

A trip on a bus in these parts is an adventure in itself. The enterprising traveler who undertakes the journey gradually comes to realize that a whole ritual of etiquette has been developed, a set of rules to which all passengers adhere. Seats are reserved, and the most desirable are those two directly behind the driver. This individual is referred to as "*maestro*," and is greatly respected. I honestly believe that if I were born to this station in life in South America, I would set my ambition as that of a bus driver. The *maestro* is looked up to more than the *alacalde* or mayor of a village. He is the only contact with other villages, the bringer of news, mailman and world traveler, engineer and raconteur, definitely a man of parts. Naturally, it is an honor to sit near him and to listen to any word of wisdom that he might be big enough to drop one's way. So these front few seats are usually reserved for officials and VIPs. Another advantage of sitting up front is that the further back the seats, the rougher the ride.

The driver's helper is the next important personage. He is a good one to get to know because he handles the baggage and the tickets. Usually he rides up front, standing next to the driver, but occasionally shows off his daring by stepping out of the door, while the bus is in full progress, working his way past the windows—where all can get a good look at him—and taking a position on the rear bumper, much as a coachman. Or perhaps he goes on top of the bus. If he takes this latter position, he stomps about to let all aboard know of his accomplishment, and then might suddenly appear hanging down over the windshield, ready to repeat the whole performance. Whenever the bus stops, he admits the new passengers and secures the luggage. Then with a tremendous thump on the back of the bus, he'll holler out, "*Ya vamos.* Now we go," and allowing the bus to get a good head start, he'll dash up and leap aboard much as a cowboy in a "B" movie mounts his horse.

Once on the trail, all aboard take a keen interest in the driver's skill, and the hour rarely passes without him receiving some audible acclaim, should a truck or another bus be overtaken. The trip is a race to the finish and life is really worth living if one is in the victor's vehicle. The code demands that one jeer at the vanquished when overtaking him, taunt him with vile names, and spur him on to mightier deeds. If one happens to be on the losing end, a pall of gloom descends over all, and only by some extraordinary feat of daring is the driver able to regain your confidence. At such a time, all is forgiven and the bus resumes its festive atmosphere.

The road that I was traveling, as were just about 50% of the roads in Colombia in the 1950s, was a one-way dirt trail. As a result, it took a certain amount of reckless skill to keep from having a head-on collision, to say nothing of just trying to cling to the mountainsides. Any living object in sight is considered fair game, and woe be the poor unfortunate being who gets in the way of a Latin American bus. Be he man or woman, old or young, octogenarian or infant, pig or dog, mouse or horse, he immediately becomes the target for a howling mass of sadists who follow the philosophy of "the closer the better."

There are no restaurants along the way, and so all food is procured from roadside vendors. These Indian ladies usually take up positions in the central part of villages where the bus stops, and swarm all over the place with their cakes, bowls of soup, bananas, and other unidentifiable hors d'oeuvres. They thrust them into your face, and ask you to hold them for a moment, and then claim you've bought them. Most of the roadside food is very unsavory; all is unsanitary.

Rest stops along the way, there are none and perhaps, the least said about that the better; although I must say in defense of my rapidly deteriorating standards, that the sight of the male contingent stoically standing along the roadside taking in the scenic wonders, with no thought of concealment, was always a bit of a wonder to me. And the ladies sitting about enveloped in their huge skirts never fooled me for an instant.

The road to Bogotá from La Dorada, on the Magdalena River is a rather rough and extremely dangerous one by United States standards. By South American standards, it was just another day's run. Never a man to tremble at driving conditions, I nearly became sick with the roads many precipices, curves, and makeshift bridges.

The day was beautiful, and I might have really enjoyed it except for the roughness of the trip. The road led through tropical lowlands to mountain peaks. Small Indian houses could be seen hanging perilously from dizzy heights or almost hidden by dense brush. At the fairly large communities, we would stop and Pedro and I would indulge ourselves in a warm bottle of beer, usually at my expense. Except in the larger cities of South America, beer is most always served at room temperature; most people preferred it that way.

At Hondo we picked up a German businessman who had gone to Colombia just after the First World War and now was as Colombian as the Indian next to him. It had been the fashion to claim that most Germans in South America were sent there before the war by Hitler to gain control of countries. I must say I never found any evidence of such a plot. Indeed, agents were working in these Latin countries, but by far the majority of Europeans in the tropics have gone there to begin a new life. The land was wide open to immigrants. Scientific and mechanical knowledge was sadly lacking in Spanish America, and people versed in those skills soon rise to financial and social prominence.

The German left us at Chaquanix to partake in the fiesta of Corpus Christi. I remember the place because there I lost a small screw vital to the operation of my still camera. Not long after, the road began to steadily rise, and towards late afternoon it leveled off on a plateau nearly nine thousand feet above sea level.

Now, the joy and color of life, the warm green feeling of the river country gave way to a bleakness almost foreign to one who thinks he knows the Latin America motif. It is the gray coldness of the Andes Mountains, my first contact with the Cordillera of South America.

The excitement of the lowlands ground down to the monotony of the highlands. More and more darker clothes appeared. Large dull ponchos replaced flower covered blouses. Civilization replaced wilderness.

It was raining hard and getting quite dark outside when our bus suddenly found itself trapped by buildings, first small and then large, that hemmed it in on all sides.

We had arrived in Bogotá and the very dark atmosphere of the city began to fill me with apprehension. The thinner air was working on my unacclimated brain and the feeling of being completely surrounded by tall structures contrasted dramatically with the past fifteen days of open river and empty ocean. Even Pedro seemed depressed.

The bus braked to a final stop before a dirty warehouse-like building and we got out. Within a moment, Pedro and I were left standing alone with our baggage on the rain soaked pavement. I could see that my associate was not altogether pleased with our predicament. I liked it that he had lost some of the cockiness that he had had while on the river. Pedro was becoming quite a human being in my book.

He hailed a car that had a little cardboard sign on its windshield with the printed words, "*Libre*." The taxicab was unoccupied. We got in and went for a very short ride through the extremely narrow streets of Bogotá. We turned into a street that I would have sworn was an alley.

Pedro indicated a door in an otherwise unadorned wall. He got out and pounded on a door and was admitted into a patio or courtyard.

He returned later and after paying the cab 30 *centavos*, I went with him into the *Santana Hotel*. We were led through an enclosure surrounded by walls. A *mozo* took us up to a veranda running around these walls. Our quarters were on the second floor.

Two large rooms with a very hard bed and a washstand in each, for eight *pesos* or $1.60, the young maid indifferently informed us. The shower and the toilet were down in the patio. Pedro had obviously botched the house hunting job, but I was too tired, sore, and discouraged to look elsewhere. Evidentially, he had once known somebody who worked here, but had now long since left. He kept reassuring me that the nice thing about the place was that it was right downtown.

The proprietor, a bustling kind of man dressed in a black suit, came up and welcomed us with a rapid volatile brand of Spanish that I could never understand.

That night I wrote in my diary. "Arrived in Bogotá at 8:00 in the rain. Pedro led me to a very crummy hotel, the *Santana*—eight *pesos* a day. We walked the dingy streets a bit, and I bought a bottle of wine. It is cold."

3 — EL DORADO

T he city of Bogotá, to a first-time visitor, can be depressing especially during a week of fog and rain. The altitude at nine thousand feet certainly doesn't add to the *joi devivre*. How it must appear to an Indian from the lowlands, I cannot imagine. Except for a few boulevards racing through the city many of the streets are narrow and hemmed in by tall modern buildings. They are made even more narrow by indiscriminate and illegal parking. A cacophony of automobile noises permeates the air. And that precious commodity is polluted beyond imagination with the odors of our time: diesel fumes, carbon monoxide, charcoal smoke, and often unattended garbage. Indeed, I saw many pedestrians, usually older ones, walking the streets while holding a handkerchief over their mouths and noses. Pedro advised me to keep my hands in my pockets and on my wallet. He might have been exaggerating—though I sometimes wonder—about the proliferation of one-hand bandits. Children as young as six years old ran in packs working the old pickpocket game right alongside of the more elegant and older light fingered gentry. They all seem to have a field day on those crowded sidewalks and streets. I took Pedro's advice, and after several trips to this city throughout the years, I have come away from Bogotá unscathed. I've accepted that this is a natural vice of the capital city. To walk the downtown streets of Bogotá can truly be an adventure in itself.

Even though our rooms in the *Santana* were on the second floor, the noise of the city clanged uninterrupted all through the night. I got little sleep, and Pedro, coming from a more rural environment, got less. I did manage to have a clean shower without the debris of the Magdalena thrown in as a bonus.

A *criada,* or maid, had absolutely no compunction at walking into my room unannounced and uninvited to place a steaming cup of strong black coffee on my bureau, and then to announce to me that breakfast was now being served in the downstairs hall just off the patio. She informed me of this as she stood face-to-face to my totally unclothed body without a nod of concern. The casual manner in which she performed this duty did not stop me from feeling immodest. I grabbed a nearby blanket and covered up. I later found out that this routine was normal in many Colombian hotels. *"No importa,"* as Pedro assured me when I questioned him.

We descended into the patio and then into the dining hall. The room was empty except for the tables to which several *criadas* brought pitchers of coffee, cocoa, or tea which were either too strong or too weak; never a happy medium to my spoiled palette. The drinks were followed up by platters of small pancakes, rolls, sausages, and bacon. These solid foods did go down well, especially Colombia's version of a Danish that is called an *empanada.*

I noticed that the majority of the hotel guests were young students from the nearby university. I was immediately recognized as a foreigner, a traveler from the States. Several of these neatly attired adolescents soon engaged me in conversation. I was pleased at first to use my own language again, but soon regretted it. I was verbally assailed by a talkative couple of fellows and a stunning longhaired girl, for being part of a government, the U. S. A., that couldn't even whip a tiny no-nothing country such as North Korea. The war in Korea was then in its most bloody throes, and my rebuttal to their attacks seemed weak, even to me. Only when taunted, "Why don't you use the bomb?" did I silence them for a moment.

"The United States," I countered, "is not in this conflict to eliminate a country; it is merely containing the spread of Communism in the world." Several others joined in the conversation, and I detected a strange anti-American sentiment. I hadn't gone to South America to discuss politics, and I now found myself being shouted down at my every statement.

The argument stepped up when an older gentleman, in a finely pressed uniform who was sitting at a corner table, set his coffee down and broke in. "Enough," he bellowed out, and the room quickly became silent. "This man here," he sternly said, "is a guest in our country. He does not make policy for his country. Let him enjoy our hospitality, not our rancor." I could see that he was a respected man, and then found out why when he was deferentially alluded to as "Colonel." He was a high-ranking officer in the Colombian Army. He finalized the debate by pronouncing, "Let his country fight their battles, and we'll fight ours." But this then was offset by a voice from somewhere in the rear of the hall.

"Yes, you *ricos* fight your battles with our blood. We the poor, get poorer while you get richer. Marx was right." That voice was immediately silenced by many "hushes." Especially when the colonel stood up and peered sharply into the crowd. Immediately to his right, two burly men stood up, their hands suspiciously tucked into the pockets of their coats. They were with the colonel, undoubtedly bodyguards.

The officer finished his coffee, stood up, nodded to me, and in good English said to me, "You should use the bomb on those people." He walked out followed by his two men.

Pedro and I rose to leave as the group broke out into a loud murmur, and a voice—probably some Marxist—growled, "Let him go out into the country and see how long his uniform stays pressed when our people there get through with him." This was followed by a chorus of approval and a few handclaps.

Once on the street, with the *pension* behind us, Pedro commented, "They all have some growing up to do." We headed downtown.

My interests never did lie in the big cities of South America, but a travel and adventure film such as I envisioned would require some reference to the capitol city of Bogotá. A short sequence would do. In 1953, world tourism was just getting restarted after the long Depression and World War. People were becoming interested in Third World countries.

First thing to do was to locate a photo store where I could find the screw that had disappeared from my still camera.

Pedro again proved my trust in him, first inquiring and then taking me to such a shop. The lost screw was replaced, and I went on to shoot stills and movies in the Plaza Bolivar and the lovely old cathedral. In the interior of the church was the banner that Jimenez de Quesada carried with him as he fought his way through the Chibcha Indians to this place and founded Santa Fé de Bogotá in 1537. (An interesting man, that tall aristocratic Cordoban. He was the model for the classic Don Quixote, the man from La Mancha. His younger friend Miguel Cervantes wrote that story with him in mind.)

Then I went to the American Embassy where, after a long bureaucratic delay, I picked up my mail. The Embassy was pretty well closed up because a couple months before it had been attacked by a mob. I was irritated that Pedro was told he must stay on the street while I did my business. And I became quite irked when I was told that the "U. S. Embassy was no post office," and would not—emphasized—forward my mail to the next Embassy down the road. I had been feeling a bit stomachy and the curt attention I received there did not sit well.

I joined my friend, and we hiked over to the large Colombian National Museum. Here again I was fascinated to see and to touch the coat of chain mail that the old conquistador Quesada had worn as he went about tilting with the Indians in his never-ending quest for El Dorado.

Here it was in the museum that the advice of the German captain of the *S. S. Karl Grammerstorf* proved his wisdom. "Mr. Wilhelmsen, in South America always carry a roll of toilet paper with you." A week of strange food on the Magdalena River caught up with me. Like an irresistible current, it now made itself known and raced through my body seeking an exit. I barely reached the elegant men's room in time to plunk my aching bowels down on one of its clean facilities. With a sigh of relief, I looked around for the necessary item with which to tidy up. There was nothing to be seen, nor have I rarely seen that most requisite item in but a few public rooms in South America. My pleas to Pedro went unheard as he was off looking at some masterpiece of ancient art or more likely, at one of the lovely ladies that beautify the city of Bogotá. I had a big "oops" on my hand, and the only paper of any kind near me were those sheets upon which all of fifteen years of research had been carefully recorded. "I'll just have to 'wing it' from now on," I said to myself as one after another of my memos went down the drain and off into the sewers of the Royal City of Santa Fé de Bogotá. I have never been caught short since.

El Dorado!!

The name literally means "The Golden Man." And yet it has come to be used as a catch phrase for any treasure trove in the world. The origin of that evocative term began right here some nine thousand feet in the Andes Mountains. A thousand years ago, the valley of the Muisca where the Chibcha Indians lived, was famous for the abundance and the quality of gold that the natives had extracted from the earth and rivers and had fashioned into exquisite figures. These pieces usually represented gods from the Chibcha pantheon of divinities. The Spaniards, being good Christians, had no respect for pagan cults and, hence, gathered up the statues and tossed them in their melting pots. For a while Quesada thought that he might be on to another tremendous empire such as Cortez had discovered in Aztec, Mexico, or as Pizarro had just conquered in Inca, Peru. But he soon realized that much of the gold that he was melting down for the coffers of Charles V in Spain came from elsewhere. The Indians pointed to the mountains east, west, and north of them. "There," they swore, "is where the mother lode would be found." They told the invaders of a large lake in the province of Bogotá from which, if His Majesty would order to be drained, he could remove a vast quantity of gold and emeralds that the Indians had been throwing into it since ancient times. The story went on that twice a year during a religious festival the *Cacique* or Chief of the Chibchas would have his body anointed with a resin-like sticky substance and then completely covered with a thick layer of fine gold dust. He would then be escorted to a large balsa raft, and with the accompaniment of drums and whistles, he would be paddled out into Lake Guatavita. Other regal noblemen would also maneuver their little canoes out into the lagoon and drop objects of silver, gold, and emeralds into the water. Their chief would be lowered into the waters and his gold dust and decorations would sink to the bottom. The tradition had been going on for several centuries which would indicate that the lake must be loaded, a veritable submerged museum of precious goodies.

It didn't take Quesada long to commission his captains Lázaro Fonte and Pedro Simón to seek out this golden pond and to drain it. Unfortunately, such an engineering project was way beyond these fighting men of the sixteenth century. Although it was reported that the Castilians did find numerous objects of gold—that ended up in the ever-present melting pot—the depth of the lake and the cold of that altitude frustrated them. They moved on to more exciting ventures near Quito.

The next treasure hunt on record at Guatavita was conducted by Antonio de Sepúlveda, who was issued a royal license in September of 1562. He set out to make a cut in the high wooded hills surrounding the lake. Eventually, his men carved a fifteen-foot V-cut and drained off quite a bit of water. Records show that he picked up quite a quantity of gold and a huge emerald that was later sold in Castile for an enormous sum. Creative bookkeeping in the Spanish Colonies in those days, with everyone's hand in the till, might not have told the whole truth of his find.

The list of the following attempts over the years is long and, sad to say, barren of results—unless finds were not reported, which is quite probable. It seems that gold, being heavier than the mountain earth, had sunk down beneath the surface. When that surface is finally drained of water, the ground soil hardens to a thick clay and a different set of searching equipment is needed.

I had no thought of digging around in this lake on a two-mile-high ancient volcanic mountain, but I did believe a few minutes of film on the subject would enhance my documentary on South American legends.

And so Pedro and I set about finding a way to get up to Guatavita Lake. Odd, for South America, no bus would be leaving for the little town of Guatavita until 3:30 p.m. That would be the jumping-off place where I hoped to rent horses to ride up the mountain. Our expedition would take more than one day. This was no real problem except that bit by bit, peso by peso, my wallet was diminishing. I had a long way to go and only so much *dinero* to get me there. Being a Depression boomer, I appreciated the value of a buck, and I had not planned on extra frills. Pedro was indispensable to this endeavor so his three dollars a day was worth it. But he would double the hotel bill. We had been told that the one hostel at Guatavita was *El Gran Hotel Del Monte Guatavita*. An impressive name. I wondered just what kind of a resort I was heading for. Nevertheless, 'faint heart never won fair maiden,' so I bought our tickets. We left that afternoon.

Unfortunately, although we were in plenty of time to make our connection, when we boarded the little school-like bus, we were by no means the first. The best we could get were a couple of seats directly over the rear axle. We were in for one mighty big bounce all the fifty-odd miles and three-hour drive. Even though the *maestro* put the pedal to the metal all the way up the grade approaching Guatavita, he stopped at every little village. Of course, there would be quite a family reunion at each of these stops, and time didn't seem of the essence. Everybody knows everybody on that high plateau and the journey evolved into a moving *fiesta*. The bouncing was not kind on the kidneys and several pit stops en route were called for. Modesty was not a virtue on those occasions. Whenever one had to go, he would just holler out, "*Momentito, tengo que ir*," and at the first open spot, the bus would pull over and people would pile out. A lot of beer had been flowing freely and a lot of stops were made. One incident stands out.

In Bogotá an extremely obese lady, say about 325 pounds, had come aboard. Upon boarding the bus with all of her bags and baskets, she had quite a time squeezing down the narrow aisle between the seats. So much so that when she finally did reach her bench near the back of the coach and settled in, she was given a rousing round of applause by all of the passengers. She graciously acknowledged those kudos by raising her arms above her head and clasping hands much like a triumphant boxer. Now, however, at this particular watering hole, the driver seemed a little impatient; he was hoping to remain ahead of another bus making this same run. For our lady to haul herself all the way out and then return, we were looking at close to ten minutes. A lot of good-natured Spanish palaver came and went, and then she, just rearranged her voluminous skirts, squatted back in her seat, and with a satisfied grin let loose. A neat little stream flowed down the walk way and out of the front door. To the accompaniment of *"Oles, muy bien,"* and *"Magnifico"* we were back in the race. The lady was the hero of the moment, and the bus aisle never looked slicker.

During the three-hour drive to Guatavita, we often seemed isolated from civilization and authority. Long stretches of open country and then suddenly dark and foreboding forest. The road was not paved and for most of its way was just one lane. When approaching another vehicle the first one who puts his headlights on had the right of way. We did not encounter much traffic, and we were all pleased when the *maestro* proudly proclaimed, *"Guatavita; El Pueblo de Guatavita."*

The driver began letting people off here and there; he seemed to know them all and where each lived. He looked back to Pedro and me and Pedro eloquently demanded, *"El Gran Hotel Del Monte."*

"No mas?" the puzzled *maestro* responded.

"No hacienda, no finca, El Hotel, no mas?"

"No mas," fired back my friend. The driver shrugged his shoulders, drove right on into the center of the little town and stopped in front of a non-descript adobe wall. It had one entrance over which hung a lopsided sign: *"El Gran Hotel de Guatavita Del Monte."*

"Aqui estamos," the man lamented and opened the bus's door. We had arrived in El Dorado.

The town of Guatavita at this time boasted no more than seven or eight hundred people. All the dwellings were fronted by a solid wall with no decorations, only a doorway. Perhaps in the whole place I could see no more than three or four pick-up trucks and here and there a larger truck. There were no passenger cars. An occasional sign protruded from a doorway announcing a *tienda* or store. I also noticed that there were more bars than stores. The whole place consisted of about ten streets crisscrossing one or another. The little town was pretty dusty, especially after our bus drove off with its klaxon blaring noisily. The place was quite a contrast to the pristine, and pure blue of the mountain sky all around us. The town disappointed but the scenery that surrounded it was breathtaking.

I had left the bulk of my belongings back in the pension in Bogotá, so we waved away the small army of urchins that immediately surrounded us, and manhandled what we had with us through the door. As expected, the walls enclosed a large patio. The rooms of the hotel opened into this courtyard. In 1948, my mother and I stayed in such accommodations in the city of Guaymas, Mexico, long before it became the fishing resort that it now is. We had quickly realized that my mother's smattering of Spanish had directed us to the local whorehouse. Now, it seemed, I had duplicated the experience. In the center of the patio there was a little clapboard building that acted as a bathhouse. As we looked on, a man with nothing but a towel wrapped around his waist darted out from it and ducked into one of the rooms or stalls, as I imagined them to be, and indeed what they were.

A heavyset lady smoking a long cigar stepped out from a desk and questioned us. It took Pedro a little while to convince her that we wanted separated beds. The rent turned out to be the equivalent of .80 per room and bed. She handed each of us a towel and turned away. After the long bouncing from Bogotá, I could well use the service of a privy. I got a good answer to my question. "Just follow your noses; you can't miss it." A small room along the back wall contained a three 'hole' board over a cesspool that literally hummed with little creatures. Needless to say, I now carried my own roll of *papel sanitario*.

We deposited baggage in our rooms, each of which contained a cot with a dirty mattress and blanket, a stool, and a table. Pedro inquired where the best restaurant might be. "Only one," the lady replied, and pointed down the street. This, the best and only, turned out to be a dark and grimy cantina lit up by gasoline lanterns. As so often in Colombia, the only item on the menu was a large bowl of soup that was filled with all sorts of foodstuffs. In mine there was a whole corncob, the wing of some fowl, carrots, peas, and other legumes. Not really bad at all, if you could stand the aroma of the place: burning charcoal from a small fireplace, horse and barnyard odors from a rack of saddles draped over a sawhorse, acrid smells of old and bad tobacco, and the faint essence of urine and unwashed bodies.

"Hell!" I said to myself and then to the wicked looking proprietor, "*traigame una bottella de ron y tres vasos*." One for me, one for Pedro, and one for the man. There was method to this charity. The alcohol cost only $1.20 but the goodwill was worth much more. Pedro did the talking. "We need a couple of horses and a guide to take us up to the lake tomorrow." The man cogitated, scratched his head, looked at the ceiling, and poured himself another drink. In effect, what we got out of him was, "That's a toughie." Apparently, the army had confiscated the majority of all the horseflesh in the area. Colombian soldiers had been chasing bandits for the last several months and their motor vehicles just couldn't go into the remote ravines of the mountains. When we pressed the man, we eventually got a firm, "No. No. Hay." He could not help us there. "But," he brightened up, "the distance to the lake is only seven or eight kilometers, an easy walk." And he could have a couple of bright young fellows available *mañana* to carry my equipment. We had to settle for that although I had really wanted those mounts. Not only to ride but because I knew they would look good on film.

The night in the Grand Hotel did not turn out as badly as I had feared. The bottle of rum eased the bumps and bruises of the day, and both Pedro and I slept well.

At daybreak, we were back in the cantina. Sure enough, two teenaged boys awaited us. They were more Indian than not, but Pedro had no trouble communicating with them in Spanish. A hidden weapon in the arsenal of my filming tricks was a Polaroid camera, one of the early black and white ones. I lined up the boys and took a picture of them, rubbed down the photo with the little sponge of hypo, or fixer, that came with each of those early Polaroid films and watched the delight on their faces when they saw themselves slowly appear on paper.

"How did you do that?" Pedro quizzically inquired.

"A little magic," I enigmatically replied, and then told the boys that once back here this afternoon, they could both have a portrait. In this manner, I assured myself they would still be around when we did return. I was right.

The 70-D model Bell and Howell 16mm camera was not heavy, but after a mile or so, it seemed to pick up weight on its own. With it in the camera bag was a canteen of chlorinated water, a Pony Kodak slide 35mm still camera, the Polaroid, and film for all of them. That and a rather heavy wooden tripod were all we took with us except for a bag of bread rolls that the lady at the hotel graciously gave us. The Luger automatic pistol I carried in an abbreviated leather holster on my belt beneath my buckskin shirt.

We were out of the town in just a few steps and into open country. Then onto nothing but a footpath that slowly angled upward as we began our ascent. After an hour, the modest climb took its toll. Step after step, always upward. Pedro wasn't in any better shape than I was, but the young guides literally flew up the slope. Once in a while they would amuse themselves by chasing a stray cow or by attempting to catch a small species of fox that frequented these altitudes. And, it was the altitude that really put the skids on me and my friend. We were now somewhat over ten thousand feet, climbing steadily, and breathing heavily. The trail itself was easy enough, mostly scrubby cactus-like bushes and a stunted tree, here and there. Up we went. Several times we did narrow down into a pass between boulders. Then I would vaguely wonder if the bandits we had heard about might be lurking around the next bend. Fortunately, once out of sight of the town, we were the only humans on that mountaintop. After four hours we came to a wooded area. I liked that because there was some shade from the brilliant sun. The woods lasted all the way to the top. On the fifth hour, we left behind the trees and looked over a quarter mile of scrub. Beyond it, I got a glimpse of the sun glinting on water. We had arrived at the place of the golden man, the lagoon of Guatavita. El Dorado.

First things first. We selected a large level boulder and settled down to feast on the rolls that our hotel hostess had given us. We washed them down with water from the canteen. All water in South America is highly suspect and so every time I filled the canteen, I liberally added several halozone tablets. The water then was pure, but had a fearful-taste of chlorine. This taste was remedied by adding a touch of rum to the tin cup that we used. This last, of course, put Pedro and me in a much better mood than during the climb. The young men didn't need any stimulant; they were naturally a cheerful and energetic couple.

However, the blissful mood darkened after I readied the movie camera for a wide-angle shot of the lake. A cloud came out of nowhere just when we didn't need it and the rains came. This did not bode well for sharp pictures in brilliant color. The rain kept coming on and off, during the four hours we stayed along the edge of this geologically ancient volcano. I hadn't expected to expose much film on Lake Guatavita so I wasn't too disappointed. As it turned out, I got what I wanted and needed. Very telling, historically speaking, was a deep cut in the rim of the crater. This man-made work could be seen across the lake which is about half a mile wide. The cut or ditch was probably made by Antonio de Sepúlveda in the 1560s. As mentioned, he did come up with gold. Not the bonanza he would have liked, but enough to sweeten his life until the end of his days. When drained of its water, the bed of the lake reverted to a hardness of cement, and even though many companies, with much more engineering expertise than Sepúlveda, have made the hard climb and set up their pumps, none has done any better. The last attempt was made in 1965 by the successful salver of several Florida coast treasure galleons, Kip Wagner. He ran into the same old problem, and the Colombian Institute of Anthropology and the Council of Monuments have now forbidden any more dredging.

My bet is that there are plenty of emeralds and golden objects just waiting to be picked up a few feet beneath the bed of Lake Guatavita. None other than Monsieur de La Kier of the Royal Institute of Paris came up with the startling figure that one billion and twenty millions sterling have settled into the bottom of the lagoon.

The one thing that I was able to ascertain before we left this place of mystery and legend was that the large boulder upon which we had made our picnic had obviously been worked by ancient hands. After clearing it off, we realized that it was a perfect rectangle about eight feet by ten. The stone had been once used for a purpose. For what purpose I have no idea.

We returned to the village just as we had come. I paid off the two guides, gave them their portraits, and had a bowl of soup in the cantina with Pedro.

I was satisfied at what I had seen and done, and we were about to turn in for the night when two weather-beaten older men furtively but respectively made themselves known. "*Caballeros*," one of them asked me, "Can we go to your room for a moment?"

I let them in. One of them closed the door behind us and then opened a dirty cloth bag that he was carrying. He reached in and brought out three objects. "*Son oro*," he said.

Gold. "They came from Lake Siecha which is nearby. We have many such things, and it is against the law to sell such things."

I looked at Pedro and we then both took those pieces and others from the bag. We placed them on the table where our one candle was burning. They were yellow and they were heavy. They seemed to be fashioned in the manner of the Indian jewelry that I had seen in the museum. There was an owl with a long beak, the stylized outline of a jaguar's head with two human feet, a thin snake-like figure, and other small objects.

I looked at my friend. "What do you think?" I asked. I had once before in Mexico been duped into buying counterfeit archaeological items. I had no knowledge of verifying ancient gold objects.

Pedro shrugged his shoulders. "I say, no," he sadly said. "It is too good to be true. They have heard that there is a gringo in town and they're after his money. Don't give them anything. They probably have a shop around here turning out these things. I doubt very much that these are gold."

I was in a quandary. Here I was in as romantic a situation as one could imagine. Right out of adventure books and movies. The left side of my brain said, "Go for it; buy a couple hundred dollars worth." But the right side argued, "Don't be a sucker. It's nothing but a scam."

"We cannot stay here long." The old man tugged at my sleeve. "We do not want to be seen spending time with you."

"Ha!" said my right brain, "the old sales pitch. I've used it before in my brief sales career." I said to Pedro, "Tell you what I'm going to do. I'll take the one little funny man with the bulging eyes. I'll give him 20 *pesos* for it here and now. No more!" (20 *pesos* in 1953 was roughly $7.)

Pedro shook his head but translated what I had said. Without hesitation the old man pressed the two and a half inch figure into my hand, looked apprehensively at the door, waited 'til I had counted out 20 *pesos*, and silently departed with his friend. They closed the door behind them.

I looked at Pedro who was grinning. "*Señor*," he chuckled, "I think you have been taken." We both laughed together and I dropped the figurine into my camera bag. I had a good feeling about it.

The next day we were back in Bogotá. In that city there is a museum named El Museo De Oro, the Museum of Gold. In 1953 one room alone contained over one million dollars worth of gold when gold was only selling at $36 an ounce. The collection has expanded since, and I have had the opportunity to revisit it. Much more Indian gold fashioned into beautiful objects has been added to it. The main attraction there now is a famous golden replica of a raft with a regal figure standing in the middle of it. Ten servants surround him. The intricate masterpiece is about a foot long and this exquisite work of art obviously represents a *cacique* (chief) and his attendants poling their way out into a lake.

The inference is that this raft was carrying the Golden Man and his offerings to the gods of the Muiscos. I returned to the museum in 1974 and was given a personal tour of the collection by the then head curator, *Señor* Dr. Jorge Gómez. He told me that the gold raft had been found by a peasant near the shores of Lake Sieche not far from Guatavita. He mentioned that many invaluable ancient objects have been found in that area by local natives. "They probably know a lot more about the archaeology of the mountains than we do. We have never been able to track down the sources of the gold that they occasionally bring into the museum to sell."

In 1953, the left side of my brain had had the right stuff. My funny little man had indeed been authentic. And I had bought it for mere pocket change. Pedro had been wrong.

(When I married in 1956, I had taken the piece to *Will Wrights*, a well-known jewelry shop in Hollywood, where I had a clasp worked into it. My wife often wore the little Colombian treasure, and when she died in 1990, I pinned it to her dress, and it went into her family mausoleum with her. She had dearly loved it.)

I never told Dr. Jorge Gómez the story of my brief stay at the mountain lake of Guatavita, the home of the Golden Man.

4 — HOLBROOK

The following morning I was packed and ready to be on my way. Everybody rises early in Bogotá, and I joined the university students in the dining room for coffee and rolls. Pedro came with me.

When we sat down, the proprietor of the Santana handed me the daily *Tiempo*. On page two there was a headlined article: "*Padre Raimondo Terabusi y Fray Antonia Selvador Estan Muertos.*" A grainy photograph showed two naked bodies hanging on hooks that protruded from a wooden wall. Both had been gutted; their entrails hung from wounds that went from neck to crotch. A sign was hanging from one of the corpses. Crudely printed on it was: "Carne de Chanchos." Pigs' meat.

The article told how they had been found four days before, nailed to the wall of a *finca* or farmhouse barn. The deadly deed had been done by Marxist Revolutionaries.

Just two weeks before, Pedro and I had talked with Father Raimondo at the village and military fort at Nare on the Magdalena River. I had liked the man immediately. He had been jovial when the salesman had hung a brassier on his cabin door. The priest had helped me with my Spanish at all of our meals, and had quite objectively explained the political problems of his country. The missionary-social worker had gone into the backwoods with the idea of softening the violent attitude of the guerrillas who were terrorizing the region. His black robe would bespeak his peaceful intentions. Father Raimondo was wrong, dead wrong. If anything, the cloth of the cleric enflamed the atheist revolutionaries all the more. He and Brother Salvador died as Christian martyrs.

My Spanish was not up to a debate, but I did take the newspaper, walked over to where the young students who had favored Marx were sitting, spread it out in front of them and said, "*Aqui están Los Comunistas; son perros de mala costa, bárbaros*…murdering curs."

Then I left the Santana, and hailed a taxi. Pedro came with me. We parted at the railroad station as good friends.

The next step going south for my rendezvous with my brother and the tall ship was the city of Neiva. I envisioned an easy trip as it would be done by railroad all the way. From Neiva I was assured, there would be a bus to the mountain town of San Agustin and the strange devilish statues that have been found in the villages and the ravines of that region.

I always wonder why, with a near empty sitting coach, a passenger invariably chooses to sit alongside of me. No matter that I am no Spanish language companion, a quite heavy Indian lady plunked herself down on my bench and started to talk. She talked incessantly most of the whole trip, that is, when she wasn't disciplining two of her toddling children. Nursing her infant gave her no pause as she blithely shoved the little fellow onto her immense bosom and continued to soliloquize. Then she asked if she could lay the little tyke on my lap, belly down, while she changed a soggy and odiferous diaper. This saturated item she then placed on the lattice rack along my head. Her droning soon put me to nodding and I was about to escape all in blessed slumber when I began to feel a slow but sure drip on my face. The diaper had sprung a leak. I immediately changed my seat, and for the rest of the trip, I was looked upon as a *gringo* snob by all the passengers in the coach.

The city of Neiva was the largest populated area I had, as yet, passed through in Colombia. Barranquilla, Bogotá, and now Neiva. The train had dropped down several thousand feet from the capitol city, and immediately I felt the heat and humidity of the southern latitudes. I liked that.

The lonely seven-story hotel where I would stay seven years later had not been built yet, so I was taken, bags, tripod, and all in a wheelbarrow propelled by a twelve-year-old, the few blocks from the railroad station to the Hotel Atlantico. Now, here was something more like it, a hotel right out of Hemingway. Surrounded, of course, by a brick wall, its patio was a charmer. Paved in tile with a ten-foot diameter stone fountain in its center. Water spouted way up into the air. It had all the beauty of a colonial *hacienda*. Everything but in-room plumbing. The proprietor, in a neatly pressed white tropical suit, signed me in for two dollars the night. He and the boy brought my goods up a stone staircase to a balcony that overlooked the patio. My spacious room with louvered shutters that deadened the intense afternoon heat was ready for me. A large circular fan hanging from the ceiling created a ripple of a breeze throughout the room. It hung above a double bed that had clean sheets and a colorful bedspread. This, I was told was Neiva's best. My dinner, included in the price of the room, consisted again of one of those large bowels of soup with everything edible crammed into it. I didn't need anything more.

My romance with the tropics took a bit of a turn that night. I had slipped beneath the clean sheet of my bed, felt the ripple of air as the ceiling fan gently murmured above me, and was listening to the melancholy strains of a Spanish guitar somewhere in the night when there came a tapping on my door.

46

"*Quien es?*" I sleepily called out.

"*Solamente la criada,*" a girlish voice responded. I went to the door and opened it. There stood an Indian lady of indeterminate age. "*Quisiere el señor una mujer para la noche?*—Would the gentleman like a woman for the night?"

At the moment, that was the last thing I had on my mind. "*Gracias,* no," I replied. "*Guizás en otra occasion*—Perhaps another time."

"*Dos dolares, señor,*" and then, "*un dollar, señor. No mas.*"

I shook my head and closed the door thinking, "That'll be a good one to tell the boys back home." I went back to bed.

Perhaps I was dreaming too much of what might have been because a disturbance in my room took more than a moment to awaken me. At 2:00 a.m. I awoke with the feeling that something was flying back and forth near my face. I could feel the breath of its wings. I opened my eyes, reached over to the lamp switch next to my bed and looked about. Sure enough, here was a huge gray moth, with a wingspread of at least six inches, swooping low over me and then diving down upon the bed behind my pillow. Not too far from my face was an immense spider hanging onto the headboard of my bed with several of its legs and flailing the air with the others. In effect, it was attempting to either ward off its assailant or to capture it.

The spider was all yellow and black and was covered with hair. At least two inches long, it looked mean, mad, and nasty. I scooted over to the far side of the bed and watched fascinated.

Time and again the moth dove down upon the spider. Apparently it was trying to dislodge the hairy arachnid. To what advantage, I don't know. But when the electric light bulb flared on, the moth soon lost interest in its furry target. The moth now began making passes at the light. The spider gratefully—it seemed—gathered itself together and quickly clawed its way down from the headboard, onto the bed, and rapidly made its ugly way to the bottom of my sheet where it immediately disappeared.

I was out of there in a moment. I checked my boots and stockings, put them on, shook out my clothing, and dressed. There was no more sleep for me that night. I sat on guard until 4:00 a.m., the time I was told to be ready for the bus to San Agustin.

(Incidentally, the moth finally lost its battle with the hot electric bulb and fell comatose onto the bed. I wondered if, after I was gone, its eight legged opponent had returned and enjoyed a meal courtesy of Thomas Edison!)

The road to San Agustin was not a road but rather a dirt trail that never let up. Ninety percent of the traffic we encountered was donkey driven carts, cattle, and mule and saddle horses. I felt as though I were in the Old West except that a saddle would have been much more comfortable than the board I was forced to sit upon from 5:00 a.m. to 2:00 p.m. Even though I had been ready to board the jitney at 4:00, as I had been told, I was already too late to get one of the so-called cushion seats. The bus was half full, and I ended up on a wooden bench in the rear. Not only did this cause my body untold misery, it also caused my mind many regrets. This last because the rugged, magnificent, and not to be duplicated scenery through which we passed was often lost to me because of the constant jostling and tumbling about in the bus. The cost was $2 for the nine-hour ride, Neiva to San Agustin.

The town of San Agustin was another one of those towns such as we see in old black-and-white western movies. All it needed were two gunfighters squaring off on its main street. Larger than Guatavita, it was even more of a movie set. The former had one-story dwellings; here some boasted two floors, many with false fronts. Where Guatavita was close to the amenities of Bogotá, which was only a couple hours away, this community was on its own. No railroad, no airport, and no paved roads. To get here, one had to brave a narrow, winding, precipitous, and often dangerous ribbon of a road. As a result, the town was pretty self-sufficient. I had been told that there were bandits at work between San Agustin and Neiva. They were mainly interested in the large emerald mine compounds along the headwaters of the Magdalena not far from this place. And, I've since been told that in 1953, the cocaine cartels were beginning to take shape. As a gringo, of course, I was highly suspect.

The Hotel San Agustin was much the same as the Grand Hotel of Guatavita, except here my room was on the second floor, a step up I would say. The tariff came to $1.50 a night without a sleeping guest. That afternoon I spread-eagled on the bed and went right to sleep. My bones and muscles were one continual ache. I had already lost ten pounds since entering Colombia, and I was near sick. No wonder the afternoon *siesta* is so popular in Latin America. Later in the early evening I took a walk to the main plaza and there saw one of those stone monsters I had come so far to film. This six-foot monolith glares out at the world with his mouth wide open and its teeth barred like a mad dog. His arms are pressed to his body and he appears to be holding some broken object. He looks like a guard of some sort; not the type of face one would care to see even on Halloween. This statue was much in contrast with the trim bronze figure across the plaza of Simon Bolivar, the George Washington of South America. Both were arrogant, but the pre-Colombian figure seemed angry and defiant where Bolivar appeared confident and in control.

The seventeenth century was a period of great expectations in the New World. As Cortez and Pizarro had proven, great and rich civilizations were somewhere out there just awaiting the plucky explorer. The seventeenth century was also a time of imagination and drama when men's fertile minds conjured up all sorts of devils and saints, monsters and demons. Anything might happen in this strange continent called America. And, often it did.

Sometime in the early 1600s, an army of conquistadors had worked their way into the headwaters of the Magdalena River, way south of Bogotá. The going had been tough and when an Indian guide pointed out a small stream of crystal clear water, the men in armor called for a halt and a campsite. Perhaps they wanted to test the waters for gold dust. But, first things first, off came the heavy boots and into the waters went the steaming feet of several of the men. Immediately these feet were withdrawn. At the bottom of this and other such pools of running water, grinning and leering at these Castilians, were scores of loathsome faces all grinning with satanic delight at the men who stood above them. They appeared to be from an underwater and underground world, to be waiting for the unwary so they could drag them down into some sort of hell. Of course, the Europeans soon realized that these faces were reliefs chiseled into the boulders beneath the surface of the water. Who and when these characters were carved is a mystery that still baffles us today.

Another member of that group of early explorers let out an oath when he realized the rock covered with moss and vegetation he had chosen as a headrest also contained one of those unearthly expressions. As the men fanned out to see for themselves just what kind of a hellhole they had stumbled into, they found many more similar statues. They were scattered about the valley as though some cataclysmic volcano had spewed them out of the infernal regions and left them here.

Hardhearted officers of this group had other ideas. They reasoned that these frightful idols might have been set up at some time in the past to frighten off would-be trespassers. Their imaginations led them to suspect that they were by a city of gold and precious stones.

And so, in time, a *pueblo* or town was charted. A *plaza* was laid out and a church was erected to ward off the many demons that were there for all to see. The church and the town were named for St. Augustine, the great writer and bishop, who in the fifth century had successfully repulsed the demons of his youth.

I now walked the streets of this little town and visited the primitive Museo del Parque Arqueológico, which contained a map of the area. The surrounding countryside has little changed since the seventeenth century Castilian dons mapped it out. Close by is the Alto de Los Idolos where the first monoliths had been discovered. All about the region wherever an idol had been found, it has been erected on the spot. The area is loaded with them, scaly creatures standing guard, unusual flat stone tables set up upon diminutive stone legs, and the now famous and imaginative Parque Lavapatas. Here it was where the early explorers were repulsed by the underwater riverbed carvings. Today, they present a mystery that is yet to be solved. Why had these grotesque figures been carved and set up here? When had they been created? Why do they look so angry? What do they mean?

I rented a horse for the day, a horse that suffered the same diarrheic condition as I. Together we both stalked and nourished the countryside as I followed my map of the region and filmed some of its bewildering stone reminders of a lost civilization. The best I could glean from the local people and the one resident archaeologist was that there were even stranger things further off in the countryside; subterranean catacombs that had been dug deep into the earth and were beautifully lined with cement and painted in brilliant colors. I was told that there are thick columns in these grottos that are covered with cabalistic figures and yet, "*No hay nada en los tumbos*," they are empty. The area in which these mysteries are found is appropriately called 'Tierrandentro' which translates to 'Underground.'

I was told, too, that much further in the mountains I might see a waterfall that descends from the "Heavens of the Andes," that beneath the cascade there are caves where marvelous things have been found.

I was certainly in no physical or financial condition to make such an exploration. Nevertheless, I promised myself that I would return and pursue this riddle some time in the future (Indeed I did, as we shall see, with tragic results).

The area gave me the creeps. It was not a nice place. To me there was an aura of evil hovering over the valley. I made the pictures and films I had come for and was gratified two days later to leave San Agustin, the strange place of fearsome stone giants.

"Now," I wrote in my journal, "for the barrel," meaning it was time to make tracks quickly and move on down to Peru for my rendezvous with my brother. Although I had many pages of notes—those not in the sewers of Bogotá—that told of intriguing areas I would pass through, I had only so much time, money, and film for the sites that I had highlighted. I was eager to move along.

I put away my notes and consulted the bus schedules. I would return north to the town of Garzon, and from there turn west over the Andes Mountains to Popayán which is on the well vaunted Pan American Highway. Then south to and through Ecuador, and finally the country of Peru.

I've seen some pretty spectacular sceneries since that first trip to South America in 1953, but the one to Popayán is probably the most awesome. One of its attractions was a steep, narrow grade where we all got out of our bus to do our thing and were told by the *maestro* to take a look way down into the valley. There, over 1000 feet below us was the bus that I had tried to book the day before but that had been full up. That bus had gone over the cliff and had tumbled unmercifully the whole distance to the valley floor through which ran a trickle of a stream. Thirty-three of its forty passengers had lost their lives. Some of the baggage lay scattered all along the mountain slope. The dead and the living had just been taken out. Within a few days this spot would be remembered by many wooden and floral crosses that always dot the Latin American landscape wherever a loved one had perished.

The city of Popayán is large and has many Spanish colonial churches and other buildings. It even boasted a modern hospital (with which in time I would become acquainted).

The next day was a long one. Up at 3:00 a.m. into a bus, and finally at 4:00 p.m. I was in Pasto. The Pan-American Highway was, indeed, a much better thoroughfare than I had hitherto been traveling. Of course, it was: The United States had contributed considerably to its construction. Still and all, it was only half paved. Mostly two lanes down to Ecuador.

I spent the night at Pasto, Colombia, before entering Ecuador.

Now came the hassle of crossing the border. I headlined my journal for June 13,

1953, "What a day!" Another crowded vehicle took me from the bus stop (I refuse to dignify it as a bus station) to the border town of Ipiales.

Then I engaged a car to take me across the border to Tulcan, Ecuador. Easier said than done. First I was told I would have to go to the military facility to have a colonel issue me an exit stamp. When I arrived at this rather well laid out army base, I was stopped at the gate and told to come back next Monday. This day was Friday and a festival was about to begin. I enjoy a festival as well as the next person, but three days here would break my bank. Brother Fritz was bringing me money from home, but he was still three countries away.

So it was here on the Colombian-Ecuador borders that I perpetrated my second crime which I am sure most judges would forgive. I literally grabbed the guard at the gate by his tunic and demanded that I speak to the commandant. Indignantly, he pulled back and briskly asked, "Who are you to ask for the colonel?" I glared at him, "Joven, young man, I am Colonel Edward Romain Wilhelmsen of the United States, Seventh Cavalry, and I am here to inspect this facility." Now in Latin American countries, a colonel is the most respected man in the army. Generals are often political appointees, but colonels are the main substance of the fighting troops.

(Once before, in jest, I had visited a close friend at an air base in California and had used the sobriquet 'Colonel' to get the attention of a self-important guard. My friend had reprimanded me severely at the time for impersonating an officer, but we both got a chuckle over it. My friend did get his colonel wings, and in a strange manner, in time, so would I.)

The only insignia of my authority I might have displayed was a battered blue mariner's cap with a visor and some gold braid. I had bought it in a boating store in California. Apparently, it was enough. The guard snapped to attention, saluted my cap, and dashed into the parade ground after an officer who was riding a bicycle. In a moment that young man was standing in front of me with the knuckles of his right hand pressed against his forehead. "*Coronel*," he blurted out, "*A la disposicion de usted*." I casually touched the brim of my cap and mumbled: "*Wilhelmsen, Coronel de La Caballeria septima cuerpo del ejéricto*." He replied, "*Bienvenido*," and pumped my hand up and down. Rather stiffly and apologetically. I presented my passport and asked for the proper stamp.

"*No problema*," he answered, and sent the guard with it to a building within the compound. In rapid Spanish—Colombians claim they speak the purest Castilian in South America, and many do—he proudly told me that he was a lieutenant, that his superiors were all in town at the *fiesta*, and that he alone was in charge of this most important fort on the Ecuadorian border. My passport would be stamped he promised, but as an international courtesy would I be good enough to inspect his troops. "It would look good on my record."

And, strange to say, this I did, cap in hand over my heart, I stood at attention and watched the Colombian border guard parade before me. When the flag passed by and was dipped in my direction, I saluted it as professionally as I could. The martial music played on and various columns of young men, in full battle regalia, stepped lively by me. My passport was returned with the proper exit stamps, and with a good handshake from the lieutenant, I made as dignified an exit as I could. (Apparently, that young officer was not aware that it was the Seventh U. S. Cavalry that was pretty well annihilated by Sitting Bull and the Sioux Indians and their allies at the Battle of the Little Big Horn in 1876.)

Still, I was in Colombia. As it turned out, I needed two more stamps. I'll quote my journal for June 13, 1953.

"A ten minute ride to the border station where I was told I needed two more stamps. Back to the Captain of the port who at first was going to put me off 'til Monday until I made it clear I would give him two *pesos*. This I did, and then I had to go to the Criminal Department where for five *pesos* I was given another stamp. A good shake down all the way."

Strange things do happen in life. Here is one of them. The young man who was driving me to all of the government places was somewhat of a hotshot teenager. It had been raining on and off and traffic was moving very slowly on the mud road. Too slow for my driver; he whipped around the line and ended up in the ditch. Several other cars were also in the same ditch. An hour and a half of pushing and tugging finally broke us free of the muddy gully. As we pulled out, a gentleman and his lady whose taxi was still in the quag-mire asked if they could hitch a ride. A big dance was programmed for the evening and they were both dressed to the 'nines.' Of course, I said and they climbed into my vehicle. Pleas-antries were passed and I mentioned that I had run out of luck, that now it was too late to obtain an entry visa into Ecuador. "*No problema*," said my passenger. "*Soy el official pub-lico de emigracion.*" He took my passport and later that evening it was returned to me in the *Granada Hotel* where I was staying. One good turn deserves another!

Overland travel in South America, especially fifty years ago, was certainly erratic. I will not go into the details of my run through the country of Ecuador. I left Tulcan, the northernmost town in that country, in what is called a *colectivo*. This is something between a four-door car and a station wagon, more like our vans today. *Colectivos* are a transporta-tion staple in Latin America. We left at 11:00 a.m. and were back at 6:00 p.m. At one point, we ran out of gas, at another the fuel pump fell off the motor nearly setting us all on fire, and finally we came to a river that was too swollen from the rain for us to cross. A new route was chosen to go on to Quito. We all had a bite to eat, and away we went again, peddle to the medal, which is a must south of the border. We arrived in Ecuador's remark-ably preserved colonial city of Quito at 5:00 a.m. Immediately I transferred to another *colectivo* an hour later, and I exchanged this one in turn for another one in Ambato. (I had dearly wanted some time in Ambato; it is the jumping-off place for one of the most famous and documented Inca treasurers, the Valverde treasure, hidden somewhere in the Llarangantis Mountains that are visible from the road where I stood.) Eventually, we pulled into the Andean town of Riobamba at 11:30 the next morning. I had been in one or another *colectivo* for over twenty-four hours, and was dead tired. I spent much of the afternoon, evening, and night in bed at the Hotel Metropolitino.

Then came another two-day run. The train ride from Riobamba was relaxing as it slowly descended the mountains to the Pacific Coast. I picked up interest when I realized that quite a few Ecuadorian soldiers were being transferred on the rails to the Peruvian border. There was talk of a war over territory in the area to which I was headed, the city of Guayaquil. At 7:00 p.m. I left the train at Doran and took a taxi to a strange ferryboat, the "*Daisy Edith.*" That vessel would take me across a body of water to Puerto Bolivar on Ecuador's most southern point of exit or entry. Quite confusing.

The "*Daisy Edith*" boasted several rooms for an extra $2. I paid it gladly; I wanted to stretch out on the cot that came with the room. I picked up an inexpensive bottle of brandy, and settled in well. I had been told that the highway in Peru going south to Lima was a dream compared to my recent roads. I celebrated a little too much.

Unceremoniously, we were dumped on the waves of a place called Puerto Bolivar at 3:00 a.m. Way before I managed the gentle sleep I had hoped would restore limb and mind, I found myself sitting on a couple of oil barrels beneath one little light bulb watching a small ant-like army of stevedores load bananas on one of several boats tied to the dock. The *Aduana* or Customs office would not be open until 9:00 a.m. A watchman informed me that a launch would then take me across another body of water to Peru.

I was soon dozing with my head in my hands. "You an American? You there; you an American?" The sound of a quite feminine voice penetrated the haze of my slumber.

I looked up and was somewhat startled to see a woman looking down on me. Her large red rimmed floppy hat fascinated my own red stained eyes.

"I am, yes, I am." I was glad to respond quickly. I hadn't spoken English since the United States Embassy in Bogotá had told me to get lost. "I sure am," I repeated as I got to my feet.

"Nice to see you," she spoke again. "I'm Barbara Holbrook, a newspaper correspondent who has just gotten herself kicked out of Ecuador. If that launch doesn't show in a couple of hours, I'll be spending the next couple of years in the calaboose." And so I met Barbara Holbrook. It turned out she was as eager as I was to latch onto a fellow American to talk to.

Barbara Holbrook was a couple years older than I was. She was divorced from an editor of the *San Francisco Chronicle* and was now making her way in life as a foreign correspondent for the magazine *Vision*. This weekly tabloid might be likened to a Spanish speaking version of *Time* or *Newsweek*. She had been working out of Quito, Ecuador, and had recently broken a headline story that had bounced around the world and which subsequently gave her the bounce from that country. In the spring of 1953, a devastating earthquake had totally destroyed several villages in Ecuador. This natural disaster was one of the first that attracted a global response. Money, doctors, medical supplies, food, clothing, and tons of relief packages poured into Quito to aid the homeless and the injured. The effort was a noble response from countries around the world. The problem was that as those bundles for Ecuador piled up on the wharves of Guayaquil or the tarmac of Quito's International Airport, much of them—more than half that was sent—was being siphoned off by greedy *politicos*. The devastation of hundreds of mountain Indians suddenly became a bonanza for a select group of high placed members of the government. Fortunes were being made as foreign relief was converted into *sucres*—the currency of Ecuador. Barbara exposed the scandal. *Vision* published the meticulously researched article and she set off the Watergate of Ecuador. The day before I met her on the wharf of Puerto Bolivar, her hotel room had been forced open by soldiers. An officer told her that unless she retracted her story, she would be incarcerated in the federal prison—not a pleasant future for anyone. Her U. S. passport did give some protection, and Barbara fired back. "Jail me, and this scandal will be even more ugly." Along with other admirable traits, this lady had spunk. "Give me a day and I'll be out of here, and you can clean up the mess anyway you care." They backed down and gave her the time to move on. She packed up and was escorted by police car to the wharves of Puerto Bolivar. Barbara was not even given the opportunity to clear out her bank account. When she was left alone, the officer told her, "If you are in the country after twenty-four hours, you will be locked up as an undesirable troublemaker, probably a Communist (Communist was a good excuse to tell the world that she was an agitator). Her spirits were low when she encountered me, but she held her head high. The writer's main regret was that she would be leaving the handsome young Ecuadorian artist who she was sponsoring for a United States education grant. She was in the midst of a romance and had hoped it would develop into more than just a romance.

My first impression of this young lady when she tapped me on the shoulder was "Ha ha, here's an American who might be able to give me a hand with the Spanish language and ease me out of Ecuador and into Peru, and make my way down to Lima a bit more easy than these last few days have been." I stood up and gave her the usual male look-over.

My quick thoughts of "She'll be of help to me," quickly changed to "This is one good-looking woman." She was well put together. My hand was extended and hers met it. We became friends. Our conversation never ceased.

At 9:30 that morning the launch that would take me through the jungle border waters arrived. A dozen or so nondescript Ecuadorians with packs slung over their backs, and two Americans, quickly stepped aboard. The boat was an open deck vessel, no shading tarpaulin over our heads. Along with the civilians were several soldiers who leveled their automatic weapons at every bend in the river. For more than a century, Peru and Ecuador had an ongoing land dispute. The delineation of the border has never been made clear. National pride in both of the countries claimed more than the other; neither wanted to give an inch. It was mainly a local affair on the frontier, but was touchy and every so often the machine guns would go off. My thoughts were, "Who would really want this swamp anyway?"

Fortunately for Barbara and for me, a Peruvian consul was also aboard our little launch. He had diplomatic immunity, and when the passports and visas and stamps were here being tallied up, he sided with us. He gave the 'okay' for Barbara Holbrook and for me to enter his country. I remember him as Consul *Señor* Carranzas. He was the kind of man who is needed to solve the diplomatic problems of different nations, a real gentleman. Unfortunately, no one else on that launch was given entry into Peru; they were turned away and sent back to Ecuador.

My lifelong affair with Peru began when I met *Señor* Carranzas.

If Ecuador was bristling with guns, Peru was more so. Our Peruvian port of entry was the small village of Hualtaca which was humming with military activity. Our newfound friend greased us through and helped us pass several inspections. With some Peruvian army officers, who were chafing to get to the 'big' city of Tumbes, we rented a truck. The vehicle bounced us through the scrubby jungle of northern Peru and that afternoon brought us to the Hotel Turistas of Tumbes.

Finally, I was able to stop in a hotel and a city that was more than a way-stop on my itinerary. This place was a well laid out and a well kept city with a quality hotel. On this site in 1532, Francisco Pizzaro made his first contact with the emissaries of the great and extravagantly rich Inca Empire. Tumbes is Peru's northern city of any size and I highly recommend it. The main hotel was one of a chain of hotels built and sponsored by the government for tourists. All of the 'Turista' hotels in 1953 were quite well run. Some were still going strong forty years later. My room cost me $1.50, and was well worth it. So was the $1 filet mignon steak and fries that Barbara and I had for our dinners. I am pleased to say that the *simpatico Senor* Carranzas joined us and contributed a bottle of fine red wine. As I have mentioned before, I liked the looks and feel of Peru with every step I took.

Tumbes has a manicured main plaza surrounded by colonial buildings and the typical Spanish church. That evening, after our satisfying dinner and wine, we three joined the nocturnal promenade around the square. A military band supplied the music and passersby contributed the hospitable ambience as they strolled round and round the gurgling fountain and greeted everyone they met. This was the Latin America that many people envision in their dreams.

We three retired early to our respective beds, well fed, well wined, and well met. I had a good sleep.

Sure enough, our consul friend was on hand the next morning to see us off for Trujillo and Lima. The road was paved all the way south and the bus was a hundred percent better than those I had recently experienced. No more impromptu toilet pit stops. Those were substituted by interesting little tavern restaurants along the way. However, we spent the first night after Tumbes in the not-as-nice city of Chiclayo, and then at 1:00 p.m. the following afternoon, we came to Trujillo, Peru's third largest city. As such, we enjoyed another of those fine Hotel Turistas on the main square (as events were to transpire in the years to come, I was to see a great deal of this area).

I have enjoyed many Spanish colonial cities but Trujillo, Peru, is the best example of a large seventeenth century Latin American town I know that has not been over-exposed to tourists. City block after city block is dominated by tall thick stone walls that open up into shaded patios abloom with flowers. Trujillo is spotted with pleasant little parks that always display a fine statue of some historic dignitary. In 1953, the military band was always in evidence after the *siesta* hours, and people enjoyed themselves on the benches of the Plaza Central. After all the effort getting down south to the town, it is no wonder that I was captivated.

Barbara and I both joined in the promenade that is still a strong custom in much of Latin America, and, arm-in-arm, we strolled around the huge fountain with its many strange statues. "*Buenas noches*," she said to everyone who passed us, and all who went by us did the same. Before the evening was over, we felt that we were on speaking terms with many of the residents of Trujillo. A drink by the walk-in fireplace in the hotel after a really good dinner, and we were indeed mellowed. I reflected, as I think she did. "Too bad about that handsome *novio* or boyfriend back in Quito." We retired to our separate rooms.

I wanted to see and film the huge pre-Inca city of Chan-Chan only a few miles out in the desert from Trujillo. Chan-Chan had been neglected because of the sensational mountaintop "Lost City of the Incas, Machu Picchu" to the south of us in the Andes. But historically, Chan-Chan is of much more interest and was also the source of much of the gold treasure that has made the Peruvian Inca Empire so well known to archaeologists and tourists. The next morning we taxied out to the immense crumbling adobe city.

Before the Incas conquered this place, a quarter of a million people lived in the city. That made it more populated than London, Paris, or Tokyo. The mud walls of Chan-Chan go up to and higher than three stories. Some are even higher. Unfortunately, with no one to tend them, all of the walls and buildings have been eroded by centuries of rain and the effects of the Pacific current, known to us as El Niño, which every so often washed ashore and inundated part of the city. This was a metropolis situated on the southern periphery of the great Sechura Desert which experiences rain of any quantity only once or twice every one hundred years. But nevertheless, after fifteen centuries, Chan-Chan has been conquered by the elements. The Incas took possession of it in the fifteenth century yet even then it was a dying civilization. Dynasties of the Chimu and the Inca armies looted the region of the gold that these people had preserved. This gold was then transported on the backs of llamas and men all the way up to the Andean Inca capitol of Cuzco. There it was reworked to satisfy the religious beliefs of the Incas until the advent of the Spanish conquistadors.

Since Barbara and I were there in 1953, many improvements and restorations have been made by the archaeological department of the Peruvian government. When we were there our taxi could drive with impunity all over and though the crumbling leavings of this once proud center. I am happy to document that we were able to film some extremely interesting and historical bas—reliefs that are no longer there, that have been washed away since that time.

Another pleasant evening in the Hotel Turistas and then we were on the road again in another bus going southward. This highway parallels the Pacific Ocean coastline which is often in sight. We had hardly settled in our seats when the *maestro* called out "Salaverry." A few folks called out and made their way to the front of the bus. Trying to be a gentleman, I had given Barbara the window seat, but I kept a weather eye on the horizon. Suddenly, there it was. All alone, silhouetted against the sky and the sea, a grand square-rigged sailing ship was etched against the skyline. The sails were furled and she was at rest.

"My God," I pressed Barbara's hand, "there it is, the ship that my brother and I will be sailing. It is the last working barque in the world!" Barbara squeezed my hand.

5 — THE OMEGA

Lima, the City of Kings. When it was first laid out on the Rimac River in 1532 by Francisco Pizarro, that is what he named it, 'The City of Kings.' Lima will always be that to me. I know Mexico City quite well, and I like it. But I prefer Lima. Smaller, more compact and much more colonial Spanish.

Our bus pulled into the downtown area and stopped at 8:30 p.m. Nightlife in the capitol was just beginning to come alive. The place had an excitement about it. My hand-written notes—those not sloshing about in the sewers of Bogotá—directed me to the hotel of my choice. The *Gran Maury*. It had been there since the nineteenth century when it was the city's finest. Many dignitaries visiting Lima stayed in it. That, of course, meant Barbara and I. A .25 taxi drive (Yes! Twenty-five cents!) took us to this once elegant hostelry on the Calle Ucali. The Maury was big and inexpensive, but somewhat rundown. Nevertheless, in those days it boasted the most tasty and elegant cuisine in the city. Yet the rooms cost us but $1.30 a night (bathroom down the hall, *por favor*). We did enjoy our best meal in some time served up by aging tuxedo-dressed waiters who all looked as though they too had been there since the turn of the century. (The *Gran Maury* lasted a few years and then its venerable walls finally succumbed to time. But so special was that old restaurant that I have heard that now, after our second millennium has turned over, it's restaurant is still going strong.)

Barbara had matters to attend to and so did I. I went to the United States Embassy, conveniently located downtown within walking distance, and asked for my brother's address. I did better there than I did with the U. S. bureaucracy in Bogotá. His name was quite well known.

Frederick D. Wilhelmsen at that time was a professor of philosophy at the University of Santa Clara in California. One of his students was from a wealthy and prominent family in Peru: the Calderón family that controlled much business and were politically influential. Frederick D. Wilhelmsen—we always called him Fritz—was then considered one of the most charismatic Thomist Pilosophy professors in the academic world. Like many of his students, the young Calderón from Lima was captivated by him. Perhaps the Peruvian was somewhat surprised when the erudite philosopher pulled him aside and admitted his life-long interest in the old square-rigged sailing ships of the past. The young fellow was, I'm sure, even more puzzled and pleased when he was told that the last commercially operating tall ship was at that time being operated by the Peruvian government…in the unglamorous *guano* trade. The bottom line was "Could Calderón manage a berth on this windjammer for Professor F. D. Wilhelmsen and his brother?" Not only did Fritz want to sail on the *Omega*, he wanted to write a book about it.

Money talks, especially in Latin America. Official Peruvian documents began to fill Fritz's mailbox. He had the blessings of the government, and he would be welcomed aboard the four-masted barque any time he wished.

Of course, in Lima, Fritz was the honored guest of his student's family. He was put up royally at the mansion of the distinguished Calderón family. Big brother would be there several weeks waiting for me. Fritz had used his time well. There were two condemned square-riggers moored in Lima's port of Callao. The German captain of one of them, the "*Tellus*," Captain Wriedt, still spent his retirement days puttering around his old ship. Fritz, whose affection for these relics nearly equaled that of the aging skipper, spent much of his time listening and taking notes of the sea yarns this gentleman enjoyed reliving. From the very shipshape and polished quarterdeck of the "*Tellus*" he would then return to the posh elegance of Peruvian high society.

My brother preferred the ship to life at the mansion. "I can't even light a cigarette," he told me, "without some liveried servant shoving a torch under my nose!" He hadn't come all this way to enjoy the small talk of the wealthy, and he hadn't brought much in the line of dinner jackets and starched collars. Intellectually, he might have been a giant among these well meaning socialites, but his lack of the Spanish language and his indifference to Peruvian politics soon had him looking about for more relaxed quarters. When one evening he was gently reprehended by his student that "Here, one never opens a door by oneself; he waits for the hired help and then goes his way," Fritz felt he had better do just that, get on his way. With made-up apologies to his hosts for the necessity of moving on, he extricated himself from the Peruvian society and took a pension or what today is called "bed and breakfast" accommodations. He went from high Peruvian aristocracy to English snobbery, *Mrs. Beach's* Pension. "The place," he told me when I finally tracked him down, "is larded with snobs. Every no-count blueblood who can't cut the muster in the British Isles is hanging around here trying to pick up a post-colonial job that will allow him to play cribbage most of the day and chase the Peruvian girls most of the night. Fritz moved in with me at the old *Maury*.

The three of us hit it off well during the couple days that we were able to spend together, before Fritz and I headed back north to our ship. Barbara, whose money was all tied up in uncooperative Ecuadorian funds, was now getting by on my largesse. Fritz had brought me money from sales accrued to my account from my late sales job and I was able to be generous with myself and with my friend. Maybe I wanted her around when I came back from the north or maybe I was just being nice. (I still don't know.) I loaned her what she needed until her freelance jobs and *Vision Magazine* would begin paying again, and she in turn was on deck when Fritz and I gathered our belongings together and boarded a 6:00 p.m. bus going to Trujillo.

Overland travel in Peru often takes place during the dark night hours. The Triple A and other responsible organizations always stress "Don't drive the roads in Mexico or elsewhere in Latin America after dark. It is hazardous." That advisory never stopped a South American traveler. Once away from the lights of the city, the Pan-American Highway stretched like a black ribbon north into apparent nothingness. The famous road was only a blacktop and only one lane much of the way. As in Colombia, when two vehicles approach one another, the first that blinks its headlights gets the right of way. Strangely enough, this system works well and only occasionally did I notice what today we call road rage.

The dust was intolerable. It was with a sigh of relief when we would stop at one of the dimly lit taverns along the way for a pit stop or a wet beer. My brother was duly impressed at one such place when a tall elderly gentleman all wrapped up in a scarf deferentially stepped aside for us, touched his forehead with his finger and respectfully murmured, "*Caballeros*." This is a word near gone in the Spanish colloquialism of today that acknowledges a gentleman or originally a man who rides horses and who is a cut above others. Fritz enjoyed that and referred to it in the book that he wrote. It bolstered us up until we arrived in the city of Trujillo and were taken to the *Hotel Turista* where I had stayed just the week before. We arrived at 3:30 a.m.

A good breakfast refreshed us late that morning, and we were even more buoyed up at our treatment at the local branch of the Peruvian Guano Company. We were expected and were told that we could board our ship any time we wanted. A taxi took us the twelve miles to the port of Salaverry. And there we got our first look at the 311-foot barque *Omega* . . . or as she had originally been christened, the *Drumcliff*. She had been launched from the ways of Russell and Greenock in Scotland and as such had a good beginning. That was 1878.

"There she is." Fritz excitedly waved his hand as we stood on the wharf of Salaverry, the last commercially operated square-rigger in the world. "She's been following the wind for nigh on to a century, and I've finally caught up with her. Let's get aboard."

I hadn't really imagined how large one of these nineteenth century tall ships could be. We often measure a large old ship along side of the great and tragic 1911 Cunard Liner,

"*Titanic.*" The ship that I was now preparing to board was thirty-five years older and nearly a third as large as that grand and classic shipwreck. The "*Omega's*" four masts reached way up into the sky. She was a barque: the masts were hung with square sails; the mizzen, or aft mast, was rigged fore and aft. The ship had seen better days, much better days. The "*Omega*" was down to hauling an even less respectable cargo than my recent tramp steamer, the "*S. S. Grammerstorf's*" hold of empty oil barrels. The Peruvian ship carried guano, the droppings of thousands—nay!—millions of birds that populate the west coast of South America. If it wasn't a fact, it would be a joke, and believe me an awful lot of jokes have been made at the "*Omega's*" expense.

We lollygagged on the main wooden pier that reached out into the ocean, and watched the flat-bottom lighters, or barges, being pulled out to the ship that dominated the harbor. They went out empty and returned loaded with fifty-pound bags of manure. These bags, in turn, we were soon told, would be trucked to the huge *Guildermeister* sugar plantation some miles inland. All we wanted was a ride out to the "*Omega,*" but such was the trickled down bureaucracy of the working class stevedores of the region that no one seemed to be in charge or could give us the OK. They were all Quechua and Aymará Indians from the Andes Mountains, and their motto seemed to be, "Ours is not to ask or answer; ours is to do only the job."

Eventually, an officer of some sort stepped out of a taxi and approached us. He was curious as to why an Anglo—I with blue eyes and sandy hair—and a dark-eyed bushy haired Jewish looking fellow, Fritz—were hanging around the docks of the Peruvian Guano Company. "Are you fellows spies for the government or are you here to fire the whole lot of us? You're certainly not Indians looking for a job." When we finally straightened out his Spanish, I was surprised to see my brother break out into a gusty laugh and into an infectious grin. "*Judío!*" he laughed, as he grabbed the unsuspecting man's hand and shook it. "I haven't been called a Jew since I interviewed Hilaire Belloc when I was writing his biography."

Sr. Eleazer Matallena Del Campo grinned back. He was a gentleman of sixty-eight years and was the first—and only—mate of the "*Omega.*" He grasped Fritz's hand and pumped it. He was caught up in the friendly mood of my brother. We talked and we showed him our papers. And he, in effect, said, "*No problemas.*" We would be guests on the "*Omega.*" (Fritz and I often reflected that the magic word here was "television." We told him that we were here to make movies of him and his crew; he thereafter always straightened up and bustled whenever my movie camera came out.) "Be my guest," he beamed and with a noble flourish he cleared a path for us through the streams of sweating stevedores and grandly motioned for us to take our places on a white guano stained and odiferous seat in one of the barges.

The "*Omega*" seemed to grow larger the closer we approached it. And when we came along side the ship and looked at the steep perpendicular rope ladder going up to the bulwark and main deck, our hearts and courage took a turn for the worse. "Crash," went our barge into the iron hull and as it did, with the agility of a teenager, the sixty-eight year old mate leaped up, grabbed the ladder, and swung himself up onto it. "Come right along," he called down to us from the safety of the deck. The ground swell separated the two vessels and then pushed us back into the ship.

"Give it a try," Fritz shouted to me. "I'll follow."

"Try," I fired back. "If you miss this thing and get caught in the middle, you won't get any more tries."

"Come right along," the mate pleasantly spoke again from the safety of the deck.

I did, and was surprised by my newfound nimbleness. I caught a rung and was on my way; no looking back until I, too, swung over the solid railing of the "Omega."

Now, I turned and looked down at the erudite university professor. And, I'll be darned if he, too, now made the leap and clawed his way up to us. His swarthy complexion was a tad less swarthy, but he was pleased with himself.

"Welcome aboard," the mate congratulated us. "If you finish this voyage with us, this will be your home for the next couple of months . . . or more."

"Two months," I grumbled to Fritz. I had a date with Barbara in two weeks.

"Two months?" Fritz mumbled back to me.

"Oh, yes," *Señor* Del Campo happily continued. "You know this is not the United States. Here in Peru we don't try to do everything yesterday; we are pleased to get it done *mañana*. Captain Hanke, after sailing these waters nearly forty years, still can't get used to our tempo." He laughed. "You'll see." And he led us aft to the quarterdeck.

We knew that our captain was German, bred and born in the old country. At the outbreak of World War I, he came to Peru as the first mate on this vessel. The Peruvian government, in an overzealous attempt to show its cooperation to the allied cause in Europe—or perhaps as a point of pique against the imperious German *Guildermeister Sugar Plantation* that controlled much of the northern coastline—confiscated the ship and renamed it the "Omega." The captain and most of the crew had been deported back to the Fatherland. Erik Hanke had stayed on with the ship and was soon elevated to Master. He had never looked back; he was now a Peruvian but his temperament definitely was Germanic.

Fritz and I had both been on a windjammer before. In the 1940s the Sausalito Harbor just north of San Francisco had the old "Star of India" tied up to one of its docks. My brother was picking up a degree at the University of San Francisco at the time, and I was trying my hand in the selling world. We both spent some hours on the old "Star" just poking around. The ship had never gone anywhere after its last run up to Alaska for lumber (as I write now I understand that eventually it was towed south to San Diego and is now a tourist attraction of the Maritime Museum there). That old timer was 200-feet long. We were amazed to realize the "Omega" was a third again as long.

Nevertheless, our quarters in the "poop-deck" would be quite cramped. Both of us are six-footers. The neat little quarters that we were given would not do for the two of us. We agreed to alternate; tonight, he would sleep in the cramped quarters—legs drawn up in the fetal position in order to fit into the five-foot bunk—and I would make up a much more commodious bed in the main lounge. This system worked out quite well.

A thickset sailor with a barrel chest interrupted the mate's proud explanation of the officers' quarters. "*Señors*," he announced, "Captain Hanke is coming aboard."

"As you say," the mate coldly answered. "Thank you." And then to us he confided, "He is the bosun; he's a strange one." We followed the bowlegged bosun out onto the deck just in time to see a slight looking man in a gray suit, tie, vest, and all climb over the bulwark. "Our guests," the mate proudly introduced us. The captain looked up at us; he was not a tall man.

"English?" he greeted us.

"No," the mate countered. "American."

"What's wrong now?" the captain resignedly asked. "What's the problem?"

We were to find out that this was typical of the master of the "*Omega*." Always a pessimist, always looking for a problem where none existed.

"Not so," my brother answered him in German. Captain Hanke looked up again and Fritz continued in the language that our grandfather had taught him as a youngster. As such he won a friend and our stay aboard the windjammer was assured. A bottle of schnapps was brought out and we three sat down and got acquainted. The mate diplomatically bowed out and saw to it that our bags were brought aboard from the barge.

Our conversation was illuminating even though somewhat colored by Captain Hanke's skepticism. He told us our ship would be the last to unload here. "The steamers," he grumbled, "get first choice. Their motors are always running and using up *soles* (Peru's currency) all day long while we have no engines. It will be several days before we are out of here. And then," he added, "the Fiestas of St. Peter and Paul are coming up. Another excuse to quit work." He shook his head. "This is not a good country in which to run a business. People stop whenever they want to. They don't care."

Fritz and I couldn't help but like the methodical German who found himself in a Latin land of *mañana* (and I sometimes think that he rather enjoyed the slower tempo of his adopted country).

We took advantage of the next couple days to go ashore. Mainly, I believe to get a full square meal at the Hotel Turistas in Trujillo, and to rent a car to take us out to the nearby pyramids of Los Mochis.

Here at the base of the Andes Mountains, in the dried-out desert lands that end up in the Pacific Ocean is the largest known pyramid on Earth, the Pyramid or Huaca of the Sun. It is much larger than the biggest structures of the Pharaohs along the Nile River in Egypt. This skyscraper is immense and is finished off with millions of adobe bricks. Research testifies that during the years of the Spanish occupation, millions of dollars of gold from ancient burials were dug out of this man-made mountain. In 1576 records of the treasury of Trujillo relate in black and white on the old vellum parchment of the day that García Gutiérrez de Toledo paid his Quinta—or royal fifth of his income—to the king. It came to 50,527 *castellanos* in gold that had been taken from this mound known as the Huaca del Sol. This measures up to multimillions of dollars worth of gold found in this mound alone. The sister pyramid, which is somewhat smaller, and is named Huaca de Luna or Pyramid of the Moon, had also yielded vast quantities of treasure to the old Castilian Colonial Empire. Today, of course, it is illegal to dig into these ancient mounds and graves, but—as we shall see—the eternal quest for gold continues. The government can't stop it (and sometimes unofficially encourages it).

I read my notes to Fritz and he gave me a quizzical look, "What the hell are we doing on this poop ship when all this treasure is waiting here in front of us?"

I know that he was being facetious, that the romance of the sea was his interest, but I finalized the speculation by saying, "Be my guest; there it is all before you. Nothing but a few grass and adobe huts around here to stop you and the Indians will probably pitch in and rent you a shovel. Anytime you want to start digging, please do so, and I'll record it on film for your students at the university."

He laughed, "I'm tempted," and then we both laughed and turned away; our ship was waiting. I knew I would be back . . . and I was. We picked up a couple of bottles of rum, a bag of that excellent Don Ofrio chocolate with which Peru is blessed, and some tins of crackers. The couple of meals we had already experienced on the "*Omega*" had shown us we were definitely not on a cruise ship.

We could never quite agree which was the most hazardous, the debarkation or the embarkation from the docks of Salaverry where the ocean moves in and out at twenty-foot swells, or the approach to the "*Omega's*" ladder. In time, we both agreed we were not meant to be deep-water sailors.

Still Fritz's feel for the days of sail drove him on. In Captain Hanke he had found a man who had experienced the days of sail from Africa's Cape of Good Hope to the turbulent storms of South America's Cape Horn. Fritz questioned him unmercifully. Fritz had read extensively about the last century of sail, but this man had been there. Captain Hanke hadn't read the books; he had personally fought the gales and had languished in the doldrums of the Pacific and had been in the Australian grain races of the 20s. They got along well.

The two of us had concocted a cocktail to ease the tedium of time while we waited for the guano bags to be shore bourn. We called our drink a "*mas o menos*"—"more or less." To our bottles of rum we added the juice of limes that we found in the galley, a tad of Coca-Cola, and a little sugar. We had some fun with that. There was no light but a single kerosene lantern, and when the sun was positioned in our portholes, we had enough light to read by. Yet, it wasn't long before we had exhausted all of the English language magazines that the captain furnished us: *Time, Newsweek,* and others. We read every word, and I do believe I was better informed on world affairs those weeks on the *"Omega"* than I've ever been.

For the next week, there was little activity. We were literally becalmed in the bay of Salaverry. Not for the lack of a breeze to blow us on our way, but for the lack of manpower to empty the ship's hold. First, there was an unusual ground swell that made it dangerous to approach with the barges. Then, it was the Peter and Paul Fiesta that took Indian laborers away from us. Nevertheless, Fritz and Captain Hanke filled the hours talking, and in time, Fritz filled the pages of his notebook. My German is nix so goot so I entertained myself fiddling with my cameras.

The barrel-chested bosun who we had met when we first came aboard was pointed out to us. First mate, the amiable *Señor* Del Campo, delighted in telling the story of the old pirate. "We got him some thirty years ago. No one would hire him or take him on. We think that he is eighty years old. He is the mystery man of the Pacific Ocean ports of Chile and Peru. Indians call him a demon, and he does have the strength of a demon. More commonly, he is referred to as a murderer, a mutineer, and above all, a survivor. In the 20s he shipped on a full rigged ship 'Escaldena' out of Valpraíso, Chile, bound for Callao, Peru. Something happened on that voyage that is as mysterious as the secret of the 'Marie Celeste' that was found sailing merrily through the Atlantic in 1872 without anybody aboard. The 'Escaldena' just disappeared in the Pacific with twenty-four hands. The *Brujos,* or Indian witches, tell us that she is still sailing up and down the coast and that on certain nights of the year, she can be seen silently and ghostly cutting through the water, her sails all set, and the phosphorous St. Elmo's fire lighting up her spars. The police in Valpraíso and Callao have a different story. 'Foul murder,' they have written on their dockets, 'Unproved, but nevertheless foul murder.' Along the sand dunes that stretch for hundreds of miles of Peru and Chile, the bodies of two men had washed ashore and were found. This was nearly a month after the 'Escaldena' had last been sighted. They proved to be seamen of that ship. Two days later, our bosun was found just ten miles from those men. He was camped out by the remains of a weather beaten longboat. The bosun was stone drunk on rum and apparently had been so for many days. He had the wherewithal, for among the supplies found in the stove-in longboat were several barrels of Chilean rum. The man was in the process of draining those barrels and obviously had been at it for some time. Hauled before the courts of Chile and Peru, the mysterious man had no comment. He couldn't explain how he came ashore or what had happened to his ship. He was in a total fog, as well he should be after downing gallons of Chilean rum, and he has never come up with an explanation. There was nothing to accuse him of. However, later in the investigation, it came out that the master of the 'Escaldena' had on board an illegal cargo of ancient jewels, gold, and silver from the tombs of the Incas or their predecessors. There has been speculation that his crew knew this and that a mutiny took place. The ship was scuttled. And then the mutineers fought among themselves. Blood was shed and only a few managed to escape the floundering ship. Our bosun was one of them, but alcohol or guilt has closed his lips. He does his work well here and has for all the years that he has been aboard. He is a good sailor. He can't get up on the spars anymore, but his work on deck is the best. But, when he goes ashore on leave, he is known to tear up the place and then sleep it off in the calaboose." Fritz and I got to know the bosun and we liked him. More than any, he was polite to us and always had a "*Buenos Dias*" for us and a tip of his cap.

A more pleasant story was the one that Captain Hanke proudly told Fritz about his compatriot Captain Wriedt of the ship *'Tellus'* who Fritz and I had interviewed. "Not long ago," the captain reminisced quite proudly, "the bulk of Her Majesty's Fleet of Great Britain paid a state visit to the ports of South America." Dozens of battle ships, destroyers, an aircraft carrier, and innumerable smaller British ships came into the harbor of Callao. Dignitaries, government officials, foreign diplomats, and politicos were all on the docks to see this might of the Queen's Navy. Now, at the same time, Captain Wriedt was poised to enter the harbor with his guano smelly full rigged square-rigger. Being German, Captain Wriedt naturally resented the British Navy. "To hell with the blighters," he said, and then, despite protocol, gave orders to up all sails and sailed right into the port among the English dreadnoughts. With the Peruvian flag billowing above a very small flag of Germany, he brought that little ship right on in among the behemoths. Not content to find a berth, he continued around the bay giving a demonstration of seamanship that very few Englishmen had ever seen. The mariners of our new age all lined the docks of their ships and applauded vigorously the efforts of this captain of another age. Wriedt dipped the Peruvian flag and the admiral of Her Majesty's Fleet then graciously dipped his colors. Captain Hanke enjoyed that story. He too had no love for the English. It turned out that Captain Wriedt was fined $25 for his display of arrogance, but the British admiral had insisted that he have the honor of paying the fine. "A splendid show of seamanship," he said, "in the tradition of Nelson."

Strolling the decks one evening, the captain pointed to the top of one of the bulwarks. It was made of thick and durable wood. We were shown a dent in the well-polished railing. "Several years ago, we were in some foul weather. Our second mate was aloft when one of the clew lines parted, just rotted through. We could all hear the scream as our second mate came tumbling down from way up there. He hit the port bulwark here with his head. It killed him instantly. We have not been able to replace the second mate."

"You know," the skipper continued, "in the old days of sail the saying was 'one hand for the ship and one hand for yourself.' The rigging is rotting, and the damned government won't give us a centavo to replace it. The guano commission will use this ship until it goes under. There are no seaman's unions here as you have up north. Most of the young men on the '*Omega*' are here only to say they have been here and to tiptoe up the ladder of experience to the Peruvian Navy where there is prestige, position, and money."

The captain took a pull on his Inca cigarette, perhaps the foulest smelling weed that was ever created, and gazed at the horizon. "Tomorrow we go," he said with finality. "The weather is good, the ship is empty, and the god-damned fiesta is over. You shall see your sail, Herr Fritz; you shall feel the deck under your feet begin its dance. It is the only good thing about this business." My brother and I both wanted to dance on the deck right then. We had waited too long for Fritz's youthful fantasy and too long for my sea epic to get underway. Besides, I had a date in Lima with a very charming lady.

Before dawn, the shouts started and the activity of setting sail began. The "*Omega*" carried no motor except for a putt-putt type of diesel engine that was used to bring platforms of fifty-pound guano bags aboard the ship and then lower them into several hatches. This barque was a true relic of nineteenth century history. No motors. We used the wind, that's all. And that, of course, was why Fritz had worked so hard to be on this vessel and why I was sure there might be a buyer for a film that could never be made again.

A good place to begin this opus of mine would be the raising of the huge anchor. Already several of the men were walking around the capstan pushing several bars and slowly winding up the great chains that held this monster in place. I scrambled out on the bowsprit, wrapped myself in some thick rope and waited for the thing to appear. I wanted to film it bursting out of the water with a dramatic splash. I waited and I waited. The process took forever. Lucky for me it did. I decided fill-in shots of the laboring crew would be appropriate. I pressed the button and got nothing. Nothing happened; the Bell and Howell was dead. I am not a profane man, but I must have said something scatological at that moment, and then extricated myself from my comfortable perch and climbed back aboard. I rushed to our cabin, shoved the camera under the covers of the bunk bed, and fiddled with uneducated fingers the mysterious inner works of the machine. Suddenly, the wind-up motor came to life. I was back in business. I charged back to the bow where I was grateful to see the same sailors patiently circling the capstan. I was in time. Out on the bowsprit, into my cocoon of ropes, and in position just as the anchor, that weighed a ton, broke water and was lifted up. It was a good movie shot, and it turned out to be very effective on the screen.

Then, aft, I hastened to the apply-named poop deck to watch Captain Hanke, all business and all German, shouting orders through a megaphone. Our first mate was the calmest of all; he stood by the wheel and quietly called orders to the helmsman. He motioned to me and proudly displayed his new uniform with a chest full of Peruvian medals. I filmed him in all of his histrionic glory. He was a delightful—if somewhat of a hammy—actor. Fritz was in the act, too. "Here," he called to me, "you must get a shot of the binnacle and the compass as we begin our run out of here." "Jeepers," I thought. "The professor has a few smarts, too."

"Crack," went the main sail. The wind caught it and it bellowed out in picture-perfect fashion. Then the foresail was let out, hung limply for a moment, and then ballooned as the shore breeze filled it. The *Omega* trembled and began to move. Captain Erik Hanke bellowed through his horn, "Let out the fore top and the t'gallents." The foremast, merely a bare pole a moment ago suddenly became a great white bird with all of its wings opened to catch the wind. First mate Eleazar Matallena Del Campo took up the litany from beneath the main mast and that pole, too, immediately became a source of energy, beauty, and life. The *Omega* was moving. Standing below the mizzenmast and the jigger pole, with its gaff rigged fore and aft spankers, the bosun boomed out a command. He didn't need a megaphone. The mostly young Peruvians, who 'til now we had seen do little but watch the guano operations, sprang into action and scrambled up the ratlines (rope ladders) as though the devil himself was after them. The masts became alive with white wings. The captain had promised my brother that he would lay on all the canvas that the ship could take and he kept his promise. White water now literally surrounded our bow and rushed along side us to the stern. I was here, then and everywhere with my movie camera. All hand-held shots. No time for the tripod. It was a scene that had been repeated for centuries. Columbus had experienced this when his *Santa Maria*, *Pinta*, and *Niña* headed out from Spain toward the New World in 1492. Sir Francis Drake knew the feeling when he and Hawkins bore out onto the Themes River and raced toward the Spanish Armada. Captain Bligh felt such a surge of sea when he set out in the long boat of his *H. M. S. Bounty* and began his epic voyage home to England. It was exhilarating.

"Mr. Wilhelmsen," the captain shouted to my brother over the scrambling, the shouting, and the testosterone of his vociferous crew, "do you like it? The men are particularly good today. They are not making mistakes. I think that movie camera has fired them up. We may reach Macabi Island too quickly." He laughed one of his rare laughs and put his hand on Fritz's shoulder (a familiarity that he had never done before). "Come," he said, "we will have us a schnapps," and he directed my brother to the quarterdeck where he kept his supply of German beverages.

Fritz called back to me, "Get it all, will you. We'll want to relive this day sometime, again and again." I hadn't seen the professor this elated since he and I had once tried to build an airplane with which to visit the Pope some twenty-odd years before when we were children, innocent, happy, and trusting.

❖❖❖

The Pacific Coast of South America from the Ecuadorian border right down to the Horn is a strip of desert sometimes fifty miles wide, sometimes only a couple miles. The greatest chain of mountains on Earth, the Andes, closes off this desert to the east. To the west is the Pacific. The cold Humboldt current flows up from the south where it encounters the warm waters of the El Niño current. For whatever reason, the meeting of those two great forces causes a climate that is ideally suited for the production of life: aquatic and bird life.

For 365 days of every year, a profusion of birds make this area their home. Millions of small fish swim the currents and a majority of them are gobbled up by the guano birds: guanaypes, pelicans, and other strange marine fowl. They rook, not on the mainland because there there are predators, but on the multitude of small islands that jut out of the sea some of which are a hundred or more miles from the mainland. They feast off of the ever-present banquet of the sea. And, of course, on these empty mountain islands they leave their droppings. Not just tons of the stuff but thousands and thousands of tons (the captain had some good German names for it and we soon did too). Our port of call was Macabi Island, and I can guarantee that on that island we saw and filmed valleys of this white excrement that measured up to six feet deep. The question then is: "Why? What's the reason for collecting all this stuff?"

The answer: This stuff is quite valuable providing one can hire cheap enough labor to gather it up and take it to the industrial world. When a person goes to his garden store and orders a fifty-pound bag of fertilizer, he pays rather well for it. Rarely will he be lucky enough to find and buy pure guano such as these islands produce. And, if during times of war which seemed quite prevalent this last century, one was in the market for fine nitrates for explosives, guano was high on the list of desirable chemicals. In other words, it has value, lots of it.

I understood guano was very profitable when I realized that the poor Indian, who was digging and bagging it, received barely a dollar a day. These men came from the high mountains where they had been glad to receive fifty cents a day working in the copper and silver mines. Like the fruit and cotton pickers who flocked in the 1930s to the United States to harvest apple, cotton, and vegetables these Quechua and Aymará-speaking Indians begged for jobs working the guano islands. Unfortunately, this work was not the best choice for them. They came from the high places of Huancayo and Oroya, and Ayacucho where they had been born with oversize lungs evolved to suck in the thin oxygen of 10,000 and more feet altitude. And now they have come down from the heights to sea level. Typically, those big and now unneeded breathing sacs collapse because there is no more use for them. Tuberculosis, respiratory problems, and cancer often follow. The mountaineers make their money but eventually many of them loose their lives. The fumes of ammonia that guano creates permeated our ship and the island. If the title had not already been used, I would have called the guano islands "Devil Islands." The Indians were not slaves; they came and they went as they pleased. The slave-master is their own doing as are the needs of modern society. They have made it their own world.

❖❖❖

I do not intend to provoke a laugh but for all the hustle and bustle on the *Omega* our average speed was about 2 1/2 miles per hour. And Captain Hanke was pleased. "We have made good time," he bragged to Fritz. "Sometimes," he wistfully added, "it is better to go slowly. It is better to be at sea, on the ocean than to be tied up to those hell holes of shit."

It took us a day, a night, and another day to reach Macabi Island.

Miles before it is reached, one can smell Macabi if the wind is right. The captain grumbled, "We'll be taking the brunt of that stink if this breeze keeps up. Our only anchorage is right where the winds gather. Mr. Wilhelmsen," he spoke directly to my brother, "you will have your fill of this sailing business very soon." He chuckled as though it was a good inside joke.

Macabi, named after the Macabee brothers of the Old Testament is really two islands joined by a wooden walking bridge. The two are about two-thirds of a mile long from north to south and half a mile east to west. Except for a two-story wooden building housing the administration, a store infirmary that is in reality a mortuary for most who enter it as a patient, and the tents of the Guaneros, Macabi is all rock, guano, and birds.

We slowly pulled in our sails and let them hang loose on the clew lines as we approached the harbor of the island. It was touchy work but the *Omega* had been there before, many times, and the crew knew the anchorage. Several rocks could be detected in the bay mainly because of the giant seals that cluster about them sunning themselves after gorging on the sea life all around them. People are only allowed to approach these ecological treasures three months of the year. Not even the workers or members of the administration can come out here. This ban allows the droppings on Macabi to increase, build up, and be worth the effort of collecting them during these three months.

Now began the process of loading the ship. We would need some 40,000 fifty-pound bags before we would be cleared to leave and head back to the mainland. Thirty of the dirtiest looking characters I've ever seen climbed aboard the next morning like a swarm of pirates boarding a Spanish treasure galleon. They were workers from the island, most highland Indians, and they were being paid a dollar a day. If looks alone could have smelled, these fellows would have driven us all off the ship. They and everything else on the island reeked of manure. Within one day we too had joined them in their unlovely essence. Barrels of sloppy-looking food were set up on the deck, and these men were all handed tin bowls. The mate was in charge of the dining of the work force, and he appeared all spruced up in his finest. He knew I would be ready with my movie camera. He had suggested that I make a sequence of this colorful event that took place twice a day. He strolled up and down the length of the line of odiferous stevedores. He carried a leather thong in his hand, not to abuse the Indians, but to show his authority. I couldn't get him to quit staring into the camera lens. Once fed, the men took up positions. Our one little diesel engine was coughed into life, and soon wooden platforms, loaded with guano, were lifted out of the flat barges along side of us, and lowered through the hatches of our main deck. Men below stacked them neatly in the empty hold. Several times the captain had the *Omega* turned around. He did this to keep us as much as possible downwind from the effluvium of the island. Nevertheless, like life itself, we soon became used to our lot for the next week or so. The nasty smells became routine and we were once again able to inhale the aroma of our coffee.

Now, that too was a problem. The coffee, the breakfasts, the lunches, the dinners were all the same; each one was as bad or worse as the last one. The bosun brought us eggs in the morning. Captain Hanke, *Señor* Del Campo, Fritz and I sat together in the quarterdeck salon and would repeat the same groans every morning. How anyone could constantly, day after day, butcher a simple egg is beyond my understanding. They tasted like vulcanized inner tube rubber patches . . . though perhaps rubber might have actually been tastier. The bread and biscuits, always so delicious in Latin America, was so hard we had to dunk them into the coffee to soften them up. There is a Peruvian spice, whose name I never put down mainly because I detested it, permeated everything. The captain wistfully lamented, "I can't get them to change it; apparently, they can't cook without it." The food got so bad that there were grumblings from the crew. Several petitions had been brought aft only to be rejected by the captain. He had no other recourse, the administration only allowed so much money per sailor per day. Resignedly, he would mutter, "When they are hungry, they will eat it."

But, we in the quarterdeck would not have to eat it while at Macabi Island. Ashore the four administrators of this whole operation were educated and proud bureaucrats of the Peruvian government. "They," the skipper confided to us, "have plenty of good provisions brought over from the mainland, enough for their three-month stay. They have a gasoline run refrigerator and they stock it well." And now he became downright conspiratorial. "I have sent word that the guano administration is desirous of a film documentary of this most important operation. I have informed them that the two cameramen and newsmakers are here aboard the *Omega* and that they are eager to come ashore and do their job." He was now twinkling, and the mate was nodding his head in agreement. "We will soon have an invitation."

And we did that evening. "Breakfast, lunch, and dinner tomorrow in the offices of the administration building." The captain couldn't refrain from a wink in our direction. The government launch came for us, not one of the guano stained lighters, but a rather snappy longboat with an Evinrude outboard engine. We chugged ashore. "Keep the camera and tripod in sight, Mr. Wilhelmsen," the captain reminded me several times. "Make it look important." We were greeted on the little pier that juts out from the island by four quite *simpatico* gentlemen. None of them was any older than I was then. Don Pablo, the boss, in a turtle-necked sweater, so out of keeping with his surroundings, greeted us cordially and sincerely. "Be our guests," he spoke and introduced us to his colleagues. "Our man is just now working on the meals." (I must mention that there were no women at all on Macabi

Island.) Don Pablo escorted us to the two-story wooden administration building. The captain motioned to me and hissed. "Take some pictures." This I did. Good ones too.

The building, except for the infirmary—or as the mate called it, "the Death House"—is a nicely built two-story frame house with verandas all around its four sides. The lower floor was loaded with boxed provisions from Trujillo and Lima. Upstairs, of course, was where the overseers made their home. It was a little above the stench of the island. Typical of Peru, these quarters were immaculately clean: trained servants made sure of that.

We were brought out onto a porch that looked out upon much of the guano operation. From our elevated position, we could see the white rocks of Macabi Island and the scores of men digging, gathering, bagging, weighing, counting, and dispatching the fifty-pound bags to the harbor where the barges waited to take them out to the *Omega*. The first day that we were there, 4800 sacks of the stuff were taken aboard. Each bag was worth two dollars before the middlemen got their hands in the pot.

From this vantage point, I took my films and was treated most deferentially by our four hosts.

A long table was neatly set up on one of the porches. Two large elevated fans, run by a generator, blew air across the veranda toward the work area below and beyond us. The air helped keep the island smell away from us. Below, at all times, we could see the Indians working the guano. These men were scantily clothed and all wore a bandana about their heads. They seemed quite content and often we heard laughter from them.

Pisco, the brandy of Peru, was served up immediately with ginger ale or limes: the one is called a Pisco Chilcano, the latter, a Pisco Sour. They are the universal cocktails of the country. Then Chilean wine was poured into long-stemmed glasses by men in clean white shirts and pantaloons. Platters of eggs and bacon were then passed around the table and pots of coffee were brought out. Good bread with marmalade was available as were pitchers of freshly squeezed orange juice.

For the members of the *Omega*, Captain Hanke, First Mate Del Campo, and the Wilhelmsen brothers all conversation ceased. We dug in. Don Pablo and his companions enjoyed our appetites as well as we did. A radio blared out the popular songs of the moment and it was a delightful repast. Fritz did whisper to me, "I wonder what those fellows out there in that shit think about all this."

"I wouldn't know," I answered as I stabbed another strip of bacon and washed it down with a steaming draught of coffee.

When breakfast was finished, we were given a tour of the island. Respectfully, the working Indians would step aside and all had a *"Buenos Días"* for us. They lived in tents made of guano sacks. The Pacific Coast weather at this time of year was balmy so no heating was needed. I dare say the workers stayed in the same clothes the full three months they spent on the island. And then, like the wetbacks of old Mexico, they returned to their mountain homes in the Andes with a fist full of *soles*. They had done much better than their compatriots and their wives were accordingly pleased—after, of course, burning the abominable guano garments. Unfortunately, many of these men were already coughing. They earned a living in one hell of an environment. The administrators, the captain, and his mate seemed indifferent to it all. They had seen it too often—but Fritz and I could not help but feel quite sorry for those Indians.

In the afternoon, a game of sorts was brought out in which players toss beanbags at a complicated large wooden box dotted with target holes. Don Pablo and his companions had a lively interest in this entertainment, and we understood that some pretty sizable wagers passed hands. The captain and the mate snoozed in their chairs during the games, and even though Fritz and I were invited to participate, we two just stared out at the wretchedness all about us.

We perked up when a light lunch was served, and then before sundown, two large lamb roasts were brought up from glowing coals below and placed on the table. These were served with the usual libations. Each roast was surrounded by many boiled potatoes.

At dusk, all in a mellow mood, we were taken back to the *Omega* where we finished the day sitting on the quarterdeck watching the great big sun disappear into the Pacific horizon.

The next day was a duplicate of the first except that I had taken all the films I wanted of working conditions on Macabi Island. I instinctively realized that only so much misery would be tolerated by the viewing public. (I was right on that; though the National Geographic Society some years later requested all that I had.) On this second day ashore we—so to speak—ate and ran. The captain had stayed aboard as was his duty, but the mate insisted on a tour by longboat around the island to view up close the giant seals. Again, he duded up in his most impressive uniform, placed a clean white towel on the thwart or seat of the rowboat and settled down to give us a lecture on the sea life of Peru. He had indulged freely of the ample stock of beverages that Don Pablo was very liberal in passing around, and this seemed to speed up his elocution. He spoke only in Spanish and most of what he said was lost to us. Fritz did try to restrain him once when he insisted on stepping on a rock and posing with one of the giant seals. He and the animal looked ridiculous, but I did get a fun still picture that I do hope is in one of his granddaughter's family picture albums. We nearly got swamped a couple of times on that little excursion, but it was a nice afternoon that contrasted with the dour business going on in the center of the island.

The third day, the mate took us out in the ship's longboat again, this time to circle the *Omega* and to make films of the anchored ship. The next day, the captain requested our presence in his cabin. "Mr. Wilhelmsen," he said not to my brother this time, but to me, "you might have quite a movie to make right here. Do you remember the movie *Mutiny on the Bounty*? Well, we've got one coming up here on the *Omega*."

Fritz really perked up. "*Vas es losh?*" he questioned the German in his own language. "Mutiny?"

73

"Ha," the captain answered, and I knew we weren't in any danger. "The worse they can do is to maroon us over there on Macabi."

Now it was Fritz whose German failed him, but whose Germanic blood prompted him to say, "No shit!"

"Exactly," the skipper rejoined. "You yourself have complained everyday about the food on this vessel. We here aft get the cream of the crap. What do you think the boys in the foc'sal are getting?" He snorted. "Crap is right. The worst. Worse than it was in Germany after Versailles and World War I. I don't blame them. But they do not believe me when I say that this is all that we have. Right now I know the petitions are being signed. They'll be coming aft now any day."

And, sure enough, "Aft" they came the following morning. A dozen or more of the sailors. Those with an eye on a future career in the Peruvian Navy, of course, stayed back. They looked mean and the tone of their voices took on an edge when their spokesman pointed to the island and mumbled, "You, sirs, are eating good food over there. Here we're eating slop."

Fritz whispered in my ear, "What did I tell you?"

The captain made an attempt to imitate the tough bully mates he had worked with forty years ago. "Are you hungry? Are you not getting enough? Tell me. It is not good, I know, but I have requested better. The government works slowly, you know."

A voice from the crowd, "You've told us that before."

Captain Erik Hanke didn't like that objection to his veracity, an objection that was not true. He had put in for better grub and for a better cook; he had told us so. Louder than I thought him capable, he shouted out, "Mr. Bosun, Mr. Bosun, come up here, now."

The hulking, barrel-chested, old pirate of fable and myth briskly lumbered up on his bowlegs. In his right hand he carried a marlinspike, a lethal weapon in anyone's hands. In his belt was a belaying pin. "Aye, sir," he simply said and turned toward the dissenters. Now I realized why the captain was so cavalier in his attitude. He had an ace in the hole, the awesome man of mystery.

To his credit also, *Señor* Eleazer Matailena Del Campo, our genial first mate, now made an appearance. Tucked in his belt was the oldest, dirtiest and most disreputable looking *Colt* six-shooter I had ever seen. "Gentlemen," he said in his quiet voice, "the captain is working on this problem. You can believe me. He is in touch by radio from the Island with Lima. Conditions will change very soon. The cook will be replaced."

A relieved voice called back, "I never wanted the job anyway. I'm a sailor not a cook."

That broke the tension. A chorus of voices hollered out to the effect, "You can say that again. That's for sure. Bring your woman aboard. I'm hungry."

The confrontation was defused, especially when Captain Hanke said in a loud voice,

"Mr. Bosun, you take the watch this evening and stay on it tonight. There'll be a ration of rum for you." The mutiny on the *Omega* was over.

We didn't fill up with the full count of 40,000 bags of guano that we had expected. Now, new orders reached the *Omega* via the radio on Macabi. "Take what you have and make for Puerto Chicama." The Guildermeister Sugar Plantation had put in an order for fertilizer.

And so we left the strange, noxious and sad Macabi Isle. We had spent eleven days there, and were mighty pleased to be on our way. The original ship itinerary had been to sail to the Port of Paita, a four-day voyage. Fritz had looked forward to that sail. But he did admit to me, as the captain had once told him, "You will have your fill of this sailing business very soon," and indeed he had. My brother had collected a wealth of information on this last, commercially run tall ship and its operation. He now wanted to be on his way home to his wife and daughters. And I had a young lady waiting for me—or so I hoped—in Lima.

The captain was good enough to put me in the longboat with a couple of husky rowers. He kept the ship trimmed while I was rowed about the *Omega* and took my films of her under sail. It was a treat, and the movie sequence that I took exceeded my expectations.

Fritz stood by the man at the wheel for most of a day and a night and enjoyed his sail into the past. Then the Peruvian coastline came into focus. A call went out, "Puerto Chicama. Bring in the sails and prepare the anchor."

Both of us stood at the bulwarks and stared at the desert shores of the coast. *Señor* Del Campo loaned us a telescope, and we made out a nondescript village of adobe houses. "Puerto Chicama," the mate told us. "We will unload the guano here, and it will go to Guildermeister. Then we will go back to Macabi for some more."

The anchor was dropped, a lot faster going down than coming up. The longboat was lowered. The mate softly came up to us and handed us two belaying pins. "A little token and remembrance of our time together." We thanked him and then Captain Hanke came forward and handed us a package.

"You are interested in the sailing ships, Mr. Wilhelmsen, here is a sail maker's kit that has been in use for at least a century. It's for sewing sails. We will soon not have any more sails to mend here. Take it as a remembrance." We were surprised by these gifts. It seemed in keeping with the *simpatico* mate, but from the cynical old German, well, that was a most appreciated gift.

The longboat was made ready. I had no need to carry our several bags; the men carefully lowered them down to it. We two climbed down somewhat more nimble than when we first climbed aboard.

Then from the *Omega* a lusty cry went up, and we were given a rousing goodbye from the crew. Many of the young men were up in the rigging, and they leaped about from yard to yard like a pack of monkeys. They gave us a good send off.

Ahead of me was Puerto Chicama. This town would prove to be a pivotal place in my life.

(In 1956 Frederick D. Wilhelmsen's book, *Omega: Last of the Barques* was published by Newman Press of Westminster, Maryland. In 1995, a Spanish edition of his book, *La Omega, La Ultima Barca,* was published by the Associacion De Maritima Yolanda: Naval Iberoamericana in Lima. And again in 1996, was reprinted under the title *Under Full Sail* along with the story of a voyage he and I made in 1988 on the briganteen *"Romance."*)

The *Omega* quietly sank one night in the harbor of the port of Callao just out of Lima. She rode tall and proud one night, and then in the morning, she was not there. It was 1972, and she was tired.

Miguel Loayza: Wanted for crimes of Indian genocide by the governments of Peru, Colombia, Brazil, the United Kingdom, and the United States.

Hermann Becker: German explorer with a 28-foot anaconda.

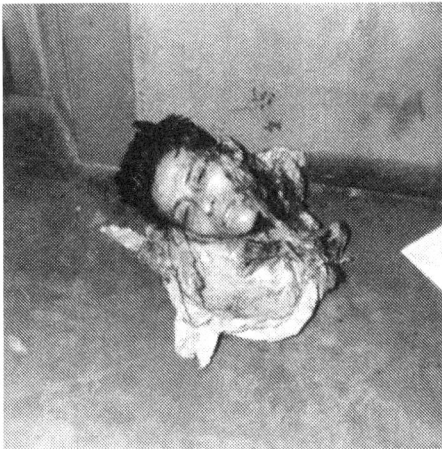

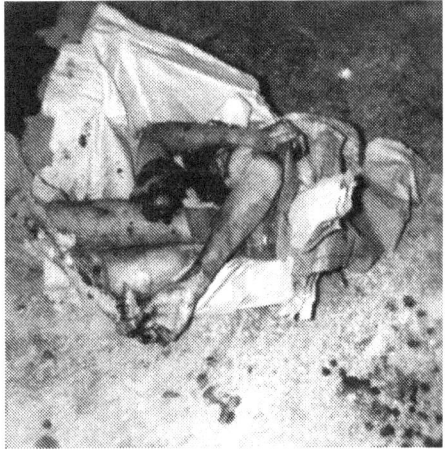

Ferdinand, our launch motorist killed by Mayorunas Indians on the Yavari River of Peru

Battle Against Indians

It could have been a scene from the days of Lewis and Clark or Daniel Boone. A surveying party of 38 was trapped on a knoll, under attack by Indians. A column of government troops was marching through the forest to the rescue.

But the forest where 30 civilian and eight army engineers were be-

SAVED—Party of engineers which set out from Requena, Peru, was saved after Indian attack in jungle.

Author with friendly Yaguas Indians.

Press releases of the Indian war author stumbled into.

Peru Planes Strafe Hostile Jungle Tribe

LIMA, Peru (UPI)—Peruvian air force B-26s flew strafing sorties Sunday in the third straight day of weird fighting which pits airplanes and modern firepower against Stone Age weaponry.

Smugglers Blamed

The Defense Ministry blamed smugglers and opium growers for agitating the normally placid Cuquimas and inciting them against the troops. The patrol was turned back by the road from Requena to the border.

The patrol, which suffered casualties of four dead and three wounded in the first two days of fighting, radioed that it was attacked again Sunday morning shortly after dawn. The column was en route to the Yavari River, which forms the border along Brazil's northwestern hump, where the gunboat

The *Jesucita* paddleboat on the Magdalena River.

Lake Guativita, Colombia, source of the legend of El Dorado, the Golden Man.

Miniature solid gold raft found at Guatavita that proves the Legend of El Dorado is true.

Author at Lake Guatavita.

Strange demonic stone statues found in southern Colombia that confound archaeologists.

Strange demonic stone statues as above.

Town of San Agustín in southern Colombia.

Pyramid of Moche in northern Peru; the largest in the world.

Inca festival of Inti Rymi in Cuzco, Peru.

Enigmatic colossal stone ruins of the ancient city of Tiahuanaco, 12500 feet up in the Andes Mountains of Bolivia.

Author and Barbara Holbrook.

The *Omega*, the last commercially operated square-rigged ship afloat.

Author on the *Omega* in the Pacific Ocean.

The *Omega* anchored off Macabi Island.

Author and his brother Frederick on board the *Omega* off the coast of Peru.

6 — ERNESTO BATANERO

Puerto Chicama in 1953 was a town of about 2000 people. There was no two-story building to be seen, just low flat, close-to-the-ground dwellings constructed of adobe or wooden slats covered over with white plaster. Many had pleasant shaded wooden porches. Geologically, Puerto Chicama is located on the southern edge of the Sechura Desert that stretches four hundred miles north close to the border of Ecuador. The Pacific Ocean parallels the desert on the west and the Andes Mountains on the east. As before mentioned, its width can be as much as fifty or more miles. The Sechura Desert receives less rainfall than most any other place on Earth: a good sprinkling once every hundred years is considered phenomenal. The Humboldt and Niño currents and the confining, often perpendicular, mountains account for this condition. The town exists mainly because it is the port of call to the big city of Trujillo, located fifty miles inland. Another reason is the need to service the huge German Guildermeister Sugar Plantation about thirty miles southwest. Most families in Puerto Chicama make their living, one way or another, through the sugar business or the government business of servicing and taxing the occasional ships that stop there. During World War II, it was rumored that German U-boats would slip unobtrusively into the port on certain nights to pick up quantities of sugar for Adolf Hitler and his sweets starved Third Reich. (I can confirm those rumors.) Of course, there is in this little town an administration that enables the government of Peru, no matter how distant, to retain control.

Fritz and I were let off at the end of a long pier that was used mostly by local fishermen. We were on our own. The usual group of youngsters were waiting for us and a pleasant looking man in a casual khaki uniform directed them to take our bags into town and to the *Aduana*. He chatted with us amicably as we tried to find out how to get to Trujillo. "No taxis in this place," he laughed. "Maybe a bus. Depends on who is going to town." But transportation was not the least of our problems. Once in the little office of the Aduana, we were met by a man with a more severe attitude. The questions came fast and then slower so that we could understand them. "What are you doing in Peru? This is not a tourist port. We have no accommodations, stamps, or seals to process foreigners here. This is strictly a business port. We've never had a foreigner leave a boat in this place." Much palaver went on between this man and a couple of other civil guard types. Our original greeter was gentler; he bought us a bottle of uncooled *Bidou* (Peru's answer to Coca-Cola). Then he brought us a nine-month-old copy of *Time Magazine* in English and advised patience. I had been picking up on the Spanish language—poco a poco—and I soon caught the drift of the conversation: "Fritz," I said, "they think that we are spies, that we're working for the Ecuadorian government, which is right now threatening their border."

"God," my brother intoned, "and here we are who cannot even understand a conversation in Spanish! Ecuadorian spies. I'll be darned."

A phone call was being placed to Lima some five hundred miles to the south of us. It turned out that this was the only phone in all of Puerto Chicama. This call took a good hour to cut through the bureaucracy of the government. "What are we to do with them?" was the question. Tourist instructions were not in the book. The line was kept open while the heads in Lima got together.

And then came the solution that we all wanted and needed. An impressive man in a Hawaiian shirt entered the door. He walked directly to us. In perfect English with just a touch of the lilting Spanish accent, he asked, "I was told two Americans were here. I want to see if I can help. I lived in the United States for some years. I am at your service. I am Ernesto Batanero."

Ernesto in 1953 was forty-nine years old. Tall, thin, brunette, quite handsome with the sharp look of the Levant about him. He did, indeed, boast of a tad of Arab blood in his veins. The man exuded charm and hospitality. As it turned out, he was all of these and more.

Mr. Batanero spoke rapidly to the officials, and it was evident that they respected him. He asked for a paper, wrote several sentences on the sheet and signed it with a flourish. They all shook hands. The government employee, who was so fierce looking a moment before, now smiled broadly and stepped from behind his desk. He shook my hand and then Fritz's. He even went so far as to give us both a gentle *abrazo*. "*Muy bien*," he repeated a couple of times.

Batanero picked up both of our bags and simply said in English, "It's all fixed up. I've signed for you. We can go now."

A husky young Indian fellow awaited us outside on the dirt street. "This is Adrián," our benefactor beamed. "We call him Quaide because of his strength, the strength of the old Inca. He is in my employ."

There was a bench on the beachfront by the *Aduana* and we three sat there and talked. Ernesto told us that he owned a small business in town that manufactured grass or straw products: The Fábrica De Junca. "We put together sandals, mats, baskets, and most anything. I employ many of the people of the town. They work for me in their homes weaving the reeds that grow only in this area. In my little factory, I have a trained few who put it all together into whatever orders we have. I'm hoping to get the United States interested. Both Japan and Italy work much the same products as we do, but their cost and workmanship cannot compete with our handmade craftsmanship and prices. I must show you," he abruptly said and stood up. "Come to my house and we'll have lunch. Coming from Macabi Island I'm sure you could do with some vegetables and fruits. Nieves and her mother will be more than happy to serve you. Nieves is my wife."

As I was to learn, everything in Puerto Chicama is within walking distance. We and our amiable friend and his employee with our bags slung over his shoulders and in his hands, strolled along the seashore. The area was quite attractive: the long vanilla colored beach, a lusty bounding surf, and in the distance, the four-masted barque *Omega*.

We arrived at the Batanero house quickly. The ocean was its front yard. The building was a neatly plastered bungalow with a flat roof. Like most the houses in town, it was white-washed a stark bleached color that made it hard on the eyes when the sun was up. Inside, the rooms were spotlessly clean.

Two steps and we were on Batanero's porch. Fritz and I were still somewhat groggy from living on sea for the past weeks and hadn't gotten our land legs back yet. But the grogginess immediately disappeared. We were met at the door by one of the most attractive—in all shades of the word—women I've ever known.

"Nieves," Ernesto Batanero called out, "meet my two friends from the United States. They'll be with us for lunch and then I'll get them on their way to Trujillo. (I was to learn, especially with Ernesto, that gentleman or not, Peruvian wives were always expected to get on with the work). She gave a whimsical nod of her head and curtsied ever so slightly, holding out her colorful skirt, as she greeted us.

She was, perhaps, five feet six, and perfectly proportioned, had a full head of blond hair—probably touched up here and there—and was made-up to perfection. . . . The woman was all woman. She greeted us and answered her husband in Spanish in a deep husky voice.

"Nieves can't get the hang of English," Batanero confided to us in English. "She is from Spain, a political refugee here from the Spanish Civil War of the thirties. She is my best friend and my wife," he proudly told us. Fritz and I looked at one another. In our minds we were congratulating ourselves for taking that final bucket bath on the *Omega* this morning before debarking. The last thing we wanted to do was to perfume her parlor with *eau de cologne de guano*. The lady was enchanting and would continue to be so for me for many, many years.

As if to answer our unspoken thoughts, Ernesto said, "If you want a shower to clean up in, I can arrange it at the Guildermeister's office just a short walk away. They have," he humorously added, "the only tub and shower in town."

That broke the awkwardness of introduction, and we three laughed as we told him that we had anticipated just such a meeting as this this morning and had done well with the mate's buckets and lye soap. This was translated to Nieves. She too caught the humor of it and let out one of her throaty laughs. "*Guano*," she shook her head. "*Qué Barbaridad!*"

Some rapid Spanish followed and an older heavy-set lady with two young girls came out from behind a curtain. "*Estan listas?*" this woman asked, and her voice sounded vaguely familiar.

"This is Nana," Ernesto introduced us. "She is Nieves' mother. We call her that because Marie and Robin call her that. Marie is nine years old and this is Robin, who is eighteen months." The older girl was tall and lithesome and obviously destined to be a Latin beauty. The little girl had great brown eyes and she, too, looked like she would be a real handful in time. They both curtsied.

We were directed into the modest dining room where a table was set with bowls of fruit, some meat cuts, a ball of cheese, and a large dish of warm bread. "We do with little here," Ernesto apologized. "But please take as much as you want." His hospitality was evident, and it would be so for a long time.

Fritz, especially, was starved for fresh produce. The *Omega* served none. He shook his host's hand again, bowed to Nana and—strange for him—gave Nieves a heartfelt hug. "*Many gracias,*" he attempted, and again the lady favored us with one of her smiles and laughs. We sat down and ate. The lunch was grand, and the warmth of the family continued. Fritz, the professor and man of words, quoted William Wordsworth to us all and Ernesto translated it to his wife who took Fritz's hand and squeezed it. "A genial hearth, a hospitable board, and a refined rusticity."

"Oh, Frederick," Ernesto beamed. "Nieves especially will like that. She came here from one of the best families of old Spain."

We settled back to talk. "May I smoke?" Fritz asked.

"By all means do," our host answered. "We don't, but we don't mind at all. I do believe Nieves enjoys the fragrance of a good cigar." Fritz blushed, and held up a pack of Incas cigarettes. Again there was laughter. "Please go ahead," Ernesto gestured. "Down here we call them in English, 'Inca stinkas.' You do not offend at all." Fritz stoked up and we talked.

Our story was quickly told, and Ernesto listened intently. Then he told his story.

Ernesto Batanero had been born in this area, but as a youngster had hoped for better things. He was always fascinated by airplanes, and when the big Pan American Airlines began servicing his country for air routes, he was determined to be a part of the action. Somehow, as a twenty-year-old, he had managed by determination to learn English and to snare a scholarship to a Pan American study course in Chicago. He paid his way by working in an automobile garage in Chicago. He often serviced the big Packards, Cadillacs, and Pierce Arrows of the Al Capone mob. "They tipped well," he remembered. Being Peruvian, he was hired by Pan American—or as it was later called, Panagra—and was commissioned to fly on many of that company's routes as they chartered the flight patterns over his country south on down and into Chile.

"Now," he chuckled, and really caught my interest, "all of my life living here with the Indians, I had been aware of a legend of a great pyramid somewhere to the north of us. Somewhere in the Sechura Desert. Supposedly it was erected by the Mochica's around the fifth or sixth century. Ask a poor man around here and he'll tell you that the 'huaca blanca,' as it is called—'the white pyramid'—holds some of the gold that Pizarro never could find. Our archaeological and historical books down here always mention it. While flying the big planes south from Ecuador, I always used my authority to direct the pilot of the plane this way and that as we flew over the desert. But I never did see any indication of a huaca blanca. But now," he confided, "some of the Pan American routes fly the path that I suggested. I never saw the pyramid, but I did see evidence of human activity and what appears to be the outline of a road. We were flying pretty high and it was difficult to make out details. Some day my hope is to locate them. See what it's all about." He looked sharply at me. I was all ears, and Batanero knew it.

"I could have done better for my family if I had continued on with Pan Am, but several years ago I took the retirement monies that I had built up and came back home. Here. I wanted to follow my instincts and desire to dig into the past of northern Peru. Every tourist knows about Machu Picchu in the mountains south of us, but many do not know that a lot of the wealth of the Incas originated right here in this area. I took my little nest egg and founded the Fábrica De Junca. A certain reed grows only in this Chicama Valley, nowhere else. This reed is so durable that when fifteen hundred year old Chimu mummies were opened in Chan-Chan sandals and other things fashioned with this reed were found intact and in near-new condition. My little factory employs a fourth of the women in Puerto Chicama. They work at home. It is a good business for this poor town." He laughed. "The chief of the *Aduna's* wife and two daughters are in my employ. That's why I had no problem signing you into the port here."

"*Señor* Batanero," I started.

"Ernesto," he corrected me.

"Have you made any significant finds? Do you work alone? I have read about this northern Peru and have notes."

"Ho," he responded, "I hire *huaceros*, keep them in beans and pisco. They are digging all over the area. When they find metal or other interesting objects, they come to me." I opened my mouth to say something else, but then thought better of it.

He anticipated me. "Yes, *Señor* Romain, I know it is illegal. It is against the law to rob the graves of our ancestors. It is a good law. But . . . " and he sighed, "the governments *huaceros*, who call themselves archaeologists, do much worse than the few men and families who I support. Take my man Chanchito . . . " he looked at his wife who nodded. "He is called Chanchito because he goes into the ground head first like a little pig. He knows much more, a great deal more than our esteemed Muséo National Arqueológico opportunists who often take from the ground that which has been dug up with our money, and place these graceful objects of long ago in their own homes as conversation pieces. Or they, more often, sell them for personal profit. Fortunes have been made. And not just by the Spaniards. I've seen it." Batanero was bitter. "And when gold is discovered, and masks, cups, plates, and the like are found, look out: There is a scramble for those valuable objects. They end up in the most exclusive houses of the rich. The museum gets but a token of their finds. No," he resignedly said, "I feel no compunction keeping what I find or what my people bring me."

I liked Ernesto's attitude, and felt bold enough to question him. "Have you come across anything really exciting?" I phrased my question carefully. I was interested in this man, and I wanted to know the full story of his treasure hunts. I even went into my bags and brought out the little owl-face gold piece that I had bought at Lake Guatavita in Colombia. He turned it over in his fingers carefully and looked closely at me. "Oh, this is good," he said, "very good. Well designed and very well made. You did very well there, *Señor* Romain."

"Please call me Romain," I interjected.

"Of course," he answered almost absentmindedly as he motioned his mother-in-law to take his two daughters out of the room in which we were talking. He then excused himself, and disappeared back somewhere in his house and returned with a wooden cigar box. He placed it upon the table, which had been cleared of the lunch bowls, and opened it.

"I have asked Nana to take my daughters elsewhere because what they don't see, they won't know. It is not fair to allow them to be exposed to my ideas and to the laws of the country that I do not respect. *No es verdad*, Nieves?" he questioned his wife. She nodded approval.

He took a handful of nondescript pieces and bits of metal from the cigar box. "Gold," he said as he handed me several fragments. "Gold mixed with copper as the Mochicas often did it. If a government employee could get a hold of these things, they would not go to the bona fide archaeologist, but to the melting fires of some metallurgist. The gold would be extracted and the profit would go into the pocket of someone in Lima. Frankly," he continued, "I do not yet know how to deal with these findings. I am at fault for accepting them from my *huaceros* and yet I know that if they are given to the authorities they will be melted down. The Spanish conquistadors have been blamed for doing the same with Atahualpa's gold, but there are a lot of people doing it today."

I looked at my brother. He tilted his head and said, "You've been romancing about this stuff for years. Why don't you go along with *Señor* Batanero and see what you can come up with." I noticed a tad of envy in Fritz's voice. He was well married and would never be able to follow such a quixotic idea himself.

Ernesto Batanero heard his comment. For a moment I was embarrassed. It was presumptuous to assume that I would be welcome in this man's private world. Ernesto talked on. "Right now I am working on a temple mound just a short walk from here. I believe it to be so promising that I have asked Chan Chita and the doctor to keep their hands off of it for the time being."

"The doctor?" I asked.

"We call him that even though he can't read or write. He has none of the prestigious degrees that our estimable museum people have, but he knows much more than they. He knows the Chimu, the Mochica, the Inca, the Lambayaque, the Cupersnique and can literally smell their remains in the ground. He has been jailed several times, not for just digging, but because he refuses to dig for the so-called professionals. Unfortunately, I can't trust him. He drinks. When I was recently in Lima on Fábrica business, he came here to Nieves and told her he had made a find. She said that I would return within the week. But when I did, I found that he was in jail in Trujillo. Not because of anything he had found, but because he had gone on a big drunk. I paid his fine and he tearfully told me that he had dug up here in the Chicama Valley, not far from us, a mummy with a golden mask covering the face. He said it was at least a quarter of an inch thick. His thirst was so great that he could not wait for my return and so he sold it to one of the big hacienda owners east of Trujillo, sold it for a pittance. His crime was not archaeological theft but too much brandy. I continue to hire him but because I come and go from here on business, I cannot trust him to bring his finds to me. I need someone trustworthy who will be here when he is needed and to help me explore the many places that I think are worthy." He looked quizzically at me. "*Señor* Romain, you could be that man."

Then quickly, as though to pad his statement, he added. "I can promise you exciting things for your film. My man, Adrián, who we call Quaide, is strong and he will fight a giant condor for your pictures. There are strange bears in the Andes east of Trujillo that are found nowhere else on Earth. They are small, but they are vicious. We can make pictures of them."

I immediately like his phrasing, "We" can make pictures of them.

"I've heard," he enthusiastically continued, "that somewhere in the mountains there is a complete city of ancient origin that no one visits . . . the Indians, yes, but not others. We could seek it out together."

Ernesto was on a roll now and I could tell it by the way his voice inflected and how his eyes lit up. I glanced at his wife. She nodded, "*Es verdad. It is true.*" He continued, "All of this region is ready for discovery. I have worked with Americans for years. I trust them. I like them. I have always been a friend to the United States. I need someone who I can trust to carry on with my discoveries."

"Wow!" I exclaimed. I looked at Fritz who pleasantly said, "You won't get a better offer than that. All you've got in your bag is a bundle of nebulous notes that don't translate to anything but hopes. I have never met a man who I thought of as more sincere than *Señor* Batanero. Tell him you're his man, and let us get on our way to Lima. I have a wife and daughters who I am eager to see."

I had made plans for this South American epic that I had hoped to film. The old Inca capitol city of Cuzco was definitely one of them, and Lake Titicaca, and the enigmatic ancient city of Tiahuanaco in Bolivia. I needed them in my film and I wanted to see them. *But*, here was the promise of a real adventure . . . the 'bird in the hand.' An adventure that would have a plot, motivation, action, and hopefully, a successful conclusion. I was excited. I stood up from the table and extended my hand to the man in the Hawaiian shirt. "Ernesto, if you will give me a couple weeks with which to finish my filming plans in Cuzco and Bolivia, I will promise you that I will return and will work with you on your finds." He stood, and we shook hands. I had a partner. We had made a deal.

"You will have your own quarters," Ernesto added. "I have a large room adjoining our house. I use it for storage. We will have it ready for you when you return."

There was little more to be said. I was given the Lima address of the Fábrica Batanero and the phone number. It was agreed that I send a wire to Ernesto here in Puerto Chicama to let him know my arrival date. Everything seemed so casual, but it was done the way gentlemen did things, I believe, for many centuries. A man's word was his bond.

There was a small bus that left the seashore every few days at 5:00 p.m. This was one of those days; Fritz and I were on it. We were elated and had much to talk about as we returned to the city of Trujillo and bunked into the fine Hotel *Turistas*.

Our bus trip the next day down to Lima was somewhat anticlimactic, except that we were all nearly killed. We naturally sat on the right side of the bus overlooking the ocean most of the way. A good place to be because the oncoming traffic on the mostly single lane road sped by mighty close to us. Finally, it happened. Either we or the opposing bus missed the headlight signals. At 50 mph, we sideswiped. A strip of chrome from the oncoming bus penetrated the left side of our bus, and completely pierced through four of the empty seats. It could have been worse; we might have gone hurtling five hundred feet to the rocks and surf of the Pacific. Both drivers took things in stride, cursed each other out, and went on their way.

By 9:00 p.m. Fritz and I were in the dining room of the Gran Maury Hotel, all dressed up in our suits and enjoying a dinner served by waiters in tuxedos. We toasted the success of the *Omega* adventure.

A message was waiting for me. Barbara Holbrook had moved to a more modest hotel, the Ventiocho De Julio. "Please do phone me there." I did, and the next afternoon we three met by the huge fountain of the Plaza San Martín. Fritz and I walked the distance and she spotted us approaching. She was seated on a bench, and when we hove into sight, she was up and running. I was totally surprised, delighted, and stirred when she threw her arms around me and gave me a long firm and wet kiss on my lips. I stood back for a moment and she purred, "Is that all you can do?" So I repeated her gesture of greeting and friendship. Fritz spoke up immediately, "I'll drink to that." And so we did in the salon of the Hotel Bolívar.

Barbara had been doing well with her articles for *Vision* and had placed a few elsewhere. She withdrew from her purse an envelope that she handed to me. It contained the 120 *soles* she had borrowed from me. She was not only attractive and fun loving, but she was also honest down to the last penny. We held hands from then on.

First things first. We had to assure Fritz's departure home with my exposed films. *Braniff* would fly him from Lima to Miami for $279.30, and from there it would be Greyhound busses all the way. That evening we three lived it up at the elegant Hotel Crillon: ate, drank, and danced. And the next afternoon, we took advantage of the Hotel Bolívar hotel shuttle bus and went with Fritz to the Limatambo Airport, wished him Godspeed, and sent him on his way. From windjammer to luxury airliner.

I had been teasing Barbara to join me on my Cuzco and Bolivia trip, and she finally agreed. I don't think that there was ever any doubt that she would. She, too, was footloose in a strange and exotic land, and her journalistic abilities enabled her to travel where and when she wanted . . . as long as she met an occasional deadline. I wanted this extra travel to use as fill-in or background for whatever adventures Ernesto could lead me to.

A smart move suggested by Barbara was for me to check out the man in question. I had his Lima office address. Her newsman's cynicism suggested that I gather whatever facts I could on Ernesto before committing my energies and plans into his hands. "Barbara," I remonstrated, "we shook hands on it!" She just shook her head. "Your brother is right, you're a dreamer. Let's just go and do it."

Ernesto Batanero's card indicated a neat little store just around the corner from the Plaza San Martín. I was surprised. He seemed to be waiting for us. He looked a little more citified than a week ago—tie, white shirt, and coat—but every bit as affable. I almost jabbed my skeptical companion in the ribs with delight. My instincts were right, and I knew it. Barbara and Ernesto hit it off well . . . especially after she suggested that she do an article on the *Fabrica De Junco*. We were introduced to Marjorie Smith who was helping Batanero make United States contacts for his products. She was the twenty-year-old daughter of Richard Smith, some sort of United States liaison for an educational exchange program between the U. S. and Peru. Shortly after meeting this friendly and lovely young lady we all trotted down the street to a French architect's office. Ernesto sold him a large rug from the Fábrica. I had no suspicions of my new friend, nor did Barbara's critical eye detect any.

Two days later, Barbara and I boarded the Huancayo Central railroad cars for the highest of all train rides in the world. "Let them climb Everest," I chuckled—and indeed,

Sir Hillory had just done that in honor of his new queen, Elizabeth—"this choo-choo will take me nearly as high up as he and his sherpas climbed into the Himalayan skies."

My enthusiastic statement was not an idle brag. This train boasts the highest railroad tracks of any other major railroad on Earth: 15,000 feet, a long and tedious and often monotonous ride except for the occasional glimpses of frightening chasms along the way. To go by the numbers, we passed through twenty-seven stations, over fifty bridges, sixty-six tunnels, and nine switch backs. The passenger cars were remarkably clean and modern. Sitting in them was pleasant. We were in first class, and I was pleased not to suffer the diaper indignities that I had experienced on my Colombian train ride. However, I did suffer the curse of high mountain travel: *Sirroche.*

Sirroche is what they call mountain sickness in the Andes Mountains. Beyond 8000 feet the oxygen gets pretty thin. We knew this, but in my newfound macho attitude, I thought I was immune from such earthbound ailments. We both sat in our chairs, talked, and marveled at the periodic glimpses of spectacular scenery. I waited for the vaunted Andes *sirroche* to strike down the other passengers. I didn't wait long. I was the first to get it. All of a sudden my head was light, my body was weak, I began to see everything before me turning a bright white, and worse yet, nausea was enveloping me. With an attractive lady at my side, nausea was the last thing I wanted. I remember Barbara gesturing to one of the porters. He immediately reappeared with a large canvas bag all blown up with pure oxygen. It looked like an immense sausage. He stuck it in my face, released some sort of lever, and a flow of pure oxygen revived me instantly, the nausea was gone, and I was again my reckless self. The railroad man went on to another passenger.

We arrived in Huancayo and went directly to the Huancayo Turista Hotel, a fine place that cost two dollars a room. It was 5:00 p.m. (Unfortunately, because of the terrorists and the Shining Path Revolutionary movement the grand Lima Huancayo railroad was shut down for some time. Only after 1996 has it reopened and the nights and delights that we experienced in 1953 are again there for all to enjoy.)

Here we were that evening, as close to the full moon as we would ever be on Earth, and our conversation turned to Barbara's artist *novio* or *enamorado* in Ecuador. "I wonder what he's doing right now? Perhaps he is writing me a letter. Or better yet, he could be doing a sketch of me from a photograph."

"Probably chasing around town with some dark-eyed beauty." I was cruel.

"We shall see," she retorted, and led me back to the lobby of the hotel where a great fire was burning in the fireplace. There was a telephone and she put in an international call to Quito. The connection took forever, it seemed, and certainly cooled my rising ardor. "Can't get him in," she dejectedly said as she came out of the telephone booth. "Too bad," I commented. "I'm calling it a night. Get a couple letters written in my room."

Barbara's face fell perceptively, and I kicked myself all the way upstairs to my room.

The road from Huancayo to Cuzco snakes along the roof of the Andes Mountain chain. There is no railroad. The tracks stopped right here. That day the road was closed to traffic going southeast toward Cuzco. The next day the traffic would travel in that direction. The system was slow but it certainly eliminated head on collisions.

We relaxed in Huancayo and that evening took in a movie, Disney's *Saludos Amigos*. Again the evening began in a quite romantic manner: the Latin songs and dances and the beat of this tribute to the glamour of South America. Barbara's hand felt particularly warm and I fancied she was snuggling up a mite closer than before. "Perhaps," I whispered as we left the theater, "we should go sit by that big fireplace, take the chill out of our bones. This air up here is a bit thin." She murmured, "Good idea," and we hastened back to the warmth of the Hotel Turistas. I liked it that she selected a dark corner of the plush room from which to view the burning logs. We settled down together on a sofa, made some small talk, and were just getting down to what promised to be a cozy evening when the bellhop made an appearance. "*Señora* Barbara Holbrook, *hay un mansaje telefónico.*" She was up and into the phone booth in a moment. I could hear her voice as she tried to determine who wanted her. At times she got a bit loud. After what seemed a long while she returned and sighed. "These South American phones; no one seems to know what's going on. They'll call back." The fire in the great hearth seemed to have lost a little of its warmth throughout the rest of the time we sat there and she speculated on the identity of her caller. Perhaps it was the thin air of this city high in the sky. I soon returned to my room. Barbara's call never came through that night.

The next morning we were on our way. I'll quote a sentence from my journal for July 24, 1953: "The most spectacular scenery and ride I've ever seen. The bus never faltered. And after the sunset, a full moon came out giving us quite a romantic ride. Particularly exotic was the thatched hut village we stopped in for dinner."

We arrived at Ayacucho at 12:30 a.m. and bunked into the Sucre dead tired. Early the next morning we were out looking for transportation. Someone told us, "The bus line stops here. Look for a truck with a Cuzco sign in the window." This we did, and soon found ourselves crowded in the back of a stake truck with a dozen or so Indians. Not at all unlike refugees escaping an enemy.

Barbara hollered above the din of our fellow passengers, "Do you know that we are now traveling on the Royal Road of the Inca? The markers you see once in a while were laid out by an Inca engineer."

"Hey," I shouted back, "you're not so bad a travel guide. You study this or something?"

"No," she bellowed back. "Read Victor Von Hagan's *Highway of the Sun*. It should be out by now. I knew him in Ecuador. He got kicked out of that country just as I did."

By now our fellow Aymara and Quechua speaking Indians had hushed and were watching and listening to the two gringos banter back and forth. One of our traveling companions produced a bottle of pisco and passed it over to us.

"Looks pretty dirty," Barbara commented.

I answered, "It's near straight alcohol; nothing can live in this stuff. I don't want to offend the Indians." I took a healthy gulp and she did the same. "You're a true newspaper woman," I joshed her.

"I do what I must," she laughed.

Our truck broke down several hours later, and we transferred to another going our way. This time hospitable Indians made room for us, and we were given seats in the cab. Out came the bottle of liquor again, and away we went. We called this truck, "The happy truck" because everyone on it was singing.

Mountain scenery, as I'm sure cannot be duplicated anywhere in the world for its ruggedness, was the norm here. The countryside was so spectacular for such a long time that I am ashamed to read in my journal no more expletives. Our mode of transportation made this trip all the more extraordinary. Only once in an hour would we see another truck.

At noon we broke down again and all our companions envied and cheered us as we managed to hop on another truck going our way. They were all good sports. I have pictures in my mind of the dirty, but smiling, little children's round brown faces as they waved us on.

We arrived in Anduyalis at 4:30 a.m. We were beat. The hotels were always open on this run, so we were, at last able to get us a couple of rooms. But at 10:00 we were up again and joined a troupe of bullfighters on its way to Abancay. García Dorán was trying his luck in any bullring that would have him. He and his banderilleros were truly itinerant toreros. I have since looked in vain for mention of him. Perhaps he ended his days on the sand of some obscure arena. Those in that little pick-up truck were gentlemen enough to give Barbara a seat in the cab. She later wrote a story telling of that truck hitting a llama on the road. The driver only said, "*No problemas, señora. No es importante*," and then sped on minus a headlight.

We were traveling on the road and in the area that sometimes later, some dozen or more years later was classified "too dangerous to even think about." The Shining Path and other Marxists revolutionaries made it their own. I understand, however, that now in the new millennium, the region has opened up again to normal traffic. We arrived at Abancay at 6:00 p.m. and were happy to see a Turista Hotel. I mentioned to Barbara, "I have some notes on an Inca ruin somewhere around here."

She replied, "To hell with Inca ruins; I'll be a ruin myself if I don't get to a room and a bed."

So much for Inca ruins.

"Cuzco: July 27—Monday:" that was the entry I had been looking forward to writing. And so it came to be at 5:00 p.m. the next afternoon. Our cargo truck dropped us off in front of the finest Turista Hotel yet. The hostelry was located in the very center of the old capitol of the Inca Empire.

Cuzco will always remain the most interesting city I have experienced. Perhaps not as colorful as some, but wherever one walks in that city, there is a feeling of unsolved mystery, of something just waiting to be discovered, of hidden stone rooms and tunnels piled high with the gold, precious stones, and the wealth of former emperors. The streets are lined with stone walls built long before the first Europeans arrived in November of 1533. An architect today would be hard pressed to duplicate one of those walls. If he did, he would be praised for the austere but striking beauty of his creation . . . that is, if he could match those ancient structures. In contrast to the studied simplicity of the ancient Inca artisans, on just about every corner of this city there is a grand colonial church which has its roots in the European Middle Ages. Their ornate towers and crosses proudly rise above all else and bespeak the conquest of Christianity over pagan mythology. Unfortunately, at over 11,000 feet the thin air of the mountains makes the city a cold place. Physically, it is not easy to get comfortable in Cuzco as it is most anywhere else. Consequently, the huge walk-in fireplace of the *Hotel Turistas*, with its great fire crackling merrily, was the real hearth of the city for me. Anyone in Cuzco who could afford the Turistas gravitated to it. The plush room with the cheerful fire was the meeting place of the tourist, the scholar, the traveler, and the gigolo. We were lucky to get a couple of rooms at this hotel. At $4.50 a day with meals, we were extremely pleased (Now, in 2002, I understand the *Turistas Hotel* has been sold. I hope to the right people).

Unknown to us in our recent travels, the first modern reenactment of the old Inti Rymi parade, fiesta, and pageant of the fall of the Inca Empire to the Conquistadors was to take place the very next day. We had not seen any announcements en route to Cuzco. I immediately realized that the show would be a real windfall for my movie camera and for Barbara's writing.

Yet, in contrast to all this historical and romantic ambience, I ended up in my hotel room doing my laundry by hand. Barbara, after dinner, decided to remain in the lobby, fireplace, and social room to interview tourists and write down their impressions.

The next morning my socks were clean and dry, and she and I were up to our old tricks. We hitched a ride on a truck full of Indians that was making its way further up the mountain to the spectacular fortress of Sacsahuaman, where the fun was about to begin. Everybody, it seems, from miles around was on the way up that mountain. (The fiesta turned out to be such a success that from then on an annual admission fee was charged to get anywhere near the action. Thirty years later I was happy to pay that fee!)

My movie camera, tripod, and the magic word, "television" meant I was immediately taken into the area fronting the fortress. I actually joined the players and almost became part of the act myself.

The fortress of Sacsahuaman is one of the wonders of the ancient world, at least in the western hemisphere. Overlooking Cuzco it was constructed of beautifully hewn stones—some of them weighing over two hundred tons apiece—by a race of people who might not have been the Incas. The Incas, after all, were warriors and organizers just as the old Romans were. There are people who say giants built the spectacular fortress. I doubt giants; but I do say that they were builders who had giant imaginations and engineering skills. Think of lifting a two-hundred ton stone, all finished and ready for placement, into a designated space in the wall a couple stories above you. And then making the stone fit so well and tightly without mortar that a knife cannot be inserted between the adjoining stones at any given spot. This was all done by hand without any known machinery.

All along this cyclopean wall hundreds of Indian actors—in reality local men who wanted to get in a word or a shot at the more wealthy equestrians who were dressed as, and were portraying, the Spaniards—were awaiting the charge of the conquistadors. The men waited with cardboard boxes that had been painted to look like stones and boulders. These they were to throw down upon the charging knights much as the Incas did to Pizarro's men in the sixteenth century.

On came the conquistadors dressed up in papier-mâché armor and helmets. They bowed and called to their friends as they rode by. Then the deluge of imitation boulders rained down upon them. The ambush looked quite authentic. A few of the horsemen had been told to slip off their mounts to make the reenactment as real as possible. They followed their stage directions, but when nearly half the riders bit the dust it became apparent that some of those empty boxes had been filled with the real McCoy, e.g., healthy-sized stones. Some old scores were being settled by those with grievances. And who was to know from where came those lethal projectiles. No one was really hurt, but a few landlords, bankers, moneylenders, and pompous *politicos* went home that night with more than saddle sores. A memorable afternoon for everyone!

Later, Barbara and I climbed into the pre-Inca ruins that dominate Cuzco. She took a photo of me sitting in the granite throne of the Kenko ruins. Thirty years later I duplicated the pose. (The throne hadn't changed a bit.)

This whole area of the Inca capitol and its pre-Inca heritage is a fascinating mystery. How artisans could have formed, transported, and put into their buildings these huge monoliths has never been explained. One of the many faceted boulders would weigh three hundred fifty tons, and yet, each of its sides fit perfectly into the wall. The Spanish found no tools that could have been used to perfectly cut and surface those massive structures. Nor have archaeologists today solved the riddle.

A disappointment to Barbara and to me was that we would have to miss the fabled "Lost City of the Incas," Machu Picchu. My pocket book was beginning to flatten and hers was not much thicker. I would have to visit this gem of the Empire another time.

I knew I would return to Peru. Once one has experienced these mystic Andes Mountains and heard the haunting music of the Quechua flute and the plaintive and sad call of the Andrita he is smitten. Once one has heard the pitter-pat of sandaled feet at sundown as they hasten between ancient walls to some small fireplace, and has watched the graceful llama plod its way to a moonlit pasture, the urge to return and to experience Peru once more, is, indeed, irresistible. I have returned again and again.

The train to Bolivia and the enigmatic cyclopean city of Tiahuanacu was scheduled to leave the next day. Another train would not be available for six days. Barbara and I were off early in the morning. We spent quite a bit of time getting the proper stamps and signatures on our passports in order to enter Bolivia, and we just made the train in time. (On guided tours one is released from those necessary inconveniences; there is much to say for guided tours.) An easy ride over the Altiplano of Peru: villages, llamas, vicuñas, and Indians in colorful clothes were the sights of that day. Along the train ride we were offered things to buy that would not be duplicated anywhere else in South America: alpaca rugs, marvelous fake Inca relics, and exotic mementos were thrust into our seats at every stop . . . and there were many stops. I still have the items I purchased. In Lima the prices were quadrupled, and in the ethnic stores of the Unites States the prices are tenfold what we paid on the puffing train that finally dropped us into Puno, Peru's port of entry into Bolivia.

The train schedule is arranged for arrival just in time for travelers to be shuttled over to the wharves of Lake Titicaca and into the venerable passenger steamer ship, the 'Inca'. This old timer had been built in the late 1800s in Lima, taken apart, literally bolt by bolt, and transported 1200 feet up the mountains on mule back, and then reassembled. The 'Inca' was the oldest of the small fleet of ships that crosses Lake Titicaca, the highest of all navigable lakes in the world, to the country of Bolivia. (The 'Inca' is long gone now.)

The romance of this trip moved along as did the 'Inca' over the black glass-like waters of Titicaca at 12,500 feet above sea level. Only half a moon out now, but it was difficult to pull ourselves away and go to our room. Barbara and I had joined up with a U. S. State Consular employee from Lima, Alice Arntz, and with a Harvard medical student, Martin Spencer. Alice was a lovely young woman, and Martin was a *simpatico* black man, who I'm sure, has made a mark in the medical profession. One wishes that one could have kept track of these interesting people who seem to come and go in life like the proverbial ships in the night.

Guaqui is the port of entry on the Bolivian shore of Lake Titicaca. The train continuing on to La Paz was waiting for us, and by 1:00 p.m. we pulled into the political capitol of Bolivia. My notes suggested the Hotel Sucre, and a taxicab took us there. The Sucre was advertised as La Paz's finest; at that time it was. Three dollars a room.

La Paz calls for another expletive. Highest large city in the world. Higher than Cuzco and Huancayo, it is every bit as cold as they are. A big up-and-down city that is extremely interesting. Nevertheless, Barbara and I had little time to explore it. My main ambition was to reach the ghost city the Incas told their Spanish conquerors was the "City of the Dead," or the "Place of those who were," the colossal enigma called Tiahuanacu. We had passed it by on the railroad ride from Guaqui and now I wanted to return for on-site exploration. The problem was resolved by Alice. With the use of her official United States credentials, she arranged for the train that returned to Guaqui to stop and leave us off near the ruins. She also arranged for the autocarril—a small gasoline railroad car that carries mail—to pick us up several hours later and carry us on to Guaqui.

Typical of the red tape—then and now—it took us much of the next morning getting our entrance papers of Bolivia signed, and then the exit permits stamped. Also, we needed new Peruvian visas. A lot of taxiing around at 15000 feet was wearisome, but we managed.

Early the next morning the train pulled to a stop at the primitive town of Tiahuanacu, and we left it. Before us stretched acres of stone works.

This ancient metropolis is the most puzzling of all America's Pre-Colombian cities. Tiahuanacu is shrouded in mystery. It forms a city limit to the miserable little Indian town where the train had left us. An alien gazing at both of these Tiahuanacus would wonder: "What happened to civilization during the two millennia that separate a once magnificently built stone city and this woebegone collection of clapboard homes where the people now live?"

From the railroad platform, we could see, on the nearly treeless high plateau, cyclopean stone ruins tumbled about as though by some antediluvian catastrophe. We could make out a grand staircase, a great stone doorway, colossal statutes, and enormous smoothly cut stone blocks. Rock carvings and a form of hieroglyphics that have yet to be translated enhanced Tiahuanacu's mysterious aura. All about this place seashells have been found. They had originated in the Pacific Ocean over two miles below us. Upon the Andes Mountains that tower over Tiahuanacu geologists have found ocean watermarks. They are easily seen and it takes no scientific knowledge to realize that those watermarks were formed after the city had been founded. In other words, Tiahuanacu had been built, perhaps at sea level, and then had become submerged by the Pacific Ocean. One theory tells us that in some ancient time, the coastline of South America might have been pushed way up into the sky by an earthquake of gigantic proportion. Thus, the Andes were formed with the mark of the ocean encircling them, and the city of Tiahuanacu was left amid them to dry off and to baffle the archaeologists ever since.

I liked the Indian approach to this question "*Quien sabe*? Who knows?" Most of the statuary and columns in 1953 were still where they had fallen. The famous Gateway to the Sun had been set up. This structure is the largest known example of single stone cutting in the world. Hewn from one block of antesite, it is seven feet and two inches in height and is thirteen feet and five inches in length. The gateway is close to two feet thick and is covered with marvelous but bizarre carvings that add to the mystery. Huge slabs of cut stone are tumbled all about the site. Some weigh up to two hundred tons. They had originally been fastened together by large silver staples or keys. Undoubtedly, many of those T-shaped staples are still buried beneath the jumble of ruins. A subterranean sewage and drainage system of pipes and conduits has been found which could make this city far more advanced than any on Earth during ancient times. No one has been able to date it.

When Barbara and I walked away from Tiahuanacu, we were more mystified than my advance notes had indicated. Alice had stopped the autocarril as she said she would; we boarded it, and went on to Guaqui and the vessel, '*Inca.*' A nocturnal voyage, Puno again, and now in the train we rolled across the altiplano, not to Cuzco, but to beautiful Arequipa. This city sits in the shade of Mount Misti which has an ever-present little cloud floating just above its volcanic peak. I was for moving on to Lima and to my rendezvous with Ernesto Batanero, but the ladies wanted to see and buy some of the extraordinary textile products this mountain city is noted for.

I must say, too, that Barbara and I were drawing closer and closer together with each day. I heard less and less about her Ecuadorian artist. The thought of leaving her and striking out on my own again in South America was becoming hard to face. Everyone we met, including Alice, assumed we were engaged. It was a pleasant thought, but neither of us intended any kind of permanent relationship. We did as the Latin Americans do—we put all such thoughts on the *mañana* burner and focused on our work.

Business was good for Alice, who ended up buying tapestries, rugs, and bedspreads for half the United States legation in Lima. I enjoyed watching her shop. What an interesting import and export business could have been headquartered at this lovely city high in the sky.

Alice and her purchases were flown back to Lima on the country's main air carrier, Faucett. Barbara and I didn't have the wherewithal to go first class, so we took a *Morelos* bus back down the mountains to Lima. It was a bumpy, scary, fantastic, and romantic drive. It was a long one. From 6:00 p.m. when we left Arequipa, all through the night and the next day, arriving in the City of Kings 7:30 that night. When we arrived, we were dusty, tired, and spent. We taxied over to Barbara's Hotel Veintiocho, and called it a trip well done.

The next day was a busy one. I packaged all the film I had shot and took it to the post office. My friend, Truman Smith, in California, was handling my exposed movies, getting them processed, reviewing them, and sending me critiques. He was a director at L.A.'s KTTV Station. I relied on him a great deal.

It seemed to me that the city had in some manner dampened Barbara's and my romantic reverie. We seemed to be doing separate things all day and in the evening Barbara's portable typewriter ate up the hours. I know that she had stories to write, but I did get a little jealous of that click-a-de-clacking machine.

I sent a wire to Puerto Chicama to inform my newfound partner Ernesto Batanero that I had bought a ticket on the next day's bus for the trip to Trujillo. I would be in Puerto Chicama the day after that. I was ready to move on.

Barbara was subdued that night. We went to the Crillon for a cocktail and then had a modest dinner at Tony's Rincón, back to the hotel where I told her I must pack and be up early in the morning. "One night cap," she smiled. "One for the road, as they say." One meant two. But, then again, our togetherness was interrupted by an American and his Mexican wife who was a real Latin beauty. He was a crop dust pilot who had lost several of his associates recently in plane accidents. "They just don't give us the money for proper maintenance," he grumbled. "Our planes are wrecks, nothing but wrecks." I had flown small planes some years before so we hit it off well. The rounds of drinks began to accumulate. Barbara, not much of a drinker, held back and picked up a story by talking to the lovely Mexican girl. It turned out to be a long night, and at the witching hour, we split up. I went to my room and slept for a few hours.

I was up at 4:30 and packed quickly. A car had been called for me. I dragged my bags to the elevator and got them into the taxi. "Hold it, just a second." I heard the familiar voice. "Just a second; you're not getting out of here that easy. Move over. I'm going to the bus station with you. I can do at least that." Of course, it was Barbara, and I was positively delighted. She embraced me passionately and I returned the favor. All I could think of was, "What a hell of a time to be moving on!"

"I must tell you," she confided, "the mail that I picked up when we returned included one from my man in Ecuador. It was not him who phoned in Huancayo; that was an editor from *Vision*. My protégé has been offered a grant to go to Rome to continue his studies. I had arranged it for him. He is grateful, and he is going. He thanked me and said in affect, 'See you around.'"

She had tears in her eyes. "And now you, too, are leaving," she sobbed. Then she blew into a handkerchief, smiled, and perked up. "You won't forget me, Romain?" she teased. "Forget your mountain traveler? Or," and she positively twinkled, "maybe you'll find something up in the north to make it worth my while to come on up?"

"Aren't I enough?" I countered.

"Yes," she sighed. "But I've got to have a story, make a living. Nobody's going to do it for me."

She sounded a bit bitter, and I limply answered, "You'll hear from me as soon as I get there. And don't you worry, I'll be stirring up more than a story for you."

The taxi pulled into a dark alley where several buses were coughing out diesel fumes. I watched as a *mozo* took my bags from the car and tied them to the roof of the bus.

Hard for me to believe it, but I had a lump in my throat. "Barbara," I whispered, "you haven't seen the end of me yet. I'll get you up north if I have to start a revolution."

"You do that," she said as she climbed back into the car. "You do that."

I noticed that the car did not move as I climbed aboard the bus and settled in. Barbara was still there as we pulled out into the misty streets of Lima and headed for the golden land of the Chimu.

7 — TREASURE IN THE DESERT

I was met in Puerto Chicama not only by Ernesto, Nieves, and their daughters, but also by the mayor of the town, Victor Ramos and his quite pretty and plump wife. *Señor* Ramos assured Ernesto and me that he would give us any help that he could in furthering our plans to explore this country. The pleasant police sergeant who had greeted Fritz and me so nicely after leaving the *Omega* was also present. He greeted me like an old friend and pledged protection and cooperation. I was somewhat overwhelmed by this hospitality.

My bags were taken to Ernesto's home and then placed in the adjacent room. This would be mine. The large room had its own street doorway entrance, a wooden table with a couple of chairs, a four-poster bed without springs or mattress, a large jug of water, a chamber pot, and a barrel in which to throw refuse. The bathroom, better say toilet, was in the back of Ernesto's quarters. This consisted of a two-holer outhouse. Ernesto showed me where he secreted his toilet paper—"You can't trust the help; they just make off with the stuff"—and I broke any tension there might have been by producing the flattened roll of paper in my jacket pocket, and used one of the Spanish idioms I seemed to hear so often, "*No problema.*" We fabricated a mattress for me by stuffing all kinds of cloth, old clothes, and useless—but clean—apparel into several bags, flattening them out, and pretending the result was a genuine Sealy. I began to realize that my benefactor was not a wealthy man by any means. He would make it big—really big—in time, but when we partnered, he was as desperate for funds as I was. His *Fábrica* products had not caught on yet. This financial situation didn't bother me in the least, and if anything we bonded closer because of it.

My next surprise was a group of local youths who came over to my place as we were settling in and lustily serenaded me in English with the "Happy Birthday to You" song. I was touched—although it wasn't my birthday. Even more touched when I was introduced to the English teacher who had coached the boys. In very poor English he told me that he was preparing his pupils to meet Mr. and Mrs. Smith of the United States Education Commission in Peru. Ernesto had arranged the visit through Margie Smith whom I had met in Lima.

Unfortunately, I took this last piece of information as a bit of a disappointment. I was told the Smiths would be arriving in their personal car in two weeks. Thus, for two weeks I would be twiddling my thumbs waiting to start our full-fledged attack on the mystery, the history, and, hopefully, the treasures of the Chimu Empire. As the weeks progressed, I came to realize that regardless of Ernesto's American ideas, desires, and abilities to get things done, he still retained some of the annoying—but still delightful—Latin American trait of "*mañana*." He always maintained that one should move slowly, make sure of his path, and then step forward. My flattened purse goaded me to get a move on, get it done and have it over. "Do not worry, *Señor* Romain, we will survive," he laughed. "Things will all work out." And they always did.

Our first order of business was to arrange accommodations for the Smith family. The Guildermeister's Sugar Company shipping offices were at the north end of Puerto Chicama. They were well constructed of wood and contained the only flush toilet and shower in the community. Important personages were put up there. At best, the quarters would be rated a second-class hostelry elsewhere, but here they were considered the epitome of elegance. The guest rooms were always kept immaculately clean. An elderly gentleman, who turned out to be a Thomist Philosopher, *Señor* Calderón (not to be confused with my brother's Lima patrons) was the manager of the sugar operation here. Of course, he knew Ernesto quite well and immediately gave his word that all would be in readiness for the Smith family. I would liked to have settled down with *Señor* Calderón for a talk. But, "He is only here every so often," I was told. He brought out a bottle of Johnny Walker Red scotch with three glasses, and I was sure I had a new friend. But, no. Ernesto was an abstainer and he nudged me along. "We must be going. Things to be done." And off we went to do good things.

We had a couple of daylight hours left. Ernesto spoke to me in English—he always spoke English to me: "Best not to let the locals know what we are up to—Let us go out and see what the *huaceros* are doing. Do not bring your cameras yet. Let us first talk to them."

A brisk walk of about an hour over hard sand and earth took us into the Sechura Desert north of town. Ernesto pointed out to me what I first thought to be sand dunes. They were actually mounds, the remains of walls and buildings of the Mochica Empire. "It rarely rains here," he commented to me, "but over the centuries, maybe fifteen or so, enough rain has come down to turn these once tall unattended buildings into blobs of mud, mounds, like cubes of ice melting in the sun. It is hard to tell what might be buried in them."

I was becoming more excited at every turn of our walk. And even more so when we moved around one of those man-made heights that rose fifteen or more feet from the desert, and was confronted by a sandy field of bones, skulls, broken pottery, and two disheveled men waist-deep in the earth feverishly throwing up dirt over their shoulders with stubby little shovels.

"Ha, we are in luck, *Señor* Romain." Ernesto hurried forward. "They are here, my diggers. They are at work. They were, indeed, two of the fabled *huaceros*. They sensed our presence, and one of them made a run for it. "No, no," Ernesto called. "*Soy* Ernesto Batanero."

They gratefully turned around and walked toward us. Fortunately for me, I had seen the worst of the worst on Macabi Island. These two men would have fit in well there. Ropes for belts and rope sandals, tattered shirts, and ripped trousers that did little to cover them.

"Chan Chito," Ernesto made contact with the shorter of the two. "The little pig," he laughed, "because he goes in head first. And *El Doctor*." He made a mock bow to the taller man. "The *huacero* who could baffle your Harvard professors with his knowledge," he added, "but not with his wisdom." The men stepped forward. They extended their hands and smiled shyly. I was leery of touching them; I had just seen one of them toss a human skull aside with his hand. But Ernesto greeted them well. "Any luck?" he asked.

"*Nada*," was the answer. "Nothing." But they had broken into a section of an ancient graveyard, and that could prove very interesting.

Repulsed and fascinated, I watched these two treasure hunters. They accepted me because of my Peruvian friend. And when we were about to leave, one of them stepped up to me, made an imperceptible bow, and handed me a bag of little things. "He wants you to have them," Ernesto said. "They are part of a necklace that he just dug up. Not gold, so they are of no value to him. But you should take them. An interesting *recuerdo* (remembrance)." The bag contained dozens of beads in different shapes, different colors, sizes, and materials: bone, stone, and seashells. "For you," Ernesto said. I still have them.

As we returned to town, Ernesto told me of his plans. He had come across some sort of marked road or trail many miles north of Puerto Chicama. He had followed it far enough to be convinced it was one of the major pre-Inca roads that connected such metropolises as Chan-Chan to some other such unknown city. "I have seen from the Pan American planes, using binoculars, many large mounds, much, much more extensive than here. I want to beat the *huaceros* to it. You can see, they destroy every thing they touch. They are only interested in the gold. I would like to further the knowledge of Pre-Colombian history of my country."

"The gold," I interjected, "the gold, Ernesto. If we find something, can we not keep a little of it?"

"Ah, *Señor* Romain, you think like a true *huacero*, and so do I. Let's find it first, and then figure out what to do with it."

I liked his attitude.

The next day we boarded a narrow gauge railway that left the port of Chicama and wound its way many miles inland and eventually into thousands of sugar beet trees to the huge Guildermeister Sugar Plantation. Of course, my friend always the PR man, stopped here and there to shake hands with the more important employees of this operation. He mainly wanted to visit with one Herman Bergman from Davis, California, who was in charge of a small fleet of crop-dusting planes that serviced the trees.

Bergman was one of those adventurous Americans I have met scattered around the world. Home in the States never seems exciting enough to this type of man even though his profession is one of constant risks and action. The pay is often more substantial across the border and the cost of living is a lot less. Bergman had a wife and three youngsters, and he calculated that in ten years or so out here, "I can salt away enough money to retire easily back home, put the kids in college, and set up my own ranch. My family and I are highly respected here. We are looked after very well by the German management, and I have no complaints."

For all of Ernesto's dalliance about our treasure hunt, I now saw in this visit a method to his workings. He was laying groundwork for our trip into the Sechura. He outlined our plans to the tall lean aviator. He left out the word "gold," and substituted it with "desire to further knowledge of the archaeology of this part of the world."

But Herman Bergman had been around awhile; he knew the score. "Of course," he replied to Ernesto's innocent look, "I couldn't have said it better." And he laughed heartily. "I'll do all I can to help you except to touch anything you might find out there in the Sechura. That's not my bag. I've got too good a thing going here for me." He put his hands flat down on the table and said in a straightforward tone, "How can I be of assistance?"

"Only this," Ernesto said with relief. "I cannot load up in Puerto Chicama all the supplies we'll be needing. It would take three or four burros to carry it. And that would be a dead give-away to the whole town. Not only would the law be watching our every move, but I guarantee we would have a gang of people dogging our heels the first day out. And some of them would not be up to any good. *Señor* Romain and I are going to leave with just one animal. I'm known for being interested in these things, and I'll let the word out that I'm escorting this North American film producer into the desert to make films of anything of interest. There shouldn't be any suspicion." He looked at Bergman and me and continued: "I can give you coordinates of our approximate position at a definite time of each day. Out in the empty desert you should have no trouble spotting us from the air. What we need is an airdrop. Mainly a bundle of tools, shovels, picks, crowbars, and the like. And, most important, a supply of water in tins, basic foodstuffs, and sterno for our stove. Will you do it?"

"Of course, Ernie, of course. But tell me," he spoke as one aviator to another airman, "how will you know the exact spot where you will be needing and using these things?"

Batanero was ready with his answer . . . as he always was. "We might need two or more flights of this kind. If we wave you on, you return here, unload our stuff, and come on out the next day. The flights shouldn't take more than an hour each way." He paused and then continued. "I know that's where I'm stretching our friendship, Bergie. Can it be arranged?"

"We're in luck. This is the off-season for dusting. All of my pilots are contract men. They're probably in Lima right now drinking up their profits."

I briefly interrupted. "I believe I met one there just this week. He was blowing off steam all right."

"I can imagine," Bergman continued. "I am alone here now and am constantly taking my planes up and testing and making adjustments on them. I like to fly. During the war, we often flew out several times a day. I can do it. I will do it. Let me know when."

I have learned over the years of my friendship with Ernesto Batanero that he was a man who evoked strong friendships. This was certainly one of them. We all shook hands. "I'm glad," Bergman told us, "that my wife and children are not here. They are in Trujillo. I prefer to leave them out of this. I've put my wife through enough by bringing her out here to this out-of-the-way pit stop of civilization. I do think she is fascinated by it all and is in control. She knows the best I could have done after the war, if I wanted to keep flying, would be an instructor for an air school. That's not for me, and sure no money in it. I don't want her to become involved in anything that might raise the suspicions of the government. You know better than I, Ernie, the crap dust that Peruvian *politicos* can stir up. We leave her out. Right?"

"Of course," was the answer. I never did meet Mrs. Bergman or her children. I would have liked to. She sounded like a winner to me.

Elatedly, Ernesto and I returned to Puerto Chicama.

The next big event was the arrival of the U. S. Educational Commission to the little-off-the-beaten-track town in Peru. Under Ernesto's and Nieves' artistic talents this town was being transformed into a United States subsidiary. Soon American flags were flying all over the place. Bunting was strung across the main street, and in particular, over the street where the small Puerto Chicama school was located. That school serviced youngsters from the first grade all the way up to the twelfth grade. It boasted five teachers—although the English teacher let it be known around town that his inability to converse freely with me was because I was using a colloquial form of hillbilly English.

The day came, two weeks after my arrival in town, when the Smiths drove up in their big American car with its little United States flags fluttering from each fender. Since Ernesto had an office in Lima and often spoke of his Factory of Straw up north, these folks from Minnesota, I soon realized were under the impression that they would be staying in some sort of Peruvian hacienda with all of its amenities. Their car was directed by a loafer on the dirt street to Ernesto's little four-room house. Their disappointment was palpable. They greeted Ernesto with the set smiles that I'm sure United States foreign personnel are trained to wear. They looked around for his army of servants. All they got was Adrian who tipped his cap and opened the door. His B.O. was the first of many disillusionments they experienced that day. Nieves served a cup of tea in her modest parlor. The lady from Spain represented gracious hospitality at its best, and naturally assumed that this illustrious educator would be able to respond to her pure Castilian Spanish. The Smiths knew no Spanish, which I thought strange for an American sent by Washington to straighten out Peru's educational system. Their daughter, Marjorie, had some command of the language, and she did the talking for the family. It was obvious that this was an awkward moment, and Ernesto—in English—proposed that we all go to the living quarters that had been arranged for them. Mr. Smith was glad for the suggestion, and we all hiked over to the Guildermeister rooms. It just got more embarrassing. Far from being an old colonial Spanish hacienda festooned with bougainvillea and teeming with servants, they found themselves in a second-rate Motel 6. It could have been funny, and I did see some humor in the situation, but Ernesto was not one bit happy. He felt even worse when Smith suggested that instead of visiting the school the next day we all drive back to Trujillo and see the famous Chiclin Museum that housed the biggest collection of pre-Inca pornographic pottery in the Americas. "Fine with me," I said, but Ernesto had to excuse himself and make a quick walk to the school to rearrange the songfest and ceremonies that had been planned for the morning. "*Mañana*," he promised.

Nieves and her mother's dinner went well. I know that they had broken the bank to get the best. I had helped them in the market of Trujillo and together we had carried the chickens, vegetables, and *dulces* on the bus a couple days before. The conversation went well enough, but the Smiths complained of being travel worn, and so they retired early to their 'place' by the wharf alongside the surf of Puerto Chicama.

The next morning, I made a quick hike with Marjorie out to the *huaceros*. They weren't there. But I did help her find a quantity of small pierced beads that she hoped to make into an exotic necklace. "A real memento of this fascinating country," she exclaimed. It was the only accolade that Puerto Chicama was to get from the United States Educational Commission.

Shortly we drove out in the big black car, with its Stars and Strips flags fluttering from the fenders, and went to Trujillo. There we visited the famous Larco Herrerra collection of *huacas* (pots) that were nicely displayed in a back room of the Chiclin Museum. Positively every form of sex, deviant, or otherwise, could be seen here in exaggerated but graphic ceramics—woman and man, or beast and woman, group sex—you name it. (A sign of the times: In 1953, these objects were kept hidden behind a curtain in a back room and one needed permission from the curator to have a look. This collection has since been removed to the big museum in Lima for all to see. Today, copies of those erotic creations are found for sale in every tourist store.) Seeing the collection was rather embarrassing with young Marjorie, but she said nothing. Ernesto and I had a few macho giggles here and there, and Nieves told us to shush a couple of times. The Smiths, in good mid-western

WASP style, marched right on through without batting an eye. Later Ernesto whispered to Nieves, "It was their idea." Again she shushed him.

We were back in Puerto Chicama at 2:00 p.m., and there we were quickly told that the Smiths would be returning immediately to Lima. "Urgent business."

"The school," Ernesto spoke up, "they are waiting to greet you."

"Another time," Richard Smith brushed him off, and he was gone in a cloud of dust in the big black car with the United States flags fluttering from the fenders.

Sadly, Nieves went over to the school and collected all of the red, white, and blue bunting that she had strung up there. I didn't show my face for some time.

My feelings were assuaged considerably the next afternoon when I received a letter from Barbara. She said she wanted to make a visit here to do a story for *Vision Magazine* on Ernesto's Fábrica De Junca, and she added a teasing postscript, "and, of course, it will be fun getting back together with you. Lima has become a bit tedious for me."

Batanero was elated; a magazine article was just what he needed for his fledging business. Needless to say, I was more than a little tickled and flattered myself. And Barbara's letter promised more. In speaking of me at a cocktail party in the fashionable Mireflores suburb of Lima, she was told a story. Somewhere in the Andes Mountains, east of Trujillo, Indians had reported to the manager of a large hacienda the existence of ruins of a pre-Inca city. My friend's informant mentioned that only mountain Indians had visited it. Barbara had done a little research, and another source passed on rumors that some of the buildings were three or more stories tall. "Better yet," she teased. "They tell me that the manager of that hacienda is one hunk of a man. He has the name for it: Santiago 'Jimmy' Flynn." He had played the lead role in the recent Peruvian movie *Sabataje En La Selva* opposite the actress Pilar Palette, who later married actor John Wayne. "The picture was so bad," Barbara went on, "that Flynn was happy to get away from the jibes of his friends and return to the mountains." Again she teased, "I'm going to go along with you; gotta meet that Flynn!" She gave me the name of the hacienda, Uningambal. Needless to say, Ernesto knew of it, and was on a first-name basis with its owner.

"We must go there, Romain," he promised me. "But first we must go into the desert. Bergman cannot be put off. He is ready to fly. Vamonos!" He spoke that quite firmly, and I liked the way he said it.

In my correspondence with Barbara, I never did let on what Ernesto and I were doing. Ernesto, the teetotaler, would wag his finger and caution, "You know those cocktail parties in Lima (which I didn't). People talk. We do not want that." I agreed.

We selected our gear carefully in Trujillo. Eventually, we had spades, a crowbar, face dust masks, buckets, canvas bags, a funny little portable rope ladder, soft brushes, and a select quantity of dry foods. We did have a hard time finding the durable type water cans that we needed, but eventually we did—no such things as U. S. Army surplus *Jeep* cans in Trujillo. Our big quandary was where to find the steel probes that are needed to feel out a possible dig site. That is where our friendly *huaceros* came in handy. They sold us theirs. They had no qualms about having new ones welded; it was what was expected of them. These probes are nothing but four-foot steel bars with a T-shape handle on one end and a point on the other. The T acts as a grip to drive the point into the earth. An experienced *huacero* knows immediately if the earth is soft enough to indicate it had been disturbed some time in the past. If something might be buried there.

And so it came about one early morning that the Peruvian, the American, and a *burro* walked out into the desert north of Puerto Chicama. A few folks waved us off, some in-jokes were cracked I'm sure when we were out of sight, and I suppose some heads were wagged at the nonsense of these two daydreamers. Also in Trujillo the government's Department of Archaeology in the North had already been alerted. The public servants yawned, "Batanero is at it again."

To me, the enterprise was the adventure I had dreamed about since I was a little boy. Not many people these days get to go treasure hunting in an exotic country. I was riding high on that theme, and Ernesto was deadly serious as we walked out of town with our *burro* loaded down with my tripod, cameras and a few supplies. We passed the area of the *huaceros*, and Ernesto clapped me on the back, "We are out here now, *Señor* Romain. We are on our way. The desert is before us. We are alone. We are a part of it." I was a bit surprised by his eloquence, but I also thumped him on the back. Truth was, I didn't know where I was going. And there were times when I wondered if he did. Was he just another of those fixated treasure hunters who never give up on a notion?

We were warm and then we were hot as we pushed and prodded the donkey along. Five hours later, the thought did enter my mind, "Have I made a wrong turn in my life somewhere? Is this guy really what he claims he is?" I had quite a dossier on the famous "Lost Dutchman's gold mine in the Superstition Mountains of Arizona," and I wondered if we too were off on one of those impossible historical treasure hunts.

I need not have troubled my mind. By late afternoon, Ernesto pointed out to me a row of stones going north into the Sechura. Then he indicated another column of good-sized stones paralleling it. "*Senor* Romain," he said quietly as though the desert and its creatures might overhear us, "this is a road. This is the road that I followed from the air when I worked for Pan Am. This is a road that is going somewhere. We will follow it." The two lines of rocks, about twenty feet apart, continued on into the Sechura Desert. We followed it in silence.

Camping in that desert was no fun, nor was it a chore. We had bedrolls, and we only needed to roll them out when the time came. We encountered very little in the way of pests. The Sechura Desert is, indeed, a dead desert. Our sterno stove, a collapsible frame that holds a pan over a can of jellied alcohol that ignites into a blue flame, and beans, pasta, and dried jerky would do for our meals: breakfast, lunch, and dinner. We both lost weight quickly on this trek.

We followed the road all the next day. Whoever had plotted it had done it well. The two lines of stone markers were as straight as a die. The Pacific Ocean was somewhere to our left. At times, we were rather close to the coastline, and at other times we were miles from it. During the third day, we came across a bit of a mystery. Some ten miles from the shoreline we encountered the corroded remains of an iron steam ship. I first thought that we were onto some ancient ruin, but as we approached, we could make out bulwarks and chains sticking out of the sand. Part of a smokestack or funnel lay within the periphery of the wreck. We figured it to be a vessel about ninety feet long; Ernesto thought it might have belonged to the guano fleet fifty years earlier. We could find no identification. All markings had been eroded by the desert sands. The ship had been covered and recovered with sand many times. Interesting to find this wreck so far inland. I took my pictures, and we moved on.

On our fourth day the trail dramatically turned east, away from the ocean and towards the towering Andes Mountains that were always in sight. We figured our pace at about twenty miles a day. The hike was beginning to become wearisome. Fortunately for me, I had anticipated a hike in the desert or elsewhere. I had purchased a pair of boots made for the British soldiers in the Sahara during the Second World War. They did me well. But Ernesto was another story. His Peruvian boots were not up to it. I know he suffered, and I saw him limp. He never complained.

On our fifth day Ernesto suddenly stopped. "There," he pointed dramatically, "there it is *Señor* Romain: the group of pyramids I have seen from the air. They are there. I knew it. I saw them from the sky, and I am here now to see them on foot." For a moment I thought he was going to cry . . . but that was not Ernesto Batanero's way. He simply said, "I can rest these tired feet of mine," and he sat down.

In the distance, about three miles, through the shimmering heat of the desert, I could see great mounds of earth, perhaps thirty or forty feet high, rising out of the Sechura Desert. They were framed by the hazy blue Andes way off in the horizon. Ernesto stayed back rubbing his aching dogs while I hastened on. I began to see outlines of walls that were either half buried in the sand or that had melted away with time, rain, and possibly ancient floods. They were all over the place. I realized that I was approaching a formerly very populous city.

Ernesto joined me. "This is it," he said. "These are the ruins of the city that I knew was here." He walked in among the hulking mounds and walls. My friend was elated. I was too. Nevertheless, that practical part of my mind asked me, "What the heck are we going to do now?"

I stood in front of a city that had probably died over a thousand years ago. Its secrets were buried beneath our feet. The remains of a city gone down were entombed in these sand dunes.

"My God!" I said to Ernesto. "We have found another Chan-Chan."

He corrected me. "Older. This is older, much older." Ernesto knew his Peruvian chronology. He had grown up with it. He had studied it. He was fascinated by it.

"How old?" I questioned.

"Mochica," he quickly replied. "Older than Chan-Chan. A lot older. Mochica. Sixth century."

We set up our evening camp right there on the top of a mound in the midst of a city where once thousands and thousands of people used to come and go, walk about, and live as we now do fifteen hundred years later. The breeze from the Pacific touched our stove light. The flame fluttered and then blew out. We settled down to a spooky night.

"*Señor* Romain," Ernesto said in those hushed tones that we used in that dead city, "tomorrow we will dig."

Herman Bergman flew over us the next day. He had done so for the last two days, but this time we signaled him to drop our supplies. He good naturedly buzzed us and then unhooked a wire that was supporting our provisions. Down they came, and hit the earth with a loud clunk. He would like to have brought the ship in and landed, but as he had explained to us before, "You can never tell about sand. If I hit a soft spot, over I go, and there goes the plane." He gunned the engine for altitude, and we could see that he was taking pictures with his 35mm *Leica*. And then, with a wave and a dip of the wings, he was gone.

"You sure do have good friends, Ernesto," I complimented my partner.

"I have been so blessed," he piously replied, and we proceeded to gather up our goods. Enclosed in the bundles was a letter for me from Barbara and one for Ernesto from Nieves. Also included was an extra pair of boots for her husband. Nieves had foreseen problems in the shoe department.

"And, you sure have one hell of a wife," I again complimented him.

"The best," he answered, "the best."

Where to dig? That was now the big question. I had absolutely no idea. Ernesto was full of ideas. "You don't want to start on the top of these structures. Nothing was ever stored up there. More likely one of the smaller buildings. We'll just have to start tickling the ground." He held up the T-shaped probe like a fencing foil, and then hiked off to the center of our city in his new boots.

Ernesto had used these probes before, and he showed me the proper technique. The secret was to calculate how much pressure was needed to penetrate the earth. If a great deal of pressure was necessary to get the point to any depth at all, we were pushing into adobe bricks, perhaps a wall or a roof. An archaeologist would probably start with a trench and keep extending it until he came across something recognizable. Then he would branch out. But, the truth of the matter, as ghoulish as it sounds, we were looking for the graveyard or cemetery amongst all these mounds, where dignitaries had been interred. As Ernesto took his bearings and gazed around the acres of mounds, he startled me. "*Señor* Romain," he shook his head. "I do not know if there is a burial ground where we will find mummies with all of their regalia. Please bear with me. I want valuables as much as the next fellow, but I am also genuinely interested in learning whatever I can about this place. I do want to add to the knowledge of my country. Give me a day to poke around here. This could be a sister city to Chan-Chan. That, I know would be of enormous interest to historians."

"Now," I thought to myself selfishly, "the man is going altruistic on me; now we are in it for the source and not the gold." Then I was embarrassed with myself for having such an unworthy thought. "Still," I mused silently as Ernesto went punching about with his tool, "the great finds of Egypt, King Tut, and other Pharaohs included the treasure with which those kings were laid to rest. For decades after they were located, people have been buying tickets and gawking at all those golden objects. And many museums are staying in business because of man's fascination with buried wealth. The Ph.D.s on the top of the pecking order of archaeologists, anthropologists, and art historians are financed by the endowments of philanthropists. Those who do the manual labor for them, the students and often underpaid local laborers, are hardly surviving. If there are gold and precious stones hereabouts, I'm for finding them." I had no thought of melting it down as the old conquerors did, but to take the findings to the proper experts for evaluation . . . and for a profit. These thoughts I brought up to Ernesto that evening as we gnawed on our beef jerky, chewed on our stale crackers, and drank bitter coffee.

He surprised and pleased me. "This is not a problem. I've done all the investigating that I want to do here. This is a job for the professional historians. I can only determine that this is a Mochica site. You saw the wall with the clay carvings on it that I exposed. This is no Chan-Chan. It is unfortunate that there is no large city like Trujillo nearby to support a major excavation. Many things would be found here. But then," he threw up his hands to express exasperation, "the bureaucrats would get into it. They would make their money all right; the bankers and the departments of government. They would come out all right while the explorers, such as you and me, would be pushed aside. Kept out of it. Forgotten." He sounded bitter. "OK, Mr. Romain," he ended his speech, "let's dig for gold tomorrow. I think I know where the burial crypts are."

At sunup we walked away from the mounds and the walls that seemed to be melting down all around us in the desert. We wanted to have a broader view; 'see the forest, not just the trees,' so to speak. Get everything in perspective. We came across what appeared to be a man-made canal that apparently had been cut into the desert all the way to the Andes Mountains. At one time, it must have been a grand engineering project. The canal was about twenty feet wide. Ernesto was elated. "We are making sense of this, *Señor* Romain. Just as at Chan-Chan, this once was a causeway or waterway that drained water from the Andes. Part of the waterworks. We can understand how people could live here so far from natural springs. And I bet if we dig deep enough, we would find underground wells or even underground rivers. You know the Sahara has miles of water running beneath its surface."

"Good for the waterworks," I chided. "Where's the bank?" We both laughed.

We were walking steadily around the periphery of the site, and we came across a walled enclosure that was a good half-mile square. It looked like a corral for horses. Whereas the walls in the center of the city were as high as forty feet, and up to ten feet thick, these walls were no more than ten feet tall and yet occasionally they were much thicker than those of the inner city.

"It had to be here somewhere," Ernesto shouted to me as I walked into the area. "The people who lived here didn't bury their dead in the middle of the city . . . just maybe a few dignitaries. Most people were interred away from the main walls. And this place where we are now standing is that place. This is the cemetery." Already he had sunk his pick handle deep into the earth.

I hadn't really thought of personally digging into a graveyard, but I was now faced with it. "You want the goodies," I sighed to myself, "you have to deal with the baddies." But my friend spared me. "No, *Señor* Romain. We won't be digging into the earth here. We will find a likely spot where the rich are laid out in crypts or vaults with much of their wealth. We will look for them. I don't want to go about smashing up skulls anymore than you do."

"Maybe we should go back for the *huaceros*."

"Oh, no. Not them. If they found something big, we would probably end up in the graves ourselves. No," he looked around, "I think I can find what I'm looking for."

All afternoon Ernesto hiked around the lesser walls and poked his picker here and there. Then he finally spoke with the authority of a bona fide Peruvian archaeologist . . . or *huacero*. "Look here, sir." He pointed to a bulge in the north wall of the mud canal. "I believe this is the tomb of an important person. You can see the adobe bricks that have been built up and away from the wall." He dug around for a short while and then exclaimed, "Ha! Stone, not clay or adobe. Stone, big blocks of hand-hewn stone. This had to have been brought in from the mountains at great effort. Take a look."

My friend was right. Forming a neat square of about seven or eight feet were obviously man-worked stone blocks. They were squared away and had been made as smooth as possible. They had been moved somewhat after their initial placement. Probably, by one or more of the earthquakes that rock the country of Peru. We began to dig.

Ernesto donned a gauze mouth mask and went to work with one of the shovels. He tossed earth or sand aside, and I with the other shovel cleared it away from the dig. He worked fast. We only stopped once when Bergman's plane came roaring over us and dropped a supply of water and bags of feed for our burro. He brought the bi-plane toward us as though to dive right into our excavation. We could make out the grin on his goggled face as he throttled back and then zoomed away. He was a welcome sight in this totally quiet and dead area.

Soon Ernesto had uncovered the blocks of stone and now as he went deeper, found himself surrounded by adobe bricks. The digging became easier. He only had to stay within the confines of those bricks. I could see that the earth was soft. He had no trouble digging in and tossing the earth up to me on the rim of the excavation that was getting deeper and deeper by the shovelfull.

We quit at nightfall and had our little meal. My friend was as elated as I ever saw him. "*Señor* Romain," he said several times, "we are onto something very big. Very important. We have made a very big discovery here. We must do this right."

"Right" was one thing. I had read quite a bit about the precise techniques and disciplines of archaeology. We certainly were not qualified to do a proper dig. We had not been trained. But—and I stress the word 'But'—we had gone to the trouble of finding this place and certainly had not destroyed anything. Batanero had tried to interest the experts in Lima only to be shunted aside by knowing looks and condescension. Now we had gone to the expense and effort of seeking out this lost city. Ernesto had been researching this place for thirty years. He had the right to dig. He had paid his dues. And, dig on he did the next day. Until high noon.

In all the thirty-six years that I was to know Ernesto Batanero, I had never heard him use a vulgar or blasphemous phrase. He always was gentle of speech. But now suddenly he let out a howl that literally came out of the bowls of the earth. To some strange word he added, "*Señor* Romain, look here. Here down around my shoulders."

He was standing quite deep in the shaft that he had created, about ten feet now from the stone opening. I peered down and saw him removing a human skull from an adobe ledge that he had just exposed. Then out came another skull, and there were more neatly lined up staring at him from their eyeless sockets. He kept turning and twisting and looking all around. His face was on an exact level with the dead heads. Ernesto was excited, and yet I couldn't help but notice that he was gentle with the relics as he carefully extracted them from the earth into which they had been placed fifteen hundred years ago.

"*Señor* Romain," he abstractly called up to me without looking, "these are skulls, but only skulls. There are no bodies, no skeletons. These heads have been severed from their necks. I can see the edges of the cuts. It was done with a knife or an axe. These people were murdered, all of them."

I had no desire to get into that hole with him, but I was transfixed by the sight below me. Some of those skulls had hair attached to them. Some had brittle parchment-like skin. When placed here, they had been intact, but as Ernesto moved them, several jawbones fell away and dropped by his feet. He quickly retrieved them and re-set them in their proper places. As he did so, he was counting them, "Twenty-four," he called up to me. "I count twenty-four."

He scraped away the earth and sand. The hole was now full of heavy dust, and it became difficult to see. Again, he let out a yell. "Look here, there are clay pots behind each of the heads. Take this." His hand came out of the gloom and I grasped an unpainted ceramic jar. I was surprised at its weight. "That's not sand," I immediately knew. I gingerly turned it over and gave it a tap with my hand. Sand and earth fell from it, but so did several man-made objects. They were personal items that had once adorned its owner. Beautifully formed beads of bone and shell, still held together by fragile leather thongs tumbled out. Three bracelets fell into the sand. They were plain but delicately fashioned. The sun, straight up in the sky, brightened them. They were metal. They were gold. One of the bracelets was quite heavy.

Ernesto handed me another similar earthen vessel with an open mouth eight inches in diameter. It contained long golden and silver earrings and two armlets. These two also proved to be gold and were decorated with platinum. Each bowl contained a large golden bead with a spider engraved on it; the head of the spider was fashioned as that of a human.

We had found the bank that we were seeking.

Ernesto handed me more containers. Then he climbed up and joined me in the sunlight. He pulled off the mask and took the gloves from his hands. And then he took the objects that I had laid out and examined them. He was breathing heavily, but he still blew the dust from each of our treasures. "Would you bring me a cup of water?" he finally said. He gulped it down.

"*Señor* Romain, we have broken into the scene of an ancient tragedy. Down, way down below us, there is the body of a nobleman. Perhaps a chief or a great warrior. When he died or was killed, his family and his subjects buried him with full honors—and with much of the wealth and beautiful things that he treasured. Believe me, he is down there all laid out, and with him are his treasures. We know that he was important because twenty-four of his servants or personal bodyguards are buried with him to serve him in the next world. They had been killed and decapitated. Their heads and a few of their valuables were placed above him." Ernesto was regaining his composure. "They were put there to keep intruders, such as you and me, away from their master. He was not to be disturbed."

"That's what they said about King Tut," I limply responded.

"I know," Ernesto seriously answered.

I watched him as he fingered the jewelry before us. "Think, *Señor* Romain," he wistfully went on. "The last time these things were touched was when they were taken off of the alive or perhaps dead bodies of those on the shelves. They were probably warm with the life of those men. For twelve or fifteen hundred years now they have been hidden from the world in this cold and frightful tomb. You know they were here before Columbus was born, before the Crusades, back to the Roman Empire. It is possible," he spoke reverently, "they were here before the birth of Jesus Christ. We don't know."

We both sat silently for a while. Then Ernesto spoke again. "*Señor* Romain, this is too much for you and me. We cannot know any of the answers. Not us. We aren't specialists. I think those men," and he gestured toward the pit, "deserve it, their story deserves to be brought to light as we have now brought these pitiful remains back into the sun. Do you not agree, *Señor* Romain? Do you not believe that we should report this to the authorities, to the museum people, the archaeologists? They will come and write a new and long chapter in the history of my country."

I remained silent.

"I know, my friend," he pensively added, "that there is a complete body down there all stretched out in the full regalia of a prince. Perhaps the tiger faced bearded god Wira Kocha himself. This is a very important place." He warmed to his idea. "We can take what we have here on the ground before us. These things are very valuable. They will prove what we have found. There will be awards enough. The discovery will be broadcast and you and I will be honored. You may take the value of these things for yourself. You have wonderful films"—indeed I did, I had captured the entire experience in my movie camera. "No more than you do, I want to see with my own eyes what this burial is. But I want to expose it properly."

I guess I am as greedy as the next fellow, but my newfound friend's eloquence and obvious desire to do the right thing greatly impressed me. "Besides," I thought, "do you really want to get down there on your hands and knees and grub about those bones like a depraved grave robber? A lot of work would be involved even if we went at it like *huaceros*." We had made a big discovery according to Ernesto, and that would go far to establishing me in the career I had planned in travel and adventure films. "And," I also thought, "we two are breaking the law of the land. Caught, sneaking out with a load of this treasure could quite possibly ruin any career I might want, to say nothing of landing us years in a South American jail."

With as sanctimonious a look as I could compose, I answered, "Of course, Ernesto, you are right. Of course. Let us take a bundle of these relics back to Trujillo or Lima and present them to the academics, and tell them the story. If we are recompensed, we'll split it down the middle." I felt holier than thou. But I did also feel relieved.

Ernesto stood up and reached his hand over to me. "Shake, partner," he said in an exaggerated Western colloquialism. We two had certainly bonded.

I was for packing up and starting back immediately, but he had a better idea . . . he always did. "We'll put every thing back as it was; we'll fill the hole back up. Keep the creatures out, you know. Keep it for the students and the archaeologists."

In so doing, Ernesto came across another discovery. A large clay pot that looked like a barrel had been placed beneath one of the ledges that contained the skulls. The container was waist high and was cracked. It was empty, but Ernesto, after manhandling it up to the surface, asked me to film it. "Maybe," he explained, "those executioners had a good side. I'm sure this big urn once contained chi-chi (the beer of the ancient Peruvians that is still popular). They put it here to provide a drink or two for the dead ones."

I filmed the large pot and joked back to him, "Do you think it did the dead any good?"

He shot back, "You'd know better than I." And so we put the excavation back the way we had originally found it. I did take pictures of one head that still seemed to be silently screaming at us from its deathblow. We placed the sad remains on Ernesto's scarf, photographed it, and were appalled at the agony of expression of its last look on earth as the knife or axe suddenly fell. This head, in contrast to the others, still contained much of its hair, and was very life-like. I was glad when Ernesto placed it back where he had found it.

Much of the next day was spent filling in the crypt. "Our work here wouldn't fool a *huacero*," Ernesto said, "but it should keep the elements away." We carefully wrapped up the contents of the three vases that Ernesto had passed up to me. Then the pots went back where they had been found. Their treasures have been replaced by slips of paper that read in Spanish, "Ernesto Batanero and Romain Wilhelmsen were here. August 24, 25, 26, 1953." Along with this we buried all of our digging tools.

We then left the place and went home.

Guano gatherers of Macabi Island dining on the *Omega*.

Guano gatherers' living conditions.

Following a Pre-Inca road in the desert.

Author and Ernesto Batanero in the Sechura Desert.

Excavation in the 600 A.D. pre-Inca city found in the Sechura Desert of Peru.

Tomb of a Mochica prince. The heads of twenty-four of his royal guard. They were decapitated to guard him in death. Some gold was found here. Much more remains.

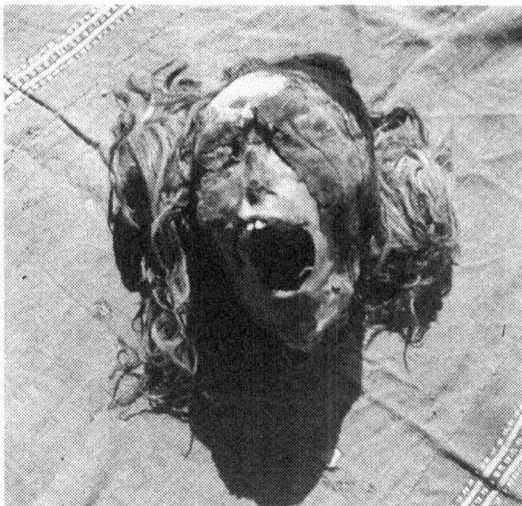

"Screaming" face of one of the Mochica guards.

"GOLD OF THE INCAS"

Romain Wilhelmsen relives his search for Inca treasure in the scorching desolation of the Peruvian desert.

KCOP CHANNEL 13

Los Angeles T.V. ad of the discovery.

Overall view of the Mochica city found by the author and Ernesto Batanero.

Professional grave robbers—
Huaceros—digging for
treasure in northern Peru:
Chanchito and the Doctor.

Nievis Batanero.

The climb into the Andes Mountains. The author, Nievis Batanero and Narciso, the Indian guide.

Author at the Hacienda Uningambal.

Nievis Batanero, Luis Seminario, Santiago 'Jimmy' Flynn, Ernesto Batanero, and author at the Hacienda Uningambal.

Newspaper story of the discovery.

Jimmy Flynn approaches the 'lost' pre-Inca city of Huasachuga.

Flynn in the city.

8 — LEGEND IN THE ANDES: HACIENDA UNINGAMBAL

The office of *Señor* José Angel Miñano García, the Regional Inspector of Archaeology for the Northern Coast of Peru in the city of Trujillo was more newspaper than museum. He was an editor of the city's major daily. "Apparently," I whispered to Ernesto in English, "archaeology isn't paying too well!" Nieves shushed us both.

Miñano, a portly man in a gray suit, vest, and tie graciously stood up from behind his cluttered desk and extended his hand. "So good to see you, Ernesto and Nieves." It was obvious that he meant it. Batanero seemed to know everybody in this part of the world. He responded in Spanish, of course, "Always a pleasure to see you, Angel, and we will both be pleased more when I show you what I have."

The fifty-five year old man was alert immediately. He knew the Bataneros did not waste time socializing for no reason. "Yes?" he questioned.

Ernesto stepped back and closed the door we had just come through. He pulled down the curtain that covered the glass door window. And he then took a chair and propped it up against the doorknob so that the door could not be opened.

"*Qué pasa?*" the bewildered official questioned. "Have you come to assassinate me?" and he laughed.

"No, Angel," Ernesto laughed back. "Although I know a couple *huaceros* who I'm sure wouldn't mind if I did." The room was now set for a jovial meeting. They both knew he was referring to Chan-Chito and El Doctor who had had many disagreements with this man.

"Better than assassination, I've got a story and the goods to back it up with." Ernesto placed on the table the boot box, in which the jewelry of the Sechura Desert was carefully wrapped. He spoke earnestly, "Angel, we have known each other for many years. I have trust in you and you know that you can trust me. I have come across something that you should take charge of. I also know that it is not my business to be snooping around ancient Peruvian *huacas*, but, as you know, we all do."

Again the man chuckled. "Batanero, we've had our eyes on you and your *huaceros* for a long time. I know that you might slip a relic past me once in a while and sell it to the collectors in Lima." He was really enjoying his own joke now, "But why not? Those egg-heads in Lima don't have a clue to what's going on up here in the north. I resent that. They are too busy promoting and cleaning up Cuzco and Machu Picchu. I trust you, not them. I would like to hear your story. I can tell you this, I do know that you and *Señor* Romain were seen marching out into the desert a week ago. My informant reported that you went with one *burro* so I know you weren't traveling far. But we did lose track of you for a lot of days; figured you had returned and gone on down to Lima. I have the feeling," and he touched the boot box lightly with his fingers, "that you weren't in Lima at all. Otherwise, you wouldn't be bringing this," he twinkled and his jowls shook, "box of boots right now. Tell me."

Ernesto told the story. However, he gave not the slightest clue as to where we had gone. Nor did he mention Herman Bergman. He indicated that we were in the same general area where the *huaceros* prowl around. He and I had agreed on our story during the long trek home. Otherwise, the facts and descriptions were as we had experienced them: the ruins, the walls, the stone crypt, and the burial. All that he left out was where the place was located. The deserts of Peru are dotted with unexplored *huacas*. (A *huaca* can be a burial mound or an object that came from it.) Our particular site could be anywhere. The fact that we had been seen trudging out with one *burro* and supplies for but a couple of days was proof—to the official—that we stayed close to the Chicama Valley. "We tell no one," my friend had emphasized to me, "until the find would be legitimized and we came back to the final excavation." That had been our agreement. I hold to it to this day.

The box was opened and *Señor* Miñano stared in amazement. "These are perfect," he exclaimed, as he fingered the armlets and earrings and the other pieces. (The bone and shell beaded necklaces I had already pilfered and kept for my own . . . with my friend's approval.)

"My God," the Regional Inspector of Archaeology exclaimed, "these are as fine as anything that has been discovered up north here since colonial days. Platinum," he almost whispered. "Do you know the Spaniards did not know the value of platinum? They melted it all down and it went the way of slag in the oven. We know that," he spoke now as a dedicated archaeologist, "very few items have come to us through the ages with platinum inlay." He sat down, pulled out a handkerchief and mopped his brow. Then he lit a ciga-rette, an Inca-Stinca.

"*Dónde, dónde?*" he repeated. "Where did you find these things?"

Ernesto stepped back—I couldn't help but admire his acting nor Nieves' innocent look—and he then carefully gathered up our treasures and placed them back in the box.

"Angel, I will tell all when we are given the rights by the government, to dig into the place. In writing. I do not trust the bureaucrats of the government's Archaeological and

Anthropological Department. It is no wonder that my *huaceros* dig behind their backs. If they don't, everything will be taken away from them. They only want to make a living. They don't have their college degrees and so they are forbidden to make an honest living doing what they are good at."

Ernesto was getting onto another subject, and again Nieves touched his arm. "Yes," he responded to her gesture, "I know."

"Angel," he pushed the box nearly into the man's lap. "Take these things. Take them to Lima, and get me the signed and sealed papers that I will need to trust them to allow me to lead them to this place." Again he touched the box.

"*Si pues,*" the official nodded. "I know of what you speak. I will take these things myself this week. I hope that I can bring you back the proper authorization and perhaps the wherewithal to examine your find. I am serious. It will be a great prestige for me also. I will lead the excavation."

Ernesto shook his head. "Miñano, you are nothing but an old *huacero* yourself."

With that, we left the building and Ernesto commented to me and to Nieves, "I am relieved. This could have gone bad. You and I, *Señor* Romain, are very illegal in all this. He could have come down on us hard.

But Nieves, in her wisdom, put it correctly, "Ernie, he knows you hold the trump card. Without you he'll never find anything out there."

✧✧✧

Barbara Holbrook arrived that weekend.

I had made arrangements with her from Puerto Chicama, told her I would be in Trujillo for three days. I was encouraged in this by Ernesto; he wanted that Fábrica story. Barbara met me at the Turista Hotel where she had booked a room for herself. Ernesto maintained a small apartment in the city and when he and Nieves retreated there at nightfall, Barbara and I snuggled up together in front of the hotel fire. She was as vigorous as before and was as full of plans to climb up to the distant and remote stone city in the Andes as I was. And, she was still holding onto hopes for her Ecuadorian artist—although one would not have thought it by the way she curled up in front of the big fireplace. She had done some research on the story that she had reported to me of a walled city beyond the Hacienda Uningambal in the mountains. Those ruins had never been listed on the inventory of such sites in the official registration of Peruvian antiquities. There was no mention of them in the learned archaeological journals nor had there been any interest in funding an expedition to explore that area. The current manager of the Hacienda Uningambal, Santiago Flynn, had mentioned in his annual report to the hacienda owner—who resided in Lima— that local Indians all spoke of the place in awe and reverence. Barbara was hot to be in on the discovery and to announce it to the world via her magazine and newspaper connections. She was so steamed up about this adventure that she decided to get some writing started right now, this very night. "The lost city in the clouds," she whispered to me as she gave me a peck on the cheek and went to her room.

We four bussed back to Puerto Chicama the next morning. The Guildermeister guest room had been readied for Barbara and she accepted it with a lot more grace than did our last American visitors. She even spoke so enthusiastically about the hospitality of the town that *Señor* Lisa, Lima's government man in Puerto Chicama, was so impressed that he sent her a bottle of Chilean champagne. In a few days he was courting her. Barbara settled in nicely.

All this while Ernesto had been working his connections. The Hacienda Uningambal, or jumping-off place for our explorations, was listed at over 12,000 feet in the Andes. No roads there, just a mule trail. Even horses were not welcome on this trail. "Too tricky and dangerous!" Indeed, we had checked with Bergman but he only laughed. "Ernie, you know I can't get my plane up that high and besides if I super-charged one, it would still beat the mercy of the fierce updrafts and the turbulence of the mountains. Sorry."

"Ever ride a mule?" my friend questioned both Barbara and me. I looked at Nieves for support. "Don't ask her," Ernesto continued. "She had her time using them in Spain when the Communists were chasing her around. (Indeed, she had. Nieves Batanero Aldana was a remarkable woman. She held the first female airplane pilot's license ever issued in Spain; I believe in 1936. She had become a motion picture actress and once showed me a poster of her and the great French/American actor Charles Boyer; she had worked against the red takeover of Spain and had barely escaped them by coming to South America.) She could ride anything.

We all joined a friend of Batanero's and went to a little desert ranch not far away. There we mounted mules and trotted around the farm for several hours. "You'll pass," Ernesto finally proclaimed, and we took our aching posteriors back to his home. "But, going up into the mountains," he added, "will be a lot more difficult." He then contacted Mario Flores, an attorney with many holdings and interests. The man controlled a *ranchito* in Chorabal, which is in the foothills of the Andes Mountains. He owned mules and was happy to loan them to Ernesto and his friends. (Hospitality and friendship go a long way in Latin America. I was to experience that over and over again.) But for all of those negotiations to come together, it took time. Barbara did a very credible story on Ernesto's Fábrica, and it was published in *Vision*. She had little else to write about here in Puerto Chicama, so we prodded Ernesto to get a move on. But he was now embroiled in a game of politics with *Señor* Miñano and Lima's archaeologists.

Our find in the desert had stirred up a controversy and Ernesto had been called into Trujillo several times to receive and sign depositions from the government. It was a touchy time for him. One incident in Puerto Chicama is worthy of comment. As mentioned, the Guildermeister Sugar Farms, a vast conglomerate in this northern area of Peru, was controlled and managed by Germans. Some of them had come from Europe after the Second World War. One who was known only as Sarth was some sort of an engineer. Sarth and his blond wife maintained a small home in Puerto Chicama down by the wharf. We, being foreigners, had been drawn together. I respected and somehow enjoyed his totally pro-German sentiments regarding the late conflict. His thoughts were much more global than those circulating around northern Peru. One evening, he and his wife invited Barbara, the Bataneros, and me to his little cottage for cognac and cookies. The evening began on a friendly note with toasts to the Bataneros, to Barbara, and to me. But then, as the brandy heated up our brains, Sarth became bitter about the war. "You know," he stammered to me. "You needn't have bombed us the way you did those closing months. My family lived in Dresden when your planes came over. Yes," he continued, "our city was one of beauty and culture. Even today the word 'Dresden' means fine, excellent, exquisite. Your goddamned government didn't have to bomb us." He had a burr under his saddle and finally had someone to blame for it.

I was no historian of World War II, and I tried to generalize that. "War is war. You bomb England, you get bombed right back." Now it was the two of us who were getting bombed. We both went back to the well for a refill.

"I lost my parents there, you know," he intoned. "But do you know something, my smart American friend, here in Peru we fooled you all. We outsmarted you. Our U-boats came right out there to the end of that wharf." He pointed to the long pier that was visible from his house. "We loaded them up with sugar—tons of it—and transported it back to the Fatherland for the little kids. We outwitted the big English Navy and the United States air patrols. We had men working for us, real men."

"Well, sir," I slurred, "let's drink to that." And again we hoisted another schnapps. The evening ended up in a drinking match. The U. S. against the Third Reich. Eventually, Ernesto led me away and with an assist from Barbara, I was taken to my room and laid out upon my bed. Barbara reported that my last statement was, "We beat them nice and proper."

The next morning, Mrs. Sarth reported that her husband had collapsed just as we had departed. We two met a couple times afterwards and both agreed. "Too bad wars can't be solved that way. Like a couple of gentlemen would do it."

The time approached when all of Ernesto's plans were coming together. A radiogram had been sent to Flynn at Uningambal. The mules had been gathered at Chorabal and the Fábrica was in good hands. Still there was concern about our desert discovery. The museum people were angry and up in arms that an American and a non-academician were able to bring out of the desert such priceless objects. *Señor* Miñano even said that he was being suspected of grave robbing along with us. Angel waved his hand, "It will blow away," he assured us, "and when they settle down and realize that there is a lot more out there, they'll play ball and start negotiating."

He, too, was extremely interested in our upcoming trip. Being a northerner he too had heard rumors of a stone city in the mountains about which the highland Indians had spoken. "They all speak Quechua up there and rumors abound. Nobody ever offered any proof of the place, and I had decided the ruins were just legends. It will be something if you can nail it down, bring back photos, and," he grumbled, "make fools out of the skeptics in Lima. I would love that!" I couldn't help but like this man. "I won't disappoint you," he promised when he saw us off on our great adventure.

And, a great adventure it was shaping up to be according to my own Pasadena hometown newspaper, *The Star News*. Barbara had mailed a story with a couple of my Polaroid photos to that daily tabloid, and on September 27, 1953, a feature article came out describing my activities as an adventurer in Peru. Typical of journalistic piracy, she was denied her byline. Regardless, we were all pleased with the write-up. My father had mailed it to me. The story told nothing of the recent fieldtrip that Ernesto and I had just made, but I had given her some photos of the dig. She knew nothing of the whereabouts of the place. The piece was the sort of publicity I would need should I attempt some sort of lecture or TV career back home. I was naturally delighted, but Barbara was steamed that her name was missing. And Nieves Batanero did much to josh me because the name adventurer was highlighted. She was never impressed by media hype.

Barbara's journalistic career was not at all flourishing in this backwater community of the world. She was at a standstill professionally. Our hike in the mountains might take weeks. Her editors had stories for her to follow up. She began to waiver about going. And then a letter was forwarded to her from the Ecuadorian. He would be making a brief trip to Chile. One night she sadly took my hand as I escorted her back to her bungalow and told me, "I'm backing out on the mountain expedition. It is really not my style. I'm a newshound, and if you find anything up there—which I suspect—my time will be wasted for weeks. In my profession I cannot allow that to happen. I'll await your results in Lima while I'm making my living there."

"The Ecuadorian?" I gently asked.

She looked at me with mischievous eyes. "You bastard," she murmured, and gave me a full and long soul kiss. "Yes, that son of a bitch has a hold on me."

Now I gave her a kiss, a good one, and then we parted.

She left Puerto Chicama the next morning on the same bus as Batanero. She continued on south to Lima and to Chile while he finalized our transportation to the mountains.

Nieves and I joined Ernesto the next day. I spent one night in their little apartment sleeping in my bedroll on the floor.

And at 4:00 a.m. our mountain expedition began. The success of it would determine the future course of my life . . . for good or bad.

No grand safari to launch our assault of the Andes. We simply started out in a beat-up old Chevy taxi that we had to push to start. The cab took us out of Trujillo onto the pockmarked Pan American Highway, which we followed south for an hour. Then a turnoff east toward the foothills on a bumpy dirt trail. My plans for a good movie exodus were dashed. We were laughable: We had a flat tire and Ernesto had to pump up a spare with a hand pump. Then we had to push the car again to start up. "Not the way they do it in the movies," Nieves jibbed.

The sun came up but a mist enveloped us as we pounded out into the desert toward a corral of adobe buildings in the little village of Chorabal. All desert with the nearby Andes looming above. Old men with white beards and little straw hats on their heads were awaiting us. A weather-beaten lady with a basket of *dulces* or cookies nourished us as we watched a string of mules being readied. The scenario was almost surrealistic as each cowboy did his thing as the mist and the dust swirled about him. I filmed everything.

A young Indian in torn pants and tall straw *sombrero* announced, "*Soy Narciso, su guía. ya,*" and he watched as we all fumbled around the mules. "*Ya vamos, la Hacienda Uningambal está muy lejos. Vámanos!*"

"Let's go," Ernesto called out. Nieves was already on her mount, talking to it, tapping it with her bridal, and telling it who was the boss. "*Señor* Romain, arriba. Let's do it." I checked to see that no one was watching and then jumped into the saddle. I made it! And so I, too, now joined the chorus of, "*Arriba, mula, vamanos.* Let's move along." And with a lurch, we did.

Ernesto, Nieves, Narciso, and two *mozos* (helpers) had begun our trek in the Andes. From an altitude of 800 feet, we would climb to 12,342 feet. As Bette Davis once said, "Fasten your seatbelts; it's going to be a bumpy ride." It was.

My mule was big-bellied, and there was plenty of girth to grip. He rode easily on the level. But once we began to climb, which was soon, he started to balk and to fight my authority. We battled all the way.

I was surprised at the gentle Ernesto's handling of his animal before me. He took no nonsense. He would take the leather bridle that contained a thong filled with metal slugs, and slap at the animal's neck or head whenever he became balky. "Ernesto," I called to him, "these are dumb creatures; give them a chance to learn."

Ernesto called back to me, "You do that and we'll be here all day. *Arriba,*" he shouted as he banged the mule front and backward. And it moved right along.

Unfortunately, Narciso had never in his life seen a mountain picture. My occasional request for a halt to work the camera puzzled and exasperated him. Nor was Ernesto eager to make the time-consuming stops. "*Señor* Romain, we have a long way to go. We must keep moving." And so we did, wearisome mile after mile.

The trail we followed was well defined, at times broad at other times only wide enough for one mule and rider. The path was worn through centuries of use. Local lore claimed that the Hacienda Uningambal had been established in 1576, which was two years before the great Spanish Armada attempted its invasion of England. There were other fine haciendas tucked away in these mountains, but Uningambal was the biggest and the oldest. The narrow trail we were following had been in use and worn into the mountainside close to 400 years. Narciso, our Indian guide, called it an Inca road, but he was wrong. Should the Incas have built such a road, it would have been much better than the one we were traveling. Their roads often rivaled those of ancient Rome. They were broad, level, and easy. Our footpath had been created over the centuries by mules, horses, and men. It followed the least resistance, winding around here to there. Except for an occasional conquest, the Incas rarely bothered with these mountains.

We began in desert cactus country quite similar to the deserts of northern Mexico or Arizona. Great prickly plants and bushes were our companions. I saw now why the locals had insisted that we fasten heavy chaps about our legs. The sun was warm, but not like the Sechura Desert. We crossed a couple of shallow rivers and I enjoyed that. They cooled off our feet and our legs and the animals always frolicked in them. There were two mules following us. They were mainly loaded down with supplies for the hacienda.

And then began the ascent! At times it seemed we climbed almost straight up. We were all sitting on McClellan saddles, and they had a tendency to slip on the back of the mules causing the riders all kinds of difficulties with balance and stability. I would have greatly preferred the Mexican saddle with its sturdy horn (I wondered how these Civil War saddles ended up down here in Peru). I have always had a mild problem with acrophobia—the fear of heights—and now I began to experience this frightful emotion. All was well when my mount stayed close to the mountainside of the trail, but when he wondered to the ledge and I looked down into a 500- or 1,000-foot drop, my heart was way up in my throat. I held onto both the front and back of the saddle with my hands at those moments when the mule, making a turn on the trail, nonchalantly—or mischievously—poked its head way over the side of the path. I stared straight down into a frightful abyss. "Never again," I mumbled to myself. (I was wrong!)

Finally, to my great relief, Nieves called a halt, and we lowered our aching legs to the ground. None of us except Narciso and the *mozos* were accustomed to hours in the saddle. Like the gracious hostess that Nieves was, she opened up a leather satchel that was strapped to the cargo mule and pulled out sandwiches for all of us. We topped them off with an apple apiece and were ready for the trail again.

I had been told that two-thirds of our riding would be uphill. It was up tall mountains, not hills. I had certainly withstood the thin air on my travels with Barbara to Cuzco and Bolivia—except for the time on the train—but now it began to affect me. The exertion undoubtedly triggered the reaction. At about 10,000 feet I called for a halt, slid off of my mount, and lay prostrate on the ground gasping for air. Nevis came over to me, stared down, and with a lilting laugh, she mockingly uttered the one phrase, "*El adventuero.*" She was referring to the newspaper article that had written me up back home. I too had to smile at the incongruity. She did spur me on to mightier deeds. I was soon back in the saddle and cussing away like an old Missouri muleskinner. Even so, I lagged way behind. There was no fear of becoming lost. The trail, cut in the side of the mountain, only went up or down. I even called to my companions to move right along, that I would be behind them somewhere. But then the sun began to go down, and in the Andes the shadows of late afternoon come quickly. Nevertheless, my animal seemed to know the way, and I gave him his head.

An experienced rider would have done much better than I did when suddenly in the growing dusk a snarling guttural roar echoed out from some clumps of bushes and boulders. The deliberate nonchalance of my mule was immediately changed from indifference to total panic. It bolted straight up the side of the steep mountain pass. It clattered up there as far as it could go and then became immobile except for the shuttering and trembling of its body. Not so gentle of speech as Ernesto, I let out a couple of expletives and reached for the Luger pistol that I had been carrying throughout all my travels. I shouted to my companion beast, "I'll get the S.O.B., don't worry. Ease off!" To my total disillusionment I found no weapon in my belt. I now remembered packing it in our supply mule's *arapajo* or saddlebag. "This is no good," I said aloud, "no good at all." I shouted to Ernesto but he was long gone. I looked about at the bushes and the boulders and the mountain going straight up. I could see no movement in the brush. "If I put in a good front," I thought, "whatever is lurking around here might leave." So I began hollering at the top of my lungs telling the menace that I could lick him with one hand. Nothing happened. I became hoarse. "Let's get a move on," I urged my shaking mule, and when he didn't, I let him have it in the belly with my spurs. He tried, but he was as stuck up there on the no-trail as was I. He couldn't turn around. And so I ended up dismounting and not to gently picking up the beast's hooves one at a time, placing them in the right direction, and guiding him back to the trail. From that time on we were friends; he never fought me again. Later, I was told that there is a form of puma or onca or mountain lion that lives in these parts. Also, a very vicious breed of small bear that was best to avoid. I vowed to never again go into such places without my gun close by. (It was a very good vow!)

Night came quickly like the touching of a light switch. In a moment, if a branch of a tree were in my face, I wouldn't have been able to see it; total darkness. But my newfound friendly mule made sure no such obstacle confronted us. He gingerly moved right along, one step after another. The claustrophobic darkness was troublesome and then frightening until I suddenly spotted a light in the distance. So did the mule; he picked up the pace. A few more lights appeared and soon I was able to identify Ernesto standing by the entrance to a corral. "*Señor* Romain, *aquí estamos*," he shouted, and I was certainly glad to hear his voice. We were home for the night.

"*Bienvenida, Señor* Romain," a deep bass voice welcomed me. "*La Hacienda Ollón*." A broad man with a round face and a bushy gray beard greeted me and guided me from my saddle. "We are at the Hacienda Ollón," Ernesto informed me. "The manager here, *Señor*

Ortega, is putting us up for the night. Everybody in the mountains, it seems, is waiting for us."

My mule was led away for water and feed and I followed Ortega and Ernesto into a quiet rustic stone and hewn wood porch and room. Not much to write about, but with its two gasoline lamps providing a modicum of light, it sure looked good to me. A small fireplace gave us warmth and I could see Nieves sitting in a chair made of leather straps. She was sipping a glass of pisco and lemon juice. I know that this was a concession of Ernesto who abstained and was actually afraid of strong spirits (His father had been an alcoholic). But the cold had set in, and it was beginning to bite at this altitude. "*Señor* Romain," my friend said, "please join Nieves, have a *copita* to warm yourself." I did, and as a matter of record, I had two. And then our host surreptitiously whisked the bottle away.

We were served a bowl of soup laden with hunks of venison. Not to my taste, but as Captain Hanke of the *Omega* had said, "When you are hungry, you will eat it." Ernesto reminded us, "We must leave early tomorrow." He and Nieves were escorted to the only bedroom in the house. Manuel Ortega, Narciso, and I ended up in the tack room surrounded by saddles, belts, chaps, boots, tanned skins, racks of horns, and other very masculine things. Whenever I think of the Hacienda Ollón, I always conjure up the smells of leather and horseflesh. It was a pungent experience. I was soon fast asleep bundled up with a horse blankets and straw pillow.

Before sunup, Narciso was shaking my shoulder and pushing a kerosene lantern in my face. "*Ya vamos*," he repeated several times, and I finally got the message. Black coffee, strong and hot, woke us all up. Hard biscuits with goats butter and a slab of bacon put us back on the trail.

"Next stop," Ernesto cheerfully called out, mainly to me, "the Hacienda Uningambal." We began to climb again. But the ride did begin to get a little easier. Longer level stretches, but still, here and there, some really scary narrow spots. On the whole, the landscape was bleak. I have always enjoyed the deserts of Sonora, Mexico, New Mexico, and Arizona (I once nearly bought a house in that old desert "OK Corral" town, Tombstone). Those landscapes have a flavor: tall saguaro cactus, the mescal, and the long come-hither look of the horizon. In Peru, as we approached the 11,000-foot altitude, the vegetation was stunted, tired and unhealthy looking. There were trees, lots of them, but they, too, were runts. We were in a land on top of the world. Not close enough to the equator to be desert, and not far enough away to produce the great gold kingdoms that the Spaniards sought. I'm sure the conquistadors paid little attention to this region as they rode through it with their bugles blowing and their commands echoing throughout the valleys. Now it was all empty. Not even a furry tarantula, a slithering centipede, or a stinger cocked scorpion. Just the endless horizon of a sterile land. "How on Earth do people live up here?" I asked Ernesto. "Why do they live up here? Hard to get here and hard to return. What's the attraction?"

He had an answer. "You just said it. Easy to get here and hard to leave. They are born up here. They know nothing better and nothing worse. They come into the world, live a while, and then die. Our friend, Narciso, he has never seen a movie. He'll never be influenced by television. He doesn't need an automobile. His life is programmed to these mountains. He is content with his environment. He knows no other."

"You're a philosopher, Ernesto," I commented.

"I've lived in Peru and in the United States. I've seen a lot of things. My motto is: 'Let it be.'"

And we rode on.

For hours we saw no habitation or even a sign of people. Where were all the llamas, the alpacas, and the vicuñas that the travel posters portray? We were now at 12,000 feet. Again, I called to Ernesto. "How can the Hacienda Uningambal make a living up here? Pretty sparse country as I see it."

"They raise a hearty breed of cattle. There's lots of space for each animal to roam and graze. The haciendas or ranches couldn't exist unless they controlled thousands of acres of land. The profit comes when every year they round up their animals and herd them off to the centers that are close to trucking roads. Santiago De Chuco, Llaray, and a couple others. Takes a lot of figuring, wrangling, and paperwork. Ask Flynn when we get there."

"This Flynn sounds like quite a man."

"I don't know him, but I like his style. He answered every radiogram we sent him. Right on time. That's unusual in Peru."

The day dragged on. Our saddle sores began to blossom. The sun started to drop off, and it all seemed endless. Our calls to Narciso were only answered with, "*Más allá.*" Further on.

Once Ernesto dismounted, unsheathed his .22 rifle, and took a long, long shot at a deer that appeared in a deep valley. I am not a hunter or a rifleman, but I know that when he brought down that buck at such a distance with just a .22 bullet, he was a true marksman. His shot had gone right into the heart of the deer. One of our *mozos* brought the animal to us. "We'll bring our dinner with us," Ernesto exulted. He was elated.

When the sun went into its disappearing act, one of our cargo mules just collapsed on the rim of an awesome mountain trail and then rolled down into the valley hundreds of feet below us. Again, the *mozos* went to retrieve it. They determined that it had broken its leg and they cut its throat. Then brought our supplies back to us, and we managed to carry them the rest of the way.

The sun and its light had left us, the darkness enveloped us, and I felt claustrophobic. Nobody else did. Nieves, Narciso, and the *mozos* were chatting away with one another as though they were on a lark. They were ahead of Ernesto and me. I was eternally grateful that my friend stayed back with me. My mule and I might have bonded, but he still moved along at his own pace, and that was slow. Batanero knew that I was unaccustomed to this sort of travel and to the Andes Mountains of his country. He kept me company. "They tell me, *Señor* Romain, that Uningambal is close ahead. Be of good cheer; we'll be there soon." He was comforting.

I needed comfort. The 30-degree chill at 12,000 feet above sea level in the darkness of the night was numbing; it went through my jacket and scarf, through my fringed buckskin shirt and into my bones. Had it not been for the exertion that generated a modicum of heat, I believe that I would have been trembling. After a couple more hours, I was.

But finally Ernesto let out a "whoop." "There she is, my friend. Look over to your left. A fire has been lit, a beacon for us. There is our Hacienda Uningambal." I was immediately alert. Way ahead of us a bonfire was blazing. It looked warm, cozy, and welcome. "That Flynn," Batanero shouted as he closed in along side of me and my mule. "That Flynn has greeted us well. He knows this is one long and hard trip. I told you I liked his style. I even like it better now."

We rode up to a long stone wall that stretched to somewhere in the night. There was a wooden archway that spanned an opening. Beyond it was the blazing fire, and beyond that was the outline of a large building surrounded by a porch. Nieves' mule was tied to the porch railing.

"*Señor* Batanero," a very friendly voice called out in English. "Come along, we are waiting for you. The fire is lit and the grog is hot. Do yourself a favor and come on in."

"I'll be damned," I thought. "Do I detect an Irish brogue?"

Indeed, I had. The voice continued. "Now get yourselves down from those beasts and join us in the parlor. You've held up the cocktail hour long enough." It was 8:00 p.m.

The voice turned to me. "And you, sir, you've come a long way to join us. Let the lads take your mule, and let us go inside where it's warm."

"Flynn," was all that I could say. "Santiago Flynn, pleased to meet you."

"Jimmy," he lilted back to me. "Jimmy Flynn to my English speaking friends. And I'm at your service from now on. Please be my guest."

Now I saw the man in the light of the porch lanterns. "Flynn is right," I thought. "Errol Flynn; he's a ringer, but he is bigger and better looking. Barbara was right." The man's smile lit up my travel-weary psyche. He extended a hand and helped me out of the saddle. A few quick words and Indians immediately led off my and the other mules. "Tis indeed a pleasure to welcome you to this place in the sky. How did you ever manage to get up here without succumbing to the terror of the heights? You must be congratulated. Come into my home and let us drink to your deliverance from the dark of the night."

Ernesto nudged me. "You're going to like this guy!"

It certainly was pleasant to hear my English language spoken again by one who could obviously do it justice.

We clomped up several steps to the porch, which was fenced by a neat wooden railing, and then through a doorway whose huge metal studded door was wide open. The room was nicely lit by several electric lamps; a generator hummed somewhere in the distance. A fireplace faced me across the room. "You are home, *Señor* Romain," Flynn informed me as he directed me to a large rustic chair along side the one in which Nieves was sitting. "May I take the informality of addressing you as *Señor* Romain? The wires tell me that's your name."

"No *Señor*," I finally found my voice. "Just Romain; friends call me that, and I am sure I am among friends here."

"Ha, ha," he laughed aloud. "Luis, get the man a drink." A shorter, slender, darker, and older man moved away from the fireplace where he had been stoking a log of wood. "Luis Seminario," Flynn said fondly, and introduced me to the assistant manager of the hacienda. "He is Trujillo born and bred, but mountain to the core." Seminario spoke no English, but was eager and pleased to hear my bizarre Spanish. We shook hands. He was obviously a gentleman. He went to a makeshift bar on one of the tables and came back with the usual Peruvian drink, pisco and ginger ale. "*Salud.*" He lifted his glass. "*Salud, dinero, y amor, y tiempo para gastarlos*," he spoke out. "Health, wealth, love, and time to spend them." I clicked Luis Seminario's glass and immediately knew I had made another friend. All of us, including Nieves, but excluding Ernesto, joined in the toast. He grinned as he sipped a cup of coffee.

The talk, of course, focused on how the trail was, how we were treated by the people at Chorabal and Ollón, and how the animals behaved. Flynn pointed to the porch of his house and congratulated Ernesto on the plump deer that he had shot and which was strung up on the eaves. "The boys will skin and clean it, and then we'll smoke it over a slow fire of mountain wood, herbs, and charcoal. They have a way up here, you know," he proudly said, "of rubbing the right spices into the meat at just the correct time it's rotating over the fire. We'll enjoy venison tomorrow. But tonight," he grinned, "we will serve you what has been roasting all day. A wild pig or boar. Not easy to come by up here, but Luis here brought it down with one shot. We should drink to his marksmanship. He is the best." Seminario didn't blush. He lifted his glass, and nodded agreement. He was quite sure of his own abilities.

Having traveled with Barbara Holbrook, I had picked up a bit of the newsman's curiosity and interviewing technique (she was always asking questions). "Santiago Flynn," I asked, "what is an Irishman doing up here in the northern mountains of Peru? From where did you come?"

"You think Ireland, don't you, my friend?" he grinned. "Not quite. But mother and father did come from the old country. They came to Argentina to join some of the great engineers of South America who were designing the railway routes over the mountains. They eventually settled in Argentina where I was born. Privileged and spoiled, but nevertheless, a healthy little lad at that. I grew up well and was educated in the best schools. I enjoyed, as we all did, the social life of the rich. I even put time in the army."

Luis Seminario broke in and his Spanish was translated to me by Ernesto. "Santiago is a member of the Bransen Lancers which is a crack cavalry riding unit of the Argentine army. He can place the point of a lance through a three-inch ring while riding a horse all out, galloping full tilt."

Flynn acknowledged his partner's compliment, but answered, "Luis talks too much, but I love him for it."

The story came out that when Juan Perón took power in Argentina, Flynn and some of his patriotic friends felt they should leave the country. His reasons were his own, but like many, he went elsewhere. To Peru and eventually to the Hacienda Uningambal. "Yes," he continued rather sadly, "there was a marriage in Lima. Very social. Very high class. And a beautiful lady, I must admit. But, after one mule trip to my mountaintop, she became disillusioned with me. She and her bridesmaids had unrealistic romantic notions about my hacienda in the clouds. She didn't like the smell of horses; they made her sneeze, she couldn't stand the odor of Indians, and she missed the elegant dances at the Hotel Bolívar, the country club, and the Crillon. She just didn't enjoy living up here all alone with her ever-loving husband. So, now she is down in Lima tasting the social graces that are lacking here. She is in the process of divorcing me." (All of this last gossip I already knew. My charming spy Barbara had reported it all to me. She had met Flynn's beautiful gadfly wife.) "How straightforward and honest this man is to me," I thought as we refilled our glasses.

"And you, Romain," Flynn asked in return. Tell me now, where might your ladylove be? And why does she let a handsome fellow like you so far out of her sight? Does she not know that the dark eyes of Lima can enchant a man right out of his skull? What's your story?"

Strangers often tell the truth. "For a long luscious year," I answered, "I was captivated by one of two lovely blond twins who were doing their best to make their mark in the theatre. Not the best sort of an entanglement. We were as close as close can get without overstepping the bonds of morality. And then the breaks began to come their way and my tall tales of far off and exotic places began to pale on her. She and her sister hired on some sort of government U. S. D. troupe of musical talent and away they went to Europe. Her letters and then her cards, and then her silence told me that she was on her way . . . without me. She came back. We tried. But nothing is deader than dead love, if she ever had it. We broke up. You may have seen her and her sister's portrait on the cover of *Life Magazine* a couple of years ago. A write-up of a musical on Broadway."

I was surprised at my flippant confession. Even Ernesto looked quizzically at me as he translated it all to his wife and to Luis.

"Ha, ha," Flynn triumphantly laughed and directed his speech to Seminario. "You see, my friend, it is not only me, but other worthies who can't keep their ladyloves to themselves." Seminario grinned at him. Apparently, there had been discussion about such things between the two of them before during the many lonely nights they shared together.

Luis briefly commented, "I am happily married to one lady and will always be. My daughter is a blessing and a beauty." I was to confirm that in time.

A dainty quite dusky and pretty young Indian lady, with long black braids that fell to her waist, came into the room. She bowed respectfully to all of us, and then went through the door which we had been told was the master bedroom. She was carrying a covered brass pan attached to a six-foot pole. I asked no questions.

The two managers of Uningambal were obviously starved for conversation from others than their farm hands, cowboys, and foremen. We talked late, until the fire began to sputter, and the savory pork had been devoured. Then Ernesto stood up and asked, "Where might Nieves and I go for the night?"

"Of course," Luis Seminario immediately stood up. "Please come with me. Your room is ready." I, too, was pretty talked out, and after fourteen hours in the saddle, was ready to turn in. "Where do you put me, Jimmy?" I cheerily asked. "The tack room will do me fine. I did well there at Ollón."

"No, no, No tack room here. That is your room." Flynn pointed to his own master bedroom. "You'll sleep there while here as my guest."

"That's your room, Jimmy."

"Not while you are here. Final," he said as he rose from his chair and moved off to the hallway.

"Jimmy," I mildly protested. "The young lady who just went into your room, she hasn't come out."

"Oh," Flynn again good-naturedly responded. "She is in there warming your bed. There is no central heating here. The fireplace doesn't do much for the other rooms. It's cold in there. You need a warm bed. She's doing it for you." He turned to go but looked back. "Do not worry. It will be warm as toast when you're ready for it. That round pan is full of red-hot coals from a fire. She is moving it around beneath your sheets. She does it for me every night."

The imp in me made me say it, "Is that all, Jimmy?"

Flynn laughed, "You are more of a rascal than you make out," he replied. "But, for the record, Luis and I have a strict rule: 'Hands off the women.' It can lead to a lot of trouble and did with the last manager."

I answered with the familiar expression, "*No problema*."

He went his way and I went into his room.

The lady was slowly drawing the warming bed pan back and forth beneath my covers. "*Está bien*," I said, and she quickly withdrew the pan and backed away with a deferential and sweet "*Buenas noches, caballero*."

I slept like a log in the Hacienda Uningambal some 12,000 feet in the Andes Mountains of Peru that dated back to 1576.

9 — LEGEND IN THE ANDES: HUASACHUGA

In the daylight, the hacienda proved to be quite a place. More like a neat little village than a cattle ranch. The great house, as it was called, stood on the periphery of the compound, and was set back from the rest of the dwellings. "On purpose," Flynn told me. "If we have a strike or a rebellion up here, we want a little space between us and the dissenters."

The house was plastered with a type of white stucco as were many of the lesser buildings which housed the foreman and other important families in the region. There was an Indian caste system that all observed. Most of the Aymará Indians lived in communities as they had for centuries, with a leader or *cacique* and a council of elders. To be born, grow up healthy, find a spouse, produce children, and to age in the bosom of the family was the ambition of all who lived and worked the Hacienda Uningambal's lands. There were no slaves here. All worked for the common good, mainly, to feed himself and his family. The *hacienda* gave them the opportunity and the means to accomplish that ambition. People were content because they knew no other lifestyle. The *hacienda* produced everything they needed. A good manager, and Santiago Flynn was a good one, kept the system honed. If he went bad, as the last two managers had, he would soon be replaced. So far Flynn, with his considerate ways and his concern for the people, was doing well. Unfortunately, just one mistake on his post—right or wrong—and he would be a marked man. It didn't take me long to realize that he always carried a .45 automatic pistol in its holster on his belt. This reality was pushed home to me when, after seeing my long barreled German Luger, he asked me to wear it in sight at all times. "Gives you the edge," he commented.

Ernesto, Nieves, and I were taken on a long and thorough tour of the whole complex. First, we made a courtesy call to the mayor or designated Indian boss, who pretty well controlled the work force. He was quite an unassuming man with sparse whiskers decorating his chin. "He can make or break an operation here," Flynn told me. "Sort of John L.

Lewis union boss. We treat him very well, and he reciprocates. So far he is on our team." He nodded to Seminario. We accepted the man's invitation into his modest but well-furnished three-room house. With gusto, Flynn spoke up, "*Cómo ésta la chi-chi hoy?*"

"*Muy bein, jefe,*" the mayor answered.

"*Muy bein, mejor.*"

He went to a cupboard, opened it, and brought out an earthen jug. Into several glasses he poured a good quantity of murky-colored fluid. He ritualistically handed each of us a glass of chi-chi and then stepped back to observe our reaction. "Drink up," Jimmy beamed, "and enjoy." I drank and did not enjoy. The beverage had a sour, milky beer taste to it. "This is the drink of my people, of all the natives of Peru. We accept the man's invitation and he takes it as an honor. Do finish up at least the glass he gave you." I did so. As did Ernesto—the teetotaler—and Nieves. I knew something was up because they all kept a smug eye on me.

"What's the story here?" I asked Batanero. Flynn saved my friend the task of telling me.

"This stuff is pretty potent. A lot stronger than Papst Blue Ribbon. It's the way they brew it that gets a little touchy. The ladies sit for hours chewing maize, and then they spit it out into a big kettle where it is heated and then set aside for weeks to ferment. It's their party drink and they can get pretty drunk on it. The trouble is, if you are as scrupulous as are most city folk, the thought of drinking down something that someone else has been salivating into is a little hard to take. It accomplishes its purpose, but I'll agree with you, it is no Johnny Walker Red Scotch."

He spoke as he directed us out of the mayor's house, "We did good there. The man is pleased that we honored his house. He will be your friend." Then in a more serious tone, "We need him, you know. He can furnish the guides that we will need to take us to the ruins you seek. We'll be calling on him tomorrow. He and his fellow Indians know everything about the land up here in this part of the Andes. Yes, we did good things here."

The mayor waved us on as we hiked beyond the main concentration of dwellings. There were many more smaller homes all over the area, but we now walked over to a rough stone circular stone corral. Several cowboys were at work taming or breaking maverick or stubborn horses. "Always interesting," Flynn commented. "They get pretty rough with the livestock, and I try to slow them down. It's a losing battle."

We watched as a short brawny Indian worked a tough little cayuse. He was rough, and he used a long leather whip with impunity; too rough, I thought. Flynn called encouragement to the man, and then hand-vaulted the fence. "*Momentito,*" he called out. The man deferred to his boss, and stepped back. There was no saddle on the horse, so I was surprised when Flynn walked up to it, called out a few sharp words, diverted it's attention, and then literally leaped onto the back of the stallion, and squeezed his long legs about the animal's belly. With the experience of many years of horsemanship, he gathered up the mane of the horse in his left hand, grabbed the right ear with his right hand, and pulled the animal's head around. He leaned over, grasped that ear with his teeth, bit down hard, and held on. The beast quieted for a moment, and Flynn let the ear go. Up and away the horse leaped and bucked, but always seemed to keep his head turned to be able to see his adversary. Away they went around the circular stone corral. Flynn yelped and whooped and the horse snorted and neighed. But Jimmy never let go. He finally rode the panting horse to a standstill. Together they stood in the center of the arena, both of them breathing heavily. The horse looked back at the rider, and the rider leaned low over its neck and challenged it. Soon it was enough, and the animal acknowledged its master. Flynn slowly dismounted, stood a moment by the horse, talked to it, and then came back to us. Ernesto said to me, "I guess those Bransen Lancers know their stuff. He sure does." I groaned, "Where was my camera?"

Then back to the great house for ham sandwiches on some of the tastiest rolls I've ever eaten. Peru, Mexico, Colombia, and I'm sure other Latin American countries do make wonderful bread and rolls. No preservatives, baked this morning, eaten today, leftovers tossed to the pigs tonight. Really fresh and good.

"Enough for you wandering people today," Jimmy pleasantly stated. "*Siesta* time for all of you. I must go about my business and you must rest. We shoot tonight. No shaky hands allowed."

"Shoot?" Ernesto questioned. "Shoot what?"

"There are pesky little birds that have taken over what Luis and I call our private preserve of trees. They eat the seedling, drive away the pretty birds, and are a nuisance. Before dinner, Luis and I often spend an hour plinking at them. Hard to hit, but it's something to do. So rest up." We three slept well. One of those good Latin American customs: the *siesta*.

At 4:00 we were all out in the grove of trees somewhat beyond the house. "The Spaniards planted these trees centuries ago, and I try to maintain them," Flynn informed us. "The Indians would long ago have chopped them down for wood, but I want to keep the Hacienda as it was."

All throughout the Hacienda Uningambal the colonial hand was evident. Another group of trees delineated the broad lane to the totally ruined seventeenth century church. The Spaniards had built for permanence; they intended to stay.

A couple of *mozos* brought several folding chairs, and they were set up for Nieves and me. Then the marksmen went to work. A couple of shooting tripods were set up. Flynn and Seminario positioned their long rifles, sighted them, and then told the *mozos* to flush out the pesky birds. The boys ran into the woods with pans and cowbells and began banging them. Immediately hundreds of little wings beat the air, and the place was full of chirping birds. The men waited until they had settled and after the *mozos* had returned they carefully lined up their scopes and tripods. They where a good city block away from their targets. "Bang, bang," the guns went off. Nothing happened. "It's a long way off." Jimmy turned to me, "and the birds are onto us. Don't worry, we'll get one of those pesky rascals." But they didn't. Shot after shot went awry. Ernesto—a marksman if there ever was one—got in the act. But, even with the tripod, he too missed time and again.

Nieves elbowed me and obviously enjoyed the *macho hombres* being bested by a flock of furry feathers. The sun was going fast and Flynn finally called it a day. "No luck, Luis. Just not our night. It'll be dark in a moment." He began to gather up the tripods. Then he looked over to me. "My God, Luis," he exclaimed, "here is our guest, and we have been rude enough to not give him a shot." He called to me, "Here, Romain, take my rifle; be my guest. I apologize for taking all the shots. I think I've been away from Lima too long; my manners are atrocious. Here, let me set up the tripod, and you take a few shots." He handed me his binoculars, "You can see some of the blighters up there."

I protested. I was no marksman and had never handled a 3.06 rifle. Flynn insisted. He thrust the long gun into my hands and brought the tripod up to me. All I wanted to do was to finish it up and get back to the dining room. I took the rifle casually, ignored the tripod, lifted the stock to my shoulder, made a flippant remark, and squeezed the trigger. A roar of applause came from all as suddenly a bird fell from its perch and crashed to the earth. No one was more surprised than I was. I remember distinctly Nieves clapping her hands and shouting, "Bravo, bravo."

Flynn, Batanero, and Seminario stood in disbelief. Finally, the Irishman lamented, "And here we were, all three of us hunters, banging away and leaving our guest totally out of it. It's a shame on us because he is the sharpshooter of us all, and he didn't want to show us up. My God, I applaud you, *Señor* Romain. Here, take another shot."

"Many thanks," I modestly declined. "One is enough." And I took Nieves' arm and we walked back to the great house. She looked up at me, and squeezed my hand. "*Uno, no mas*," I whispered to her, and she silently laughed. It had been one of those lucky occasions that comes rarely in a lifetime.

Venison was the menu this evening. Not my favorite dish, especially when the head of the buck was placed on a platter by the cook and wrapped with herbs and leaves. We were honored, I realized to be served in such a manner, but it was a little too graphic for me. Nevertheless, basking now in my posture as "Sharpshooter of Uningambal," the meal tasted just fine.

❖❖❖

The next morning we began our preparations for the ascent to the ruins that the Indians called Huasachuga.

When we had all gathered for our breakfast, I noticed that the attitude at the table was all business. Jimmy Flynn quickly spread out several maps. They were old ones. Two of them looked like leather parchment or vellum. They had the smell of age—if age can smell. Not merely must, but archival, like something that was put away a long time ago and then forgotten. "These charts," Flynn began, "have been in the records of the Hacienda for a long time. Two, maybe three centuries. They were the result of surveys made of Uningambal to mark out the boundaries of the ranch and to establish the tax structure for the King of Spain. They are quite accurate, and they cover a lot of territory up here. But they show no sign of pre-colonial Indian ruins. Nothing. Just a lot of taxable land. They will do us little good except as a curiosity, and to tell us where we should not go exploring."

Flynn put aside the first two maps and positioned the third one on the table. "Other than the Indian legends," he said in English and then in Spanish to Nieves and Seminario, "this chart gives us proof that the Spanish *hacendados* were aware of a group of ruins two days from here." He pointed to a well-done line drawing of a tower and wall some distance from Uningambal. "The Hacienda is indicated here on the map by the flag and seal of Spain with the name Uningambal written beneath them. Down here in the right corner of the document is written in archaic Spanish—'It is said that in this region there is a city that is deserted and that is very old. The Indians speak of it. It should be investigated'—it is signed, Alejandro Rojas, mayordomo to Uningambal."

We all gathered around and took a look at the chart. Flynn continued, "There is nothing at all in any of the documents that I have been able to find here that mentions a follow up. I don't know if the Spaniards ever did look for the place. I certainly imagine they would have, and if they had, that activity would have been mentioned in the account books. The colonial Spaniards were very meticulous in recording everything they did."

Luis broke in, "Santiago and I have scoured this place for any other shred of information. If there was any, it has disappeared. We haven't been obsessed by it, but we are curious, and it has given us something to do other than to keep cattle and cowhands in line." Seminario was a cautious and serious man.

"Exactly," Flynn kept going. "So, of course, we put out some feelers to our local Indians. We were surprised at the response. Most of those who we questioned, such as the mayor who you've met, agreed that in the area marked on the map there are—and I quote the Indian—'homes of the people who were here before we came.'"

Ernesto questioned, "Were they at all in awe of the place? Would they be willing to guide us there?"

Luis again spoke. "That is why Santiago is the boss, the manager; he knows how to do things and get things done. He has coaxed the Indians to guide us there. They wouldn't have done it for me, but they will for him."

Jimmy was pleased with his friend's approbation. He acknowledged Luis' statement but added, "No, Luis, I think they would have gone along with you. They just know I'm the head man and so they talked to me."

He gathered up the maps and explained, "We won't be needing these at all. They're just good background. We'll go with the Indians tomorrow morning at 6:00 a.m. There will be four of them to act as guides and three to work the mules. The mayor has arranged it, but he, himself, will not be going. Too old. He has given explicit directions to his men. We'll spend one night on the way in bedrolls that I'll supply. The second day should see us there in the afternoon. We'll spend a night at the place; give *Señor* Romain an opportunity to take his pictures. Then we'll leave that noon. One more night on the trail, and then back here." He had it all planned. Santiago Flynn was indeed the boss.

The managers of Uningambal went about their business the rest of the day, and Ernesto and I wondered about the premises. There was activity by one of the stables. The old mayor was directing several younger fellows, including our recent guide, Narciso, in shoeing mules, bringing saddles from the shed along with straps, tack, and stirrups. Other men were carefully packing *aparejos*, the packs that are fastened to the saddles. The Hacienda seemed to be going somewhere.

Then Nieves approached us. "Ernesto," she said, "I will not be going with you to-morrow. My sinus condition has worsened at this altitude. I do not want to aggravate it. You know what the doctor told us."

Batanero was truly taken aback. "We've come so far, Nieves, just four more days." But then he shook his head. "No, it is better you stay here and relax. It would not be worth it."

She answered, "Ernesto, this is your and *Señor* Romain's moment. I am a Spaniard. These Indian things do not interest me as they do you. Please go on, and I will regain my strength. I do not want to be a burden." And so Nieves chose to stay behind.

With bells ringing from the necks of our lead mules, shouts from our muleteers, and good wishes from Nieves and the old mayor, the next morning at sunup we were off. The moment was exhilarating. The sky was clear, a soft pale blue, with perhaps a touch of frost to invigorate us. I was on the same mule that had already served me so well. I liked that. But when I saw Jimmy Flynn glide by me on his beautifully groomed mount—tail fluffed out, withers scrubbed down, a haughty manner that perfectly matched his master, a pro-nounced strut that exaggerated his gate as he trotted by us—I was envious. "There goes a *caballero* and his steed," I thought. Flynn was cognizant of the impression he made.

"Romain," he called to me as he pranced by, "this is my friend who I call 'Gringa.' I paid half a year's wage for her. She is the best mule in the mountains."

"I can imagine that," I hollered back as I goaded my beast on. Santiago slowed so that I could approach him.

"She is the best. I've worked her hard. I spend a lot of time in the saddle, and I cannot allow my subordinates the pleasure of besting me in our roundups. I've got to be the best." He easily trotted to the front of our little safari into the high sierra.

Seminario rode up to me. In Spanish, he good-naturedly called to me, "Santiago is in charge. He knows what is best. He wants to be a step ahead of all the Indians around here. It is his edge. If he looses it, he will go the way of the last two managers."

"What happened to them?" I asked.

"They had been playing pit-i-pat with some of the pretty Indian girls of the area. Husbands didn't like that. One was ambushed as he rode out to a roundup. Shot to pieces with a double-barreled shotgun. The other never woke up one night. His throat had been cut."

"Ouch," I croaked as I felt my neck.

"That's why it is so lonely up here," Luis laughed and rode on.

"What a unique place this is," I mused to myself. (Indeed, I was to see in the future, the flaw and the fate of Santiago Flynn of the Hacienda Uningambal.)

We rode out on the old Spanish road with its tall eucalyptus trees proudly framing our way. After the arduous ride up to Uningambal, that hacienda complex had come to mean a real haven of civilization. Now, as we left its avenue of trees, we were back in the primitive country of a truly unknown land.

There was no sniffing of the grounds and sifting of dung as Indian scouts of the movies are portrayed. Our Quechua Indians just boldly strode out and led the way as though they had done it before. (I use the phrase "Quechua Indians" for lack of an ethnic name to give these people. During the reign of the Incas, their Quechua language was forced upon all the tribes they conquered. Today, people who speak Quechua tend to be called "Quechuans.")

Within an hour, we were beyond the influence of the hacienda. We rode through scrubby and non-luxuriant foliage. Soon we came to a *quebrada* or deep canyon. From there, we entered a land of abrupt ravines and abysses. These were sometimes awesome, but I felt much more comfortable in the saddle now, and I managed these challenges with a great deal more confidence than I had during the ascent to Uningambal. I even began to enjoy the difficult places and picked up a few tricks for maneuvering a mule. Flynn, who admitted that he had not traveled this far away from his duties at the ranch, went riding here, there, everywhere, up over ridges to see what was on the other side, and then down into dark and obscure gorges. He was enjoying his freedom from the worries of keeping some thousand Quechuan peasants content. Seminario said it well to me as we rode side by side. "Santiago is conscientious (I had a hard time translating that Spanish into mine); he looks into every detail of the Indian's life. He wants to do right by them. But, not being of their blood and background, it is hard to guess just what is right for them. Flynn comes from a wealthy family who live in Argentina. They have been there for generations. But now the Perón region and the frivolities of Eva Perón have made it difficult for people like them to pursue their traditional lifestyle. No matter how they conduct their affairs and pay their employees, the Peróns accuse them of robbing the poor. In this way the Peróns gain the support of the less fortunate and capture their votes. They have started to take away the land and wealth of the rich. Santiago and many have left and now live in Chile or Peru. I have heard that Santiago had a run-in with Eva Perón. He was too good looking for Juan Perón to have around. I believe he was lucky to get out of there."

Luis rode ahead and took a long rifle shot at a huge condor that swept down from the heights and made a pass at one of the mules. The whole trip was strange to me, and I wondered at the complexities of life south of the United States' borders. "If Barbara were here," I thought, "what a story she could drag out of that charming and handsome Santiago Jimmy Flynn!"

When the sun goes down, as it quickly does in the high Andes Mountains, the pleasant sun warmth of sixty degrees suddenly drops in minutes to a thin cold of twenty degrees. Flynn called a halt. He chose a flat meadow that was sheltered from the winds by a stony ridge. "This is as far as we go today," he happily called out. "Let's not overdo it. The boys will fix up our shelters and supper. We can sit down, soak up the fire, and have a cocktail or two. We'll make it as pleasant as possible."

I'm sure the stop was as welcome to the others as it was to me. I hadn't raised calluses on my buns—not yet—but I'm sure they were as red and as chafed as they ever were. There was no wind that night so there was no chill factor. With a big fire that the Indians quickly got going, it was actually enjoyable. The locals themselves were pleased with the outing: not the drudgery of home. Away from their nagging wives, and on a lark with the big boss.

We slept well, but not long. The Indians were up and about at 4:00 a.m. They started up the fire, hung a kettle of water over it for coffee, and dropped some puddles of dough into a large iron skillet. The dough rose to light brown, some too much so, and between those biscuits were added slabs of pork from last night's meal. It sufficed. We were back in the saddle by 5:30, just as day began to break.

We had started out at the Hacienda Uningambal at 12,000 feet more or less. We had been climbing slowly and I do believe that we might have reached 13,000 feet above sea level. The vegetation through which we now passed showed the effect of the height. Everything was stunted. Trees were underdeveloped, not a shade under any of them. But then toward noon we began to descend. Gradually, but for quite a distance. Maybe 2000 feet. Then we leveled off.

Flynn rode ahead. He always rode the point. We became used to seeing him a mile ahead of us. He wore a bright red *poncho* that covered him down to his knees and a broad brimmed Mexican style *sombrero*. Santiago Flynn was quite picturesque.

At high noon of that day, he abruptly stopped and stood up in his stirrups. He pulled his binoculars from their case attached to the saddle, and stared intently at a high but flat plateau that I assumed we would be bypassing. He had seen something up there. He replaced the binoculars and took off that big *sombrero*. And then he waved it back and forth. His Indian guide rode up to him. Flynn said something to the man and gave his mule a slap

149

across the rump. The guide came racing back to us. He galloped up to Luis Seminario and shouted to him. Luis turned and called to us. "He has seen it. I think he has found *Huasachuga. Vamanos.*"

As we spurted forward, Flynn came pounding back with a big grin on his face. "Come along with me," he yelled. "Come on up closer. You'll see it then. It's up there all right. We're here. We've found the city. The Indians were right all along." He cantered his mule along side of mine. "Here, take the field glasses. Have a look yourself. Those aren't mountain outcroppings. Those are walls, big ones." He leaned over to me and handed me the binoculars. I focused in on the large plateau that rose majestically ahead of us. The sight that filled the eyepiece startled me. I brushed the grit from my eyes and stared at a row of ramparts that jutted upward from the ridge. I could make out doorways, apertures, staircases, and passageways. They were obviously old, very old. There was a geometric pattern to them. They were man-made.

"We've got it," I shouted to Flynn, and turned back toward Batanero and Seminario who were trotting up. "We've got it," I called again to them. "We've found it. Right there ahead of us. Up there," I called again, and nearly fell off my mule pointing it out. We all had a laugh as I struggled to regain my seat. And then we all raced hell-bent-for-leather toward the rim rock ahead of us.

The city still eluded us. At the base of this steep *mesa* or plateau, we were stopped. We were confronted by a near thousand-foot wall of rock. To get to our objective, we faced a very steep, almost impossible climb.

"May the good Lord preserve us," Jimmy intoned. "Whoever built this place sure didn't want anybody wondering in on him. There is no way we can climb from here to there."

Ernesto and Luis had not been idle. As Jimmy and I speculated, and I set up my tripod and movie camera, they began circling the *mesa*. Before long they and the Indians found a narrow pathway leading up into the plateau. Once it seemed to end but then they saw a cleft in the stony escarpment large enough for them and a mule to enter. They led their animals through it, and soon they were waving and shouting to us from the edge of the butt. They were in the city.

We followed them.

This was no Machu Picchu with its well-dressed polished boulder-like smooth walls. These were made of all sizes of rocks, big and small. They had been leveled off, or dressed, to give a fairly smooth appearance on the outside and did look quite attractive. The style of masonry is called by archaeologists *pirca*. It was used sometime before the advent of the Incas. This would mean that Huasachuga had probably been built and abandoned before the Inca Empire sent its conquering legions into these formidable mountains. Sometime before the thirteenth century.

Exploration was remarkably easy. Because of the altitude the foliage and dirt that most always gathers about, and eventually covers many abandoned sites, was lacking. Lots of tall grass but nothing to hinder our wanderings. We were intrigued by the walls. Some of them were almost forty feet tall. Many of them leaned way over as though the mountain winds had been blowing them in one direction for many centuries. They had stood, we speculated, for perhaps eight hundred years or more. These walls had been built well. They had stood here alone, tall and unattended for a long time. The silence of the place was only challenged by the natural breezes blowing through empty hallways, windows, and doorways. The ruins comprised an area of about a half-mile by a half-mile. Not too large, but quite concentrated or centralized like an inner city or ghetto. Perhaps 10,000 people may have once lived here crowded into this mountaintop citadel. What they did is hard to fathom. Not being archaeologists, who most always have an answer for these questions, we can only assume that this bastion contained the government that controlled and directed the agricultural activities of the population around it. The potato was the big crop in Peru. (That's where those tasty McDonald French fries originated), and I'm sure there were other homegrown products also. We saw no llamas, vicuñas, or alpacas in these northern Peruvian mountains so I doubt those productive animals with their luxuriant fur coats were a factor here. The city will remain an enigma until some university or state sponsored archaeological project decides to work it over. So far those institutions are concentrating on the better-known sites such as Machu Picchu, the Nazca Lines, and Cuzco. More recently an interest in the Chimu of Chan-Chan has been growing.

"*Señor*," one of the guides approached Flynn. "We can take you to the cave of the graves of those who were here first." He noticed Flynn's interest and that of Seminario and Batanero. "Three days ride, maybe four, maybe more, there is a large cave. In the cave are many of the old people all sitting in a circle. They are long dead and dry. But they are dressed and their possessions are with them. We can take you there."

Flynn looked at me. I looked at Ernesto. He looked at Seminario.

"Speak it again," Flynn gently asked. And the man repeated his story. "*Es verdad?*" Jimmy asked.

"Of course," the Indian answered. "We all know that."

"Who told you?" Flynn pressed.

"Oh, it is something we all know. It doesn't matter. Those people are all out there, sitting in a circle. We know that."

"Have you seen them with your eyes?"

The Indian hesitated; then quickly spoke up. "No, *senor*, but we all know it is so."

"*Mil gracias*," Flynn sincerely thanked him.

He relayed the man's story to us, and then he shook his head. "I have no doubt that all that he is telling us is the truth. None whatsoever. But I do not have the time. Two, three, maybe four days to get to that place. And even then, they admit that they don't know for sure just where this cave is. The Indians up here have no real sense of time and distance."

Luis interrupted him. "It might be less far than he thinks, Santiago."

"Quite possible," Jimmy answered. "But you know as well as I do that we have a ranch to run. I have an obligation to the people who hired me. And who pay you, too." He pointedly indicated Seminario. "We've taken all the time we can to be away. We'll leave here in a couple of hours."

Santiago was a bit brusque. I could see that he was fighting the temptation to go on, to follow up this man's story. But as he pointed out, he was the manager of a huge operation. He was alone in these mountains except for Luis. He had to attend to his responsibilities.

As mentioned, there was not much for us to see in this city of Huasachuga, and there seemed no place where a dig should be begun. Leaning towers and falling walls. One of those walls was close to four stories tall. We gathered there, and had our picture taken by an Indian who pushed the button of my still camera on the tripod. In front of this building was a well laid slightly raised platform constructed of large smooth stones. Ernesto brought up the suggestion, "I wonder if there might be something underneath this nicely laid out patio. Sometimes pre-Colombian people placed their more treasured images in such prominent places. Like a cover stone or tombstone." He poked around. "Just a thought."

"Lead a mule over it," Flynn suggested. Narciso did so. We were divided as to the result. Ernesto and Luis thought it sounded hollow beneath the large stone slabs. Jimmy and I didn't think so. "Leave it to the archaeologists," Flynn spoke rather abruptly. "Let them look into it. I do not want to break this place up."

"If only we had a metal detector," Ernesto wistfully suggested. "Save a lot of trouble."

"But, Ernie," Flynn answered him, "it is not only metal we should be looking for. There's a whole culture of life that once lived here that we should look into. Not just the gold and silver of a few noblemen. We are out of our realm; let's leave it to the professionals. I cannot stay much longer."

"Of course," Ernesto added, and began to prepare his mount for the exodus.

I sided up to Batanero. "Ernesto," I confided," I can get us a metal detector. I can come back with one."

He looked sharply at me. "If you can do that we can find untold riches, secrets of old haciendas, gold and silver buried before and after the conquest. I have dozens of places where I would like to pass a gold detector. Too bad they are illegal in Peru." He turned away.

My old romantic dreams were overpowering me. "I can do it, Ernesto. I'll bring one in from the States. I can bring it in in parts. No one would be the wiser. With your connections I know we can get it into Peru."

The old treasure hunter looked me in the face. "*Señor* Romain, do that. We can make a million."

I looked at him and winked. We had agreed.

We left the pre-Inca city of Huasachuga around noon of that day, October 10, 1953. We had emptied a coffee tin and placed in it a slip of paper with all of our names and the date written on it. (We would see it again when we would return with the promised gold detector.) We also included the name of Narciso the guide. We placed it in a prominent niche in the wall of the largest building. It should still be there today.

Unfortunately for me, my 16mm Bell and Howell movie camera took this time, at the apex of my adventure, to quit. The spring became undone and there would be no fixing it until Hollywood, California. However, I had already captured 200 feet of this never-before-filmed city. That translated to about five and a half minutes of screen time. As it turned out, it was enough. (I had been such a novice on this first foreign trip to only take the one camera. I never did that again.)

I surprised myself at the horsemanship—or would it be called "mulesmanship"— that I displayed as we returned to Uningambal; I was getting good at it. And I was pleased with myself. In my film bag were the documentaries and stories of the *Omega*, the desert, and the mountain adventures, plus my travelogue on Colombia and Peru: 'Off the beaten track.' They were enough, I was sure, to begin a lecture career and maybe even a beginning in television.

Nieves was now feeling normal, and the day after we arrived in Uningambal we left for Trujillo. Jimmy went down the mountain with us. He and I had bonded in a way. We got along together. We had rapport. He had a recalcitrant wife in Lima to look into, and he continued on to the big city. Ernesto, Nieves, and I went on to Puerto Chicama. It was good to get home.

After a refreshing cleanup in the showers of the Guildermeister guesthouse, we all felt ready to confront the problems of our desert gold. They came quickly. A message was awaiting us: Angel Miñano urgently wanted to see us.

We rested for a day and then took the rural bus back to Trujillo. Miñano admitted us immediately into his newspaper office. He closed the door behind us, and brought us up to date.

"The government authorities of the Department of Archaeology in Lima have attempted to get a warrant for your arrest!"

Ernesto was dumfounded. "Arrest for what?"

"You can imagine, Ernesto," Angel answered him. "You and *Señor* Romain have been accused of digging into Peruvian antiquities without the authority of the government, without the seal of their approval. They claim that you are not bona fide accredited archaeologist and that you have been breaking the law. They call you common *huaceros*." Miñano wiped his brow with a large white handkerchief. "They wanted me, Ernesto, to have you and *Señor* Romain placed in irons as soon as you came back from the mountains."

"I cannot believe this," Ernesto replied.

"But," Miñano quickly interjected, "I have talked the Lima people out of their drastic action. You are known for many civic activities here. You have a good reputation. And you do have friends in the government. They will be content with the objects that you brought back. And they want me to put a watch on you to see that you never go back to that city in the desert. And, of course, Ernesto, they want you to tell them exactly where the Mochica city is. They would like that."

Batanero looked at me. I kept my tongue and my expression. "They took the things that we found?" Ernesto questioned. Without an answer, he continued, "They did that in the name of science? Where are those things now? The objects that we worked so hard to bring back? Are they on some politicians trophy shelf? To be bragged about at the next cocktail party?" He grunted. "And they want to put me in chains?"

Ernesto was working up to a tirade, but Angel wisely calmed him. "Ernesto, you know you could never have sold those ancient things on the market. Nor do I believe that you ever would. You are right. The articles that you brought back are now in the hands of private citizens, and I agree with you that they are being privately displayed as the finest antiquities to come out of a hitherto unknown archaeological dig. Now, the director of antiquities wants to know where they came from."

"By giving up the treasures I'm off the hook?" Batanero asked.

"Yes."

"Thank you for saying so, Angel. They have taken our priceless finds with no thanks to us or any recognition whatsoever," Ernesto definitely explained. "*Señor* Romain and I will never reveal where we found those things. The State has our treasures. We have the location from where they came." He leaned into Miñano's face. "It will snow in the Sechura before we'll tell anyone."

My friend was angry. I had never seen him so.

But, Miñano placated him. "Good friend, you are in no danger at all from the police. It has already been concluded. They have your goods, and you have your freedom. I am sorry, but I do hope that in time perhaps we—you and I—might go back there together. For now I will simply write the department that you decline the invitation at this time to lead them to your dig."

My friend was relieved. He knew quite well that legally he, Bergie, and I had been breaking the law. He could not fight that in court nor did he have the resources with which to do so. He shook Miñano's hand and said, "Let it be." I knew then that he and I would never see what lay in the bottom of the tomb in the Sechura Desert, the sepulcher that was guarded by twenty-four skulls.

Our moods abruptly changed and Angel asked, "And what did you find in the mountains? More treasure?" And he laughed and nodded to us.

"We found the ancient city of Huasachuga," Ernesto quickly answered. "And the tons of gold that we have already sent off to Brazil." It was a joke, and we all laughed.

We left the regional inspector, and went out into the cobblestone streets of Trujillo. "I knew they would take us," Ernesto mumbled. "I knew they would cheat us. But," with a sigh and spreading of his hands, he wisely concluded, "I shouldn't have thought otherwise." He added, "We could have taken a couple of the *huacas* and put their treasure in our pockets. We really got nothing."

I whispered in his ear as we walked down the street, "Not quite nothing, Ernesto. I kept a necklace out of that tomb."

He looked at me and laughed, "And so you did, *Señor* Romain. Keep it. It is yours." I still have it.

❖❖❖

Two days later, Ernesto and Nieves watched me board a bus for Lima. I had come to love that couple and they had reciprocated. The departure was nearly tearful. We were at that time, all poor as church mice, and the best I could do for my friend was to present him my German Luger automatic pistol. He feebly protested, but was glad to get it. I had nothing else to give him.

"You will be back," Nieves called to me as I stepped into the bus. "Please do."

"I will," I shouted. And I did, indeed, return.

❖❖❖

Barbara was waiting for me at the little bus station when I arrived in Lima the next morning at 8:00. I did not believe that I would be so glad to see her as I was. She looked good. She was enthusiastic, and she was physically affectionate.

"My God, Romain," she purred, "you are a sight for sore eyes." She was as glad to see me as I was to see her. "Let's get you home and tell me about your adventures."

Home was the Hotel Veintiocho De Julio, a businessman's hotel out of the tourist high rental district downtown. I was a dazed, not only by the long 'red-eye' nocturnal bus ride but also by the concern and interest that this lady put upon me. I had lived as a bachelor for twenty-nine years and suddenly was being greeted by a mother, lover, daughter, and long lost friend. I loved it.

"There's a small but fine restaurant here," Barbara informed me as we stowed my possessions in a rather commodious room that she had reserved for me. I ate a copious breakfast, and she then took me by my hand up to her room. It had a porch overlooking a working section of Lima. It was all so much more modern than my recent views of Puerto Chicama, Trujillo, and Uningambal. We settled back in lounge chairs and sipped rum and cokes. Her reporter curiosity went to work immediately, and she dragged the whole Huasachuga story out of me. Then she firmly said, "I can get this in the newspapers. The Lima papers. Not a big story because we have no proof, no pictures."

I was really relaxing and nearly asleep, but I did pick up on her conversations. "But we do, Barbara, we do. I have several Polaroid pictures that I took up there. (I would never have trusted my color slide photos to a Peruvian processing lab at that time.)

"Romain, you dear," she exploded and gave me a big kiss. "Where are they? Give them to me. I can write a story this afternoon and have it in the *Commercio* tomorrow."

I wasn't expecting this sort of activity so soon after the bus, but I dutifully went to my room, dug out the Polaroids, and brought them to her. "Excellent," she exclaimed. "Let's get this story going," and she proceeded to bang away on her typewriter.

Late that afternoon, we both went to the offices of Lima's *Commercio* and Barbara sold my article immediately. The next morning, October 17, 1953, a large article with two photographs of Ernesto, Luis, Jimmy Flynn, and me made the front page. Peru is proud of its heritage and always plays up a story concerning it.

I was quite pleased with the whole situation, especially when I received a phone call from the Lima offices of archaeology. They wanted an interview. As the man spoke on the phone, I was feeling quite smug and successful until he brought up the Mochica city in the Sechura Desert. I then knew I was in trouble. I stalled. "Better do this next week. I am tied up at U. S. Embassy at the moment." Those were the right words.

"Of course, Mr. Wilhelmsen, we know that you are busy. We'll be in touch in a few days."

That night Barbara had been invited to a party of newspaper people. I joined her and was received quite well. She had scooped the story but these men of the media were quite gracious to her and to me. They were full of questions. Among them was Ed Movious of the *Movious Productions*. He and his company had been attempting to start a motion picture production company in Peru. They had produced one film, *Sabataje En La Selva*, which had starred Pilar Pilette (later, Mrs. John Wayne) and Santiago Flynn. Pilar had run off to Hollywood with Wayne, and Flynn had escaped to the mountains and Uningambal. The picture not only bombed in Latin America, it stink bombed. Movious had then turned to documentaries. When he heard that I had a complete film in the can on the ship *Omega*: "Last of the Barques," he wanted to deal. My interest in the man was that I had eight rolls of commercial 16mm Kodachrome film that I had not used. The sale of those would grease my way home. We made a deal. He bought the unused film—a good deal for him—and I dangled the thought that I might sell him my *Omega* film. I admitted that it had already been sent to Hollywood, but that he would get top priority. As it turned out, Movious Productions shortly went belly up and thoughts of becoming the MGM of Peru went down the tubes.

Barbara and I had one glorious day to do nothing but see the sites of Lima. The lights at night. The fountain in the Plaza Bolivar. The dramatically lit up statue of Pizarro on the Plaza San Martin which is surrounded by the illuminated government buildings and the colonial cathedral. We walked down between the two historic squares and stopped in the old Maury Hotel for *pisco chilcanos*, and then into the sophisticated Hotel Crillon for a dinner. We ended the night back at our Hotel Veintiocho De Julio.

We had one last nightcap in the small six-stool bar in the hotel. "You are off to civilization tomorrow." Barbara toasted me, "Back to Hollywood and the la-la-land of bathing suits and starlets. You'll be surrounded by the sweet young things of tinsel town. You will be a celebrity. I have already written an article for the *Los Angeles Times*. They'll be after you." She began to tear up. "And I have that wretched Ecuadorian who I can't seem to let go." She squeezed my hand, leaned up and kissed me. "I wish I were traveling with you again."

We finished the evening and I took her to her room. Rather flippantly she gestured, "You had better go to your room." I did so.

Barbara was at the Limatambo Airport the evening of October 20, 1953, when I boarded a Braniff plane. She gave me a kiss, and I have felt that kiss upon my lips ever since.

10 — THE RETURN

My adventures continued after I arrived home.

My father and mother, both staunch supporters of their two sons, were at the bus station to greet me. They had offered to send me air fare to get me home from Miami where my Braniff plane landed, but a certain macho pride—the bane of many accomplishments—prompted me to take what moneys I had left and board a Trailways bus from Florida to Los Angeles. A long tedious ride over non-interstate highways. I was at least able to say, "I did it on my own."

I was told at the L. A. Bus Terminal that the *Los Angeles Times* had phoned and wanted a personal interview. Barbara's letter and *Commercio* article to that newspaper had done the trick. And—as had happened to her before—her byline and her writer's fee had been denied her. It might have been a considerable fee because the *L. A. Times* is an important paper with a circulation spread all over the country.

My folks and I drove back from downtown Los Angeles on the Pasadena Arroyo Freeway to our large flat on California and Hudson Streets. I bunked into my old familiar room, but I was vaguely restless. How did that old Irving Berlin song go: "How you going to keep them down on the farm after they've seen Paree?" Home life would never be the same. I knew it.

The news media works quickly. The very next morning two reporters from the *Times* came a-knocking. My father had informed them of my arrival. They had the article from the Lima *Commercio* that Barbara had included in her write-up. It had impressed them. Fortunately for me, there was no earthshaking event taking place that week, and the media was in need of a story. I became the story.

Without waiting for my 35mm slide photos to be processed, they took my few remaining Polaroids, shot a portrait of me, and went to press. They published a fine story, a bit distorted here and there, but enough to really launch me on a career.

The next people to approach me were Bob Stevenson and a couple members of the prestigious Los Angeles Adventurers' Club. In 1953, and even more so now, it was hard to find a genuine adventurer who was not a promoter or an impostor. I promised them a presentation of my film whenever I got it all together. My big TV contact, Truman Smith, had been taken back into the Air Corps, so I turned elsewhere. One of my actor friends, John Pimley, was now a professional film editor for the Telefilm Studio. We had known one another for years, and he agreed to help me edit, cut, and put together the forty-five hundred feet of 16mm film that I had. That translates into about one hundred thirty minutes of film on the screen. Totally ignorant of the lecture business, John and I attended one such lecture at the esteemed Pasadena Civic Auditorium, one of the top auditoriums in the country. Count Byron De Prorok, whose exciting books of African exploration had long been in my library, was giving a lecture on the glories of ancient Greece. We timed it at eighty minutes: two reels of forty minutes apiece. John then went to work, and—often over my objections about cutting a sequence here and there—we pared my film down and made a travel and adventure lecture documentary out of my stock. As a trained actor, I was easily able to put together and to recite a good and snappy narration to go along with this film.

My father, E. D. Wilhelmsen, then went to work. No *Kiwanis* or *Rotary* luncheon groups for him; he went right to the Pasadena Civic Auditorium which was just then staging the Motion Picture Academy's Oscar presentations. Dad had had his own taste of adventuring as a young man chasing Pancho Villa all over northern Mexico with General Black Jack Pershing's expeditionary force. He was now a salesman, one of the best, and Elmer Wilson, the impresario of the Civic Auditorium, was no match for his persuasive pitch. I was booked on a 50-50 deal. Win or lose, we were in it. The date was set for May 5, 1954.

Now, I was already getting the old familiar butterfly feeling in the stomach. I would rather have been back in Peru!

Knowing the value of a good performance, especially a premier, I went to work with a vengeance. Twice a day I repeated the narration that I had written to accompany the scenes in the film. I am not a perfectionist, but when it really counts, I do work hard. The film, the script, and the delivery soon began to come together. I had picked up an old used 16mm projector, and so was able to perfect my timing. I decided to try my presentation at the Los Angeles Adventurers' Club.

The delightful cigar smoke-filled hall was loaded with men who had accomplished many things in their lives: explorers, adventurers; a man who drove one of the cars in the round-the-world auto race of 1906; Dana Lamb who took his kayak from San Diego to the Panama Canal; John Goddard who was the first to descend the full length of the Nile's headwaters to the Mediterranean; Doc Peterson who negotiated a Chinese junk across the Pacific to escape the Japanese onslaught in 1941, Doug (Wrong Way) Corrigan, the flyer who started from New York for a non-stop flight to Los Angeles but ended up in Ireland;

big game hunters, world travelers; Spanish American War veterans; World War I vets, and a sprinkling of World War II vets. The assemblage on this occasion was also honored by wives, girlfriends, and a few mothers. It was Ladies' Night.

I was prepared. The lecture was a success. I was immediately nominated to become a member of this esteemed group of gentlemen. My father was suddenly proud of his son and my mother beamed. Life was good. Yet, I still thought of Peru, Ernesto, and Flynn, Nieves, and Barbara.

They and Chan-Chito and the Doctor came to mind when the exclusive Pasadena Art Museum and Gallery asked me to set up a display of my *huacas*, necklace, the funny owl face gold piece, and the ancient things I had brought back with me. I was even pressed into giving a slide presentation of my experiences.

The *Pasadena Independent* boasted a fine feature writer, Russ Leadabrand. Seeking publicity for my up-coming lecture at the Civic, I approached him. We got along well, and he began writing of me in his columns. Even better, he took my stories and pictures and worked them up for the quite popular men's magazines of that era: *Saga, Argosy, True, Men In Danger*, and others. Russ sold everything that he submitted, and we split the profit. Not an awful lot but $200 a story in 1954-55 was a fairly respectable sum.

Leadabrand was a fast and exciting writer. His style didn't quite fit the format of the fastidious National Geographical Society. They paid well, I believe at that time $750 for an article with the photos to back it up. Russ went for it, and we were both quite nettled at the reply that one Andrew H. Brown returned to us:

". . . I find it hard to believe that in this day and age one can stroll out into a desert in South America and uncover the remains of a city and buried site that we of the National Geographical Society and others know nothing of. Nor do I believe that there is such a pre-historic city such as you claim you found 12,000 feet in the Andes Mountains of Peru. You are probably referring to the pre-Inca city of Huamachuco that we here at the Society are quite familiar with . . . "

Perhaps the fact that I did not give the exact locations of these discoveries prompted this letter, but nevertheless, I was being called a liar, and I strongly resented it. The Geographical Society is an accepted authority on many things. I wanted their recognition, but I did not get it. In time, with—of all things—the help of the regional inspector of archaeology in northern Peru, *Señor* Angel Miñano, I would get it and the august Society would eat its words.

I had finally met Dana and Ginger Lamb at the Adventurers' Club. Their books had inspired me to embark on this sort of life, and they now entered it personally. "Watch your step," they cautioned me. "It's a jungle out there in the world of the media." They were quoting the great humorist, Edgar J. Guest who had so informed them.

Dana and Ginger had recently completed an exploring trek in southern Mexico and Yucatan. *Harpers Brothers Publishers* had published their book *Quest for the Lost City*. As had their first book, *Enchanted Vagabonds*, this work went right into the New York list of best sellers. Hollywood took a look at it, realized the potential, and Sol Lesser—producer of the early Tarzan movies and more recently Thor Hyerdol's *Kon-Tiki*—made them a deal: "Go back, pick up all the film you can to expand your adventure, and we will produce it. Big screen, national distribution." Back into the jungle they went, and eventually the 16mm film that they brought back was converted into 35mm and was ready for the big screens of the nation's movie houses. Football great and World War II hero, Tom Harmon, was hired to say a few words on the screen, and the movie, *Quest for the Lost City* was launched. Dana and Ginger made not one cent on that release. Nothing. The creative booking of Hollywood saw to that. "After the expenses of production and distribution and publicity are covered, *then* you will get your percentage." That was the contract. The Lambs received nothing at all.

They were bitter people but lovable people. I liked and enjoyed them for many years. It was often hard to do that because they had taken to drink. Not a snappy martini or two but the insidious all day sipping of wine. It slowed them down and eventually put them out of business.

✧✧✧

May 4, 1954, was the big day for me. I arrived in the parking lot of the Pasadena Civic Auditorium in my new tuxedo. In those days such an event was almost always a black tie event. The Civic seated 3200 people. Even to one who heard the rumble of a large audience from behind the curtain, it has to be one of the most exhilarating and frightening sounds of his life, especially since only I was going out there to meet it. The thought kept gnawing into me, "I should have stayed in sales." But the die was cast, and a stage manager standing next to me checked his pocket watch and whispered in my ear, "It is eight o'clock. The curtain is going up. You are on!"

I walked on stage. The spotlights made it hard to see anything but the floorboards. I made out a microphone in a stand slowly rising from center stage. I went to it and stood there. "Take a good pause," I said to myself. "Let the audience see you, let them settle down and wait for your words." There were 1470 people out there staring at me. This was considered very good for a travelogue. My family was out there somewhere, but I couldn't see them because of the bright Klieg spots pinpointing me. Pasadena friends were there, too. They had paid their two dollars to see me do my stuff or to fall on my petard. Talk about a moment of truth. The noise died down, and I uttered the words that I was to say for

161

the next forty years. "Thank you very much, and good evening ladies and gentlemen." I made $417 that night.

In 1954 not many people had traveled abroad, just those in the Army or Navy, none at all compared to today. Soldiers, back from the war, were content to stay home. The economy hadn't picked up enough yet to allow for travel on a whim. Much of civilization was putting itself back together, and Russia was rattling its saber. These were serious times and the travel film lecture business was booming. Television was just getting its start and was still showing only black and white programs. Yet, we lecturers bragged about the "living color" of our films and the big screen on which to see them. I was in the right place at the right time. I gave the audience my best, and it was enough.

I was surprised at how many people came up on the stage to talk to me after the lights came on again. And in that throng there was an agent. She was booking the most humorous travelogue artist on the circuit, Stan Migley. Within the week, we had signed a contract. And that began my lecture career. It would finance my adventures abroad.

To broaden my potential, the agent suggested I make another film immediately. If a lecture course did not want an adventure subject I could be in a position with another topic.

I chose Mexico. My mother and I drove down and through that country in her little Hudson Jet car. I did not do well. I love Mexico, but a straight travelogue of Pátzcuaro, Guadalajara, Mexico City, Taxco, Acapulco, and Oaxaca, didn't do well on the circuit. I made that film the summer of 1954, and it did more to slow my progress than to advance it. Nevertheless, my adventure film, *Legend in the Andes* was a grand success. The Ralph Windows Travel and Adventure Courses booked it for some fifty cities; and it was chosen by the majority of the program chairmen as the best of the other five speakers who were on the circuit. "Forget that Mexican film," old Ralph Windows leveled with me. "Go back and get another adventure."

Not only Ralph, but Hollywood also came knocking. The word was out, and Jack Douglas, who was putting together a television series called *I Search For Adventure*, gave me a call. My film was screened in his offices and three segments were chosen from it. The *Omega*, the desert adventure (without maps), and Huasachuga. All appeared on Station KCOP television live from Los Angeles. It does sound like the 'Big Time,' but each performance paid only $150. The 'Big Time' would come with syndication. I couldn't help but think of Dana Lamb's Hollywood shafting. Nevertheless, I signed the contract with Jack.

The season was spent getting my feet wet lecturing around the country under the auspicious of my agent Grace Humphrey, a frustrated diva left over from the Chautauqua Circuit. It paid expenses and my name did get around. I also got to see again my actress one-time ladylove while in New York City. She had been appearing in the immensely popular *Fanny* with Ezio Pinza while I was appearing in the renowned New York Town Hall. Just as good that I moved along to the Brooklyn Museum of Fine Arts. We met and respected one another.

1955 was suddenly upon me, and I was delighted to receive a letter from Santiago Jimmy Flynn. "Old friend, you said you would be returning. Get your body up here. I've got another ruin for you. The Indians say there is a place they call 'Aque.' Just like Huasachuga. Bring that metal detector and let's go to work."

And then there was one of several letters from Batanero. "*Señor* Miñano has given us the all-clear with the government—although a return trip to our Sechura site is still forbidden. But, if you can bring that metal detector, I know that we can come up with something right here in Trujillo or back at Huasachuga. Nieves sends you an *abrazo*, and while in Lima I saw Barbara Holbrook; she sends you more than an abrazo."

I began to make plans.

My *Legend in the Andes* lecture film was being received well, and I was booked ahead for the next season of 1956-57. I realized that I could not bring in another mountaintop discovery lecture to the circuit so quickly after *Legend*, so I planned on an Amazon adventure.

On May 24, I booked a Pan Am plane at the International Airport of Los Angeles at 12:30 a.m. destined for Lima, Peru.

Ernesto and Nieves were there to meet me when the plane touched down. Right away I was given the unwelcome news that Barbara Holbrook had accepted a hefty advancement in New York City and that she had left several days before. My dream of traveling with her was crushed. I would be on my own again.

Spread about and in my several suitcases and suit bag were all sorts of strange mechanical devices. Those days there was no such thing as electronic surveillance in airports. These little toys of mine only came to light when the Peruvian Customs man opened my bags and rummaged through them. "What are these things?" he asked as he examined them.

"Ah," Ernesto smoothly answered. "So you have brought me the components for my shortwave radio. I thought you might have forgotten them."

"Radio, you say," the official repeated. "Radios are not duty free. There is a tax on them." He consulted a book. "Twenty dollars American to the government," he laughed as he looked at my friend.

"We're in free," I thought. "The metal detector is here free and clear."

But Ernesto surprised me. He knew the value of a buck. "*Señor* Inspector," he responded, "this radio is all apart. It won't be a radio until it is assembled with my components. If twenty dollars American is the tax on a full radio, this should only be ten dollars American because it is but half a radio."

"*Señor* Batanero," the man grinned at him, "ten dollars it is."

"Give the man an extra dollar, *Señor* Romain. He is a gentleman."

I counted out eleven U. S. dollars, and handed them over the baggage counter. The .38 caliber revolver taped to my inner thigh had also arrived without a problem. No one was interested in frisking me because of the presence of a reporter and photographer from the *Commercio* newspaper. They hustled me by the Customs people and set me up for an interview and photo. The inspector happily stepped into the background and made sure that he, too, would appear in the morning edition. Ernesto had staged it all.

We taxied out to the Hotel Veintiocho de Julio. It was a nostalgic moment for me. Lots of Barbara hung about the memories of that hotel. It was good to get back.

"First things first," Ernesto said after my bags were stowed away and my one suit bag hung up in the closet. "Let's see the gold detector."

I had worked with that cantankerous machine at home with my writer friend Russ Leadabrand. It was a Goldak, manufactured in Glendale, California. Russ and I had managed to detect a tin can on the front lawn, so I knew it had some value. We reassembled it in but a moment, and Ernesto, Nieves, and I now attempted to detect a handful of Peruvian coins. We got a reading and a sounding all right, but we also got the same results when we passed it over nothing. "Probably the pipes in the floor," I optimistically proclaimed as I turned the battery off and folded it up. I had my doubts about this contraption. "No matter," Ernesto happily said to me. "Nothing works well in the big city. Wait till we get to Trujillo and the desert."

Nieves looked at me with that quizzical look she often had. "It is of no importance, Romain," she said to me. "What is important is that you are here, back with us. We have missed you and talk of you often." That statement made the whole flight south worth the effort. We gave each other a hug.

The usual nocturnal bus drive north to Trujillo took place three nights later. I spent the time picking up fine movie shots of this "City of Kings"; these I would add to my *Legend in the Andes*.

The Bataneros had moved a step up in the world during the two years that I was gone. They had left Puerto Chicama and were now living in the city of Trujillo. They had a fine single story house, big enough to have a nice little guest room for me alone. They also had modern plumbing. The shower was, I admit, a strange one. A circular series of half-inch brass tubes that passed in and around and through several butane-burning jets which when lighted heated the water as it came down through the pipes. It never would have passed the codes in the United States.

Ernesto was eager to get to work with the Goldak metal detector. One of the oldest large homes in Trujillo was owned by the Bracamonte family. It dated back to the early eighteenth century. The building had once been a colonial Jesuit Convent. The tenant before the present Pedro Bracamonte, we were told, went "crazy when he saw a ghost" here by the massive fireplace. Two years before Pedro's son Gaspar saw the same specter and fell unconscious in front of the hearth. It took three months in the hospital for him to recover (the hospital records confirm his treatment). And the year before our visit, Gaspar's sister saw the spirit and nearly suffered a nervous breakdown. These strange events all took place in the parlor in front of the fireplace. Don Pedro told us his family refuses to come into this room anymore, but he confided to Ernesto, "There are family traditions that a Jesuit treasure is buried right here in front of the fireplace. Right where you are standing, *Señor* Romain."

I quickly stepped aside.

"Perhaps," he said, "something is secreted here that the long dead do not want to be found. I am not afraid to look. Our family fortunes have taken a turn for the worse, and all that is left to us is this old rambling house. Please work your magic, Ernesto. I promise to split 50-50 on anything of value we find."

We went to work. First we passed the Goldak over all unsuspected areas of the room. A faint 'ping' here and there but not enough to tear up the beautiful inlaid floor. We then zeroed in on the fireplace. The little arrow in the dial swung wildly to its highest number, and the sounding device pinged into action.

"We've got it," Ernesto exultantly proclaimed. "Something down there. Let's get some picks and dig it out."

Strangely enough the tall, thin, and aging Pedro Bracamonte suddenly demurred. He was obviously pleased but also concerned. "You know, Ernesto, these floors are three centuries old. It would be a sin to trash them up. What I will do is see if somewhere I can dig into this area from the side. Tunnel in, you know. Save the floor. I will look into it and when the time comes, we will get together and share what lies beneath us. You have been most generous with your time and your machine. Of course, I knew all along where there might be something, but I thank you, *Señor* Romain." Bracamonte gently put his hand on my elbow and eased me out of the room. "We do thank you for bringing this metal detector into our house."

Then he said the words that Ernesto and I knew doomed our enterprise. "I've heard that these metal detectors are strictly illegal in Peru. Is that not so? Electronic huaceros," he snickered in his high nasal voice.

We were out of the big studded doorway in a moment, and Ernesto said to me, "So much for the honor of helping an old acquaintance. We won't be hearing from him again. I misjudged my countryman."

(Indeed, he had. Within six months the Bracamonte family had sold their house and moved to Lima where they bought an elegant modern ranch house. Whispers abounded in the social set of Trujillo that they had suddenly come into some sort of an ample inheritance.)

More to my liking were the stories that Batanero's next-door neighbor told us one night in his pleasant parlor where we were warmed by a modest fireplace and a few rum and Cokes. Osman Ravitch was an Austrian engineer married to a stately Peruvian beauty. He had been hired by the government to look into possibilities of new roads and maybe even a railroad north of Cuzco. Osman worked that area for ten years, and was familiar with the country and the local Indians. "I am not a treasure hunter," he exclaimed, "nor am I a bullshitter." He peppered his vocabulary with earthy Germanic expletives. "But, I have heard rumors and actually seen things in those high Andes Mountains that defy logic."

He settled back, took his lovely wife's hand, fired up his pipe, and went on. "I was headquartering out of a little village way north of Cuzco. I had a crew with me, and we were plotting the possible route of a road. Walking to work every morning from the little three-room house where I was staying, I always dropped a coin into the lap of a legless old Indian who enjoyed sunning himself on the town plaza. We talked, became friendly, and he asked me to be the godfather of his new grandson. He claimed it would be an honor for him, and I was happy to do the old man this favor. He soon got to telling me the story of his past and how he had lost his legs. Some fifty years earlier around the turn of the century, while hunting pumas some four days from the village, he had spotted white stone buildings in the distance, beyond a great wet swamp. He and his two companions sloshed out into the marshland toward what he was sure were Inca buildings. According to him, there is an old Quechuan legend that told of a tambo, or resting place for Inca runners who traveled between Cuzco and other large centers those days, where one of the pack trains carrying the Inca Athualpa's ransom was secreted. The legend told of several buildings in the area that had been used to place many llama loads of gold and precious stones.

Osman continued, and he shook his head almost in disbelief at his own story, "This man, then young and full of energy, stalked out into the swamp toward the buildings. But suddenly he and his companions were startled by a loud rustling sound. The swamp became alive with thousands of poisonous snakes that had made this their breeding ground. He was struck several times in his legs. He never saw his friends again. Painfully, he managed to reach his village. Both of his legs were amputated by the local *curandero*. Now he sat in the plaza and sunned himself."

Osman Ravitch, at that time, copied what directions the old man could give him after half a century. And, with four European engineers and some Indian trackers, went out seeking those stone buildings. After five days of mule travel, they did find the swamp, and they did see through their binoculars the very white stone Inca buildings in the middle of it. Osman was well mounted and rode out into the morass. Immediately a rustling sound hissed through the quagmire. His horse reared up, threw him, and was quickly covered with dozens of long snakes that fastened themselves upon its neck. The horse went down screaming, and Ravitch made a beeline back to firm ground. He was not bitten but his horse was gone for good. "My fellow engineers pondered ways to get out there but we finally gave it up and came back home. I do think something is out there."

I liked that story.

Two days later, we made plans to return to the Hacienda Uningambal. Radio contact had broken down but Flynn had arranged mules for us at the Hacienda Llaray. It would be a different route than two years earlier when we had left from Chorabal. Ernesto sensed problems up there somewhere along the way. "The Chorabal and Ollón Indians seem to have had some sort of quarrel with Santiago. There seems no cooperation along the way at all. If I read the signs, Santiago is in trouble."

Nevertheless, Luis Seminario had sent a message to us to "Please bring along my daughter, Maria." He also reported that Flynn was not at Uningambal at this time, but that he was due back. His message was very cryptic. I dearly wanted to see Jimmy, but regardless, I had to get some film of that region. The ascent was scheduled and we made ready.

Maria Seminario was a solid full-figured young Peruvian woman of twenty-two years. Dark eyes, and long black hair almost to her waist. She was full of mischief. We hit it off immediately. She knew not one word of English and somewhere along the line had decided never to learn any. My Spanish had improved somewhat, so I did most of the conversing. We got along well. She was a flirt, and what man doesn't appreciate that?

We rented a car and on the early morning of June 9 we started up the Andes. Ernesto sat with the driver who charged us 400 *soles* or $21 for the eight-hour climb to Llaray. Nieves, Maria Seminario, and I sat in the back seat. The dirt road was very rough, originally a horse and cattle trail. I have one memorable recollection of that drive—other than the flat tire and a gas pump failure. At a small village we stopped to ask for directions. There I saw five or six year-old children who were nearly naked. They were picking through the steaming droppings of horses that had just passed by. They were collecting the undigested kernels of corn that were visible in the manure. They were that hungry! Ernesto told me that they will follow animals and gather such undigested things from the dung, take them home to their mothers who would wash them off and put them into the soup of the day. (Since then I have never been very sympathetic to the many people I see who drive to their welfare office in their relatively new automobiles to arrange for their handouts.)

We arrived at 2:30 p.m. at the Hacienda Llaray, and were met by its administrator, Victor Pinillas. He was a rugged leather-faced man of fifty-some years who was quite handsome. His hacienda was a storybook place that could have served as a setting in a period motion picture. The main house was surrounded by bougainvillea plants, the big red ones. It overlooked a little brook that bubbled in front of the door of the main dwelling. Shade trees surrounded the place. The complex had been laid out three hundred years before by those great colonizers, the Spaniards. In the great room, we were welcomed by a huge fireplace, which is a prerequisite in the high mountains. Servants took the luggage upstairs to our rooms. Refreshments were laid out. When one is welcome in an old and grand hacienda, one is really welcome.

On this occasion, both Ernesto and Nieves seemed to succumb to the effects of *sirroche* or mountain sickness. They asked for an hour or so in their feather beds on the second floor where balconies overlooked the green valley about us.

Maria, Victor, and I settled down to coffee and talk. My questions were to the point. In my best Spanish I asked our host, "Santiago Flynn. You know him?"

"Everybody knows Flynn."

"Will he be in Uningambal when we arrive?"

"I doubt it, *Señor* Romain," was the dour answer.

"Why?"

"He is a marked man. The Indians will kill him. They are waiting for him. He would never dare come back here."

I was confused. "But why, what has he done?"

"He whipped an Indian cowboy caucho style."

"Guacho style?" I questioned.

"Yes, that is a form of punishment that is used in the Argentine. Only the tip of the whip touches the victim. It stings more than it hurts. It is more of an insult than a whipping. It takes a well-trained man to handle a whip that well."

"Why did he do it?" I asked.

"I don't know," he answered, "but knowing Santiago Flynn, he had a good reason."

"I'm sure he had good reason." I rose to the defense of my friend.

"Indeed, but the Indians do not look at it that way. He has insulted one of them. Trust me, Santiago Flynn will not return to Uningambal. If he does, he'll never leave it."

"Maria," I asked Seminario's daughter, "do you know anything about this? Has your father mentioned it by letter or radio?"

"Yes," she answered. "He has written us that *Señor* Flynn is in bad trouble. My father is now managing the ranch. He will probably continue to do so. Your friend has gone to Lima to tell his story. He will be away from there all this week while the big *fiesta* takes place.

"*Fiesta*?" I asked, envisioning something colorful to film. "*Fiesta*?"

"Oh yes. A grand week of drinking, fun, and dancing. You and I," she flirted, "can have a dance together. And watch the bullfight, too. No wonder *Señor* Flynn is staying away. It will be a brawl there all week."

The idea of such colorful activity excited me, but I also was terribly disappointed. I had dearly wanted to see Flynn again. I had even packed in my bags a fifth of Johnny Walker, Red, that we had joked about two years before. I grumbled to myself and to them, "I'll bet he'll come. He knows I'll be there."

Victor Pinillas spoke up, "No, *Señor* Romain, I believe that Santiago Flynn has had his day up here. He has lost his edge with the Indians. He would be crazy to come back up here and expose himself to them."

I stubbornly replied, "He'll come; he knows I'll be there."

Pinillas shook his head. "I hope you are right for your sake, but it is one messy situation up there in Uningambal."

The Bataneros pretty well stayed in their beds the rest of that day. A snack for supper, and we all turned in for the night. I went to my room overlooking the babbling brook and the bougainvillea, and the grand view of the Andes. Pinillas called after me, "Lock the blinds on your window shutters. The Indians out here are not all that friendly either." I had heard that Pinillas was a hard taskmaster. I closed them up as well as I could, and laid my revolver alongside of the bed on a little table. I tucked in but did not sleep well that night.

There was a fine breakfast awaiting us the next morning: eggs, bacon, sausage, and toasted bread. A real treat. (But I thought to myself, the children out there are eating the leftovers of your stables. I have never been able to forget that roadside scene.)

A truck took us to the Hacienda Santiago De Chuko. There Flynn's horses were waiting for us. Horses, not mules, this time. They were spirited animals, not fully broken, but after mules I felt quite confident.

Our little caravan marched north and up the crest of the Andes Mountains. We had another of those long rides. This one even seemed even longer when the left stirrup broke loose of the saddle and fell off. The leather straps were rotten. At first, I treated this mishap as just a little discomfort to endure. But as the hours dragged on, my leg, with no support, began to tingle and then to hurt. Faithful Ernesto dropped back and rode along with me. We had a long and—for me—agonizing four more hours to the Hacienda Uningambal.

Nieves, Maria, and the *mozos* arrived well before us, and Luis Seminario was on the watch. That good man came immediately to me and extended his hand. I needed it. I was too stiff to move. He lowered me to the ground and helped me onto the porch and into the great house of Uningambal. He sat me into one of the easy chairs, removed my chaps, pulled off my boot, rolled up my pant leg, and began vigorously rubbing my left leg. He was familiar with this sort of rider's dilemma. The blood in my leg began to circulate again, and soon I was hopping around the room and warming myself at the fireplace. I knew everything was okay when, of all people, Ernesto said, "Give him a glass of rum. That'll bring him back to life!" Luis did just that, and my circulation and my mind were immediately revived. I thanked Seminario profusely, and he in turn thanked me for bring-ing his daughter to him. "*Señor* Romain," he said, "Maria has never had the opportunity of seeing her father at work. You have made it possible. I do thank you." I accepted his grati-tude and then asked—perhaps a tad too quickly—"Where's Flynn?"

I could see that this was a touchy subject. Luis looked around at Ernesto and Nieves and his daughter. Then he spoke directly to the point. "Santiago is not here. He is in Lima. He still retains control here, but he knows if he comes back, he might well be killed. Even now he is working with the managers of Uningambal to find a suitable replacement." Then sadly, almost to himself, he muttered, "Even though he and they know that I am here." I took a long gulp of my rum and limejuice and answered, "I am sorry. Sorry to miss him, and sorry to hear that you are being bypassed. I am sure he did not want to leave you out of the negotiations."

"Of course not," Luis quickly added. "Santiago and I are friends." He said it, but I could still see the hurt on his face. Maria took his hand and held it.

Indeed, the Indians were restless that week. The very next night they began to blow off steam. The *fiesta* began. Seminario took great pains to admonish his daughter not to leave the porch of the great house. He asked me, "If you need your pictures, go out and get them, but please don't encourage my daughter to go out there. It is not safe. Look, they are already drunk." He was right. Dozens of Indians were milling about, singing, sometimes dancing, and most looking quite unstable. "No," he said again, "keep my daughter out of it." I had noticed that he was wearing a pistol in his belt, had a shotgun leaning against the door jam, and an automatic rifle close by on a rack above the fireplace. They were all loaded.

We holed up that night in the great house. Again and again Luis repeated to his daughter, "You don't want to go out there." He repeated it because she had mentioned several times, "I'd sure like to join in on some of that dancing." He firmly stated, "No," and such a paternal "No" in South America means "No."

We were all surprised when the next morning the old mayor came a-knocking at the porch door with his hat in his hand. "Would you and the *señores* and *señoras* like to enjoy the parade and the *corrida*?" This man was well aware of the situation regarding Flynn, and yet apparently none of Santiago's sins had spilled off on Seminario. He was welcome. I was elated. A real Country Peruvian parade would be quite a boost to any of my films. "Of course," we all answered him. "We'll be there."

We were. I positioned Ernesto on top of a house along the route. He would run my 'second,' or back up, camera as this miniature Rose Bowl Parade would file by him. I chose to stay with the pageant in order to grab as many close-ups as I could. Between the two of us, I filmed a slice of life on a remote Peruvian mountain hacienda. The sequence proved to be very good. Better yet, no way along the route were we molested by Indians.

After the parade, a bullfight had been planned. A *matador* and his troop had been hired but when the *toreador* jacked up the price, Seminario balked. The assistant manager was already economizing. The *corrida* had been announced and was to have been a highlight of the festivities. Luis came up with the solution. He sent out the word that anyone who wanted to fight the bull was now welcome to try it. Several local stud bulls were ready and willing to mangle anyone who got in their way. I was surprised, delightfully so, when half the male population wanted to get in the act. "Better than I thought," Luis grinned. We all trouped out to the little bullring that most of these *haciendas* have had for centuries. This one was enclosed by wooden bleachers. The ring had been built and maintained quite well. The place filled up quickly and, as in an old gladiatorial contest, the bulls were herded into the arena. On came the macho men, most of them drunk, and one by one they were bowled over by the bulls. These were not the killer fighting bulls of a professional *corrida*. These local bovines just wanted to get a shot at the pesky cowboys who were always bothering them. They didn't have the killer instinct, but, one by one, they sent the Indians who challenged them flying. No goring, just a good butt on the butt. The sport provided one of the most comical film sequences I ever made. The audience loved it. Husbands, sons, sweethearts, were all being knocked about. The ladies finally had a good laugh at the expense of their men folk.

That night we were sitting on the porch watching the fireworks when one of the foremen approached Seminario. "The Bishop is coming. His man has come ahead to inform us. He will be here very soon." The *hacienda* had been expecting this prelate of the church to arrive there on his annual tour of the diocese. Perennially, he would make the mountain trek to officiate at baptisms, marriages, and to perform memorial services for recent deaths. The tour was his ecclesiastical duty, and in this case, so far from Trujillo, it was a real hardship.

Being Catholic myself, I was interested in seeing this dedicated churchman. He came riding up at dusk right after the bullfights. He was dressed in a long black tunic or cassock that was buttoned from collar nearly to his heavy riding boots which contrasted to the miter or clerical hat that jauntily topped his silver hair. With him was a young seminarian leading a mule that contained a hand pump organ. And, behind them, riding tall on Gringa came Santiago Flynn!

The crowd of Indians who had run forward and gathered around Bishop Ortega quickly gave way and let their administrator, Jimmy Flynn, ride into the main area of the Hacienda Uningambal and up to the porch of the great house. He did so with a nonchalance and style that belied any impression of trouble. He reigned in his mount, swung it around, took off his broad rimmed sombrero, and bowed to the people of the ranch. He pointed a finger at one of the Indians, dropped the ruins from his hands, and gracefully slid from the back of his well-groomed Gringa. The Indian quickly took the animal by the bridle and led it away. As Flynn stood legs apart firmly on the ground, I could see that he not only had his customary .45 caliber automatic in a holster on the right side of his belt, but that he also had a holstered revolver on his left hip. In his hand was a double-barreled shotgun. This last weapon he now raised in the air and pulled both triggers. It went off with two explosive 'booms.'

"*Estoy aqui*," he shouted out. "*Viva la fiesta!*"

There was a moment of silence, and then a great roar rose from the people of Uningambal. "*Viva la fiesta!*" they repeated, and the merrymaking began anew, the dancing, the singing, and the frolicking. Flynn was back and he was in control.

I stepped down from the porch and approached my friend. His arms went out and we both embraced one another in a lusty *abrazo*.

"You old fox," I murmured to him. "You did come back. They said you wouldn't, but I knew you would."

"Indeed, I did," he replied as he looked me in the eye and held me at arm's length to get a better look. "That I did," he continued. "When they told me you had come up here to see me, I said to myself, 'The man has come thousands of miles to visit me, by Saint Brendan, I can ride a day up the mountain to see him.'" We embraced again.

Santiago turned to the Bishop who had dismounted and was directing his companion to do the same. All in Spanish, of course, "My American friend, *Señor* Romain." To me he slightly bowed and said, "Bishop Ortega of the Diocese of La Libertad. He will say Mass here for my heathens and give them a taste of the Sacraments."

The ecclesiastic, who was a good six feet tall and of ample girth, shook both of my hands. "My pleasure." His smile then froze on his face as he let out an explosive and very odiferous fart. "Whew," he sniffed. "*Porfin*. Finally."

What does one do when a Bishop lets one go audibly and then proclaims his satisfaction? I stepped back—I had to—and attempted a gentle smile.

No way!

Behind me I heard Nieves giggling and then letting it all out. Ernesto joined in the laughter. Soon Seminario, Maria, and all of the nearby Indians were guffawing. And so was I.

The prelate sniffed, stepped out of his own aura, and joined us. He chuckled to Flynn and Jimmy in return translated his words. "He tells me that this was one of his better entrances." And we all again cut loose. (Why do such earthly emanations always evoke such hilarity? Especially when they come from a dignitary, better yet, a man of God?)

We all marched into the great house. I went to my room—Flynn's—and began gathering my belongings. I assumed that the good father would naturally take the master room. But, no, Flynn waved me back. "That's yours. It will always be yours. I have a perfectly good room for the Bishop, one close to the bathroom." And he led him into the hallway.

Later that evening, when dinner was finished, the priest had gone to his room, Ernesto and Nieves had turned in, Maria and her father had gone off somewhere to talk, Jimmy Flynn and I settled down before the fireplace.

"Jimmy," I was happy to say, "you told me a couple years ago that you liked Johnny Walker Red. I've been hoarding this bottle throughout the trip just for you. And me."

"You are a true gentleman," the Irish-Argentinean answered. "You realize that when a Flynn has a thirst up he must always go to the well. Pisco is good. Rum is better. But nothing takes the place of good old Scotch. Shall we have at it?"

We did for much of the night.

We sat on the porch and watched the fireworks going off all over the place. They were crude, but they were loud and they were bright. Under the circumstances they seemed almost surrealistic.

"Tell me," I finally got around to asking, "what is this all about you and an Indian and a whip? Doesn't sound like you."

He answered immediately. "The man was a troublemaker. He had come from Lima, and I believe he was trying to put together up here a Communistic cell. He defied me at every turn. He was dirt poor as they all are and somewhere along the line his arrogance got the better of him. The outsider thought he could get away with stealing from the *hacienda*. Just minor things, some tackle here, stirrups there. A saddle disappeared. I suspected in time some cattle would go." Flynn poured another Scotch and continued. "One of the younger workers, a rather dimwitted young fellow, came to me and told me that he had seen this agitator taking things and even bragging about it. Of course, all the other cowboys thought that was a good joke: stealing from the big boss and getting away with it. Then the young man disappeared and was found deep in a valley dead from a fall. I do not believe it was a fall. The lad was pushed.

"Well, Romain," Flynn sweetened my glass, "I waited until I was sure I had the goods on him. I was told that he had taken several leather straps and belts and that he was hiding them on his person until he could leave the *hacienda* for a few days and sell them at Llaray or De Chuko where you picked up the horses last week. I called him out. In front of his peers—who probably knew he had them—he swore that he had taken nothing. My patience was up, and I knew that the whole *hacienda* was testing me. I had him spread-eagled on the wall of one of the corrals, brought out my ten-foot leather cattle whip, and gave him one more chance. He spit in my face. I uncoiled the horsewhip and gave it a crack. It nicked him. He began to holler when I gave it to him again and then again. I had quite a crowd around me, but Luis was there, too, and he carried a gun. One more time the man took it, and then begged, 'All right, all right, I do have a horse bridle wrapped around my waist beneath my shirt.' And, sure enough, there it was. We took it off of him, but I wasn't through. 'You have more,' I demanded. 'No, no more.' I knew he did and I started up again. Sure enough, wrapped around his thighs were more of our trappings. I ordered him stripped of all clothing. A real insult to those people. But, I did find other things. I ordered him and his family all off of Uningambal property forever. He left, I think to De Chuko, but the rancor lives on. I, a white interloper in Quechuan country, had truly insulted one of them." Flynn did not go to the bottle this time; he just leaned over to me and said, "My life isn't worth a plugged sole up here now. Right or wrong, I have insulted their race. I have been to Lima and to the owners of this place, and I have recommended that Luis be given full charge. He doesn't know this yet."

I had the whole story. I asked one more question, "Jimmy, why did you come back up here? You are a target. Tell me why."

"Romain," he said as we finished our bottle of Johnny Walker Red, "I came up because I heard that you were coming with Ernesto and Nieves. I told you that I would be here when you returned, and by God, I intended to keep my promise. I will leave here forever and will return to Trujillo when you leave." I was overwhelmed by this statement of friendship, and even more so when he brought out a huge iron key of great age and gave it to me. "It is the key to the *hacienda* Uningambal. It is yours." We finished the night with an embrace just as the sun began to peak over the Andes Mountains. The key to the oldest *hacienda* in northern Peru is now prominently displayed on a shelf in my den.

Our next day was spent close to the big house. Flynn was not reckless. He knew that many of his people at the ranch respected him and accepted him. But he also knew that somewhere out there a group of men had sworn vengeance. He was wary.

Not so Ernesto and I. We mingled with the *fiesta* revelers and were accepted. While so doing an event occurred that eerily resembled what happened to me at Lake Guatavita in Colombia. An elderly man with a long white beard approached us. He claimed to be one hundred years old, and he looked it. He drew Ernesto and me aside and furtively told us that he was in possession of a large trunk of colonial coins. "Very old," he whispered. "Seventeenth century. You can have them all for a few soles. I have no one else to sell them to. I need the money." Needless to say, we two old treasure hunters were all ears. The man lived a distance from the *hacienda*. We planned to meet him the next day. We mentioned this to Luis Seminario, and he immediately pooh-poohed it. "An old man with a long beard?" He shook his head. "That *Viejo* has been telling that story for years. Santiago and I followed up on it. He has nothing to show you; he is a little loco." As a result, Ernesto and I did not meet the man as scheduled. A couple of days later, Luis pointed out a bearded man and laughed. "There goes your treasure man; he's probably looking around for someone to believe him." We did not have to look closely.

"Luis," Ernesto said to him, "that is not the man who spoke to us. He is not the man with the trunk full of coins." Inquire as we did, we never did see the old man again. He could have been genuine and his coins might have been a priceless collectors item. Ernesto said it well, "*Señor* Romain, we goofed it."

Bishop Ortega performed baptisms and marriages out doors, in the sunlight especially for me so that I could film them. My documentary on Uningambal expanded each day. Another of the better sequences was a marinaro dance that Maria and I joined in at one of the local gatherings. The Indians liked that, and we were invited to a lunch in one of their houses. A little pisco had emboldened me, and I accepted. A lot of deferential bowing and hustling went on in the house, and we were finally served. I did not expect chicken here to be the best, but it did go down all right, stringy and tough. We all toasted ourselves and Maria and I left. "Not the best chicken," I said to her, "but better than nothing."

She laughed at me. "Not chicken, *Señor* Romain, rat. That was a rodent you just ate." And Maria, who had a great sense of humor, laughed all the way back to the great house.

Flynn relieved me somewhat. "Yes, Romain, it is a rodent, but technically not a rat. We call them cuy, a form of guinea pig. They're considered a delicacy up here. You must feel honored." He let out one of his hearty laughs.

Two days later, Flynn, Ernesto, Nieves, Maria, Luis, and I with a group of locals, mounted up and left the *hacienda*. First to the ruins of Huasachuga and then to its sister city Acque. Maria brought along with her a box of cuys that she was constantly sneaking into my belongings. They are really cuddly furry little white animals and are quite tame; she had her fun with them. Luis was riding high; he had been told by Santiago that upon his return he would be the big boss of Uningambal. Flynn was somewhat silent; he was experiencing his last escapade in these mountains. Ernesto was excited about using the metal detector. I was happy to be with the group.

We camped out for one night. Ernesto and Nieves shared a tent, and the rest of us slept under the stars by a great fire. I wondered if Santiago Flynn slept that night.

Huasachuga, of course, had not changed. It hadn't in the last millennium. We found the coffee can with our names and added Nieves and Maria to them. I picked up all the extra film shots I would need for the next lecture season and, hopefully, for some television presentations. Ernesto spent all of his time fiddling with the obstinate Goldak. He couldn't get a 'ping' or a movement on the dial. Only when he put the tin can beneath it did it come to life. If there is gold or silver there, we certainly did not look in the right place. We questioned our Indians regarding the cave, "four or more days away with circles of mummified dead in them," but we received so many confusing answers and directions that we gave up on the project. "Besides," Luis proudly explained, "I must get back to my duties at Uningambal."

Another day took us to the ruins of Acque. They were extensive, but not as impressive as its sister city. They were quite obviously built at the same time as Huasachuga. We did not spend much time there. Eventually, our little expedition would go into the Peruvian archaeological record books as having discovered this hitherto totally unreported pre-Inca city. But, to me, it was a disappointment.

My Andes adventures were completed, and several days later all of us, except Luis Seminario, made the long arduous descent to Trujillo. I had filled in the blanks or—as we call them—the slow spots of my lecture film. I was satisfied.

Santiago Flynn went immediately from his faithful mule, which he turned loose in Trujillo's finest stable, to the *Moreno Bus Line* office. He had had an offer from the Anaconda Mining Company who needed a manager for one of its eastern Andes copper operations. We all saw him off. I do believe he was reluctant to leave his position high in the mountains of northern Peru. We would meet again.

Ernesto and I let no time go by before we were at Angel Miñano's office. Here he handed me a statement attesting to the explorations that Batanero and I had made:

"The writer, Regional Inspector of Archaeology of the Northern
Coast of Peru, certifies:
    That he knows Mr. E. Romain Wilhelmsen, North American
Explorer, who has for the first time, taken motion pictures of
the ruins of Huasachuga and Acque in the mountain section
of La Libertad, still not known to the scientific world; and it

can be said that these are the first accounts that have been made.

In the same way, I certify that coastal archaeological sites have been filmed with a profound current of spiritual nearness.

I issue the present to acknowledge the outstanding labor which Mr. E. Romain Wilhelmsen has displayed.

Trujillo, June 4, 1955
José Angel Miñano García
Inspector of Archaeological
Monuments of the Northern Littoral

(This document I sent on to Mr. Andrew H. Brown of the National Geographical Society in Washington, D. C. Eventually, I got a half-hearted apology for the response Russ Leadabrand and I had received after submitting my story to the Society. I could tell those learned folks didn't like being corrected.)

❖❖❖

My plans now called me to fly to Iquitos, Peru, located on the Amazon River. From there as the song at the time went: "What will be, will be."

The main airline of Peru, *Faucett*, did fly from Trujillo to Iquitos, but the fare was $10 more than the fare of an upstart airline called *Rapsa*. Naturally, I chose *Rapsa*, and reserved a seat. Two days later, Commander Owen Williams, an old World War II B-17 Bomber pilot showed up at our door. "We'll be leaving tomorrow at 4:00 a.m. We will pick you up." Now, that was service! Owen was a big man, tough looking, and efficient.

"What are we flying?" I asked. With pride he answered, "A B-17. I wouldn't fly over those Andes Mountains in one of Faucett's two-engine planes. You've got to get pretty high up there, and we'll have four motors to lift us."

At 4:00 a.m. Williams was at our door in Trujillo. Nieves had breakfasted me, and she and Ernesto waved me off. The landing strip was dark, but the big silhouette of the World War II bomber loomed up in front of us. "Might be a little rattly," Williams apologized, "but it'll get us there." He was attempting to start a competitive airline against the established Faucett. This surplus B–17 was his only plane. (He never got another, and in time the Rapsa line folded.)

The flight was quite noisy and the plane smelled of gasoline all the way. I hoped that none of the six passengers smoked. We took off quickly and smoothly. We passengers sat in metal bucket seats in the belly of the plane. We were crowded in by a cargo of huge boxes, bags, heavy equipment, and bundles strapped down all around us. Once I went up to the cockpit and made my presence known. Owen hollered over the roar of his motors. "This is my co-pilot. He got kicked out of the Bolivian Air Force for joining the wrong revolution. He's a good flier, but a lousy judge of politics." I shook the hand of a dark-skinned handsome man.

Owen Williams continued, "You know Faucett flies those two engine jobs all over the country, but I don't trust them. Getting up this high, 20,000 or more feet, I feel a lot more comfortable with four motors banging away behind me. How about it?" I agreed.

We landed at Pucallpa and discharged some cargo, and then flew on. Shortly thereafter, Owen shouted to me, "There she is, Iquitos, 2400 miles up the Amazon River. About as far as you want to get." He went into a turn, a glide, and then leveled off toward a runway somewhere below us. The American expatriate was a good pilot, and he set us down smoothly. Then he taxied us over to the ramshackle buildings at the other end of the strip. He cut the motors. "Grab your bags and let's 'git'," he hollered to the passengers. I did so. Dropped my legs out of the trapdoor in the belly of the plane and lowered myself to the ground. Immediately, I experienced and smelled the strange and pungent odor of the jungle.

11 — THE JUNGLE

I had experienced the feel, the odor, and the humidity of the jungle on Colombia's Magdalena River. But this was different. The atmosphere was heavy and pervasive. It encompassed one. Especially as the little jitney drove us the several miles from the landing strip through a clump of tropical trees, and then an area of overgrown foliage and primitive straw houses. The feeling faded as we entered the city limits of Iquitos. The roads lost their dirty look, and I could see that they were tarred. Tall buildings replaced the huts of the outskirts. One building of many stories was positively beautiful, all covered with blue and white tile. I had read that Iquitos was at one time one of the capitols of the infamous rubber business of Amazonia; the other was the much larger city Manaus, located down the river in Brazil. The glory days of those cities were past, but much of the opulence was still quite evident.

I was a little surprised to see more than trucks on the streets; there were also automobiles. Iquitos was a moving town.

Owen Williams assumed that I would be staying at the Hotel Turistas Iquitos, in the same chain of government hostelries that I had enjoyed before. At $2.85 a day, I didn't complain. The new boy in town was immediately approached by the local travel agent, a Swiss national with the last name of Authouse. I never learned his first name. Just as good. He was a weasely fellow who first ascertained how much money I was prepared to spend on a jungle trip, and then told me that was exactly what it would cost. I distrusted him right off.

More to my liking was Hermann Becker who occasionally worked for Authouse. He stayed in the background as the Swiss agent put the hustle on me. And when Authouse went off to make a pit stop in the hotel's public facility, he approached me and said in a pronounced German accent, "Mr. Wilhelmsen, I am Hermann Becker. I do work for Mr.

Authouse. He is a son of a bitch and leaches off all of us. I will take you wherever you want to go and will do it at three times less money than he quoted. He has never been fifty miles out of Iquitos; his main office is in Lima. I have been moving about these jungles for years. I will do right by you, Mr. Wilhelmsen."

How could I not like that approach? I hired him on the spot.

Iquitos in 1955, and I'm sure today, was one interesting town. Set 2400 miles up the Amazon River in a scorching jungle, it is part modern and much primitive. At the time I was there, the city was loaded with the flotsam and jetsam of the tropics. I quickly met them all. There was Scotty, a sergeant in the United States Army who was here with some sort of a PT boat that serviced the United States geological oil exploration team working several rivers that touched Iquitos. He was from Brooklyn and talked Brooklynese. Scotty was proud of the oil paintings that a young local Peruvian artist had made for him depicting him in the battles of Anzio, Monte Casino, and the Bulge during World War II. Each painting, full of action and fury, also had a Peruvian llama serenely standing by overlooking the European landscape. Somehow, Scotty thought this would be a good touch.

Then there was a Swede, Captain Larson, who ran a little river launch once a month up some river to service the Texaco oil exploration group who were drilling there. He had three weeks, out of each month, free in Iquitos, and spent that time drinking heavily. So much so that he was proud to explain to me one morning over a bottle of whiskey that he had come upon the perfect plan for a business. "Frogs' legs," he cheerfully explained. "You know how much frogs' legs cost in a good restaurant. I intend to make a fortune by breeding frogs and centipedes. Just imagine how many frogs' legs I'll be able to come up with. We'll deep-freeze them here like they do shrimp, and market them worldwide. Imagine: big Amazon frogs. He even took me to his experimental farm where he had placed several large frogs and a ganglia of sinister looking centipedes together. "Trouble is," he confessed, "I don't know which is the male and which is the female." I really thought the big Swede was putting me on, but Hermann Becker assured me he was dead serious. "He is also on the verge of having the d.t.'s."

Then there was Jim Andersen, a thirty-year-old writer from southern California. Big, blond, and enthusiastic, Jim and I immediately got together. He was on assignment for an English speaking tabloid in Lima, *The Peruvian Times*. This periodical dealt with happenings of interest to English-speaking residents of the capitol. *The Peruvian Times* paid very little, but Jim was hanging in, waiting for a good story that he might be able to sell elsewhere. Perhaps, he thought, my objectives would help him. The trouble though with Jim was that he was totally enamored with a young Yugoslavian blond beauty in Lima. He wanted to get back to her so much that, as he said, "it hurts." I liked him.

Hermann Becker was the most interesting person I met in Iquitos. He showed me his scrapbooks and old newspaper clippings. Before World War II he had gone to South America and as a very young man enjoyed traveling the remote rivers of this mysterious continent.

In 1928, he even thought he had a clue to the puzzling disappearance of Colonel Percy Fawcett who dropped out of sight in the vast wilderness of the Mato Grosso jungle of Brazil in 1924. He had been following a map or description to a magnificent stone city of antediluvian age. The colonel vanished with his son and a friend. That mystery with its decaying city had been a favorite of mine; it still haunts me. Hermann Becker's historical claim to fame is that he, as one of Field Marshal Erwin Rommel's chauffeurs, he was with the legendary tank commander when his car was strafed and he was wounded. Becker was the man who rushed to his aid and pulled him out of the burning vehicle.

If my old friend Barbara had been with me, she would have pulled the full story out of Hermann. She might have come up with a best selling book about this man. He was genuine.

"Mr. Wilhelmsen," he addressed me a day after I had decided to go with him, "you are a film man. You are a reporter showing North America how the other half of the world lives. I have a story for you. There is a man living up the Ambigaqui River who has been accused of the murder of thousands of Indians during the time of the rubber atrocities. He is one of those men who would capture the Indians and force them to work the rubber trees. In the early decade of the century, the world was demanding rubber, especially the Detroit auto industry. The only place to get rubber at that time was right here in the Amazon jungle. We have the trees. Wicked men came and, under the pretense of giving work to the local Indians, enslaved them. The Indians were forced to bleed the trees of their rubber. Vicious men got the best of local natives. The men were sadistic. An Indian would bring in a quota of latex and ask for his pay; often he would be shot dead and thrown to the piranha fish. The man in charge was Julio César Araña, who lived very well in Manaus. He gave the orders. Taking those orders was Miguel Loyasa who did the dirty work not too far from here. Although that genocide of Indians is now long past, that man is still alive. I can take you to him. I have visited him before. He is old, in his late seventies; he is alert and aware of his name in South American history. You can tell his story, Mr. Wilhelmsen." Becker was full of enthusiasm. "And then," he continued, "we can go up the Yavari River. I have recently made contact with the Cocomas tribe. They are very primitive, and have never been touched by the outside world. I have taken them salt and bread as gifts, and I am sure they will allow you to film them. Herr Authouse would only hire me to guide you to the nearby Yaguas people. I can take you much further on my own and can do it at much less cost." Hermann was scabbing his rival, and apparently he had every right to do so. I shook his hand. The handshake was the only contract we ever needed.

I spent several very interesting days in Iquitos. Scotty was a delightful companion with his stories of Italian Brooklyn, the Army in Normandy and his wife back home who had been a neighbor and friend of Frank Sinatra's wife. "You going down the river?" he said to me when he heard my plans. "You going with Becker?" He added, "He's the best." Then he continued. "I don't believe it one bit, but I've been told the Jews are after him. You know, Wiesenthal and his bunch. But I do not believe that Hermann was ever mixed up in the Holocaust. He was a Rommel man, and Rommel was never involved in that stuff. Hell, I fought the old 'Desert Fox' in Tunisia; I might have even been taking shots at Becker myself . . . " and Scotty was off on another war story.

I was glad to hear Scotty's take on that subject, and from the German and Spanish clippings that Hermann had shown me, I never did see a connection between him and Hitler's "final solution." Becker was too decent a man.

Jim Andersen came along with us. He had no money to put in the pot but he had become a friend and I wanted him. Scotty furnished several crates of American Army rations that dated back to the war. "You'll like them," he said, and then added, "once you're hungry enough."

The morning we left, I was awakened in my room at the Hotel Turistas by a Jivaro Indian from Ecuador who worked there. At 3:00 a.m., it shocked me to see this man, from the traditional headhunting tribe, leaning over me and shaking my shoulders. I looked up and saw his bowl-shaved haircut and my confused dreams became a reality: I was in the hands of savages. Actually, he seemed quite gentle. In a strange accent he said to me in Spanish, "It is time for you to go to the Amazon." I quickly came back to the present and dragged my body out of bed.

Like smugglers in the night, we gathered at the little pier where our launch was waiting. Becker was already there with Jim Andersen, and shortly the motorist, Fernando, "Ferdie," arrived to take charge of the riverboat. The type of vessel is often coded a "monteira."

Several large gasoline tanks had been stored aboard and Scotty's K-rations were laid out for all to see. I was grateful when Hermann, after checking every detail of our cargo, told Ferdie, "*Vamos.*" I was grateful because all along the high riverbanks of the Amazon, leading up to Iquitos, I saw and heard literally thousands of big, corpulent, rats swarming along the river shores. Slipping out into the clean and powerful current of the river felt good. I was glad we were on our way.

"Mr. Wilhelmsen and Mr. Andersen," Hermann Becker announced when we had left Iquitos behind us, "first things first, we must drink a glass of rum, 120-proof rum. That will keep the mosquitoes and the miseries away from us. I always do that when I travel in the jungle. He uncorked a bottle and poured Jim and me a good shot of lethal alcohol. We dutifully downed it and did feel ready to face the dawning day. A negative thought about Hermann never developed. Except for that morning eye-opener he rarely indulged himself. At night, a nightcap, but no more.

The sun began its ascent. The river looked beautiful. Very tall trees towered above us on either side. They swayed with a little breeze. We moved by dark jungle foliage as we putt-putted down the Amazon. Here and there a light twinkled along the riverbank where people were stirring and heating their coffee. Jungle smells enveloped us, punctuated occasionally by the fragrance of brewing coffee. Hermann stood at the bow of our launch and peered into the mists and vapors that were now evaporating as the brilliant orange sun slowly arose in the east. He was all explorer. Jim and I promptly dozed off.

We were awakened soon by the monkeys and the birds in the tall trees as they, too, greeted the new day. There were fish that followed us and would dart out of the water and then dive back into it. We also heard the constant chirping of myriads of strange and unseen creatures.

"Ah, Mr. Wilhelmsen and Mr. Andersen, we are now on our own in the jungle. This is a different world from where you have come. Stir yourselves and take a look." Becker was fully awake. He loved this country, and it was evident. He constantly pointed out birds and fish and the ever present butterflies that seemed to gather about us. He was a very competent travel guide. His enthusiasm even broke through the effect of that 120-proof drink.

The tropics were exotic, swaying palm trees, greenery everywhere, vivid birds, and flashing fish. But I was mostly fascinated by the huge pull and force of the Amazon, this largest of all rivers, as it pulled us along in its powerful current. I wondered how that little outboard motor could ever get us back up the river. I asked Hermann.

"You stay out of the center of the river, out of its current; you hug the riverbanks where the force is much less. Do not worry, Mr. Wilhelmsen and Mr. Andersen, I'll get you back all in one piece." I never doubted it for one moment.

At 5:00 p.m., near sunset, we pulled into a little river mission town called Pebas on the Ambigaqui River, a tributary that enters the Amazon from the north. "There is a Franciscan mission here." Becker winked at us. "We'll get a free dinner." We sloshed through some mud, mounted the riverbank, and walked to a neat long, single story wooden house. "Oh, Mac, are you there?" Hermann irreverently called out to the priest who, he informed us, was usually at this station. A roly-poly man in a long gray tunic waddled out onto his porch, and waved us on. "Father Mac McDonald," Hermann proudly introduced us. "He's been here for years preaching to the pagans." He shouted to the grinning prelate, "Got any new converts?"

Father McDonald answered in English; he was from the United States. "Only when I feed them, you old Nazi. But they're getting interested." They both laughed. "What characters," I thought to myself, "one meets out here in the boondocks!"

"Come on up, Herr Becker, and bring along any spirits you might have on board. I'm about out." I noticed that Hermann had tucked a bottle of pisco in his pocket.

We entered a very neat, clean, and orderly frame house that was elevated on sturdy logs to compensate for the floodwaters of the Amazon. "Sit yourselves down," Father Mac motioned to several chairs that were almost the only furniture in the main room. "Where are you off to now, Herr Becker?"

I was carrying a letter from Cardinal McKentire of the Diocese of Los Angeles, and

I whipped it out to prove to him that I was one of the fold. "No need for that, son," he waved it off. "Out here, we're all alike," and then he winked at Becker, "unless you're bringing me a donation from the good man. You are as welcome as that old Nazi there," and he thumped the German a good knuckle blow to his shoulder. He brought out a tray of small glasses. "Pour your spirits, Hermann, and tell me why you're here."

The glass held no more than a shot, and I noticed that that was all he had the couple hours we talked. He enjoyed the taste, not the effect.

"Father Mac, are the Yaguas Indians on the Ambigaqui River? I've heard they are around here somewhere. My colleague here, Mr. Wilhelmsen, is an explorer and would like to make some movies of them." He turned to me, "The Yaguas are the most colorful Indians you'll ever care to see. They'll make a good film sequence."

"You're in luck," the missionary answered. "A couple hours up the river, the Ambigaqui; they've been working with José Ruiz who has a farm on the river. The whole group should be there. They're a nice bunch."

The Franciscan had one of his half-breed Indian *mozos* serve us a span of spareribs. Not North Carolina ribs by any means, but they were filling. He furnished Jim and me pads to sleep on, and Hermann went back to the launch. "I'm responsible for it," he told us, "and I'll sleep in it."

The next morning, Father McDonald waved as we left the Amazon and turned north onto the Ambigaqui River. One hour later, we arrived at José Ruiz's farm. His house consisted of a fairly long thatched roofed building propped up on poles or logs that were fifteen feet tall. Visitors are rare in this part of the world, and the youngish swarthy Ruiz greeted us like long lost friends.

Becker had never met him, but with his German's charismatic personality, they were soon deep in conversation.

Several men were working his *manoic* farm. They looked strange. They were completely enveloped in red straw garments. They wore flat hats from which long strands of red dyed straw hung down to their shoulders. Their bodies were also completely painted red. They were Yaguas Indians, a colorful and peaceful tribe that wandered around the jungles from campsite to campsite. I knew right away that these folks were made for color television. Becker confided to me, "I've been trying to get these Indians to settle down close to Iquitos so that I can bring in day tourists. They can make a little money that way, live a little better."

"Are you sure, Hermann?" I asked him. "Are you sure they would live better?"

He simply answered, "I guess I really don't know." (In time Hermann's plan for those Indians did come true. The Yaguas are now quite an attraction for the tourists who fly into Iquitos for a day or two, take a motorboat ride out to the village, get their pictures of a blowgun shoot-out, and then fly back to Lima.)

Several of these colorful men were glad to leave their digging and take us to their dugout canoes. They paddled us a ways further up the river to their village. I believe my 16mm Bell and Howell movie camera recorded their lifestyle for the first time. Of course, I did what eventually all tourists want, a film sequence of their blowgun marksmanship. They can hit an orange dead center a hundred feet away. Their women are quite pretty and dainty. They are lovely people, and I did return some years later to record their language on a tape recorder. Becker had done me well taking me to the Yaguas Indians.

We returned to the Ruiz farm and then the following day, we set out to meet the infamous Miguel Loyasa. "He is and has been literally in hiding, or should I say in retirement for some twenty-five years. He has with him a tribe of Boros Indians who are in his pay. They protect him. Those Boros are not the gentle people that we have just visited. They are more like guard dogs. Loyasa and I have met. He knows me, and trusts me. We can get our interview and pictures."

❖❖❖

In the first decade of the twentieth century one of the most macabre episodes in that bloodthirsty century took place. In retrospect, perhaps it was a harbinger of the crimes that were to take place: The Japanese in Manchuria and Nanking; Germany's holocaust, Russia's purges, Cambodia's death camps. This episode took place in the area through which I was now traveling, Amazonia.

Quite similar to the California and Klondike gold rushes, in 1900, men hurried into these jungles and began harvesting and bleeding the rubber trees to fill the demand of the industrial world of Europe and the United States. Eventually, one man cornered the market. He was the steely eyed Peruvian, Julio César Araña. Through astute manipulation and then by brute force, he gained control over the major rubber forests of Brazil, southern Colombia, Bolivia, and eastern Peru. Foreign workers going to those areas were discouraged not only by the environment, but also by Araña's legions of vicious and unscrupulous field managers. One of his foremen was Miguel Loyasa. After discouraging foreign labor, this man relied on the thousands of forest Indians who inhabited the jungles around him. They were the innocent victims of one of the first crimes of the century. Multitudes were rounded up by Loyasa's army of Winchester-carrying Huitotos Indians. He had recruited the Huitotos, paid them well, trained them from their early teens, and used them to round up as many Indian tribes as possible. These slaves—for that is what they became—were often chained together as they worked the rubber plantations. Quite often, after bringing in a quantity of rubber, where they asked for their pay, they were shot down. It is an eye witness report that Loyasa and his henchmen would often throw parties where they would sit on the shaded porches of their grand jungle houses, make bets, and then turn a few poor souls loose as targets of their rifles. Spectators reported that occasionally Indians were doused with gasoline, set afire, and as they ran screaming to the nearby river, they were shot by revelers on the porch. Some estimates claim that Loyasa was responsible for the death of 30,000 of those Indians of the rainforest. The native population of one section of the jungle fell in five years from 50,000 to less than 8,000.

Eventually, the anti-slave crusader Sir Roger Casement, after his work in the Congo, went to Amazonia for a look, and eventually exposed the genocide. The Victorian government of England called for a cessation of this slave trade and the whole business came under fire from many nations around the world.

In 1911, one W. E. Hardenberg traveled into the area to substantiate Casement's accusations. He found that they were all true. In the process, Hardenberg was captured and imprisoned by Loyasa and witnessed some of the above atrocities. He managed to escape and write about the experience in his book: *The Putumayo, the Devil's Paradise*, published in 1912. I have that book. And more recently in 1968, Richard Collins' book retold the whole story: *The River That Time Forgot*, published by E. R. Dutton and Company.

In time, Alexander Wichem managed to smuggle 70,000 rubber seeds out of the area and, in so doing, to begin the great rubber plantations of the Far East. Within just a few years, the monopoly in the Amazon was broken. Araña was taken to court in England with the backing of the United States, Peru, Colombia, and Bolivia. He had the wealth to fight the charges and to avoid the prison of the world court. Julio César Araña went scot-free. Miguel Loyasa just faded away in the jungle. He was still out there, and that is where Hermann Becker, the ex-Nazi, was now leading Jim Andersen and me.

✧✧✧

The first indication we saw of a powerful man was Loyasa's employees. We spotted them here and there along the Ambigaqui River. They watched us from the riverbanks, and soon we could see runners hurrying along ahead of us. "Boros Indians," Becker informed Jim and me. "A bad bunch. Loyasa has hired them to protect him. Many of them are the sons and grandsons of the Boros who worked with him during the rubber days. They are loyal. And notice, they are all armed. You don't want to challenge them. They are dangerous."

We chugged along for another hour, and then saw a large house on our right. The house was the largest we had seen on the rivers. As others, it was raised up from the riverfront by those usual sturdy stilts that keep all these river homes dry. There was a long shaded porch and the house was obviously a comfortable dwelling. For a dock, there was a floating platform that rose and fell with the motion of the water. We tied up there.

Hermann told us to stay put while he stepped from our boat and went ashore. Two Boros Indians approached, and he spoke with them. (Becker could converse easily in German, English, Spanish, Portuguese, French, and several Indian dialects; he had a flare for languages as do many Europeans.) One of the Boros trotted up to the house and entered. A moment later a man in a white shirt and trousers came out of the main door. He nodded and the Indian returned to Becker. Hermann motioned us to follow him. We mounted the wooden steps and entered a broad porch that literally wrapped around the whole house. I could not help but notice that at every ten-foot interval a 10-guage automatic shotgun was in brackets on the wall. They were within easy reach. The place looked like an arsenal. It was.

Miguel Loyasa was not young, 76 or so, but he carried himself well, quite straight. He was about five feet ten and had white hair. Loyasa looked strong, not necessarily physically, but mentally. His distinguishing feature was his eyes. Black as sin, and shifty as a cobra preparing to strike. "*Señor* Becker," he addressed us, "why have you come here? What do you want? You always want something."

Becker threw him off. "For starters, *Señor* Loyasa, rum. My colleagues here and I would like to tap the grape and enjoy a drink with you. If you are dry," he said with a chuckle, "I've got my own rather potent stuff."

"Ha," Loyasa responded. "I'll send for some. I don't know why you are here, but I'm a lonely man, and you always make me laugh. Let's put the drinks and the cards on the table." He murmured to an attendant and several bottles of rum were brought to a sideboard on the porch.

"English?" he asked Becker, and nodded toward me.

"American," Hermann answered.

"Good," he said in English. That surprised me.

He looked at Jim and spoke in poor, but understandable English, "You know I do not like the English. That queer Roger Casement gave me a bad time a long time ago. The British are not my friends. I don't know much about the Americans. They never bothered me." He turned to me, handed me a glass, and graciously asked, "Would you care for a lime with your drink?"

"Thank you."

"Are you with the press? I don't want any reporters here," he rather bluntly said. "They want nothing but bad from me."

I answered him, "No, I'm not a newsman. I just take pictures of interesting people."

"You do?" he questioned. "My time goes back a long, long way. Most people aren't interested anymore." He lit up a large cigar. I interpreted that as a good sign. He took a couple of puffs, looked out over the river and his guards, and remained on the subject that apparently was deep in his memory. "Sir Roger Casement," and he spat into a spittoon, "he came here as a troublemaker. You know he was queer as a monkey's prick. He accused me of all the bad things on Earth, and yet he was corn holing all the Indian boys he could find. And yet they prosecuted me for every other crime under the sun. As though I was the criminal. He was the one who should have gone to the stocks." He glowered and gulped his rum.

I already had a story. Except that I needed films. I wasn't a news reporter.

Hermann Becker changed the subject. "Miguel," he asked, "have you ever seen television? You know, movies in a radio. It has become quite popular. This man here, Herr Wilhelmsen, makes moving pictures that they show on television."

"Of course, I know of it," Loyasa shot back abruptly. "I may be far away from those who would persecute me, but I have a family and they have been educated. I read magazines. I come and go to Iquitos when I please. Why shouldn't I? I helped make that city. My rubber business created it from a river front backwater village to a modern city. The tile building, our money erected that. I am no Indian, Hermann Becker. I am a man of the world. I made things happen. Did you ever do that?"

Loyasa's dander was up. He lashed out at Becker. "I helped build more of this country than anyone else. César Arañá and I. This was our country and it should still be ours except for that busybody homosexual Casement." He stood up and paced the floor of the veranda. "Do you know the Royal bluebloods of Buckingham Palace knighted him because of his snooping around in my backyard?" He coughed, stared at me, and kept going. "And then they put him in prison when he snooped into the Irish business over there. The Irish Republican Army. Turned out the man was a spy for Germany all the while. He sold out César Arañá just as he sold out his own country. And the dukes and duchesses of the mighty British Empire hanged him for that." The old man settled down and poured himself a glass, a big one, of rum. He squeezed a lime into it. "No, I am not an Indian, my friend." To be an Indian obviously bothered him. "I do know about television. I see that magic box occasionally in Iquitos. Don't think of me as an Indian." He settled down.

Becker was up to the challenge. He stood and walked over to Loyasa, looked him in the eye, and in a jocular tone, said to him in Spanish, "You know, *Señor* Loyasa, I worked for a fellow who eventually lost the war for my country. You, too," he continued, "worked for a fellow who lost his war. Let us not fret about the past. I am here for a schnapps or two and to see an old acquaintance." I don't know the exact translation of what Loyasa responded, but it was something like this, "You old bullshitter." Whatever it was it broke the mood and they laughed. Jim and I, of course, joined in.

The conversation slipped into small talk: the price of rubber at the time and how the market had changed from the old days. Loyasa was still working the product on his holdings. Huge balls of dark gray latex were piled up beneath his veranda ready for shipment. He was living well. His defensive mood had changed, and he called into the house. Two very well endowed young women came out. By anyone's standards they were beautiful. "My daughters," he introduced them to us. He smiled and was obviously pleased with them. He certainly had every right to be. They were centerfold girls. They were dressed in blue jeans and loose blouses. We all stood up and shook hands. Loyasa beamed as one of them openly flirted with Jim. And they then bounded down the steps of the compound and off to a motorboat tied to the raft-dock. They were going to a party at some other family home up the river. There is a social life along these lonely Amazon tributaries.

Becker did manage to get Miguel Loyasa off of his porch and out in the open where I was able to take a few minutes of film. What I took was sufficient, and with the background footage, the Yaguas Indians, and the dramatic setting all around us, I was able to produce a solid and interesting show. (I have done as much research as possible into the crimes of this man. Having been entertained by him and been given his hospitality, I would like to excuse him in some manner. But the truth is that he was a murderer in the league with Hitler and Stalin. He was a beast along the rivers of the Amazon.)

The drinks that Miguel Loyasa kept flowing eventually inspired Jim, who seemed to have a rather active libido, to suggest we take a boat trip up the river to where Loyasa's daughters had gone. I was surprised when the always prudent Becker said, "Let's go." So, off we went, one horny Jim Andersen, one fledgling film producer, a curious German explorer, and one tired boat motorist, Ferdie.

I do not know how courting is done along these rivers, and I never did find out. We missed the party somewhere in the darkness of the night. Our energies gave out, and we soon returned to Loyasa's dock and zonked for the night in the launch.

The next morning, we left the compound. Loyasa seemed reluctant to see us go. He was obviously a lonely man. "Where now do you go, Hermann Becker?" he asked. "Remember, as I told your American friend, if he wants to take pictures of primitive Indians, he should go to the Cocomas on the Yavari River. They are quiet and peaceful. Take your pictures of them, Mr. Wilhelmsen. Maybe I will see them on the Magic Box in Iquitos some day." He stood on his dock and watched as we chugged away.

"Seems like a nice sort," Jim remarked, but Hermann Becker surprised us by snarling, "The man is an animal. He is a killer. He should be shot. I've heard enough stories of his brutality. The man is friendly to me, but he was anything but friendly to the Indians. He thought that they were little more than jungle animals. That man would capture hundreds of women and put them in his brothels to be raped and used by his henchmen." He changed the tone of his voice, "and yet, I accept him and we communicate. I believe because he likes me and I am one of the few older men of the area to whom he feels he can talk. Truth is, someone should shoot the son of a bitch."

Jim moved up to the little cupboard, that we had on the launch, and pulled out Hermann's bottle of 120-proof rum. "Time for a drink, Hermann." Becker agreed, "Ya, of course. You are right. Let us put this man behind us. You have your films, Mr. Wilhelmsen; let us now take a look at the Cocomas. Loyasa is right. They are a tribe that hides in the jungle and have not been eager to be contacted. A feather in your hat, Mr. Wilhelmsen, if you can get some film of them. You know, there are a lot of Indians here in the forest that are totally unknown to anthropologists." (There still are, helicopters or not!)

Becker directed our launch back down the Ambigaqui River and into the Amazon. Then up that river to the Yavari River, and south into relatively unknown country.

We spent a night at the little compound or house of Guillermo Rapoz. He received us well and was pleased with our company. Ominously, he reported, "The Mayoranos Indians were on the warpath. They are killing and pillaging all of the farms up river. You don't want to go much farther."

Becker thought awhile and then spoke. "The Mayoranos are always stirring up trouble. But the Cocomas aren't involved in all this stuff, are they?"

"No, no, not the Cocomas. They are never mixed up in that sort of thing. They are not too far away, and they are quiet. They often come here for this or that. They were the ones who warned me about the Mayoranos. No, I like them."

"Let us go on," Hermann suggested, and we followed his advice. We continued up the Yavari River. We traveled until sunset, and then stopped for the night by a small clearing.

Here it was that Ferdie decided to take our little dugout canoe and make a reconnaissance up an unmarked tributary of the Yavari. He was an adventurous but a quiet young man. I am sure that he hoped to make points with his boss, Hermann Becker, who would hire him again. We all knew that the Cocomas Indians were a skittish bunch and might panic at the sound and sight of a motor launch (Loyasa and his minions had done just that years ago: Come up the river in their steam launches to kidnap the fathers and grandfathers of the people.) So, Ferdie went ahead to contact them. He, instead, was ambushed by the hostile Mayoranos. They killed him and literally chopped him up. The Mayoranos let the current take Ferdie's remains back to us.

When we found that canoe, caught upon the snags of the river, it was the biggest shock of my life. The man was all in pieces: head, legs, and arms. Our friend Ferdie!

"My Gott," Becker lamented. "What have I done? The young man was my friend. His mother and my wife go to the market together. Now I must bring him home this way." There were tears in this stoic German's eyes. "I will run the boat," he quickly recovered. "I will take him home."

We, of course, reversed direction and, with the little dugout canoe containing the bloody remains of our motorist lashed to our launch, we charged back down river at full speed.

We hurried on to Guillermo Rapoz's farm, and he too quickly hustled his wife and two young children into his motorboat and joined us. We were relieved to enter the Amazon where we knew we were safe, and with but two night stops we returned to the big city in the jungle, the city that Miguel Loyasa helped build.

Jim and I, like guilty cowards, drifted off to the modern Hotel Turistas while Hermann Becker took on the task of going to the local police and military where he reported the murder of Ferdinand. Then that poor man's remains were removed to a funeral home.

Jim and I drank more than we should have that night. The Indian uprising was quickly subdued. With bombs and napalm falling all around them, the hostile natives just melted away in the dark recesses of the forest and disappeared. They are still in there somewhere perhaps gathering their strength for another attack on modern civilization. However, the odds are growing against them. Their lifestyle will eventually go the way that the Indians of the western plains of the United States went.

Jim Andersen and I, along with Hermann Becker, his Peruvian wife, and his two-year-old son mingled with the crowd of mourners who stood by while Ferdie's remains were lowered into its final resting place in the cemetery of Iquitos. His priest read the last rites, and we dispersed.

I lingered on in Iquitos a while. I liked the place. Jim's desire to return to his novia in Lima hastened him on his way, but I hung in and enjoyed my time with Hermann and his wife. We made plans for future trips, but my longing for unexplored and unknown jungles had been dampened considerably by this last tragedy.

One morning, Scotty drove me to the airport and Owen Williams flew me back to Trujillo. I was loaded down with Indian blowguns, drums, and Adrita Yaguas flute, and other curiosities from the jungle. I would return again.

The faithful Ernesto and the lovely Nieves were awaiting me, and I accepted their hospitality once more. The Peruvian papers were full of stories of the Mayorano uprising and the Bataneros were all ears when I related my participation in it. I even did a newspaper interview with our archaeological friend Angel Miñano.

Northern Peru had become a second home to me; yet, I could see no reason to plan for more film adventures there. I had pretty well squeezed it of stories. Ernesto had had no luck with the Goldak Metal Detector. It proved much to erratic as did all metal detectors of the 1950s. I left it with him when finally I took the bus for Lima. (Eventually, as we shall see, that detector was used to *very* good work.)

The Lima Hotel Veintiocho De Julio was comfortable and nostalgic, but I soon flew back to California.

I didn't stay in the States very long.

Pre-Inca gold found with author's gold-detector.

Ancient buildings of Huasachuga.

Luis Seminario, Ernesto Batanero, Jimmy Flynn, and the author in Huasachuga.

Santiago 'Jimmy' Flynn on his mule, Gringa.

Author and Jack Douglas on the set of the *I Search for Adventure* show.

Lima Comerciio reports the story.

L. A. Times coverage.

Ernesto tries out the *Goldak* Metal Detector.

Author on the windjammer, *Omega*.

Author with Spanish conquistador armor found in the Sierra Madre Mountains of Mexico.

Author with Roy Moore with the loaded 1863 Winchester rifle found in the Mexican Sonora Desert.

Julie at the ghost city of Baroyeca.

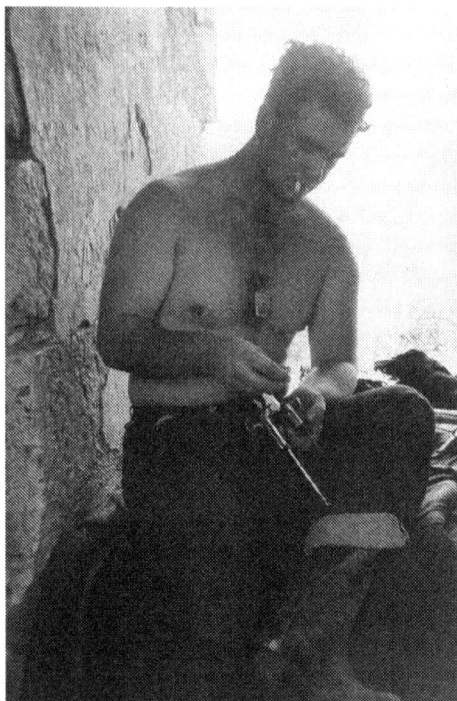

Roy and his 'cannon' in the church tower of Baroyeca.

View from the tower.

Author with the flag of *the Los Angeles Adventures Club* in the
Barranca De Cobre Canyon of Mexico.

T.V. ad.

Padre Trampas with Tarahumara guide.

Author with 16th century cross-bow and Indians.

12 — THE SIERRA MADRE I

The Los Angeles Adventurers' Club was a haven for restless men. The members were not all pillars of propriety, wealth, and dignity. We had a few rascals in our club. However it happened, I became one of the directors of the club in 1956. My lecture season, October to May, kept me away from the very masculine cigar-smelling club rooms, but apparently I was good enough at what I did in and for the club for the members to keep me on the board for a couple of years.

One of those members told me an interesting story.

In the state of Sonora, northern Mexico, along the Pacific Ocean, there is a remote and totally unchanged Spanish colonial city called Alamos. It is about three hundred miles south of the Arizona town of Nogales. Drive down the Mexican Pacific Coast Highway 15 to Hermosillo, continue on to the port town of Guaymas and keep driving south to Obregón, and a little farther to Navojoa. Leave the pavement—in 1957—and take the dirt road No. 10 east toward the Sierra Madre Mountains for some thirty miles and you will, finally, come to one of the best preserved Spanish colonial towns in all of Mexico, Los Alamos. By government decree, no new modern buildings may be constructed there, and no old ones may be torn down. It is as it was in the eighteenth century. Electricity is about its only modern feature. Believe me, if you enjoy historical settings, this is one real find, a gem. Some Anglo Americans have decided that Alamos is the place in which to retire—go back a couple centuries and live in the past.

One of these expatriates from the United States was Herbert Moss. He settled in an old *hacienda* and then renovated it. Moss was known for his ranch-style barbecue cook-outs. In 1956, a Los Angeles friend of his planned to visit him. This man piloted his own light airplane, and requested identifying features of the town to enable him to spot this somewhat remote city in the foothills of the Sierra Madre. He was told: "You can't miss it.

The cities of Obregón and Navajoa on the highway are modern. Only Alamos has the colonial look. We have a large old Spanish church right in the center of town; you'll see the tower easily."

The gentleman took off from Lockheed Airport in Burbank and cruised south. He soon crossed the border and followed the Mexican coastal highway. The air charts were accurate, and he recognized Navajoa and Obregón. He turned inland towards the mountains and began a search-and-seek flying pattern. Quite close to the foothills of the great cordillera Sierra Madre he spotted what he was told to expect, a tall four-story church tower surrounded by adobe buildings. He throttled back and glided in close looking for the landing strip that he was told was there, and floated over the city block after city block of buildings and houses. An extensive water dam came into view. There were large earth ovens and other man-made structures, but there were no people. Nor was there a landing strip, just a Mexican desert of cactus trees. The confused pilot buzzed the place a couple times and then realized that it was a vast ghost city, a very old one. He turned south, and after a while he spotted the lively city of Alamos. He landed and was taken over to the *Hacienda* Moss. That night while sipping a salty margarita and sucking the bones of a Mexican spitted lamb barbecue he mentioned what he had seen.

Immediately the attention of all present was upon him. The reaction was, "My God, that's the legendary city of Baroyeca that the old Mexicans and Indians talk about. They say it was a good size Spanish city, built over wealthy silver mines, that the Yaquis Indians finally overran after more than a century of constant warfare. Everybody in the place was massacred. The area became untenable and nobody ever moved back. It's a good legend around here. Some call it a myth."

A group of folks from Alamos decided to take a half-track and go out for a look. They charged out into the desert several days later with a good supply of iced beer, picnic baskets, and skepticism. After ten hours in 120-degree heat, they dejectedly returned. That was the story that I got from Henry Kehler at the Los Angeles Adventurers' Club.

This story was just the sort of thing that fascinated me. Furthermore, it was relatively close to home. I could make a whale of a good TV film without the long expensive trip to South America. I packed my bags.

However, not so easy now to do that. I had recently courted and married a beautiful and sensuous woman who had been present at my first lecture at the Pasadena Civic Auditorium. She was as interested as I was with the legends of the past. "Could I go along with you?" she asked. "I would have it no other way," I answered. It was hard for Julie Troll Wilhelmsen to part with her two young daughters and younger son for even an afternoon, but now she arranged to leave them for a full month in good family hands. Julie turned out to be a flawless adventure companion and would travel with me whenever possible on many trips in the future. (She is the lady who is interred with the little golden Colombian pendent.)

With us also was Roy Moore, a 20-year-old college student. He was big, brawny, and willing. Very pleasant. We never had any conflicts.

A club member recommended that we go directly to the Bougenvilla Motel in Hermosillo. I was given a letter for its manager, Manuel Ortiz Varga. *Señor* Ortiz laid out the red carpet for us and gave me good advice on travel in Sonora. He also put me in touch with a pilot who flew for Mexico's Aeronaves Airline. The pilot turned out to be another fine link in the chain of Mexicans with whom I was to work for the next couple years. We were in the air the following morning. Back and forth we flew over the region north of Alamos, ever widening our flying circle until finally we spotted the tall church tower with its huge sunburst cross jutting high into the sky. The dead city of Baroyeca lay all around it. We zoomed down low over the crumbling adobe buildings. My pilot was as excited as I was and for a moment I thought he might clip a wing on the tall tower. But he was an excellent pilot, and he enabled me to take marvelous aerial films of the old ghost town.

He was then happy to plot a ground relief map on a geological and geographic chart of the area that I had had the foresight to obtain from the offices of the U. S. Geological Survey in Los Angeles. The chart was not totally accurate, but good enough for my experienced pilot to mark out the site of Baroyeca, just west of the Sierra Madre Mountains.

Next, we had to find a local man with a four-wheel drive vehicle who could take us out there. "*No problema*," as they say south of the border. Every cowboy in the Hermosillo area was sure he could speed us out there in no time. Our Aeronaves pilot, who had taken an interest in the project, called a friend and we had our man.

Then followed an evening that I remember well. Manuel Ortiz, with a guitar that he played well, entertained us in the parlor of the Bouganvilla Motel; he made background music to our conversation. Mike Ramirez, the chef of the restaurant, served us great T-bone steaks that he insisted came from the States. Our pilot and his driver friend were there also. The conversation went beyond the immediate project of Baroyeca. "You go a little farther east from that place and you are in the Sierra Madre Mountains. Up there you will meet with the Tarahumara Indians. They are part of the mountains. They can take you to places and show you things that we here in the cities know nothing of." Our driver was speaking. I liked that kind of talk and my wife Julie liked it even better. "What kind of things?" she questioned.

Manuel stopped strumming his guitar; he had been listening and now he entered the conversation. "Those of us who listen to Sierra legends have a *sombrero* full of tales. The Indians up there talk about extensive cliff dwellings; they even speak of the burial tomb of a giant in one of those caves."

"A giant?" I asked.

"*Si pues*," he answered, "a huge container where a god or a giant is entombed." He turned to the driver. "You've heard that?"

He answered, "All the Indians up there have heard it. Other things too."

I broke in. "The mystery writer Erle Stanley Gardner (whose Perry Mason stories were very popular) just published a book, *Neighboring Frontiers*. I've read it. He wrote about the legends up there. He especially mentions the Mexican Sierra Madre. And so did Frank Dobie in his book *Apache Gold and Yaqui Silver*. There were references in both those books of Indian tales of caves stacked with old Spanish armor and weapons. Maybe even treasure. Have you heard any such legends?"

They hadn't. But my curiosity had been more than piqued.

Julie leaned into me and whispered, "Go for it." I was surprised.

✧✧✧

But, first things first. Baroyeca.

The young and clean-shaven Honorio Sabastion Alberto Gonzales y Hermanito—"Just call me Al"—our driver loaded us up in his pickup truck: Julie, Roy, he, and I. Cozy. We left Manuel's motel and drove south. We passed the miserably dirty area near Guaymas where the '*coyotes*' (human flesh peddlers) were camped out in miles of mud wetlands. With them were hundreds of Mexican workers they were preparing to smuggle across the border of the United States.

We reached Ciudad Obregón, and Albert turned his four-wheel drive vehicle east. Away from the city and towards the distant range of mountains. He consulted the map that the pilot had given him. Then he literally plowed through many cultivated fields until we abruptly left all semblance of farm and ranch. The dirt trail quit, and we were on our own. Our man wasn't fazed. He took the logical and easiest route east.

When the cultivation stopped, the graze land commenced. There was a sturdy breed of long-horned cattle that do well in this near desert land of cactus. Each cow or steer in this land needs a great deal of space in which to survive. The animals eyed us suspiciously as we made our way by them. We were startled when Julie called for a halt. We had passed a wild bull with a large prickly cactus plant sticking out of its snout, obviously quite painful. "Hold up," she demanded and then got out of the truck. She walked over to the bull that warily eyed her. She strode right up to him, took a firm grip on the offending spinney cactus, and quickly pulled it from his tender nose. He stared at her, shook his head, backed off, and trotted off to where the other cattle were browsing. Julie got quite an "*olé*" from our driver. I was very proud, but did say, "Why'd you do that? You could have been killed." She answered. "Old Bossie couldn't graze with that painful thing sticking out of its face." I tossed in another "*olé*."

We moved along, but now ever more slowly. Here was no semblance of a trail. We were guided only by the airman's directions that he had set down on the charts and those didn't take into consideration the conditions of the terrain. We passed a little hillock and

202

Roy spoke up. He did little talking and was good at seeing things that Julie and I missed. "Is that a pipe?" he called, "sticking out of that little hill. It looks like one to me." We backed up and got out of the pickup. It was not a pipe. It was the muzzle of an 1863 octagonal-barreled Winchester rifle.

"*Aye Chihuahua*," exclaimed Alberto. "*Miren*, look," he said, and then carefully pulled the heavy weapon out of the earth. The stock or wooden handle was gone, rotted away by years of exposure to creatures and the rains that do come and go in this Sonoran Desert. The workings were pretty well seized up, but Roy gave out a Texas yell (He was from the Lone Star State), "Lookee here, there's a bullet. There's a bullet still in the chamber." He pulled back. "I wouldn't touch that; it could go off."

Julie went right ahead, took it in her hands and gingerly inspected the breech. "This sure is a cartridge," she exclaimed, "but I think it has been fired. There's a hole in the rim of it." She saw it right; there was an indentation where the firing pin had struck and fired out the bullet.

Roy looked around at the open cactus dotted horizon. "I just wonder where that slug went," he speculated, "and what was the man shooting at."

Julie continued his thought, "And why was he shooting?"

Albert spoke up and was probably correct in his summation. "Yaquis, the Yaqui Indians. They didn't go to the earth like your Apaches; they stood firm and held their land and those mountains." He pointed to the haze in the distance that shrouded the Sierra Madre Mountains. "Nobody came out here alone back in the days when that gun was being used. They had to deal with the Yaquis. Even the Revolution armies of 1915 didn't want to have anything to do with them. They left them alone. I would say that the 'warriors of the Monté' brought this man down."

Quite a talk from a rather stoic fellow . . . until we found out later that he was part Yaqui himself.

Our simple find remained a mystery. Our guess was that the gun's owner had fired his rifle, and then kept moving without ejecting the empty shell. He was probably wounded but managed to elude his killers. Otherwise, they would have taken the gun. He died some-where close by and the creatures of the desert finished him off.

Such is a plausible and good story; I have that old relic of a shoot-out in the desert hanging on a wall of my den. I enjoy pointing it out and telling the story. My guests come up with all sorts of theories. It's kind of a game. And yet, somewhere out there in that lonely landscape, a life and death drama was once played out, and all of our speculation will never recreate the full story.

We continued to drive. I couldn't believe that the truck could take the jolts and bumps or that the tires could survive the sharp rocks and stiff cactus spines of this ride. But it did! We had begun this drive at 5:00 a.m. and it was 3:30 p.m. Albert took his truck out of gear, slowed to a stop, and simply said, "There it is *señores*. There is your city of Baroyeca."

Perhaps a mile in front of us the tall four-story tower of the city stood out like a lighthouse in the desert. Its huge iron sunburst cross was silhouetted against the afternoon sun. It was a sight to behold.

"Hold everything," I bellowed. "I must get my pictures." No matter how curious a cameraman might be, the good photographer always records his first impression; often it is the best. Then we slowly drove into the center of the jumble of ruined walls and buildings. We took the truck right up to the tower. The roof of the church, of which it was a part, and the roofs of all the other buildings had collapsed. The walls still stood. All of the buildings were constructed of adobe except for the church. In several of those shells of buildings, we could see through doorless openings and glassless windows earthen ovens still intact waiting to be fired up. We were surrounded by a genuine ghost town, not of the nineteenth century Old West, but of the seventeenth and eighteenth century colonial Castile.

Albert unloaded our equipment, asked if we were sure that we didn't want to return with him and then headed back to civilization. He was to return one week later for us. He drove off. We were not worried to see our lifeline depart. On my travels I had learned to trust a man's word. Albert was worthy of that trust (Besides, I hadn't paid him yet!).

The first life that we noticed as we began to set up our cots, folding table, and a couple of stools, was a two-and-a-half-foot reptile that waddled into our space like a teenage alligator. It paid no attention to us but slowly crawled along its way. "That's too big for a Gila monster," Roy learnedly proclaimed, "and they sure as hell don't have gators out here. What is it?"

"Damned if I know," I answered. "But I surely would like to get a movie of it. Grab it by the tail, Roy, and we'll tie it to a tree. The light is too dark now for the movie camera. We'll film him tomorrow."

Roy looked at me. "You want him, you grab him."

"You afraid of him?"

"I don't like his looks."

Julie popped up, "How do you know it's not a she?"

"Let it be," I gave in. I wasn't too happy about its looks either. "He'll be around tomorrow when the sun is out."

"Hey man," Roy exclaimed, "I don't want that mother prowling around here while I'm sleeping. I'll shoot it. There'll be others."

Now Roy fancied himself an old time Texas cowpoke. He dressed all in black even in the heat of this desert, and he wore the biggest, longest, and meanest looking .45 revolver in a low tie-down holster. He made a quick draw and blasted away at the strange creature. Those big slugs went into it and through it several times. They didn't faze it one bit. The beast just kept waddling off into a bush of cactus. It wasn't affected by the .45s. "Before it gets away," Roy shouted, "I'll blast it with the shotgun." We had a 12-guage scattergun and Roy let fly with it at our mysterious visitor just as it shambled into the brush and was lost. "Well, I'll be a Texas sidewinder," Roy muttered and went about the business of setting up camp. (Let me speak of this creature from the desert that we encountered. It is found only in the Sonoran Desert. Albert, our driver, later called it an escorpión—not to be confused with the tail stinging scorpion. Big brother to the Gila monster, it is twice as large and twice as venomous. Most people of northern Mexico go throughout their life without ever seeing one. Believe me, they do not want to see one. The escorpión acts sluggish, but can turn on an enemy as quickly as a fox terrier. The curator of the El Paso reptile farm told me that one of his workers had grabbed an escorpión by the tail to transfer it into another cage. The beaded monster had spun around so quickly that it had gripped the man's arm before he could pull back. With the zookeepers trying to dislodge it, the thing just kept chewing the man's arm and dripping very potent poison into the wound. They couldn't seem to kill it or incapacitate it. The man went into intensive care for two weeks before the poisons were controlled.)

Things began to look cozy at our campsite, even though we all cast occasional suspicious looks at the clump of cactus where the creature had disappeared. We hung our Coleman lantern on a branch of a tree in front of the church tower and Roy set up the stove. We opened some cans and settled down to our first meal in the Mexican wilderness. However, things were not as they appeared to be: quiet, serene, and peaceful. We began to catch fleeting glimpses of movement out of the corners of our eyes. No noise, just a rustling along the periphery of the bright Coleman gas light, fleet scatterings here and there and all over the place. Tarantulas! Big, fat tarantulas had come to pay us a visit. Our bright light had immediately drawn myriads of moths, beetles, and flying insects who, when they flew into the very hot lantern, fell to the ground. The giant spiders never had it better.

Now, Julie's resolve dissolved. "They're all over the place, hundreds of them." Actually we counted up to one hundred and then lost count as they scurried closer and closer to us. Julie pointed to the church tower's three belfries. "Let's go up there, anything to get away from the ground." And that's where we spent seven nights at Baroyeca. There was a stone spiral staircase that led up into the bell tower. We followed it up to the first landing. This cozy spot with large openings meant we could lay out our sleeping bags and look right out on the city below us. Our heads and feet stuck out over the ledges of the belfry, but at least there were no more menacing creatures crawling around us. There were, however, winged ones and ticks. I picked up a case of dengue fever in that church tower that fortunately didn't manifest itself until I was home a couple weeks later.

Our first night in the tower went well. We three managed a fair sleep and did not wake up until the sun made its early appearance at 5:00 a.m. We stirred and enjoyed our lofty perch as the cool, clear and fresh morning arrived. And as the sun came up so did the Yaqui Indians. First we heard the rustling and the hoof beats and the muted conversation as they approached.

Roy removed his ever present gun from its holster beside him. Julie whispered to him, "Watch that gun, Roy. We'll talk to them." I had my doubts, but I peered over the rim of the belfry and called down, *"Buenos días, amigos. Como estan?"*

I was answered with a hearty, *"Olé hombres; qué tal?"*

I was relieved. I saw not only three Yaqui cowboys, but a small herd of cattle.

"Qué Linda, el día." I hollered down, and said to Roy, "Put away your pistol."

"Gringo, tiene usted una copita? Tenemos sed."

"Sí pues," I responded, *"Aqui hay un poquito de tequila."* I handed down to one of the men a tin cup and a small bottle of tequila.

"Muchas gracias," he grinned up to me and took the bottle. He pretty well filled the cup and took a good drink. He then passed it on to one of the others, and on to the third rider.

"I don't like the looks of this," said Roy.

"Just keep your canon ready," I cautioned him.

But there was no need.

The man looked at me and grinned, *"Hasta otra vez, muchas gracias, gringo. Aqui tiene la botella y la copa, duerme bien, y hasta la vista, hasta mañana,"* and he and his men rode off with their cattle.

When they had gone, we came down from our fortress in the sky. There were no tarantulas to be seen; the escorpión had gone forever. Roy lit the stove and brewed the coffee. That and rolls were our breakfast. At sunrise the little beasts of the desert came out to prowl and bedevil. They are the insects, and bedevil us they did. Julie's bug repellent stood us in good stead, but we were constantly flailing our arms and hands at unseen assailants.

We started exploring by tracing and walking along the adobe walls that made up the houses and the defensive system of the old city. They were weathered but most of them still stood erect; some a good twelve feet tall. Occasionally, a *viga* or crossbeam was still in place. We got the feel of the place and hiked here and there mapping the remains of a once populous city. To think that Baroyeca was here, a city full of life, business, homes, love, and romance for over two hundred years—before the United States had won its independence—and that now it was a crumbling ruin of adobe bricks. A lifestyle that had collapsed.

Each morning at sunrise the cowboys came riding in. They would shout greetings to us up in our belfry, and would then request their *copita*. Fortunately, I had taken along with us a plentiful supply of tequila. The Indians would take their one drink and then move along. For a week we became a watering hole or bar in the desert to these roving herdsmen. They, in return, saw to it that our large Jeep water cans were always filled from a nearby stream.

Roy continued to practice with his big .45 revolver. During the 110-degree heat of midday, we would return to our belfry perch in order to catch the little breeze that blew down from the mountains. Roy would pull out his gun and start firing away at anything that moved. Mainly, that would be the large gray iguana that stretched out to sun themselves on the many walls and buildings of Baroyeca. The .45 would make hell of a racket, but Roy never hit a thing. He was a lousy shot.

That is, he was a lousy shot until one afternoon when the Yaqui cowboys came riding in. This was unusual for them to come that late in the day. We noticed, too, that they had no cattle with them. Also, on this visit, three others had joined them. They had been drinking, and when I offered them our bottle, the six of them drained it. They dismounted, tossed the empty bottle onto the ground, and demanded another. They were in a belligerent mood. They stuck out their hands, and in no uncertain terms called for more. One of them casually drew his long machete from a loop in his belt and began nonchalantly lopping off buds from a barrel cactus.

"*No, no ha más*," I said.

"*Sí, ha más*," their spokesman corrected me.

Roy walked up from behind a wall where he had been excavating an adobe oven. He had, as usual, his long .45 revolver strapped to his thigh. He challenged the Indians in English. "You boys looking for trouble?"

They didn't understand him, but they got the message. They all started to laugh. One pointed to Roy and scoffed, "Tom Mix." They all roared. They now pointed at his gun and said in effect, "You couldn't shoot a hole in a barn." It was obvious that they had been observing us or spying on us. The situation had become ugly, and it didn't get any better when Roy took on a Matt Dillon of *Gunsmoke* stance, and said to me, "Throw that empty bottle up into the air."

"No, Roy," I hissed. "Don't try it."

One of the Yaquis got the idea. He leaned over, picked up the bottle, and tossed it way up into the sky.

With marvelous precision Roy drew, cocked, and fired. The bottle exploded in the air. Roy had done it.

The Yaqui Indians applauded him, began their normal chatter, and then mounted, and rode away. They waved and shouted back, "*Adios, amigos*."

"Let me give them a parting shot," Roy eagerly asked. "I'll shake them up a bit."

"One is enough," I said, and Julie gently guided his pistol back to its holster.

There was what appeared to be a well some 3500 yards away from the church tower. We came back to this opening in the earth many times. It intrigued us. Here was a perfect square with sides of seven feet all surfaced with neat well-worked rectangular stones. I had read of a similar northwestern Mexican city of colonial times that utilized such a device as an escape should the community be surrounded by Indians. Another shaft would be sunken somewhere in the town, and it would then be joined by a tunnel underground that would connect up with the remote shaft. This system must have been similar to the escape routes used by the prisoners in the Nazi camps of Germany. We did dig down several feet beneath the church and found that the stone spiral staircase continued down way beneath the earth floor of the church. We never did find a satisfactory solution to the vertical pit so far from the city limits. We ruled out a water well when we lowered a Coleman lantern into it and could see where it had been shored up with wooden beams and that there was an opening of some sort at the bottom. That Coleman went down at least 200 feet.

Baroyeca is certainly worthy of full restoration. Unfortunately, its distance from any major city or tourist center probably precludes the possibility. Maybe that's for the best: only someone really interested in history will attempt to go out there. As Roy commented, "That's sure a long way from nowhere!"

❖❖❖

Once home, the films I had taken, including the Yaqui herdsmen, made for a very good television show. First on KTTV in Los Angeles, and then in syndication. Jack Douglas' *I Search for Adventure* had caught the imagination of the viewing public. The program's charm came from the premise that nonprofessionals who traveled to remote areas and took films of strange and exotic sites and customs, and told their own stories, were of interest to the armchair traveler. Folks in their living rooms casually thought, "Why, I could do that; I might just chuck it all one of these days, and go traveling." Of course, very few did, but the basic idea gave the TV series a definite fascination and excitement.

My winter months were being filled with travelogue lecture dates. Most of my peers stayed strictly to the tourist travelogue theme. These men, and occasionally a lady, were good at what they did. The profession that began when Burton Holmes showed "lantern slides" shortly after the turn of the century had now blossomed into an industry. Name the country, and there was a film being made about it. Some of the real pros were Kirt Nagel, Thayer Soule, Stan Migely, Cliff Kamen, Howard Pollard, and of course Lowell Thomas. On the adventure side there were: Nicol Smith whose book and subsequent movie, *Burma Road*, were quite successful; Martin and Oso Johnson, whose book and movies of capturing animals for zoos around the world, excelled in their "Bring 'Em Back Alive" subjects; my friends Dana and Ginger Lamb: Lou Cotlow whose *Passport to Adventure* book, lecture, and movie, were very appealing. John Goddard's kayak trips down the full length of the Nile River—and then one down the Congo; Colonel John D. Craig's book *Danger is My Business* and his TV series, *Of Lands and Seas*; and others. I had joined this latter group of adventurers.

Our exciting moments on stage and interviews for local newspapers were contrasted with long hours of driving through all kinds of weather in just about every state in the Union and in all the Provinces of Canada. Way before the Interstate Highway System came into being we were indeed "getting our kicks on Route 66," and we were pounding the pavement; and just like the postman of yore, we worked in all kinds of weather and endured all kinds of accommodations. We travelogue artists have a wealth of stories to tell.

I gave a film lecture in the opera house of Racine, Wisconsin. My friend Dana Lamb was with me. We were headquartering out of the Commodore Hotel in Chicago; Dan had the day off. This particular engagement was a matinee. I was wearing my tuxedo—the uniform of the lecturer—and had just made my usual final pit stop in the restroom. There, to my consternation, I found that I could not close the zipper of my trousers fly. I stepped out on the darkened stage and called Dan. "I can't get this zipper up, give me a hand." There was but one dim stage light bulb hanging from the ceiling illuminating a patch of center stage. The curtain was down so we both went out to the middle of the stage, where the light was the strongest, and Dan had a look-see. He tugged on the stuck zipper, and then knelt down before me to get a closer view. "Aha," he triumphed, "there, I can see it now." He reached into my gaping pants and grabbed a hold. From somewhere backstage we heard the order, "Curtain time. Curtain, screen, floodlights." This was a union house and everything went according to pre-written specifications. Up went the curtain, on come the lights. And off went Dan dashing to stage left while I, with a quite visible white shirt hanging out of my fly, made a beeline to the cover of the lectern at stage right. Dan and I were never invited back to the Racine Opera House.

The travelogue—adventure lecture profession was not the best career move one could make. There were no pension plans, no medical plans, and there was no security. We were on our own. If one were to prepare for the future, he had to do it on his own. The lecture fees were generous, but the traveling expenses whittled down their value.

I thought often of the gold that I had seen and had held in my hand in Peru. I still harbored the thoughts that I had grown up with: that treasure is out there awaiting me—just beyond the next mountain. "Over the mountains of the moon, down the valley of the shadow, ride, boldly ride if you seek for El Dorado." So wrote Edgar Allen Poe. I vowed to try it again.

So close, and yet so far: the Sierra Mountains of Mexico. My friends in Hermosillo had painted visions of them and their secrets in my imagination. They had whispered haunting words into my ears. The melodic strains of Manuel Ortiz Varga's guitar occasionally played again in my memory. The intoxicated look in Julie's eyes when she listened to the stories of cliff dwellings hanging from the mountain tops, the tomb of a giant, and the rumors of armor from Spanish knights. I began to consult my maps.

A letter to Manuel was answered immediately. He wrote, "I have just the guide for you. He speaks perfect English, and has been in those mountains. He could be of great help. Come back to Mexico and we can talk about it."

My mind had already been set. I would return to Mexico not to talk about it, but to head for its mountains.

I learned through library research that the Sierra Madre is one rugged piece of real estate. I couldn't just drive my Hudson Hornet automobile up into those mountains and canyons; I would need a vehicle more adaptable to that terrain. With a wife and three children to feed, I was in no position to come up with a four-wheel drive half-track or Jeep. Besides, my mechanical smarts didn't include any knowledge about such rugged cars. I went back—once again to my youth—and bought a 1931 Model A four-door Ford.

Not as whimsical as it sounds. My first car in 1941 had been one of Henry Ford's "Ladies." I paid at that time $45 for it—$5 down, $5 a month. I got to know that old timer so well that once my buddies and I took the whole motor out and replaced it with another. In 1957, I again paid $45 for a four-door coach. She had been down the pike a few times, twenty-seven years, but it was still going strong. I felt that should something go wrong with her, I would be able to repair it. The Model A was, and still is, a reliable car. The high clearance of the vehicle was not lost to me; it will go where very few modern cars would dare to go. I glued a little red sticker on the back window that read, "Don't laugh, it's paid for," and I was ready for the Mexican mountains.

Julie helped me with the packing. She would dearly have loved to hop in beside me, but she had her family responsibilities. I left the checkbook with her, and carried with me $310. The day was March 29, 1957.

At its best, a Model A Ford can rumble along a good road at a steady 50 mph to move along hour after hour was pushing those four pistons a bit. I held the speed down to 35 or 40. The Interstate Highway System hadn't been built yet, but the road from the Los Angeles area east to San Bernardino, Indio, and on to Yuma was mostly four lane. Lots of room for the Oldsmobile Rockets, the Hudson Hornets, the Studebaker Champions, and the Edsels to boom by me. Most drivers would wave a friendly hand when they saw this boxy little relic of an auto museum put-putting along the mighty big highway. I got thumbs up all the way. The drive was fun, but it was too long. Down in the Yuma area, the temperature ran to over 110 degrees. Of course, there was no air conditioning. I had the front windows open and had one leg hanging out over the left windowsill like a teenage hot-rodder. The A has a throttle on the steering wheel yoke so I could control my speed with my hand.

I pulled into a little roadside rest area at 11:00 p.m., somewhere between Yuma and Gila Bend, Arizona. The name "Gila Bend," is enough to dampen many campers enthusiasm. I pulled out my sleeping bag and laid it out on the table. The Coleman stove heated up some 'Dri-Lite' dehydrated Spanish rice for my dinner. Before long an Arizona State Patrolman drove up and settled down to talk with me. "Would you care for a glass of red wine?" I asked.

"Sorry, not now, I'm on duty; some other time."

We talked a bit, and he then boomed off into the desert night. I settled into my bag—it cools off out there at night—and dozed off. Two hours later, I was awakened by headlights. The cop was back. "I'll take you up on that drink," he happily said. "I'm off duty now and am on my way back to my wife in Gila. I could use a drink now. The wife and I aren't getting along as well as we should." For two hours, I heard his tale of marital woes. And then, with a fond farewell, he drove off to Gila Bend. It is hard enough to sleep in a sleeping bag without being regaled by the local constabulary, but what does one do when the man in charge of the night's highways wants to unburden himself? You listen.

Years after this, Willie Nelson wrote and recorded a stirring song, *"On the Road Again."* That song was a long way in my future, but I had the spirit that Nelson had captured, when I drove out the next morning to Gila Bend and a truck stop where I shaved in the restroom, and then on to Tucson, and south to the border town of Nogales. My motto then and now is, "Be nice to them, and they will be nice back to you."

I headed due south into Mexico, a country that I have come to respect and appreciate. My travels in that country over the years have all been extremely interesting to me. The people have been most friendly. Here and there the hand has been out for a bribe, but so is it elsewhere in other nations of the world. The first town worthy of the name south of the border is Magdalena, where Father Eusebio Kino's bones were yet to be found. He was the great missionary of northern Mexico. And then onto the modern city of Hermosillo.

Manuel was waiting at the Bouganvilla Motel, and he escorted me to my large room (Less than $3 a day—over $100 today!). I was treated to a sixteen-ounce steak by Mike Ramirez, and we then retired to Manuel's parlor. His guitar came out and his hospitality and bar were generous. We had a party going very soon. Varga's knowledge of strange phenomena in the Sierra Madre Mountains was extensive. I did, however, begin to wonder if he was a bit too romantically optimistic about the yarns he reeled off between the melodic strains of "Poinciena" and "Perfidia" on his guitar. He was a true Mexican.

Manuel's exuberance was slowed when a very handsome young fellow of twenty-two years appeared at the door. My new partner had arrived. "Sergio Camalich," said Manuel as he put his guitar aside. "Come in." I met Sergio and shook his hand; he had a strong handshake.

"Mr. Romain," he seriously addressed me. "I am Sergio, and I hope that we can accomplish what you want."

I immediately liked his approach, his mixture of modesty and confidence. I answered him, "Sergio, you are now in charge. I am leaving it up to you to take me into the mountains and to seek out the objects that Manuel has told you I am interested in."

Manuel attempted to break in, but Sergio continued, "I understand you want to go up into the Sierra and to the Barranca De Cobre (the Copper Canyon). I have been close, but not into it. You know (I didn't) that right now a railroad is being built over the Sierra from west to east. I suggest we drive along the proposed route of that railroad where some clearing has been done. We can approach the mountains that way."

"Yes," is all I could answer.

The young man continued, "I don't think much of the railroad bed has been laid down yet, but we should be able to use whatever there is. Better than going all the way down to Mazatlán and then crossing over to Durango."

"Where on earth did you learn such fine English?" I broke in.

Sergio stopped talking and grinned. "I wanted to improve myself and so have been listening to American television day after day." He almost apologized, "I can tell you anything you want to know about the soaps." I knew that I had the right man.

The next morning Sergio came to my room, and we went over our plans. He had heard nothing of a cave of armor, but he had heard of cliff dwellings. Usually, when we think of cave dwellings we think of Arizona or the pueblos of New Mexico. Not until we get down into the Valley of Mexico do we think of such ancient cities. I carried with me two books that are now almost forgotten. They were written in the first years of the twentieth century by the anthropologist explorer Carl Lumholtz. Using the marvelously detailed and researched writings of Bandelier and Bancroft—historical detectives of the last century—he had sought out the Tarahumhra Indian country of the Sierra Madre and had seen and actually photographed several quite impressive cave dwellings. They were ancient mountain pueblos that science had no idea were south of the United States border. Lumholtz's books have been relegated to the back rooms of libraries today, but they do represent the first and the only descriptions of the spine of the Sierra Madre Mountains. I was impressed when Sergio asked if he could take those two volumes home with him for the night. I now believe that he spent the whole night going over them.

The next morning, Sergio arrived at my room and suggested that we take the Ford—which he had dubbed, "La Mula"—to a garage where he knew and trusted the mechanics. He wanted it to have a complete look over (I have found Mexican mechanics to be practically wizards with automobiles. Never doubt a Mexican alley mechanic; he will get the job done correctly, most often better than the job will be done at a dealership). His man spent an hour on the Model A. There really isn't a lot to go over on that simple machine, and he proclaimed, "You could drive this to China; it is ready to go anywhere. Would you care to sell it to me?" Then he scratched his head, "Tires, that's another story. Where you are going you had better have a good jack, air pump, and tire repair kit." He was right on every count.

On April 2, I picked up Sergio at his family home and we chugged away. A beautiful sunny day as so many of them are in that part of the world. We putt-putted south on Highway 15. Sergio requested a stop at Obregón so he could touch base and say 'goodbye' to his grandmother. I joined him for tea in her parlor and sat with this elderly patrician as she and several of his relatives fussed over him. The Mexican family is quite close; the young respect the elders and the elders esteem the young. When we left an hour later, I was presented with a liter of a high quality drink called *Ricilla*. It turned out to be palatable and quite potent.

Our campsites along Highway 15 were all we could ask for. Almost picnic perfect. Lush grass and trees and often a river or brook nearby. There were no commercial campsites along the road at that time; there are many now. Sergio and I were having a good time. Four hundred fifty miles from our starting point in Hermosillo we came to Los Mochis. From there we would leave the Pacific Coast and turn east toward the Sierra. The fun and games were over. The ascent into the mountains began. We knew it immediately, and so did the car.

We had but two flat tires on the run south. The highway was all paved. Tire trouble is easily handled south of the border. Every village has some sort of tire and vulcanizing shop. Folks down there drive their tires until they are no more. Changing a wheel on a Model A was quite easy, and local people and truckers usually stop and give a hand. Unfortunately, we now began to run out of people and vehicles. The road, still paved, took us to San Blas on the Fuerte River that flows out of the heights. Then onto the very interesting town of El Fuerte which was named for the seventeenth century Spanish fort that guarded the mining community from the warring tribes of Indians that dominated the area. This is a city somewhat comparable to Alamos, but without the restoration. There are no tourists here, so the place has its own unspoiled colonial charm. We weren't at this point interested in charm, and so we drove east and north to the end of the road, just a few miles farther into the foothills. Then we followed dirt wagon trails for several miles until we reached the beginnings of the railroad bed for the Chihuahua Al Pacífico Line.

A group of cowboys pointed out the way. They told us that the train company had gone bankrupt and that most work had been stopped. They pointed out a proposed trail and, for a while, the driving was easy. But, the trail soon ended, and we soon were traveling cross-country. We boomed along, usually in second gear, northeast in scrubby desert and mountain terrain. Once we crossed a river where a half-finished bridge mocked us. We had no idea how deep that river, the Fuerte, would be, and Sergio walked ahead of the car making sure it wouldn't slip beneath the water. It was tiring work for both of us, and I admired my guide's enthusiasm. Here and there we would encounter farmers or cowboys who always waved to us with a cheerful word.

Our immediate destination was Creel which was the major town in this part of the Sierra. Today in 2003, there is still no road going up from Mochis, just the railroad that is now completed. We depended on the roadbed of that railroad. When least expected, it would appear again, and we were able to go into third gear once more and move along at 25 mph. We drove through a couple tunnels that I'm sure were over a mile in length. They were quite spooky. Finally, the sun went down and we were forced to make camp on hard boulders. There was little sleep that night.

The following day was a day of sunlight that enhanced the rugged beauty all about us. We fired up La Mula and finally drove to the summit of the Sierra Madre Mountains at about 7500 feet. We hailed a group of horsemen, and they pointed us in the right direction. Soon we were racing along a dirt road at 30 mph. It was exhilarating. A couple hours later, we came to our first road sign: Creel 125 kilometers. We brought out Sergio's grandmother's

Ricilla and we both toasted her and our success in climbing the Sierra Madre from the west. I believe that it was the first automobile to do so in that section of the mountains.

We arrived at Creel late that afternoon. In 1957, there was but one hotel in town. I have described the hotel at Lake Guatavita, Colombia, and I will apply the same description to this one except that here we had to hike up to a second floor for our room. I experienced a tad of deja-vu when Sergio asked for the restrooms and was told, "Follow your nose."

I was back in the Old West once again. It sounds like a well-played record, but it was true. I felt as though I were on the western Mexican frontier when Sergio and I walked out into the street that night looking for a restaurant and the first person who tipped his Stetson to us was wearing a frontier model Colt six-shooter in a holster belted on his hip. He was the sheriff. A man closely following him was his deputy, and he was sporting a pearl handle .45 automatic on his belt and an automatic shotgun in his hands. The two of them were off to quell a disturbance in one of the cantinas. We found out later that no one would argue with those two guardians of the law.

Sergio and I went in the opposite direction. The first thing that we realized was that this was not a good town for food. Absolutely no tourists were anywhere near here in 1957. (Now in 2003, with the train coming and going from El Paso and Chihuahua City things are very different.) Sergio and I ended up in a poor Chinese restaurant. "If this is it," I told him, "I'll eat my Dri-Lite in my room."

Sergio had an acquaintance in town, Don Estolfo. He gave us what information he could. The best of which was an introduction to Father Juan Martínez, S. J.—or as he was fondly called, Padre Trampas because of his magic tricks. I headlined that day in my journal when we met him as: "A remarkable day!"

I had read about this man in Erle Stanley Gardner's book, *Neighboring Frontiers*. Several years before we arrived, Gardner and a party had gone up to explore "one of the last unknown areas of our North American continent." He had written about this Jesuit priest who had given up a comfortable position as a chemistry professor at the University of Guadalajara to live on the frontier and to do what the original Black Robes did: work among the pagan Tarahumara Indians and attempt to bring them to Christianity.

We met the priest on the porch of his little frame house next to the Catholic Church of Creel. He greeted us with gusto. And when I told him I was here to take motion pictures for television, he got right into the act. He spoke excellent English, and he started off with, "*Señor* Romain, there are so many things up here to talk about, to tell the civilized world, to broadcast the story of this remote region." He motioned us into his parlor. "I will give you a copitá of the best brandy in the mountains. I do not indulge, but well-wishers give me much." We accepted the hospitality. The man was a library of stories. He obviously wanted to tell them to someone outside his immediate area.

"You, of course, are going to the Barranca De Cobre—the Canyon of Copper. You must go down into it. You must walk down and get the feel of it, of the country, and of the Indians you will meet. They are the Tarahumaras, very handsome, gentle, and honest people who have outlasted the Apache and the Yaqui. They now inhabit the country. The Apache are pretty well all gone, and the Yaquis—the 'wild ones'—have been forced back into the *sierra*. By remaining peaceful as they had been taught by the Black Robes, the Tarahumaras did inherit the earth as the Bible might tell us. The Apache and the Yaqui fought the white invasion at every turn, unmercifully, and as a result, they were removed. They lost the war. The Tarahumaras never fought a war and they are still here. I work closely with them."

Father Trampas stopped and poured a cup of coffee. "You must go to San José Huacaibo, an old Jesuit mission," he continued. "Some of the walls are still standing. The Tarahumaras have quite a village close by. They live around the old walls. I was there not long ago, and since those Indians trust me, they showed me several objects that they say came from a burial pit near the ruined mission church there. They are solid small gold pieces in the form of church bells." He showed us one. Rather crudely molded, it weighed in at about ten ounces of solid gold.

Father Trampas coughed and blew his nose. I noticed that the black robe that he wore was old, mended, and dusty. He continued, "I told this story to Mr. Stanley Gardner and he arranged to have sent up to me from Los Angeles, a metal detector. I took it back to Huacaibo and passed it over the area where the Indians had spoken of a burial." His eyes lit up. "The needle on that detector jumped like a Mexican jumping bean. The arrow on the dial nearly flew out of the gauge." Again he chuckled at his hyperbole and flatly said, "Something is buried there. I know it."

I was fully alert with this story. There it was again, the treasure at the end of the rainbow. "What will you do about it, Father Trampas?"

Almost in desperation, he spread his arms. "What can I do? This is their heritage. They might have allowed me a peek into their treasured past and maybe even given me a piece of it. But what can I do with it? Turn it into cash and the Mexican government would be on my back. We Jesuits have had enough trouble here in Mexico. The government would then come into the close-knit Tarahumara community and would begin their digging. The whole region would be disrupted. The Indians, I can say with knowledge, would be cheated out of their land and its valuables. It would be disastrous." Again he spread open his arms. "I will not take a part in disrupting the historical laws and mores of my charges, the Tarahumara Indians." After this definite declaration, he continued, "I will give you directions to San José Huacaibo. You should be able to reach it in your car. There is a small trading post there run by a man we call Ramón Mendoza and his wife. Don Ramón is a veteran of Pancho Villa's Dorados. He might be wanted by the federal government. I believe he has buried himself in this remote area to keep a low profile. The Dorados were Villa's private guard. I am sure he can be of no danger to Mexico now because he is totally blind. His very competent wife is his eyes. We are friends, and I will give you a letter for her. Please treat them well."

My little tablet of notes was rapidly filling up. There were stories in there that I knew Russ Leadabrand could turn into lucrative magazine articles.

Now, the Jesuit looked at his wristwatch and excused himself. "There is a boxcar of fourteen tons of cheese that has come up on the railroad from Chihuahua and from the United States." He nodded to me, "A major industrial company of your country has contributed it to me and my Indians. Mr. Gardner is responsible for that. I haven't had a nibble on that cheese yet, but I just might." He smiled and escorted us out into the brilliant sunlight. Please return and be my guests. Stay with me if you can't stand the smell of that brothel where you're staying. He strode rapidly to the railroad yard where he said his Indians were awaiting him.

Let me explain about those railroad tracks. They had reached Creel in 1956, all the way from the city of Chihuahua. But they had gone no farther. The auto and the truck road from the east had yet to be completed. That, of course, was the reason we had come up from the west.

Sergio and I were quite dazzled by the revelation that we had just heard. I said to him, "If Erle Stanley Gardner—with his incisive and analytical mind—believes in that strange missionary to the Indians, I do too." My partner agreed.

At our next visit with the priest we brought up the subject of the rumors of Spanish armor in the Sierra. Gardner had mentioned this legend in his book as had Frank Dobie. "The Conquistador armor," Father Trampas mused. "Yes, I have heard of it. Somewhere in a cave. I am sure the Spaniards got into this area in the sixteenth century. Their documents, those of Francisco Coronado and our more modern chroniclers, were consistent in relating that a group of Coronado's soldiers broke away from their captain's main column and came up here. This was when his whole expedition was retreating from his explorations in the southwest of the United States. They hadn't found anything except mud dwellings and were eager to try their luck in the mountains. They never rejoined Coronado. Historically, they're still up here."

The priest promised to look into this tradition with his Indians, and sure enough, the next morning a tall, lean, near-naked Tarahumara was at the hotel. He spoke very little Spanish, but made it clear that Father Trampas had the information that we wanted. He indicated that the cleric had been up much of the night with a quite sick pregnant woman.

Sergio and I arrived at the church shortly. The priest's battered Jeep was there, so we knew he was home. We felt guilty for disturbing him, especially when he appeared at his door in his old-fashioned flannel nightshirt. He looked haggard, but wiped the sleep out of his eyes and ushered us in. Sergio helped him with the coffee pot.

"I have spoken to the man who once mentioned the Spanish things that you asked about. He can help you, but unfortunately, he left this morning on the train to Chihuahua.

He is with a small delegation going to speak to the governor of the state on some sort of Tarahumara business. I am afraid he won't be back for some time. Once a Tarahumara gets into the big city, he'll wander around for days taking in the sights." Father Trampas savored his coffee, and then continued. "He did tell me that in the community of Samerchique he has seen what appears to be an iron crossbow. It is kept in one of the ruined Jesuit churches of that area. He works for the protestant mission there that is being run by the Linguistic Bible Translators."

Father Trampas took a good gulp of his coffee, and grinned. "Naturally, Pablo or Paul Carson of the Linguistics and I are on different sides of Christian theology, but he is a nice young man and his wife is a gem. They headquarter out of Samerchique."

I impatiently broke in, "But the man we would like to talk to has gone to Chihuahua? We can't see him?"

"If he's not here, you can't see him," the priest quickly replied.

"Is there no one else who might help me?" I almost pleaded.

"Go to San José Huacaibo. Don Ramón Mendoza might have the answer. Of all the people in this area, he is the most respected by the Tarahumaras."

I had hardly said, "Thank you," when Father Trampas wiped his brow and said, "Please excuse me. I must go back to bed."

The next day, Sergio and I were on our way to San José Huacaibo.

The problem was, that no one but Father Trampas seemed to know where that place was. He gave us directions, but he was no cartographer. He knew the way, but like so many of us, he was poor at giving directions. There are few roads leading out of Creel and there are no signposts. Sergio and I and La Mula floundered about going from one dead end to another. The driving conditions were near impossible. No need to go into details. The old Ford met every challenge. Our break came when we spotted a lone man hiking down the trail that we were following. We hailed him. "Do you know where Huacaibo is?" We had run across the right man.

"Give me a ride, and I'll take you there. That is where I am going, to visit my Uncle Ramón and my Aunt Evita."

The Ford was four-door and we had plenty of room. We noticed right away that this lean and clean-cut-looking man was prominently wearing a large .45 automatic pistol in a holster on his belt. Such is highly illegal in Mexico unless one has the proper credentials. This man, Salvador, was a federal agent of the Mexican government. He could pack a pistol or a machine gun if he wanted. He modestly explained, "I'm not on business, just a visit to my dear uncle and aunt." Sergio translated to me, and I knew that we had a good turn of luck. Toward evening we arrived at San José Huacaibo. "Blow your horn," Salvador eagerly asked me, and I sounded the old claxon. Immediately a fine-looking, middle-aged woman came out from the adobe building in front of us. She shrieked, "Salvador, my good nephew. Oh, Salvador, it is so good to see that you have come. Oh! Oh!" And she turned back to the building. "Ramón, he is here. Come quickly, Salvador." A nicely dressed man came to the doorway and walked assuredly to his wife. We knew that he was blind, but if we hadn't, we would never have guessed. He was sure of himself.

Evita bounded off of her porch and threw herself in the arms of her nephew. A touching scene. The couple had tears in their eyes. Their separation had been too long, as I later heard, but that was the way these family-conscious Mexicans reacted. Salvador disengaged himself from his aunt and walked over to his uncle. They shared not one but several strong *abrazos*.

Eventually, we were introduced, "You drove Salvador here?" Evita seemed to speak in wonderment. "You are a dear man," she said to me, and I was in the *abrazo* business. Sergio got in the act too. "*Yo tambien*," and he was greeted like a long-lost son. I said to Sergio in English as we were escorted into their neat little parlor, "I think these people like us." He answered, "These people are genuine. They are the real people of my country. They are family."

Don Ramón unerringly walked to a cabinet along the wall, opened a door, and brought out a bottle of Cuervo Tequila. "Here, we must drink to this occasion," he exuberantly said. His wife poured the drinks and we all raised our glasses. "To my favorite nephew" our host toasted and downed his drink in one gulp. His wife handed him a slice of lemon that he sucked on for a moment. She then guided his hand to a saucer of salt. He took a pinch and put it on his tongue. And down went another shot of Mexico's finest. I don't know why I uttered it, but I think it was appropriate. I spoke out, "*Ole!*" The gentleman turned toward my voice and let out a typical Mexican, "*Ui, ui.*" I think we bonded right there.

Most of the evening was taken up with intimate family talk that excluded Sergio and me. But eventually, Salvador came to our rescue and told his uncle why we were there: films of the Indians. A flurry of words went on between him and his folks, and then they all turned to me. The prognosis was better than I could have hoped for. Within four days all of the Tarahumara Indians of his region were gathering here for an annual *fiesta*. The best title I could get for it was, "The Banquet of Death."

"You stay with us," the *simpatico* Evita patted me on the knee, "and you will see something that no outsiders have ever seen. You are our guests."

The trading post that Don Ramón ran was a private enterprise with no connection or subsidy from the Mexican government. He admitted to us—after a day of hospitality—that technically he could be prosecuted by certain factions of the federal government who might still hold a grudge against him for fighting against it some forty years before during the Mexican Revolution. With the help of his nephew Salvador, he explained, "When we fought along side of Pancho Villa against the army of General Huerta, who had assassinated our president, Francisco Madero, I always thought that I was fighting for Mexico, not against it, as the history books now claim. I lost my eyesight in the battle of Ojinaga on the Texas border. I was blinded by a bomb. I have never seen a sunrise or a sunset since that day.

Evita tells me when it is time to go to bed and to rise. She is my life." He reached over and she was there to take his hand.

Salvador, with what I am sure was a tear in his eye, took up the story. "This is Villa country, the northern Sierra Madres. The Federalistas of those days wouldn't have dared to come up here. My uncle and my aunt have found a home with the Indians. I am very proud of them." He put his arm around the blind man and held the hand of his aunt.

For four days we stayed with these people. They dragged a spring bed with no mattress into the room where they held classes for the Tarahumara Indians. Sergio and I soon brought in our sleeping bags. One night on the springs and I was happy to go back to the floor.

Two days later, we were becoming bored. Nothing of interest was happening. But each morning Evita brought eggs for breakfast, and once she came in with a cake covered with frosting. Salvador and Sergio went hunting with one of four rifles I had smuggled in with me (which makes me a gun runner!). They returned without anything to change the dinner menu of frijoles, tortillas, and whatever would fit in the tortillas.

On the morning of our fourth day, Evita pounded on our door early in the morning. "*Señor* Sergio, they are coming now. The Indians are gathering just beyond the rise. Come quickly." We followed her for over half a mile. I was impressed by the swift steps she took as she climbed steadily up a grade of rocks, stones, and sand to the summit of a hillock.

We had been up there before and had seen the adobe buildings with a few Indians working around them, but now there were scores of people. As the day progressed, we saw hundreds of Indians coming from all directions. The men wore little more than a diaper-like breechcloth and a band of fabric around their heads. Their ladies were very well covered with voluminous skirts and blouses. Herds of goats were being brought in from the countryside. They were corralled close to the cluster of buildings.

Evita led us right down into the center of the shallow valley where the majority of the people were gathering and milling about. She called out, "Isidro," and then in his native tongue she called again. Isidro, the 83-year-old governor of the Tarahumara Indians of this district, came out from his adobe and stone house. His language was a total mish-mash to Sergio and me, but we did hear the distinct word, "Evita." They touched hands and said "*Querava*," and then they embraced. Don Ramón came up behind his wife guided by Salvador and an Indian boy. With more formality than the *abrazo* given to his wife, Isidro clasped the hand of Pancho Villa's old Dorado. Sergio and I were introduced, and we felt welcomed. There seemed no problem with my motion picture camera.

One by one, Indian men came into the area of their governor, and the proud gentleman greeted them with a handshake and an *abrazo*. By count, there were about four hundred Tarahumara Indians present on this occasion.

The proceedings were barbaric to our way of thinking. In the center of the main group of adobe buildings several men stood and waited for another to lead a goat on a tether to them. They would then grab the legs of the animal, throw it on its back, and quickly slit its throat with a razor-sharp machete. Perhaps the operation was no different than in the Chicago stockyards, but to watch it and to hear the bleatings of the animals was a shock to both Sergio and to me. Twenty-three goats were slaughtered in this manner. The blood that flowed copiously from their throats was collected in gourds. Thirty-four chickens were also put to death, and their blood was added to that of the goats. Tesvin, the fermented alcoholic drink made of corn by these Indians, was then added to this blood. Several huge *ollas* or jugs of this beverage were put over fires. Eventually, all present, men and women, dipped their cups into the concoction and like vampires they gulped down the blood. Sergio and I turned down the proffered cups—graciously, I hope—and went back to our room at Don Ramón's.

My friend quoted an old Mexican colloquialism: "*Aye, Chihuahua, cuántos Apaches, con pantalones y huaraches,*" which fit the description. "Oh, Chihuahua, how many savages with trousers and shoes." We both took a slug of tequila. "Better than what they're serving," Sergio grinned.

We returned to the festivities in time to see a huge bull, hamstrung and helpless, receive the same treatment as the other animals. All of the carcasses were then stripped of their skin—which was quickly claimed by the women—and then put on spits over fires throughout the valley. Despite the brutality of the proceedings, the aromas that now filled the air were delicious. And here is where Sergio and I entered the scene as participants. Father Trampas had strongly recommended that we take a quantity of salt with us to give to the Indians. In Creel it was plentiful and moderately priced. So now, we retrieved from the back seat of the Ford some twenty pounds of it. We brought it to the Indian ceremonies and we were greeted as members of the tribe. They took the condiment and rubbed it into the pieces of meat on the grill. They looked at us, grinned, extended their hands, and said, "*Querava.*" We were now part of the Banquet of Death."

Tesvin was being liberally passed about. Several huge clay vats were spaced around the area and anyone who wanted a drink would just go to one of those vats, dip his or her cup into it, and have a draft. The party was getting into gear.

When we saw Ramón and Evita withdraw and return home, we too followed them. I had my film, and it was good. I could ask for no better. The few inquiries we had been able to make about the cave of conquistador's armor all drew a blank. We hadn't scored on that story, but I had filmed an unknown Indian festival for TV.

That night our sleeping quarters were surrounded by Indians. They were drunk, but they were happily drunk. They danced around our room, sang, and shouted. I was all ready to go out and join them and was in the process of putting on my trousers when Evita came quietly into our room. "It is best that you do not go out there," she cautioned. "You can never tell when the Indians might sour. They have a savage streak in them that drink brings out. It is better that you keep out of their sight." Sergio and I heeded her warning.

The next morning was as quiet as I had imagined it would be. The valley was subdued by one horrendous hangover.

We said very fond *adios* to our hosts. I gave them a picture of me that they insisted they wanted. Salvador traveled back with us. Sergio and I stood well aside as Don Ramón and Doña Evita Mendoza bid goodbye to their nephew. He would see them again, but we knew that we never would.

We took a last look at the several stone walls that are the last of the Jesuit Mission San José Huacuibo, and speculated just where the legendary burial of gold might be. Then we moved on with Salvador as our guide. We were back in Creel late that afternoon.

Father Trampas was delighted by our story and was amazed at what we accomplished. He wrote the following testimonial:

"For 15 years I have been working with the Tarahumara Indians
with the purpose of bringing them civilization. Their beliefs are
rooted in the Sun, the Moon, and the Squirrel. In their ceremonies,
they sacrifice animals and offer them to the Sun.

They have never permitted white people to photograph their rituals.
I greatly admire the abilities of Mr. Wilhelmsen and Mr. Camalich
in being able to take these pictures. I can assure anyone that no one
before them has taken such photographs.

J. Manual Martinez, S. J."

Regardless of Father Trampas' tribute, we still had not come across any concrete information about the so-called 'Cave of the Conquistador's armor,' as mentioned by Erle Stanley Gardner. "You must go into the canyon, the Barranca de Cobre," Father Trampas insisted. "Just go," he said. "There are marvelous things there for you to see. Someone will know about your cave. Just go."

And so Sergio and I went. We loaded up La Mula and drove toward the rim of the Western Hemisphere's greatest canyon.

13 — THE SIERRA MADRE II

The Barranca de Cobre or Canyon of Copper is a canyon system that cuts through the Sierra Madre Mountains of the states of Chihuahua and Sonora, Mexico. It is four times as extensive as the spectacular Grand Canyon of Arizona. Our Grand Canyon has the Colorado River running through it. Mexico's Barranca has several rivers: the Urique, Verdes, Batópilas, and others. Each forms a canyon comparable to the Grand Canyon. None of them have been completely surveyed or explored. They are mysterious, often concealed by the reluctance of the Tarahumara Indians, who live there, to speak of them. They are wrapped in clouds and they are enigmatic. The railroad survey that Sergio and I used to arrive in the area is now complete, and passengers stop at a lookout place called La Divisadora. From there they gaze down into the 6000 feet or so of Canyon. The train conductor allows them an hour to buy a hand-made drum, flute, or violin from the Tarahumara who gather at the little station. They take their photographs

—perhaps for a dollar a piece—and then they reenter the passenger cars and continue on to either Mochica or the city of Chihuahua. In 1976, when my wife and I took the train ride, we remained up there in Divisadora in a fine little rustic bungalow. The entertainers put on a good show for us, and we all clapped and stomped and enjoyed the gutsy female guitarist and dancer. It was delightful and highly recommended.

In 1957 things were quite different.

The dirt road from Creel—all roads were dirt—began well, but as we approached the rim of the canyon, it deteriorated into huge slabs and boulders of rock that had been pushed up there by natural forces eons ago, during the formation of the canyon. Both Sergio and I took turns walking ahead of the Ford and pointing out a possible route. Some 40 miles took all day, but as night closed out the day, we knew we had arrived. The atmosphere changed.

Heat rising up from deep in the ravine pushed away the local haze and made clear the great ditch in front of us.

"Watch it, Sergio," I facetiously called to him as he motioned me to continue in the car. "Don't step back into the canyon."

He shouted back, "Check your brakes, Romain. I don't want to watch you sail out into the abyss."

Both of us were delighted to be there. There was still light enough in the sky to enable us to drive right up to the rim of the Barranca de Cobre. I pulled up, turned sideways, stopped, and stepped out of the car. "You want wilderness," Sergio exulted, "there it is. Take a look."

I was awestruck at what I saw. The shadows in the canyon had lengthened but here and there spurts of sunlight still clung to outcropping ledges and boulders. Reds and oranges, and purples and blacks formed a mosaic of colors all through the canyon. As the sun continued west, all color was suddenly gone and a black void stretched ahead and below us.

"Are we going down there?" I almost whispered to Sergio.

"That's what you came here for," my friend answered.

We set up camp where we were. Not a bad place at all. A little tree gave us cover that we didn't need. But that made it cozy above a plot of grass on which we could stretch our bedrolls. We talked into the night longer than before. We lay on our backs and looked up at the stars. It was the kind of night where one spoke intimately and was not afraid of revealing secrets. The stars and the moon and the blackness about us brought out an honesty in our conversation that is rarely achieved. We talked of everything: family, home life, ambition, beliefs, the girls, hopes, and fears. It was a night to remember.

When we awoke several Tarahumara young men were hunkered down a respectable distance from us. They were obviously awaiting to hear what we were there for and how they could profit by it. I fired up the Coleman stove and got the coffee going while Sergio engaged the young fellows in conversation.

We struck a deal. Julio, one of the teenagers, would guide us down and the other young man would watch the car and our goods.

My idea all along had been to go down into the canyon and to return *pronto*. There was no hope of exploring that vast maze of ravines. This hike would be mainly for photography and for publicity purposes.

Down we went with Julio carrying the camera and tripod. Down and down on a little foot trail that hugged the canyon wall. We literally passed through all the seasons of the year. We started in pine forests at 7500 feet, moved down about 5400 feet to oak, and then into the more tropical and very hot and humid conditions at 1500 feet. We finally arrived at the bottom. And what a chore and pain it was to get there. Even Sergio was bushed after four straight hours of scrambling over rocks.

A booming river ran through the canyon.

Far from being the first to get down there, we saw a group of Indians standing in the stream. They motioned us to back off. We did so, and these primitives then set off an underwater explosion. They were fishermen and as stunned fish surfaced, the Tarahumaras gathered them.

I was carrying the flag of the Los Angeles Adventurers' Club and I brought it out and had Sergio take a photo of me displaying it. The flag had never been down into Mexico's largest and deepest canyon.

We hiked alongside the river for a few miles, but were really oppressed by the breezeless humid heat. Father Trampas had told us about an iron door that would be in this area. Many of the old treasure trove books dealing with the southwest and northern Mexico had included a legend of a treasure hidden in a cave that was sealed by an iron door. Frank Dobie liked the story and put it in his book, *Coromadós Children*. He had heard it from travelers in the region. He never did get into the canyon, but he wrote several stories about it in his *Apache Gold and Yaqui Silver*. Now Sergio and I came face to face with the source of that iron door legend. Julio took us to it. It was there all right; a large very heavy and well made solid iron door with bolts, hinges, and a complicated locking system. "This is the door, *señores*," Julio explained, "where the early mining companies of the region used to store their explosives. It is cool in there and there was no danger of an explosion. I will show you." He gave a push to the big door that was fastened to the canyon wall, and it slowly opened with creaks and groans. Behind the door was a large hollowed out cave that had been empty for a long time. Other than destroying an old romantic legend, Sergio and I were pleased to enter the cave and enjoy the very cool ambience of the dark hollow space. We did joke together that if this cave was the keystone of the legend of the treasure behind an iron door, we had solved its mystery. We also hoped that the story of Spanish armor in a cave might not also prove to be nothing but a natural phenomenon.

We returned to the fishermen and asked if we could rent some mules that they had. "Just to get us out of this inferno," we pleaded. And so, Sergio and I rode out of the Barronca de Cobre in style. I had a good film and I was satisfied.

We slept the night on the rim of the Barronca, and the next morning drove away. La Mula was stronger than we were, it took us right back to Creel without a miss.

Father Trampas' Tarahumara Indian, the man who claimed knowledge of our Spanish cave, had disappeared in the maze of Chihuahua City. He would return but as Father Trampas admitted, "*Quién sabe cuándo*? Who knows when?"

I decided to call it a successful trip. For me it was. I had the films of the Banquet of Death, and perhaps the first movie films of the descent into the legendary Barranca de Cobre. With Father Trampas' blessing and a promise to return, we drove back as we had come. The return was no easier, but knowing the way eased our drive home. Nevertheless, it was a rough trip. Again the car did better than we did. Back in Hermosillo I almost had to carry Sergio into his family home. He had picked up a bug and was weak, very weak. When I returned to the Bouganvilla Motel, Manuel had to unload the car for me and tuck me into bed. Mike Ramirez, like a Jewish grandmother, brought me a big bowl of chicken soup. Two days later both Sergio and I were up and about. He was ready as ever to turn around and go right back to those mysterious mountains of the Sierra Madre. We made plans for the future.

I had no problem driving my vintage Ford back to California.

The media was quite generous to me once I let it be know where I had been and what pictures I had made. The *Pasadena Star News* heralded me as a local celebrity and the *Los Angeles Times* gave me an interview and published a front-page story with photos of the trip. Jack Douglas made two *I Search For Adventure* television programs out of my films, and I had the makings of another travel and adventure lecture film.

The problem with my lifestyle at this point of my career was that from October to May, I would have to take to the road and travel the length and the breath of the United States giving my lectures. Without the revenue that these lectures generated, I would not be able to go on with the legend-hunting that I so wanted to do. People often believe that to go on television in some sort of a series is an automatic source of riches. Jack Douglas in 1957 paid us $300 for a live show. Pretty good money for that time, but not nearly enough to cover the expense of making the film. As time went on and Jack syndicated his series, we began to receive residual checks that increased our income. Even they were never enough to keep us in business. That is where the weekly grind of travel and adventure lecture film personal appearances kept us going. The lecture platform was our bread and butter.

A few months after my trip to the Sierra Madre, while dashing about here and there all over the United States and Canada, a great gulp of fresh air came to me by way of a letter from Sergio Camalich in Mexico. "I have just returned from the mountains, and have found the clue that we are looking for. As Padre Trampas had suggested, I visited the Linguistic Bible translator, Paul Carlson. We talked about the Spanish cave and, though he knows nothing of it, he brought in one of the Tarahumara Indians with whom he is working. The Indian went to his home in the canyons and brought out an ancient crossbow. I had it in my hands. The weapon is definitely from early vice royal colonial times. He spoke vaguely to me, but I do think that he knows something about the Spanish cave." Sergio ended his letter, "I spent the profit of my last trip with you and can go no further. Tell me if you are interested in following up this clue." I do not have Sergio's letter in front of me; it has been lost. But the above is the gist of his message.

I did not return a letter. I sent him a telegram. "I will be in Hermosillo the week of May 10, 1958. Let us go find it."

✧✧✧

The lecture season had finished and I was free. Again I left my dark-eyed beautiful wife Julie the checkbook. I put $420 in my pocket. Again La Mula took me straight to Nogales, Arizona, with but one overnight stop near Gila Bend (I had hoped to see again the State Trooper with the troubled marriage, but he didn't make an appearance).

I had an interesting incident on the Mexican side of Nogales. As was usual when one would drive his car across the border, a minor Mexican customs man would direct it to a parking area. He would then direct the driver into the *Aduana* for a travel permit. I was hardly in the building when the young man who had pointed me there came running after me and shouted out to his superiors that he had discovered a quantity of cocaine or opium in my car. I knew this could not be. We all marched out to the Ford. Sure enough, spilled about the back seat area was a small pile of incriminating fine white powder. The young employee was elated; he had discovered a dope smuggler. I knew exactly what it was. In anticipation of the Spanish cave, I had brought with me a bundle of flares with which to light up the cave should we find anything. These flares were in the form of two-foot cardboard tubes. Like Roman candles. One of them had sprung a leak and spilled white powder on the floor of the car.

I was about to laugh it all off when the head *Aduana* man gave the eager young employee a vicious backhand slap on his mouth. He turned then to me. "*Señor*, many apologies but our young associate is new to the border. He doesn't know the workings of the *Aduana* here. Please forgive him and be on your way with our blessing."

I drove on down to Hermosillo where Manuel was waiting for me. When I explained the strange border encounter, he roared with laughter. "*Señor* Romain, that border is a thoroughfare of smuggling. Everybody there is part of the operation. They thought that you were a narcotics dealer, and as such was one of their people. The young whistle blower was not yet in on the take." Manuel shook his head. "Ah, Romain, you have arrived back in Mexico."

This story became a favorite of mine, especially after the big cocaine involvement in the United States. And the story is all the more bizarre when I ponder that I was not smuggling narcotics into Mexico, but that behind the back cushion of the Model A were five rifles. I was bringing in guns. Not semi-automatic weapons for a revolution, but single shot .22 rifles for the Indians with which to shoot small game for the pot.

Manuel had a thriving trading business with the friendly Apache Indians still living in the Sierra. Many of them had retreated from the United States after they had been subdued, and a lot of them still owned the old Frontier Model .45 caliber Colt six-shooters. Those guns are now highly valuable as collector's items. The .45 bullet is too big a slug and too expensive for hunting small game, and the old single-action piece was surely no target pistol. Aging Apaches had heard that at the Bouganvilla Motel they could trade their ancient fighting guns for an inexpensive and much more accurate .22 rifle. Manuel had a fine collection of vintage nineteenth century weapons. The rifles that I brought into Mexico would buy me much goodwill with the Tarahumaras.

Sergio was with me the next morning. He was full of stories that he had gathered. He even brought me a 16mm film that his priest had loaned him detailing some of the country that we would be traveling. We rounded up a projector and with Mike Ramirez's bags of popcorn; we gave an impromptu film presentation to Manuel's and Sergio's close friends. The film was all scratched up and not too well taken but the missionary had gotten far into the country, even to the Basaseachic Falls. These are the third highest waterfalls in North America; they drop an impressive 806 feet. But I, of course, wanted more. I wanted more than a good travelogue—there were already too many in my colorful profession. I wanted a real adventure, and perhaps the treasure at the end of the rainbow.

I was soon to get that.

"Romain," Sergio earnestly said to me once we were alone in my motel room, "I saw it with my own eyes. I had it in my hands. What is left of an ancient crossbow? It must be hundreds of years old. It has to have something to do with our Spanish cave. Where else could it have come from?"

Where else, indeed?

We made a shopping run in the new *mercado* or supermarket stores that were becoming the norm in Mexico. I bought what I needed. Good substantial canned goods this time instead of the primitive condensed Dri-Lite packages we had subsided on before.

We put the Ford in gear and rolled out of Hermosillo May 15, 1958.

On this trip we took a detour down to the ocean side town of Puerto Vallarta. I had friends there who were convinced that this place would be the next Acapulco in Mexico. When we finally got into this charming beach town, we were told that ours was the first car to drive into it and then to drive out (An American had driven a Cadillac here, through the Amaca River, and he said he would never drive it out; it went out on a boat). My friends had started well with a building they were converting into a hotel, but they didn't have the experience that would be soon needed for the expansion that Puerto Vallarta was about to experience. They soon returned home and others reaped the benefit of this now Class A tourist resort. The several wealthy American expatriates whom we met did not impress us. Parties were the order of the day. Drinking, bedding, and gossip were the excepted practices. The lifestyle was frivolous. It would have been easy to fall into the beachcombing party atmosphere of the place, but Sergio and I had our own plans. (I have been back to Puerto Vallarta. My friends were certainly correct in their original assessment of the resort: It does in many ways rival famed Acapulco.)

We drove back to the main north and south Pacific Coast Highway of Mexico, joined it at Tepic, and continued on down to Mazatlán. Then over the spinney ridge of the southern Sierra Madre to the city of Durango, capital of the state of the same name. We only experienced two flat tires. Durango is an interesting city. Anyone who is a fan of the John

Wayne movies of the 1960s might recognize some of it. He and his company with director Burt Kennedy made this area their home as they ground out several of the Duke's oaters. We now drove north to the city of Parral where I took a picture of the early seventeenth century church and the bridge where the legendary Pancho Villa was ambushed and killed in 1923. We continued north to the city of Chihuahua. This would be our point of departure for the mountains. We splurged on a good room for the night and a thick T-bone steak. Then, the next morning it was west toward the foothills.

The road was paved all the way to Cuauhtémoc. I stopped once to take pictures of a large lone mesa to the west of us. It is called Muñaca. This plateau, according to Frank Dobie, is the first clue to the location of the fabled lost Spanish gold mine of Tayopa. Our pavement stopped at La Junta. This is the railroad junction of the Sierra. Tracks running south from Ciudad Juarez and El Paso stop here as do those coming west of Chihuahua City. One little track then continues on to Creel (These railroad lines are all finished now and will take one right to the rim of the Barranca de Cobre and on west to Mochis and the Pacific).

We camped in Cuauhtémoc beneath the crumbling ruins of a famous old nineteenth century "villa of prostitution." We gathered wood, lit a bonfire, enjoyed a meal, and settled down to one of those very pleasant nights under the stars. An evening of talk, reminiscences, personal histories, a couple of drinks, a smoke for Sergio. Another evening to long remember.

But, just when one thinks he has it made, things can change. Just after midnight it began to pour rain. Sergio and I ended up beneath the car. I slept looking up at the oil pan of the motor, and Sergio was stuck with the differential of the rear axle. The old brothel had a reputation of being haunted. Neither Sergio nor I would care to spend another night there. We both compared our strange dreams the next morning, and wondered about the curious noises we had heard coming from the ruined buildings all around us.

The following day we were back in Creel consulting Father Trampas. His Tarahumara Indian had never returned from Chihuahua. "Probably got a job offer that he couldn't resist," Father Trampas excused him. However, after Sergio's independent reconnoitering the last winter, we felt we didn't need him. We set our sights on Paul Carlson, the Linguistic Missionary of Samerchique, where Sergio had seen the crossbow.

We stopped at an old church that had been built by the Jesuits, and then taken over by the Franciscans, called Basihuare. A Tarahumara fiesta and dance was in progress. Again, I had a field day with my cameras. Round and round the Indians danced. Then they began wrestling one another. Once a couple had embraced in combat that contest would not end until one had been thrown. Some of these matches lasted for hours. A great deal of tesvin corn alcohol was being consumed, and after a few hours Sergio and I decided we had seen and filmed enough. We had no contact at Basihuare as we had had with Don Ramón and

Evita at Huacaibo, and as Evita had warned us "drinking and Indians don't mix well." We drove on.

We had lost some time so we hustled La Mula along. It was getting dark when we spotted a pickup along side of the dirt road. The left rear tire was flat to the ground. We stopped, as is the Mexican custom, and Sergio called out, "Do you need some help?" A clean-cut young man came from behind the vehicle and answered in Spanish, and then in English when he saw me, "I sure could. I've got a flat, and I don't have my jack with me." We immediately got out of La Mula and introduced ourselves. He answered, "I am Paul Carlson of the Linguistic Institute. They call me Pablo. It is a real pleasure to meet someone up here who knows something about a car. Do you have a jack? Just call me Pablo. Everybody else does."

On Sergio's winter trip here, he had not met this man, only his Indians. And so we both now met this Bible translator who Father Trampas had told us to contact. We liked him despite his aggressive religious zeal. Carlson was young, still in his twenties. Very personable, and full of life. We fixed his car in a hurry.

If nothing else I had two tire jacks in the Model A. Lord knows, we needed them. They had been worked to death on the two Mexican trips. We were experts at changing tires, and soon had Pablo on the road again. He led us back to his neat little mission complex and introduced us to his pretty blond and lovely wife. "You must be our guests in the spare room," she quickly offered. "We are lonely to talk English with someone. We are so involved in working with the Tarahumara Indians, translating the Christian Bible into their language. We just don't see any Americans at all any more." She looked me in the eye, and asked me the fundamental question, "Have you been saved?"

I shot a look at Sergio, and then quickly answered, "Yes, of course."

My friend came to my rescue. "Your Indians, can they read? Can they read the Bible?"

"Oh, we'll have to teach them that, too," Mrs. Carlson gaily responded.

As Father Trampas had told us, she was delightful, as was her husband, Pablo. After a service of some sort she made a couple of excellent grilled cheese sandwiches. We enjoyed their company, and were more than gratified to hear that the Indian with the crossbow was in the area. "We'll have him here for you tomorrow," Pablo eagerly told me, and then went into a long religious sermon. Sergio began to nod, and soon so did I. Mrs. Carlson had already dozed off, so mercifully Pablo showed us to a very clean guest room. "This is for you," he said. "Please sleep well."

We began the next day nicely with pancakes and bacon. Pablo was off of his pulpit this morning and spoke to the Indians who had arrived to worship with him. The one I wanted to see was the one with the crossbow. "I'll call him in," Pablo said.

The Tarahumara Indian who was brought before us was a stocky man past middle age. He had a thick body and a broad face. Sergio recognized him. "That's him," he whispered to me. And the man immediately recognized Sergio. He went to him, and gave him an *abrazo*. "*Amigo*," he muttered.

"Did you bring it?" my friend quickly asked him. The man reached into a gunnysack that he was carrying and brought it out.

I could hardly believe my eyes. I took the old weapon in my hands and turned it over and over.

Pope Innocent II, in the twelfth century, had called the crossbow the "weapon of the devil." Some hundred years later Innocent III had banned its use in Christian warfare. In the later middle ages, the crossbow was regarded as the ultimate weapon. I thought of these things as I fingered this relic of the past. And I also thought, "What is a primitive almost Stone-Age culture Tarahumara Indian in the remote Sierra Madre Mountains of northwestern Mexico doing with it?"

The wooden handle was gone. The iron shank was pockmarked with age. And yet there was still a light spring to its bow.

The man answered our question before we asked it.

"It is from the trophy room. For a long time it has been there."

I knew that the Tarahumaras had places, loosely translated as 'trophy rooms,' where they kept venerable objects of the past. Lumholtz had written of such places in his books. These Indians don't keep written records, but they do gather mementoes. They pass down the stories of these keepsakes from one generation to the next. The stories often become confused in the retelling.

The Indian mumbled apologetically to Pablo, "To the south there is a valley with many similar things. We call the valley Rayabo Otsheloa. Nearby is Maula Rachki." Roughly translated, he was telling us that somewhere south "There is an obscure mountain ridge in which there is a cave that looks like the mouth of a yawning dog."

❖❖❖

The history of the northern Sierra Madre Mountains is sketchy. Missionaries and Spanish soldiers did not explore and prospect this region until after 1600. By then, the conquistadors had quit wearing the heavy cumbersome Spanish armor that they had brought from Castile and had used during their earlier conquests. The slow loading crossbow or *arquebus* also fell out of favor and was not used after 1550.

I am now referring to the notes that I had copied from the historical archives of the Los Angeles Library and the Southwest Museum that specializes in such matters.

A classic historical book on northern Mexico by H. W. Bancroft contains an obscure footnote to history. It relates how in 1532 one Diego Hurtado de Mendoza—a remote cousin of Cortez—wrecked his small exploratory vessel along the rocky coastline of northern Mexico, perhaps near where the Rio Fuerte flows into the Pacific Ocean. He salvaged his supplies and his arms.

With thirty-seven soldiers, some on horseback and many encased in armor, he set out towards the mountains. Then, as today, peaceful Indians pointed to those mountains and told of strange tribes and abandoned cities. These stories have never been disproved because even now there are many areas in Mexico known only to the Indians. Mendoza and his men rode on in pursuit of riches.

The Spaniards clanked over the horizon and disappeared. No word about them has ever come from the heights. History forgot them except for the soft whispers Indians use when they talk of the myths and legends while hunkered around the campfire on a chilly night.

And now, after all of those centuries, here was a crossbow where none should have been. We had found the 'smoking gun' of a mystery.

Or had we?

The Indian could tell us no more. He was reciting by rote the stories passed down through his family for many generations. When questioned by Pablo and Sergio, he had absolutely no clue as to where the landmarks that he mentioned might be. They were but a blur of many tales told to him by an old Indian now long gone who had himself heard the words from an older Indian long, long ago.

The man knew that he had disappointed not only his religious mentor, Paul Carlson, but also Sergio, the man to whom he had originally shown the crossbow. He actually teared up, but he would not fabricate the truth. "I can say no more," he whispered, "because I know no more." He sat down on Pablo's davenport, put his head in his hands as though trying to remember more, and then suddenly shook his head, thrust the gunnysack with the crossbow in it into Sergio's hands, and said, "Take it. It is all I have to give."

It was obvious, the man was telling the truth. He had no more to say. Sergio looked at me.

My cupidity surfaced. I said in English. "Take it. It is no more use to him," and I grasped the bag.

I looked at Paul. He nodded and said, "Take it. It is nothing but a reminder of the Papist Church's conquest of the Indians."

I didn't like the connotation. "They came to Christianize, Paul," I responded, "just as you have."

"But I don't bring any crossbows or weapons," he retorted.

"They made the country safe for you to bring your Bible." Then I softened, "It really didn't make much difference. In the end, the Indians killed whoever carried the crossbow."

Mrs. Carlson broke in, "Talk theology and history somewhere else. Not in front of this bewildered Indian."

I turned quickly to Sergio, "Take one of the .22 rifles from the car and give it to this man; give him a box of shells, too."

Carlson, I could see, did not like this trade off. Nevertheless, he replied to his wife, "You are right; I will not confuse Serifino with words." And then to me, "Take the cross-bow. I can see it means more to you than to him, or," he added, "to me. And, once he has given it away he will not want it back. That is the way it is with these Tarahumaras."

And so I came in possession of the survivor of a battle in the Sierra Madre Mountains long ago.

The stocky Indian soon left us. He firmly grasped in both of his hands his new rifle. He walked alone through a field of flowers. He looked back once and smiled at Sergio. Then he was gone.

I tested the steel spring of the bow, and said more to Sergio than to Carlson, "Now I know that the story, the legend is true, that it has substance. Somewhere in these mountains there is a Spanish cave." And then both to Sergio and the Carlsons, I said, "We will be leaving."

With but few words we gathered our things and drove away. I am sorry to say that our mood was not as it had been the night before. He withdrew from his former jolly rapport. We all shook hands, Sergio fired up La Mula, and we waved farewell.

(Years later, while lecturing in Atlanta, Georgia, I read this article in the *Atlanta Constitution* entitled: "Congo rebels may slay second missionary." The piece was datelined "Leopoldville, Africa, October 29, 1964. Several days later I read in the papers that 'Pablo' Carlson had been machine-gunned down. I have remembered him in my prayers.)

Sergio and I drove back to Creel. We were elated with the relic that we had. Nevertheless, we were right back to square one in our quest.

We immediately visited Father Trampas to show him our trophy. We found him sitting with a grizzly white-haired Tarahumara Indian. "Meet Clemente Cruz," the priest eagerly greeted us. "When I realized you were back in Creel, I sent for him. He is your man. The one I have told you about. He has returned from the big city."

Sergio and I were especially taken aback. We had driven to Creel in a quandary, not knowing where to turn. And now, here was another piece from that jigsaw puzzle of a Spanish cave.

"He has a story to tell," Father Trampas gleefully proclaimed. He put a huge pot of coffee on his stove and brought out four mugs.

Clemente Cruz looked at us from beneath hooded eyes. He turned to the priest who nodded to him. He told his story. Roughly translated, this is what he said. "I am one who is entrusted by my people to remember what has taken place during our past. There are several of us who do these things." He turned to Father Trampas, "Ignato Torino is one also." The priest prompted him to talk on.

"Several lifetimes ago," the storyteller continued, "before the coming of the Black

Robes (the Jesuit, Father Juan Fonte, who in 1607 was the first missionary to make his *entrada* into the high Sierra Mountains) there came a group of bearded Spaniards. They were looking for gold. The friendly Tarahumaras led them through a valley in which flows a river. The river was known for the gold in its bed. The Indians had scooped up the gold and fashioned ornaments. There were many nuggets to be found there. The white men camped. They had with them several horses that frightened the Indians. They had long spears, and very long swords, and some of them wore metal suits of armor. There were twenty or thirty of them. Several were ill and were being carried. Here they stayed and worked the riverbed and a mountain ridge for some months (not at all unlike the Adam's diggings of the nineteenth century in New Mexico). They maintained good relations with the Tarahumara Indians who kept them supplied with corn. In turn, they shared the deer that they ran down with their horses."

Now, the word 'Apache' has often been translated to mean 'enemy,' and, according to Clemente Cruz, "One day without warning, scores of our enemies raided the valley." The Tarahumaras were used to such incursions, and they managed to escape to the hills. But, taken totally off guard, the Spaniards were overrun. They were killed to a man. The horses were driven off and all forms of mountain creatures arrived to feast on the remains of the men. Soon even the bones were gone . . . consumed or scattered. All that remained was that which could not be eaten, Spanish armor, weapons, and (I like to think) gold. The Apaches were a nomadic people; they were not interested in these things. Eventually, the Tarahumaras did return to tidy up the mess. What little could be used was taken. The rest was placed in trophy 'remembrance' rooms, probably caves. It should still be there. We Tarahumaras do not disturb the memories of our past, nor do we steal from the dead."

Clemente Cruz looked at Father Trampas. He had a question in his eyes. The priest nodded encouragement. "Tell them where," he said. The thickset Indian did just that. He gave the same names that Paul Carlson's man had given us. I compared them to my notes: a valley called Rayabo Otsheloa and nearby Maula Rachki, the mouth of the dog. He was even better; he named rivers and geographical landmarks.

I had with me a very good geological map of the border region of the states of Chihuahua and Sonora. The Indian had somewhat different names for rivers and features on the map, but Father Trampas was able to sort them out for us. There is a large valley boxed in by tall craggy promontories where the Rio Piedras Verde enters the mountains. Clemente told us to hike them all. He hadn't been there since he was a boy, and there were reasons, he said, why he would never go back. But, he promised, in one of those gorges there is a cave with an entrance shaped like a dog's open mouth. This whole region is dominated and, in many cases, watered by the larger Rio Urique which flows through part of the Barranca de Cobre. The Urique River was on my map, but frequently the rivers depicted are as much as twenty or thirty miles removed from where they are shown to be.

I asked Father Trampas a delicate question in English, "Can this man be trusted? Is he telling old fables, or do you think he knows that what he tells us is true. There is a lot of country on this map. We have just so much time. I cannot waste it."

"The Tarahumara always speaks the truth," he answered, "or what they believe to be the truth."

Again, here was the big question mark. The "If."

"You game, Sergio?" I asked my partner.

"Of course," he answered.

That afternoon we put La Mula in the best condition that we and a local mechanic could. We topped the tank with gas and loaded up on oil. We went over Father Trampas' maps and our own, and worked out a course from Creel to the mountains.

I had good references from the 1902 Lumholtz book, and from a couple of other sources, that there is a valley of caves in the area toward which we were headed. We drove northeast to La Junta and then south into, what has been called for a hundred years or more, Mormon Country. When Utah was finally admitted into the United States in 1896, the Mormon practice of polygamy was, of course, outlawed. Many Mormon families disagreed with this restriction and some left the Saints of Utah and moved into northern Mexico. There nobody cared how many wives a man had. In 1958, and still today in 2003, those families and their descendents are still living as they have for over a hundred years. The way Brigham Young had said they could. They are close-mouthed and defensive. In order for us to get into that mountain country that Lumholtz had mentioned, we would have to seek assistance from those Latter Day Saints. We would need horses. The jump-off place would be a town marked on the map as Pacheco.

The road from Creel through La Junta, and partially down from the mountains that we had been traveling, was no problem. We arrived in colonial Juárez (not to be confused with Ciudad Juaraz next to El Paso on the Texas border), and were directed to the village of Pacheco fifty miles farther east and close to the foothills of the eastern Sierra Madre.

One could hardly believe that he was in Mexico by the looks of these Mormon towns. They looked more like Wisconsin than Sonora. They reminded me of little Midwestern rural farming communities.

I could only imagine what people inside of one of these neat little farmhouses thought when they looked out of their parlor windows and saw the 1930 Ford rattle up to their porch. We did see several pairs of eyes staring at us from behind hastily drawn curtains. When we stepped out of the car, their faces quickly disappeared into the obscurity of the house. I had been alerted to such behavior. These ladies were the wives of their common husband. They kept a low profile.

We clomped up on the porch and wrapped on the door. It was immediately opened by a middle-aged man who was the quintessence of what the movies portray as a man of the West. Everything but the six-shooter. Broad of chest, thin of waist, slightly bowed legs, homespun trousers tucked into Texas boots, a flannel shirt, and a red kerchief around his neck. He had steel-gray hair that contrasted with his slightly red, weather-beaten face. I liked his looks right away.

I tried English, and he answered in kind. I introduced myself and Sergio, and told him that we would appreciate it if he would let us camp out in his pasture. "Come sit on my porch swing," he suggested. He seemed relieved at what I had said. I have read that these Mormon colonies have been subjected to all kinds of harassment from American hoodlums and from Mexican officials who are envious of their wives and of their well-kept and fairly prosperous farms and ranches. He excused himself and went into the house. We noticed that he carefully closed the door behind him until he came back out with a pitcher of water and three glasses. "You fellows might like a glass of water from my spring well; it's the best around here. My name is Webber M. Cluff, and you're welcome to camp here as long as you want. I suggest the big tree over there. It's got a lot of shade and a brook running by it." He pointed to a really full tree about half a mile away. There were others closer, but I'm sure he would just as soon we weren't too close to the house. Some pleasantries followed, and then I asked him if Sergio and I could rent riding horses from him.

"You ride?" he sharply eyed me and Sergio.

"Oh, yes," I jumped in. Not quite true; the only riding I'd ever done was with Batanero and Flynn in the Andes. "I've ridden all through the Peruvian Mountains." Sergio chimed in, "And I belong to the Hermosillo Riding Club." I gave him a quick look.

"That answers that," Mr. Cluff grinned and continued. "Now, don't you start asking about renting from me or anyone else around here. We loan things. We help each other out. You'll have your horses. I ask if you can ride because they're only half broken. Don't want you to get hurt."

With that settled, I asked if he were familiar with cliff dwellings that Lumholtz mentioned in his book, *Unknown Mexico*.

"That would be Strawberry Valley; that's what the Indians call it. I've never been up there. I should have a look-see sometime," he reflected. "Sorry to say, I don't have anyone around here that could take you there." He chuckled, "I don't know nobody who went up there. Just stories I've heard all my life. To hear the old Indians talk about it, you'd think a giant is buried up there somewhere."

My eyes widened and I gave Sergio a sharp look. We had read of and heard of the legend of a giant burial ever since I became interested in the area. "Giant?" I questioned.

"Oh, those Indians will tell you anything." Again he chuckled. He was enjoying us. "Don't have a guide, but tomorrow morning I'll bring the horses to you, and tonight I'll draw up a little map showing you how to get from here to the valley of caves."

We set up camp by the designated tree and settled in for the night. We were congratulating ourselves on our good fortune when shortly after dark, Mr. Cluff returned into the light of our Coleman lantern. "Fellows," he called out to us as he stepped out of the darkness, "brought you a little something that the Misses fixed up. A bag of popcorn, warm off the fire and buttered the way I'm sure you'd like it."

We stood up and took the steaming bag from him. "I'd sure like to thank her," I said.

"No need," he quickly answered, "I'll tell her myself. We don't get many visitors here. Now, you sleep well. The weather looks good," and he faded away into the shadows.

"That is one nice man," Sergio commented, as we dug into as savory a bag of popcorn as I've ever tasted.

At 7:00 a.m., Cluff was back again, leading two horses. Big ones. Both saddled. He spread a paper map on the hood of La Mula, and let his fingers do the walking. "You'll be riding east into the sun," he pointed to the neatly drawn map. "That bunch of mountains over there," he now indicated with his arm the foothills in front of us, "you can't miss them. Keep your eyes open for a valley opening that enters from those mountains. It's the only way you can get into the mountains. Once inside you'll find other canyons leading into that valley. I am told there are caves all through those canyons and that in some of those caves there are cliff dwellings." He was a man of few words, and left us at that. He waved and called, "Let me know when you're back, and I'll stable the horses. And," he added, "keep an eye out for cougars. There's a lot of them around here." He stalked off to his house.

We had prepared a sack of supplies: canteen of water, a small bag of beef jerky wrapped in oil cloth, Sergio's smokes, a half liter of tequila, iodine and bandages, and other practical things. I strapped on my short barreled .32 caliber revolver, and Sergio tied one of the .22 rifles to his saddle. And off we went.

For riding a half-broken bronco, I surprised myself by doing quite well. And I could see that Sergio indeed was no stranger to the saddle.

The mountains seemed a long way off, but we ate up the miles at a steady pace. Their distant purple hue gradually changed to green, brown, and black as the haze evaporated, and we could make out the details of the craggy range or sierra in front of us. Three hours from Cluff's ranch, and we were in the foothills. Sergio, who liked to ride ahead, shouted to me. "There's the entrance," he called. "The mouth of the canyon that Mr. Cluff told us about."

We turned our horses into the canyon and followed a dry *arroyo* that seemed to lead past a maze of ravines and outcroppings in front of us. It was a very pretty and colorful area. There were lots of scrubby trees, huge boulders, brush, and stony crags through which we had to ride. There was no trail at all; we just went the easiest and sometimes the only way possible. "Sergio," I bellowed to him, "keep an eye on your landmarks. We're going to have to come back this way. Don't let us get lost."

"I will," he enigmatically called back. He was eager to continue forward into the labyrinth of the mountain range. I was right behind him. We had emerged from a quite level grassland into a confusion of stone and chaos as though a long time ago an earthquake had tumbled the sierra into a jumble of bewildering pathways. "Where do we go, Sergio?" I called to him.

He shouted back, "Toss a coin. I don't know which way. It's here or there. Come on up and let's talk about it. I don't want to make the wrong move."

We paired up and speculated. Our first choice ended up in a box canyon, a dead-end blocked by some old landslide. We backtracked and took another route, another canyon. Again we had chosen wrong. There were caves up along the canyon walls, but Sergio, who was the climber, went up to them and reported nothing but dung and a few bones.

Deeper into the maze, Sergio was getting a bit ahead of me when he suddenly stopped, turned around, and shouted, "Come on. We've got it. Here are cliff houses." I put spurs to the horse and joined him. Up on a cliff side I could see buildings. Not just one or two primitive shelters, but a whole metropolis of well-built stone and adobe buildings protruding from a cliff not more than a mile from where we stood resting our horses.

I had been to Mesa Verde, Colorado, and had marveled at those sensational cliff dwellings, but I now saw a canyon wall lined with ancient houses much more impressive than that very stirring Mesa Verde. And among those buildings along the mountainside, we saw a couple of huge strange structures that dominated them all.

We nudged our horses forward to the base of the cliff in which the ancient city was located.

"Sergio," I called to my amigo, "we have made a discovery. We're here where not even the Mexican archaeologists have been!" (I had visited the great anthropological and archaeological museum in Mexico City—considered one of the finest in the world—and, though it had displays of this northern area, there was no mention of anything like this at all.)

We dismounted and tied up the horses.

The climb into the caves was not a difficult one. Neither of us had trouble reaching them. The focus of our attention was a huge pear-shaped structure some thirteen feet tall and twelve feet wide. It was hollow with eight-inch thick walls that were covered with many coats of plaster or some sort of whitewash. It was an *olla* or granary, a fifteen-hundred-year-old silo that had been used to store the corn harvest that annually was gathered by the people who once lived in these silent houses all about us. No wonder timid Tarahumaras, peering from a cliff top or tiptoeing into this canyon and gazing into the cave, thought giants were buried here.

The Tarahumara, the Yaqui, the Apache know nothing of the builders of these cities in the sky. They knew nothing of the Anasazi, that strange and mysterious race of people who suddenly appeared in the southwest, built their cities, and a few centuries later just as strangely abandoned their elaborately constructed cliff dwellings and disappeared from history. Those well-built metropolises were in turn taken over by the Pueblo Indians who always referred to the vanished race of people as "the old ones who were here before us."

It is understandable that the primitive Tarahumaras of today, who often live in un-adorned caves and often bury their dead in those caves, are confused when they see such well laid out structures high upon a cliff side. The huge *ollas*, and there are several in the caves that Sergio and I explored, the Tarahumaras thought could only have been used as burial crypts for giants. Even in 1958, the Tarahumaras rarely stored food for the winter. They would never have understood that a millennium or more before they were born a race of people lived here who were culturally much more advanced than they are today.

By the time I had made my films of the place, and we had gone through three of these caves—all filled with walls, roofs, window frames, and doorways—and had had our lunch, the sun was beginning to make its way west. We both agreed that we did not want to be caught in this valley in the dark, and so we turned back.

And again we were in for a surprise. Shortly before leaving the mountain valley and entering the Mormon prairie, we saw the smoke of a campfire. We could see it a short ways up one of the ravines that we had bypassed. We turned away from our trail and went for a look-see. First, we heard the rustlings and the bleatings of a score or more of sheep. Then by the fire we saw a typical Tarahumara Indian with his woman and three small children. They were obviously preparing to spend the night.

"*Quevara,*" Sergio greeted them with an upraised arm. The man stood up from where he had been sitting. They began talking, and it was evident that my friend was having a difficult time understanding the man. He called to me, "He's a sheep herder and he's bring-ing his flock from up north somewhere to sell to the Mormons. He says he gets a better price there."

"Ask him if there is anything else around here worth taking a look at other than the cliff dwellings."

Now Sergio hunkered down and the two talked for several minutes.

"*Ay Chihuahua!*" Sergio suddenly shouted and leaped up. He rushed over to me and my horse, so swiftly that the animal shied back and reared up.

"Easy," I said to both Sergio and to my mount. They settled down.

"He told me," Sergio said with a rush of words, "that further up this valley where it widens there is an old Tarahumara burial or, if I got it right, he called it a trophy room of the 'people of long ago.' He says that the Rio Piedras Verde runs by it."

I was off of my horse in a moment. Rio Piedras Verde was the one concrete clue that Clemente Cruz had spoken of. Sergio continued, "He says there are green boulders along the river bank and in the river. That's why he called it the green stones river."

Sergio continued to talk with the Indian who had accepted a cigarette from him. And he now came up with the clincher. I made out the words in their conversation, and Sergio blurted them out to me. "He says this particular valley is called by the Tarahumaras Rayabo Otsheloa and that the big cave in it is known as Maula Rachki. He says that no one is supposed to go into that place. That Tarahumara chiefs as far back as memory have said that it should be left alone. Something to do with the Apache Indians. He apologizes that he is only here on this trail because it is much less of a journey, a shortcut from his ranchito in Temosachic.

They spoke again and Sergio laughed. "He is asking me not to tell anyone he came this way. He might get in trouble."

"Tell him our lips are sealed," I too laughed. Then I reached into my saddle bag and pulled out the little bottle of tequila. "Here, give it to him," I exuberantly said. "It is his. Take it all. He has just given us the whereabouts of the Spanish cave." I had no other way of thanking him. Sergio handed it over along with his pack of cigarettes.

We questioned the Indian some more and were convinced that he spoke truthfully and that the valley to which he referred was just a few kilometers up the ravine. We were satisfied.

There was no question of us going into the hills again this evening. Shortly it would be dark, and we would be lost. "We'll come back tomorrow," I told Sergio. "It is too late now." Both of us were pretty excited but neither one of us wanted to be out there after sunset. We could well imagine the cougars about which Mr. Cluff had warned us.

We said *adios* to the Indian, who was more interested in getting his new treasure open, the bottle of tequila, and we rode back to our trail. By the time we got to the Cluff ranch, it was dark, but we could see its lights from quite a distance. His dogs set up a clamor as we approached, and he greeted us heartily. "See you made it. Was getting a little concerned when it got dark. But, here you are. Find anything?"

"We found the caves and the cliff dwellings, and I did right well with my cameras. Really a good success."

"Glad to hear it," Cluff said as he unsaddled his horses and led them to a trough. "Looks like you had no trouble with the animals. Good to see you didn't froth them up. Thanks."

"Mr. Cluff," I came right to the point, "can we use them one more day? I need to go back and finish up one of the caves. We'll take good care of them."

"Got no use for them right now. Sure, you can have them. What time?"

"A little earlier," I answered. "Sunup."

"You got 'em. I'll bring them to you 'bout 6:00. Now, you fellows have a good rest."

We left him and hiked over to our camp. There was a lot to talk about. We had already gone over every aspect of the Indian's story. We played the 'devils advocate' with it, and we still came up with the thought that we had identified the location of what we had been seeking. Sergio admitted that the Indian had used different pronunciations of the clue words. They were Tarahumara words, and who were we to challenge them? There was, of course, a nagging feeling that maybe we had overreacted to the man's story. Should we have stayed with him, camped with him? But, no, we couldn't have done that; those horses had to be returned. Maybe, we speculated, we'll see the sheepherder tomorrow as we ride out that way. "Perhaps," I suggested, "a few dollars would persuade him to return with us, or maybe the .22 rifle."

Sergio thought not. "No, he was dead-set against having anything to do with that valley. He was afraid of it."

We didn't sleep well that night.

By 6:30 the next morning we were on our way, back on the horses, to the mountains. Added to our bag of supplies was a flashlight, a Coleman lantern, a shovel, a couple of large canvas bags—in case we got lucky—and the flares that I had brought from the States. We hoped we were prepared for any contingency.

We were worried when we did not encounter the Tarahumara Indian and his flock of sheep, and we were beset with doubts all the way into the mountains.

We made much better time than the day before. We knew the way. Our trail led us right into the valley opening and into the foothills. "Here," called Sergio, "here is the *arroyo* of the Indians, the one we had bypassed." We turned into it and soon came across the campsite of the Indian, his family, and the sheep. There too we saw the empty tequila bottle.

Now, we were riding into new country, east into the narrow gorge. "Kind of spooky," I shouted to Sergio who was in the lead. The gorge kept narrowing, and then suddenly the trail widened into a very pleasant looking valley. A narrow river ran through it and nourished vegetation for the whole area. The striking feature of the river was the many green pebbles of the riverbed and the green moss of the boulders along side of it. "Las Piedras Verdes" . . . the green stones.

The story was all coming true.

I was suggesting to Sergio that perhaps the green in the rocks and environment might indicate copper deposits when he, who was slightly ahead, hollered out, "There she is, the mouth of a dog. The cave. It is up there just to our right."

And, so it was. A yawning cave-opening that seemed intent on taking a bite out of its surroundings. "That's it," I shouted back to my friend. "There is no mistaking it. There can't be another."

We tied the horses to trees at the base of the cave, and scrambled up to it. An easy climb.

I was immediately disappointed at the shallowness of the cave. I had envisioned stalagmites and stalactites and all sorts of dramatic background. The depression in the mountain was no more than fifty feet. Then it quit. There was nothing to be seen but black earth, black walls, a high ceiling, and the smell of centuries of dung.

We backed off holding our noses. I took a good breath and went back to the horses. There I retrieved the Coleman lantern from its carefully insulated box. I undid the surplus green World War II collapsible shovel, and returned to the cave.

Sergio was already on his hands and knees pulling out of the earth what I thought

240

was a good size boulder. It was not a boulder but rather a mid-sixteenth century European iron helmet, an officer's helmet with earflaps, neck and back guard. The metal helmet was heavy, and it was complete.

I lit the Coleman and set it down by Sergio. He took the shovel and stuck it into the earth, and struck something solid. He scratched around the object, put his hands on it, and gave a pull. Clouds of dust swirled around us. We were patient. The dust settled and Sergio pulled from the loose earth a breastplate. The armor was solid and heavy and Sergio took some time to drag it from its grave. He marveled at the weight of the piece. Right beneath it was a back plate with metal fittings that matched the breastplate. Sergio wrestled it from the floor of the cave and laid the two together.

We said very little but kept poking the earth. Close by was a helmet with a big hole in it. And then there was another breastplate.

But then, after an hour of mining the cave, there was no more.

We searched for another five hours, but there was nothing else to be found. We dug, we sank the tripod rods into the earth, but there was nothing else to find.

We were not in any way disappointed. We walked out of there with an officer's helmet, earflaps and all, a breastplate with a matching back plate, another crudely fashioned breastplate—probably fashioned in Mexico—and a pike man's helmet that had at some time been repaired, but that now had a gaping hole in it. We had hit the jackpot.

While Sergio was digging, I had lit several of my flares and the moments of brilliant light enabled me to shoot a roll of movie film. It was sensational.

Carefully, we placed each of these articles into the canvas bags that we had optimistically emptied of our canned foods, and brought along with us. There was evidence of leather on the breastplate, but it disintegrated when we handled it. The back and breastplates fitted nicely together and iron hinges fastened them to each other. They would fit a man about five feet six inches. When later weighed, they tipped the scales at forty-two pounds together. What a load to carry around ones torso! They must have been transported on mules and then buckled on for combat. They had the look of fighting armor, all business. There were no decorations, no scrolls, no etchings. On the corner of the back plate is the armorer's proof mark . . . a neat round indentation created by the impact of a musket ball. Perhaps, if the bullet could penetrate the armor, the soldier would not have to purchase it.

We divided the loads, and securely tied our precious finds to the saddles of the horses. And we then rode back to Webber Cluff's ranch. Before returning the horses, we tucked the finds into the Ford and covered them with our gear.

We thanked our host profusely—we never did get as much as a glimpse of his wife or wives—and then we left immediately. I didn't want to linger in the area too long. Instead of driving back to Creel and returning on the closer but very difficult trail, we turned off of the dirt section of Highway 10 and were glad to see pavement the rest of our way. Forty-five miles took us to Highway 46, and then north to Juarez and El Paso.

Sergio was happy with his bonus, and when we reached Tucson, Arizona, I put him on a bus that would drive him in luxury south to Nogales and home to Hermosillo.

❖❖❖

The adventure had been successful and my story, pictures, and films caused quite a commotion. Jack Douglas TV Productions immediately signed me up for two live and syndicated shows. The *Los Angeles Times* and the *Pasadena Independent* carried feature stories about the trip. The Jesuit University of Santa Clara, that specializes in Spanish colonial history, requested me to bring up my findings and to give a lecture before their historians; and the University of Southern California sent a group of academics to my home to look over the relics, and, I suspect, to see if I would donate them to their museum. Best of all was Dr. Denzel of the prestigious Southwest Museum. He was an authority on ancient armor, and for six months all of these pieces were put in a special glass display case in that museum. He told me that the armorer's proof mark was truly unique. He had heard of only one such renaissance armor in existence today that contains one. "It makes your find priceless."

He also had a theory somewhat different than mine about the source of the armor. If true, it would make them all the more priceless.

Dr. Denzel speculated that these pieces came from the third greatest conquistador in the New World. First, of course, was Hernán Cortez. Then Francisco Pizzaro. And then the "Knight of Pueblos and Plains," Francisco Vázquez de Coronado.

In 1540, this man—much more humane than his predecessors—traveled north along the western foothills of the Sierra Madre Mountains. He was seeking his own El Dorado, the Seven Cities of Cibola. In the area of the Rio Sonora, Mexico, Coronado's friend the missionary Fray Marcos de Niza, was told by local Indians that to the northeast "where the chain of mountains end" there would be a large valley or, as he called it, an *abra*. There, he was told, lived people who "had vessels, nose and ear pendants all made of gold." Fray Marcos was excited. He had been with Pizzaro and had seen firsthand the riches of the Incas. This might be the same. His excitement, though, was immediately channeled into another direction. Scouts had come in from the north reporting cities with great buildings, and undoubtedly treasures just waiting for the plucking. Coronado's army moved north and eventually came to the Pueblo country of our southwest.

For close to two years, Coronado searched in vain for his Seven Cities of Cibola and his El Dorado of gold. Eventually, he was thrown from his horse in what is now New Mexico. His spirit was broken. He nevertheless held his army intact, turned around, and returned to Mexico City.

242

There were, however, men of his company who gazed greedily toward the *abra*—or opening in the mountains—as they rode back by the mouth of the Sonora River. Fray Marcos told them, and later wrote, what he had heard from the Indians regarding that area: "I heard in that canyon that there is much gold, and that the natives of this open canyon area in the mountains, make the gold into vessels and ornaments for the ears and *paletillas*, small spatulas, with which they scrape themselves to remove the sweat; and they are people who do not permit those on the other side of the *abra* to trade with them . . ."

History recounts that a group of Coronado's men—fired up by these stories of gold in the northeastern mountains—slipped away from the main column of over three hundred returning soldiers, and disappeared into the east and into the Sierra Madre Mountains. They were never heard from again.

Some relics of Coronado's *entrada* have been unearthed as far east as Lindsberg, Kansas, where they are on display. Why then, in a much more remote region, the shadowy Sierra Madre Mountains of old Mexico, might there not be more?

As the Tarahumara Indians often said to Sergio and to me: "*Quien sabe?*" Who knows?

14 — THE HAUNTED FORT

While I was studying at the Pasadena Playhouse State School of the Theatre of California in the 1940s, I met some interesting people. I missed out on some of the students who became the movie stars of the 1930s and early '40s such as Dana Andrews, Victor Mature, Bob Preston, and others. They were a bit before my time at the school, 1943 to 1946. And my time was a little bit before the Dustin Hoffman, Gene Hackman and several others who are currently in their prime. I did interest Raymond Burr, before his Perry Mason days, in my treasure and legend hunting plans. We actually formulated plans to charter a ship to bring out of Mexico a golden treasure that I had yet to find (and still haven't). However, at the Playhouse I also met—and am still in touch with—Truman Smith, who briefly studied there, and who was responsible for my going on one of my more interesting adventures.

Captain Truman Smith had flown the B-17 Flying Fortresses of the 8th United States Air Force over Germany during the Second World War. He too had some hairy adventures that he recently wrote of in his book, *The Wrong Stuff*. He continued flying after the war and ended up air lifting rubber out of the Amazon River basin. During World War II, the Asian sources of rubber were choked off by the aggressive Japanese Navy and Army. Then, right after the white flag went up and the fighting was over, the request for rubber skyrocketed. Detroit was back in the automobile business and couldn't keep up with the demand of car-starved Americans. The assembly lines were booming.

The Rubber Development Corporation was set up to return to the original source of the product, South America, and to bring rubber out of the Amazon jungle. Truman got a job flying the large P.B.Y. amphibious planes in and out of Manaus, Brazil, carrying tons of the bouncy stuff to the industrial world. The job lasted little more than a year because then the cheaper Asian plantations began to produce again.

While flying over the Amazon jungles, Truman and his crews saw some pretty open and unexplored country. He often took shortcuts, left the major river highways, and flew over unmapped jungle. Truman had bought an old Keystone 16mm movie camera and took films of whatever was unusual. What was unusual, on several of his flights over the Brazilian and Bolivian border, was a huge stone fortress a good hundred miles from any sign of civilization. There were no roads, no trails, and no people anywhere near the place. Yet, here were those massive European-style walls pushing out of the tangle of jungle. Poking out of its ramparts were dozens of centuries old canons. Truman's co-pilot made a couple of low passes to enable him to take some pictures. Their plane, on its second pass, was greeted by numerous arrows flying their way from the dense forest. They quickly gained altitude, and flew on. The closest landing strip was by the jungle town of Guajara-Mirim on the Mamore River. This river town was one of their regular stops to pick up a cargo of rubber. They were informed there that often planes coming into this place or flying out of it were the objects of arrows. Truman told me that the Indians even stole the landing light lanterns that were placed alongside of the runway for night arrivals or take-offs. When he asked the name of these belligerent Indians, he was told "Pacas Novas, and you stay clear of them!"

Truman and I met in 1947. One night he invited me and a few of his Playhouse classmates to his apartment to show us the movies that he had taken during his Amazon flights. I was all eyes and ears, and when I saw the large eighteenth century trapezoidal fortress suddenly appear on the screen I called, "Run it again." Truman did so, backed up his old Keystone projector and gave us all another look. Completely surrounded by an impenetrable jungle here, on what he told me was the Guapore River, was this relic of the past. When the aspiring young actors and actresses had all gone home to their artistic endeavors, I asked 'Smitty' to play it again. It lasted no more than 45 seconds, but it was all that I needed to put the Brazilian fort in the state of Mato Grosso on my agenda for a future look.

✧✧✧

"Julie," I said to my ever loving and lonely wife, "I'm going to go for Truman's fort. It would make a whale of a good show."

"You want to see Ernesto again," she teased, "and Flynn, and your tropical pals."

I agreed. But she continued, "Just promise me that one of these years when the brood is pretty well grown, you'll take me with you."

I promised again, and I was able eventually to keep that promise. In the meantime, Julie was there when I flew out of L. A. International Airport at 12:30 a.m. July 9, 1959. "No more Barbara Holbrooks," she admonished as I mounted the steps that took me up into Mexico's Aeronavis plane.

In those days, the flight to South America was somewhat slower than it is today. Mexico City, and a layover. Tegucigclpa, Honduras, for a night, and then TAN Airlines and on to Lima. TAN was a new airline in need of exposure and offered me a free flight if I would include a picture of their plane in my television and lecture presentations. No Barbara Holbrook, but the faithful Ernesto and Nieves Batanero greeted me at 8:00 p.m. at Limajambo Airport. Not only them, but also a reporter from the *Commercio Newspaper* was there to record my arrival and to interview me about my plans. "Do you have another pre-Inca city to track down? Are you planning new discoveries?" I was treated as a celebrity. Ernesto enjoyed the spotlight, and Nieves kept her consul.

None of the people who met me at the airport—including my good friends—knew that I carried a contract from the enigmatic Mr. Olds of the United States CIA I had been contacted shortly after an *L. A. Times Newspaper* press release had announced that I was returning to South America. I had been asked to report any Communistic sympathies that I might encounter, especially in "high places." Cuba, Bolivia, and perhaps Peru appeared to be targets of the "Red Menace." I kept those thoughts to myself.

On this visit to Lima, I stayed in the Hotel Wilson right downtown where, as they say, the action was. It was a better address than Barbara's and my old nostalgic Hotel Ventiocho de Julio, and it put me within walking distance of the presidential palace. Although asked to do so, I was not at all happy about snooping into the private doings of a country and people that I liked. I made the decision to myself to cut out the chaff and go right to the top, to the president of Peru himself, and to ask him *mano a mano* his political views. I wanted to get it behind me. With Ernesto's help, I got an interview with President Odria. As a travelogue cameraman, I had easy access to high profile government people who always want any publicity they can get. I did not at all enjoy the process of going through all sorts of self-important *politicos* in order to get to the top man. Stamps, counter stamps, seals, and signatures, and finally the man himself.

President Odria was a soldierly-looking man of broad face and features. He wasn't a dictator, but some said he was headed that way. Odria had been the top general in the army, and as such, it was said, gained the highest office in the land. He was a no-nonsense man, and I liked him.

We had an interpreter. (Ernesto had been left out of the meeting; I don't know why.) Odria was straightforward in our conference. "Sir," he said to me, "I will speak to you very frankly and not politically as I must do with the ambassadors of your and other countries. I came to this position because of my rank and popularity in the army. The government is afraid of me because I have come up from the ranks and am not a political appointee. I work for my country, not for the bureaucratic establishment. Because I am liked by the workers of the nation do not think of me as a Communist as some do. I married an Indian woman from the Yungas (jungle region). We are much happier than most. She has no ambition or social standing. They all consider her an Indian, someone way beneath their station in life. So, Mr. Wilhelmsen, we have been ostracized from polite society. We are not invited to the grand balls and social events for which Lima has been famous for centuries. We are outcasts in our own country. But," and his voice now had an edge to it, "I have the power. I have the army. I will build this country as my predecessors never did."

President Odria allowed me to make a film of him with all of his medals, and then my time was up and I left.

(President Odria, at the end of his first term in office, opened up the election polls for a free democratic voting process. He was sure he would be reelected—as he had told me—but he wasn't. His Indian wife was not acceptable to the power brokers of Peru. The soldier and his modest wife stepped down quietly and faded away. The man had done well: new schools, roads, and good works. Once he was gone, the Peruvian sol went to pot and inflation became the norm. I liked the man and so reported to Mr. Olds, my CIA contact. I saw no particular threat of Communism in Odria, although, in time, the Marxists would surface in Peru.)

Now there was the obligatory bus drive up to Trujillo to meet with the Batanero family and friends. I couldn't go all the way to Peru without seeing these people to whom I felt so close. We all enjoyed our visit. I walked the Spanish streets of the city, felt a kinship to it, paid my respects to the burgeoning beauty, Marie Seminario, and then announced to Ernesto and Nieves, "I must go on to Bolivia; it is why I came here."

"*Señor* Romain," Ernesto reverted to his old nickname for me, "go slowly and cautiously in that country. I have traveled there in the past when I was with Pan Am. I met and married Nieves there in Cochabamba. If you think Peru is a touchy place, you will find Bolivia much more so."

After a couple days of the Batanero hospitality, I boarded a Morelos bus and boomed through the night to Lima. And two days later I was on another bus heading into the high country to Arequipa. No Barbara to keep me company on this twenty-hour climb into the Andes . . . just the usual jolly Indian lady who apparently didn't mind when I occasionally dozed off on her shoulder or ample bosom. She had only one baby to nourish, so she found room for me. We arrived there at 5:00 a.m., and I had five hours in which to stretch my legs and pick up coffee and rolls. At 10:00, I was off again for the twelve-hour drive to Puno on the shores of Lake Titicaca. Bad timing. The traditional tourist hotel was all booked. But, typical of this friendly country, I was given blankets and a pillow and told to make myself comfortable on one of the voluminous sofas in the lounge in front of the fireplace. I needed that fireplace because it was bitter cold at over 10,000 feet. Puddles of water outside were frozen.

The next day I was moved to a small, but cozy, room that had no heater. No wonder everybody in Puno seemed to be bundled up in two heavy sweaters and a jacket. Once in the sun one's bones do warm up, but the difference in temperature from shade to sun was at least 25 degrees.

In 1959, and for a thousand years before, a tribe of Indians called the Uros lived on floating islands of Totura Reed on Lake Titicaca. I was told that some of these people never leave the thickly matted islets. They are born there and they die there. Some never come over to the mainland or even show an interest about what goes on in the rest of the world. There was plenty of fresh water, sun-dried tortura reed to burn for heat and cooking, and an undiminishing supply of fish and other aquatic creatures to put in the cooking pot. As did the Incas before them, the Uros worshiped the sun, and in the distance they could see two mountainous islands called by the Incas the Island of the Sun and the Island of the Moon. Buildings and altars had been erected on those islands a thousand years ago. They are now abandoned, but I was told that the people of Puno believe the Uros still go to those altars and leave fish as a sacrifice. The Uros of 1959 were gradually becoming extinct. Only a few hundred of them were there when I approached them. And now in the twenty-first century, I do believe they are all gone or have been moved by the government.

Uros Indians would make an intriguing film sequence. I teamed up with an aging French couple and a honeymooning Chinese couple to rent a little launch and to go out into Lake Titicaca for a look. It was a very interesting afternoon made all the more entertaining by the Frenchman's volatile temper and vociferous comments to our motorist. Like many French travelers, Monsieur found fault with much that was not French, and couldn't keep his comments to himself.

The Parisian couldn't fault the Uros Indians though; they were hospitable, courteous, and helpful. Like all highland Andes Indians, the ladies wore voluminous skirts and blouses made of colorful cloth that their fishermen bring from the mainland where they trade them for fish. The men are all expert fishermen. They were nice looking fellows who seemed honored at our visit and our interest in them. They were totally at a loss as to what I was doing with my still and movie camera, nor did they shy away, ask for money or turn their backs on us. Even Monsieur was pleased. And, of course, later on, my television and lecture audiences enjoyed with me again these solitary people.

While in Puno, I also hired a car and driver to take me out to the little visited chulpas of Sillastani. Chulpas are well-built stone silos, some over ten feet tall, which are found all about a small lake called Umayo. This lake is about fifty miles from Puno in a rather lonely area. Archaeologists are still debating the reason for these well-built hollow tubular buildings. Hard to believe they were watchtowers because there would be no reason for so many of them. Bones have been found in them, but it is thought that these bones were placed there long after they were erected. The chulpas are one of the many mysteries of the Andes Mountains. I was seriously told by my driver that on one day of the year, if one goes out into the center of Lake Umayo and looks down into it, he will see a large stone city totally immersed in the frigid waters. So far, no one has come up with that one correct day of the year . . .

On the drive back to Puno in beautiful twilight, my driver and I passed a small village where a *fiesta* was in progress. I halted the car and got out hoping for some good 'grassroots' film footage. And, I really did get some quite wild stuff. Women, whirling around with those big round skirts spreading out around them were worthy of a well-choreographed Broadway or Las Vegas musical. Men, leaping in the air swinging their partners in all directions became almost a dream sequence. I got it all in the camera. But then the scenario turned ugly. The whole community had been imbibing freely of chi-chi, the native brew, and suddenly they resented this alien intruder with his inquisitive camera. Fingers were pointed, and then arms were directed my way, and soon I was surrounded by a mob of villagers. Fortunately, a couple of the Peruvian Civil Guards were on duty—they often stand watch over these all-night parties—and I was gently eased out of the area and into the car. In no uncertain language I was told, "Move along. Leave these people alone." I did just that.

My experience has shown me that often a little touch of fate or luck gives us all, once in a while, a helping hand. In the Hotel Turistas I met a Swiss engineer and his wife who spoke perfect English. They had an automobile and were preparing to drive around the southern shores of Lake Titicaca to La Paz in Bolivia. As gracious people, the offered me a seat in their car, and they did drive me the whole distance. We left Puno at 9:00 a.m. and arrived in La Paz at 6:00 p.m. I produced my wallet but they vehemently objected to any thought of payment. This man worked on one of Bolivia's sky-high railroads. While we had stopped for lunch, a picnic basket lunch, he had pulled up his shirt and showed me a string of bullet holes in his back. He told me that a couple years before he had been machine-gunned by Marxist Indians who had decided to take the railroad from its foreign operators. "They got rid of us," he laughed. "They sure did. They shot us up and put us on the train that took us to a hospital in one of the big cities. And then, after realizing they didn't have the training to run the train themselves, they decided to hire us back again. Watch how you handle yourself when you are alone with these people," he admonished as he and his wife drove away from the Hotel La Sucre where they had deposited me.

The Sucre was La Paz's best hotel at that time, and I was not at all averse to paying the $6 per day for a quite nice room.

Again, it was my destiny to run into a German. The manager of the establishment was a big strapping man from Mainz who spoke excellent English and played classical music on his hi-fi all throughout the lounge. I told him what I was doing in Bolivia, and he immediately turned the desk over to a Bolivian and escorted me to the adjacent bar and bought us a drink.

In the 1950s, the hunt for ex-Nazis was going strong and such countries as Uruguay, Argentina, and Bolivia undoubtedly had their quota of Third Reich ex-soldiers on the lam. I doubt if this man was one of them. He talked openly and intelligently about the political situation in his adopted country. Like most Germans in the west, he was deathly afraid of the network of Communistas that were spreading like a red dye through the governments of Latin America. "The countries are poor, have always been," he said, "and yet there are some very, very rich people living here. The poor resent that, and when the agitators tell them that they too can get into the pockets of the rich by joining the Soviet movement, well, there's a lot of fertile ground that the red seed falls into." When I told him that my next stop would be the city of Cochabamba, he cautioned me. "That's the main center of unrest. Go carefully there and quietly. There are some pretty mean *hombres* down that way." He placed a thundering piece of Wagnerian music on his turnstile and I gave him a sideways glance—Wagner was Hitler's favorite composer. He continued on, "You must meet Charles Perry Weimer. He is staying with us. He, too, is a camera man. I'll have him in the coffee shop at 9:00 a.m. for breakfast. You should get together." One certainly encounters interesting people in Latin America, I thought.

Charles Perry Weimer was tall, taller than I am. He had an intriguing look about him, and an engaging manner. Weimer featured a long neatly waxed mustache, hollow cheeks, mischievous eyes, and an elegant casual demeanor. He always wore his trench coat and always had three still cameras hanging from his neck. We got along just fine.

Over bacon and eggs, Weimer told me his story. He, too, had been a travelogue film lecturer and had appeared in many of the same lecture platforms that I had. The premier travelogue impresario of the United States, George Pierrot of the Detroit World Adventure Series, later told me that "when Charles Weimer was good, he was the best, but when he wasn't, he was the worst. He'll tell you that he has the greatest film ever made, and then prove it. He'll tell you the same thing next season, and he'll drop the biggest bomb this side of Hiroshima."

Charles wasn't working the travelogue circuit when I met him. He admitted that he was living on the largess of his wealthy eastern socialite wife, and was now traveling Latin America looking for opportunities. He was paying his way by freelance still photography. We had a lot in common—except the wealthy socialite wife.

"If you have a camera," he said to me, "you must be in Cochabamba this coming week. The president of Bolivia is flying there to confront his opposition. Many are Communists. The meeting is going to be interesting. Very interesting. There may be some fireworks, and I don't mean just the fun kind. I'm going."

"Perry," I answered back after his speech, "I already have my ticket bought." In order to get to the jump-off place to Truman Smith's chimerical fort in the jungle, I would first have to go to Cochabamba and from there to Guajara Marim on the Brazilian border.

That afternoon, Perry Weimer took me to the main newspaper of La Paz, the *Nación* and I again made the front page. Weimer was a man who got things done.

That night in La Paz, Bolivia, I became a millionaire and I made a movie sequence of my recently acquired wealth. At 8400 Bolivianos for $1 American—at that time the rate of exchange —my $120 came to over 1,000,000 Bolivianos. I piled them up on my bed and had quite a time pushing them around in front of the camera. I've been trying to get up to another million ever since.

The ex-German-run airline, Loyds of Bolivia, flew me out of La Paz at 5:00 p.m. This flight is always tricky because the air is so thin at over 12,000 feet. The plane literally needs miles to become airborne. The problem had been solved by running the main airport landing and take-off strip right to the edge of a plateau which allowed the plane to drop a couple thousand feet in order to pick up sufficient speed to be on its way. Several wrecked planes alongside the landing strip were not encouraging. Spooky! It was a one-hour flight that gradually dropped us down from those chilling heights to semi-tropical Cochabamba. I taxied to the Hotel Colón and found Perry in the bar sipping a biblia, which is the cocktail of Bolivia.

I had been told that Cochabamba was a hot bed of Communist intrigue. On many of the city and building walls, for all to read, were innumerable Communistic slogans. There were enough to make any American feel ill at ease. Perry and I stayed with those people of the United States we could latch onto. We almost immediately received a dinner invitation from the director of the U. S. CARE program and his wife. The next day, we were taken out to lunch by Dan Stewart of the International Corporation Administration, and that evening we stayed up until 2:00 a.m. at a party thrown by Sergeant Stan Burges of the U. S. Mission to Bolivia. Social life for an American in Cochabamba was booming.

The L-O-B planes flying to Guayaramarin (note the Bolivia Spanish spelling of that city which is bisected by a river) ran an erratic schedule at best. They were booked way into the next week. Waiting that long was hard on my budget, but it did work out very well otherwise. My new social contacts included Carlos Manning, a *político* who in turn lined me up with a *Señor* Cañedo, the secretary to the governor. And that gentleman put me into a V.I.P. group who would meet with President Silas Suazo when he flew in for his rally (I was fast learning how to do business in Latin America). The president's arrival would take place fifty miles out in the countryside where airplane landings could be controlled. My filming luck was hanging in there.

On August 2 at 8:00 a.m. I was downtown in front of the building of the Prefectura. There I was joined by some twenty extremely colorful and dangerous looking men. They were to be the local guard for the *presidente*. Apparently, in this region, Sila Suazo felt that he could not trust his own army officers; these loyal partisans were to be his personal guards. Some were dressed in casual business suits, and others were in hunting outfits. All of them were armed to the teeth. Each man carried a revolver or automatic pistol on his belt. Many of them carried .306 rifles. I saw a couple of model 94 Winchesters, and several carried portable machine guns. This reminded me of photos I've seen of Pancho Villa's men in 1913. These wealthy Bolivian businessmen, hacendados, and mining people all had a personal stake in the stability of their government. Cañedo introduced me to them; they

251

greeted me and my cameras quite enthusiastically. One of them shoved a revolver into my belt and shouted, "Now he is one of us!" they then all posed for a photo.

We piled into the stake-bed of a large truck and drove fifty miles to where the plane was landing. We passed through several little communities and wherever there was a group of people assembled, my comrades would shove their guns over the sides of the walls of the truck and shout, "*Viva Silas Suazo!*" A few bottles had been going the rounds, and the boys were all in a good mood. That mood occasionally necessitated a few rounds of gunfire into the sky.

We came to an open field surrounded by rolling hills and pleasant little farms. We were just in time because a DC-3 plane was then circling the landing strip that had been recently plowed and leveled. Several thousand people greeted the aircraft as it came in for a landing. The president stepped out. He was dressed in a neat blue business suit, tie, and felt hat. He was directed to where I and a couple of dignitaries were waiting. He joined them and I got my pictures. Then he was put into a 1952 Chrysler Town Car. Off we went for another hour with our armed truck leading the caravan of several cars.

We came to a stone monument where we stopped. We were ushered into a large rustic building nearby and luncheon was served. For whatever reason, I was directed to sit directly opposite the president of Bolivia. We used the same saltshaker, and the same coffee pot, and we shared a few thoughts. The president told me that the man he overthrew in the recent takeover of the government, ex-President Lachine, was "red as a beat." He told me that that man walked off with $60,000,000 from the Bolivian Treasury. Another politician with Communist leanings, Nueflo Chavez was now trying to unseat Suazo. I lost a lot of the story through interpreters and language differences, but what I did get was one hot item for our CIA. (A few years later, when Che Gueverra attempted a Castro-like takeover in Bolivia, the men in this area that I was visiting stopped him and ended his revolutionary ideas for good.)

We were all ushered out to a raised wooden platform and podium where the president made his speech. Much of it was lost to me. Language and a poor mike system.

I was pleased, though, to feel a friendly touch on my shoulder. Perry Weimer was right behind me. We joined forces.

A railroad track ran through the valley and several railroad cars were waiting to take the president into Cochabamba. He was afraid, and refused to fly into the airport there. At lunch, he had told me, "What you can't see will someday get you." All of the *carabineros*— as my escorts were called—were loaded into a pullman car that bore the seal of the President of Bolivia. He would be well protected. Perry, a few others, and I were directed to a second-class car.

So back to Cochabamba we clickety-clacked on the tracks. Once there we found out that just six seats behind Perry and me sat the president and a couple of his most trusted politicos. There had been intelligence rumors that a plot was afoot to blow up the presidential car. The *carabineros* had acted as decoys while Silas Suazo slipped unobtrusively into our second-class chair car. When we arrived in Cochabamba, he awaited Perry and me as we stepped into the railroad station platform. With a smile the president greeted us. "*Muy interasante*, but you didn't get an international scoop, did you?"

Perry and I celebrated our fruitful day with a filet mignon steak at the English Club in the center of Cochabamba. I hadn't gone back to my hotel room, and was still carrying the long barreled revolver that had been thrust into my belt. The next morning, I carefully wrapped up that gun and took it to *Señor* Cañedo in the Prefectura. He marveled at such prompt honesty, and when I asked for the favor of placing me on the next plane to Guayaramarin, he held up his hand to stop my request, picked up the phone, dialed, barked several commands, and said to me, "Your plane leaves tomorrow morning at 7:00 a.m. You are confirmed."

The flight out of Cochabamba ended well, but I began it with great misgivings. The passengers climbed aboard a DC-3 and settled in, and there we sat for two hours. The left motor wouldn't start up. We waited for a mechanic to come on duty, and eventually, at 9:00 a.m. a ladder was wheeled to the plane and the mechanic climbed up to the motor. He reached into his leather bag, brought out a screwdriver, and removed the cowling of the motor. He poked around the insides and motioned for the pilot to fire it up. Nothing happened. He fiddled around somewhere and still no action. Finally, in disgust, he removed a heavy open-ended wrench from his belt and gave the obstinate motor a couple of hefty blows. He leaned back and waved to the pilot. The motor started immediately. He refastened the cover, got out of the way, gestured to the pilot, and off we went. Like a prizefighter joining his hands together over his head after a successful knockout, the mechanic waved us off in triumph.

We flew north into jungle country. The green savannas with their herds of cattle gave way to spotty forests, less humanity, and more rivers containing, what looked like little toy boats covered by straw roofs, coming and going on South America's great inland waterway system. Our first stop was Trinidad. We were there for a couple of hours and all got out to visit, sightsee, or, in my case, to take pictures. I was quite surprised to see many Communist slogans and graffiti on the walls and buildings of this pretty little tropical town. The hammer and sickle was everywhere. The next touchdown was Magdalena, then San Joaquin.

I had in my file of notes several good stories that I would dearly have liked to look into. One has since been pretty thoroughly examined, and I can now scratch it off of my list. The Bolivian town of San Vicente was in the news in 1969 when the blockbuster movie *Butch Cassidy and the Sundance Kid* was released. Butch and the Kid shot it out with the Bolivian Army and were killed there. Being a Western buff, I had been well aware of that dramatic encounter many years before it hit the silver screen. Knowing the value of guns that once belonged to famous and infamous old timers—some bring $1 or $200,000 or more by collectors—I always thought that if I could go to San Vicente with some U. S.

dollars and locate one of the guns that Butch and Sundance had on them, I might be able to make a favorable deal. Their bodies were buried, but I'm sure not with their guns. Perhaps some old resident might want to part with that rusty six-shooter in his papa's trunk. An American crew recently exhumed what may or what may not have been the remains of those two romantic outlaws. They had permission from the San Vicente officials—paid a lot for it, I'm sure—but nothing conclusive was found. Those heavy revolvers didn't disintegrate. They're down there somewhere in someone's house.

The other site that has interested me since I first read about it in 1946 is the buried Jesuit treasure of Sacambaya. The story goes that just before the Jesuits were expelled from Bolivia in 1767, they gathered the wealth that they and their Indians had been accumulating for over a hundred years of successful gold mining and buried it in a hill alongside of the Sacambaya River. Of course, a couple of old documents have surfaced that tend to authenticate the hoard. In 1920, an Englishman, Cecil Herbert Prodgers, dug into that hill, found a huge egg-shaped boulder that the documents mentioned, dynamited it, and began his dig. He found a jewel studded crucifix. But then poisonous fumes came pouring out of the mound. They nearly killed him. Prodgers recovered in England, and then returned. But the local workforce was so unreliable that he soon gave it up, went home and wrote a book, *Adventures in Bolivia.* There have been other attempts, but from what I read of them, they were only halfhearted. I know that I would never have the funds and collaboration to seriously attempt the project. Nevertheless, the story, the existing documents, the crucifix, and the egg-shaped boulder are all proof of something hidden alongside of the Sacambaya River in eastern Bolivia.

And so, I flew over those Bolivian rivers, pampas, villages, foothills, and mountains, and let my mind do the dreaming. Perhaps another time!

In that mind of mine there are two varieties of jungle: the bright emerald green that pleases the eye and is inviting, and that today we call the 'rain forest.' And then there is the very dark, almost black green, that has a foreboding look to it; that I call 'the jungle.' As we approached Guayaramarin, Bolivia, this unattractive jungle came into focus as we descended and touched down on a lonely strip that stretched out into the forest. I noticed also that the pilot gunned his engines as he turned around and then taxied back to the tired looking hanger and buildings that were quite close to the town proper. I remembered my friend Truman Smith's story of Indians who shot at his PBY on this very landing strip just nine years before.

There were no cars or trucks, so a young boy piled my baggage into a wheelbarrow, and we walked into town. Not much of a town. Guayaramarin consisted of several blocks of wooden buildings surrounded by small farms with their respective buildings. We walked to the Hotel Royal, which was anything but royal. My stuff was wheeled into a room where several hammocks had been strung, and I was told, "This is it. Seventy cents American." I tried to be humorous when I pointed out several five-inch spiders clinging to the walls, and said, "Does that include them?" In effect, I was answered, "They live here. They keep out the bad ones." Each hammock had a mosquito net draped over it.

I left my bags and went into town to the Maryknoll Mission Station that I knew was here. This is mainly an American Catholic mission, and I hoped that the Maryknolls could help me with my plans to go up the Mamoré and the Guaporé Rivers to Smitty's fort. I banged on the screen door of a large one-story cottage-like building, and the door was quickly opened. A tall good-looking young cleric in a long white tunic greeted me, extended his hand, and introduced himself, "I'm Father O'Brian from New York, and who might you be?" I told him my story, and he more than welcomed me. These missionaries, all from the United States, were deep in their duties here in this isolated jungle post. They were very happy to see a fellow American who was also now in this same jungle hole that they were.

One of them, a clean-cut-looking blond priest, asked, "Where are you staying?"

"At the Hotel Royal," I responded, "with a bunch of monster spiders."

There were some laughs, and another prelate said, "Not any longer. Get your bags and come on over here. We've got a spare room, and you're welcome to it." I moved in immediately, and not just to save seventy cents a night.

My luck continued to hold. I set up in a small but neat little room with the Maryknolls and left the spiders behind me—for a while.

I seemed to be the star attraction that evening at dinner. These men were pretty well talked out and a visitor from the States was a source of all sorts of information. They served a big bottle of wine and kept pushing it my way, so I became quite loquacious. I enjoyed the evening and the rather tough beef dinner they served; they did their own cooking. We all had a good visit.

I spent five days with these fine gentlemen, and I learned a lot. Father Ambrose Graham was a great source of information. He had just come down the Mamoré River from the Abuña River where he had been doing missionary work among the Pacaguara Indians north of this station. Father Ambi, as he liked to be called, originated in Brooklyn, and he had a very pronounced accent to prove it. He was more of a vagabond than his comrades. They seemed more content to stay at their mission and tend to their school for children. Father Ambi preferred cranking up his outboard motor and traveling the rivers in search of untamed Indians. "It won't be much longer though," he told me one night over a beer after the others had retired, "before they'll be sending me back to the Mother House in the States. I've got a case of malaria that nobody seems to be able to tame. I do think I've used up most of my energies." He looked it. His face showed the effect of years in the tropics; it was marked with the bites and stings of innumerable bloodthirsty jungle insects. On his back was a vicious looking scar, now long healed, where a giant anaconda had bitten him. He pulled up his tunic so I could inspect it. "Anacondas aren't poisonous, you know," he explained, "but they have a couple of long and very sharp teeth. Their jaws are articulated so they can unhinge them. This flexibility allows them to stuff animals like pigs, tapirs, does, and other game into their gullets and then let the strong muscles and juices of their body pull the unfortunate creature in where it will be slowly digested. You've seen photos of them, anacondas and boas and other constrictors with a huge lump inside of them. The anaconda uses those long teeth to bite into a prey and to get a good secure hold or grasp while the coils wrap about the victim's body." He indicated his old wound and said, "This mother dropped out of a tree hanging over the river as I came by in a canoe. I'll swear it was thirty feet long, heavy and fat. He got hold of my back and before I could get to my gun, had me pretty well trussed up. I knew if it tumbled me into the water, I was a goner. So I held onto the boat with one hand while it kept encircling me. With my other hand I managed to reach my machete. I keep it razor sharp, and I was able to nearly cut the snake in two. It finally let up, and I extricated myself. The head and jaws were still locked into my shoulder, and I literally ripped them out. I came down with quite an infection after that and nearly died." He laughed, gulped his beer, and continued, "but so far they haven't been able to kill this old body. But, I admit, it's pretty well used up." He stood, stepped out into the tropical garden, and relieved himself.

Father Ambi came back and sat down again. "Pacas Novas Indians. That's who you might meet where you're going."

"Tell me about them," I asked. "My pilot friend said that thirteen years ago when he was flying rubber out of here, they were pretty wild."

"They still are." Father Ambi got serious. "Every month or so when a plane takes off, we have reports that at the end of the runway a few Pacas Novas step out and let fly with those five-foot arrows they have. We had a young daredevil brother with us here at the mission. He would once in a while jump on his bicycle and peddle like mad down the runway. Then he would make a quick U-turn and race back, his white robe flying in the wind behind him. Naturally, none of the Indians knew when he was coming so he could get away with it and show off his daring-do. But one afternoon, he was out there, and two arrows came whizzing by him. He never tried it again."

"Why aren't you trying to tame them?" I asked.

"Tried to. They won't communicate with us. They just shout insults and fade away into the forest. The army has gone after them several times, but it's a losing proposition. If it's the Bolivian Army they slip across the river to Brazil. If it's Brazilian soldiers, they're back here. And once in a while they do manage to sink an arrow into some unfortunate trooper or civilian. Stay away from them."

"What do I do if I encounter them?"

"Get out your rosary and run like hell."

"Have you ever been to that old fort that I want to reach?"

"No, I haven't, but I would like to see it. It's pretty far up stream, I'm told. I believe it was the Pacas Novas Indians who forced its abandonment. That's why now Brazil has an army post on the river."

"Why would anyone build a stone fort out there in the wilderness?"

"Politics," was the simple answer. "The territory over there, across the Mamoré River, was Portuguese. Here, this area, used to be Spanish. The two countries were often at war, especially when Portugal would ally itself with England, as it often did, to fight Spain. There is a lot of history connected with this region. I understand slavery was big around here in the eighteenth century. Blacks were transported from the West Indies, chained in riverboats, and brought up the waterways to work the gold country or the sluice boxes of the streams. Blacks who managed to escape joined up with the Indians. You can imagine how those blacks and their offspring thought about us 'blancos' or whites. There still is slavery among the Indians, but the blacks are out of it now."

"Any suggestions on how I can get up the river? I was told in Cochabamba that airplanes do land at the Brazilian Army outpost that you mentioned. What planes?"

"That's across the river," Father Ambi yawned, "in Guajara Mirim, over there in Brazil. You'll have to go there. I'll set you up. The Franciscans have quite a place, even a Bishop. They'll have the straight poop."

With that we both retired.

The nights in Guayaramarin were not conducive to sleep. August 6 was Bolivia's Independence Day, and gunfire went on all through the nights of that week. Many men carried weapons openly as in the Old West. Their pistols, rifles, once in a while an automatic piece, and here and there a canon, banged away the whole five days I stayed with the Maryknolls.

The next day a Franciscan, Father Marcellos Smith, came across the river from Brazil to visit us in Bolivia. He was quite American and when introduced to me by Father Ambi, stuck out his hand and, in a real Midwestern accent said, "How ya doin'?" Later, I asked him how he came to choose the Franciscan Order. He answered, "They do things. They come here to the boonies. They are interested in the very poor and unknowing people of God. Like Saint Francis, they seek out and work with the weak and the underprivileged . . . "

"Enough!" Father Ambi, the Maryknoll, boomed out. "Keep your sermons for your converts." He laughed as did the other missioners who were present. "This man wants to know how to get up to Fort Principe da Beira. He doesn't want to be saved now. He wants to know how to save his life once he gets there. If you Franciscans would just ease up on dogma, we'd all get along a lot better." For his statement, that I thought a bit harsh, he got laughs and a few handclaps from the Maryknollers there and from the two Franciscans who had joined us. Father Smith blushed, and admitted, "I guess I'm in the pulpit again." We all settled down to lunch.

I was asked, "You are going up the Guapore?"

"Yes."

"All the way to Principe da Beira? That is, the garrison? The Brazilian garrison?"

"That's my hope," I answered, and then outlined why I was interested in the project.

Father Marcellos spoke again. Your friend flew over there in 1946 or '47? Those days this whole area was cringing under the threat of the Indians. They were vicious. I don't recommend you going up there."

"But, Smitty," Father Ambi butted in, "the man's a sport; he wants to see the place. Can't you Franciscans get him an intro to the Brazilian Army up there? You know if you give the word, they'll cooperate."

"You're going, aren't you?" the Franciscan asked me.

"I'm going."

"I'll get you on the Cruzeiro Del Sol plane that stops at the army post. The plane schedule is erratic. It would be best if you were across the river and ready to go. If we could, we would put you up at the mission, but we're all full up. I understand the Guaja Hotel is adequate. We can feed you, would love to have you. The Bishop loves drop-ins. Get a room at the hotel and come on over. We'll make sure you get to that fort."

✧✧✧

Going from Bolivia to Brazil was the easiest border crossing I've ever made. A ten-year old boy from the Maryknoll school was "volunteered" to wheelbarrow my goods down to the river front where, every morning, a launch makes the run for Guajara Marim across the Mamoré River. The few passengers were mainly day working people who commute. There was no custom house, no inspection, or border guard. Technically, I was supposed to already have obtained my proper stamps in La Paz or Cochabamba. A trip to the police station would have been in order, but I just let sleeping dogs lie and commandeered another wheelbarrow to take me to the surprisingly large and surprisingly bad Guaja Hotel.

Here I realized that I had a real language problem. For years I had heard people say, "If you speak Spanish, you can understand Portuguese and vice versa." Less than half a mile from Spanish-speaking Bolivia, the Portuguese speaking Brazilians could not understand their neighbor's language. I was back to sign language again. I managed to book a room for $3 a night, to evict a couple of those four-inch spiders, and to find my way to the Franciscan Mission.

The majority of the missioners here were from France, and like Frenchmen everywhere, they greeted strangers with gusto. They all spoke English—one way or another—and I was accepted like a brother. The Bishop, Father Armond, looking very Episcopal with his acetic face and sharp goatee, came out from his study and pumped my hand. "You are welcome here," he said with a heavy French accent. "You must always eat with us while you are here. Father Ambrose from over there," he gestured, I thought rather condescendingly toward Bolivia, "has told me that you are a fine fellow. We will have a glass of wine and you will tell me about yourself."

Such a nice hospitable greeting! We sat and talked until dinner was served, and then we continued to talk. The French Franciscans liked the American Maryknolls quite a bit, but I detected a tad of jealousy toward the so-called big bucks that the American missioners received from the States. In contrast, these men seemed to operate on a shoestring. The rivalry was friendly, but it was nevertheless there, at least on the Brazilian side of the Mamoré River. I remained neutral: anybody who wanted to give me a dinner was OK by me (and I must say the French cuisine was far superior than the American). Bishop Armond did apologize for not having a bed for me. "The place is full. We have novices here at this time, and we must nurture them. But, do come back for breakfast, and lunch, and dinner. And do take some pictures of us here. We could use a little publicity." I was overwhelmed by this Bishop, and even—shame on me!—facetiously wondered for a moment: "Did he talk his way into his bishopric?"

I found out otherwise. He was a very competent administrator and spiritual leader of his flock. The photos and films I took of him, that I still have, remind me of Saint Francis and his animals. Bishop Armond had a yard full of deer, tapir, and other creatures that followed him wherever he went.

Unfortunately, for my needs, except to get me a seat on the Cruzeiro Del Sol Airline plane for the Brazilian Army garrison on the Rio Guapori, the friendly and outspoken French Franciscans did little to further my trip. If anything, they hindered it by their talk of dangers and uncooperative Indians. However, they did get me on the one plane that flew off into the remote Mato Grosso jungle. I was indeed grateful for that, and the fact that there was no charge. Free, all the way!

Within two days of my crossing the river into Brazil, I was up at 6:00 a.m. and shaving by candlelight in the Guajara Hotel. A *Jeep* took me to the landing strip. There, a two-motor aircraft was being loaded with bundles of cargo, and I was directed aboard with a few rough looking characters who were my fellow passengers. No nonsense at all; no kicking of the engine, we were off when the last bag was tied down. We rumbled down the runway and zoomed into the sky. I was flying into real jungle country, and I couldn't help but think of my last Amazon trip with Hermann Becker and the unfortunate motorist Ferdinand.

The day was clear, and we could see everything below us for miles. There were no mountains to consider, and so we flew close to the tree tops. We followed the Mamoré River as though it were a map. In a little while we turned off on its tributary, the Guaporé River. Now we were away from river traffic. Very little was to be seen down there on the streams.

I tried to engage my fellow passengers in conversation, but the language barrier soon silenced us. Most of the seats of the plane had been removed to make room for cargo. Large wooden crates wrapped in canvas and a number of bundles were stacked about, all securely tied down. They were being shipped to the small Brazilian army outpost and to the rubber gatherers who worked under the protection of that troop of soldiers. I noticed two wooden crates that were stamped Winchester Arms-U.S.A. I pointed to the boxes and said to a wirery tough-as-leather-looking fellow sitting across from me, "*Por que?*" He scratched his head at my Spanish question, and then nodded. "*Señor, son indios malos.* Bang. Bang." He looked at the other passengers, and they all laughed. There was no more conversation.

There was not, in any case, much time for conversation. The flight lasted hardly an hour. We came in low, buzzed a narrow landing strip that had been cut through the jungle alongside the river, and then the pilot—who was wearing shorts and tennis shoes—cut his engines and brought us down.

Right away I could see that we were definitely away from the broad Mamoré River. We were on the Guaporé. There was a little shed on one end of the strip; a river launch was tied nearby. A man emerged from the thatched canopy of the boat and stepped ashore. He carried a semi-automatic machine gun in one hand. He waved us toward him with the other arm. We quickly taxied over to the shed. Half a dozen heavily armed soldiers came out from the little building and took positions around the plane.

The door was opened and a little metal staircase settled to the ground. We all descended. Four quite hard looking men stepped from the boat, briskly pushed by us and began unloading the plane. They stacked up the cargo on the deck of the river launch.

Later, I was told that those men and those on the plane were *serinqueiros* or rubber gathers. They make a living tapping the trees for rubber just as those unfortunates during the rubber boom had done decades before them. The rubber here is considered the finest in the world, so, even though it is much cheaper to purchase from the Asian markets, this product goes into the industries that need and demand the very best. I could see by the demeanor of these rough looking men that theirs was a hard, dangerous, and ill-paying job.

A man, who may have been a foreman, asked me where I was going, and all I could mumble was a little Spanish, "*A los soldados; al fuerte.*" He pointed to the launch and manhandled my baggage into the boat. Within an hour the motor was started, and we drifted out into the Guaporé River.

It was an uncertain time for me, and I forgot to unlimber my camera. I just stood in the vessel, hung on to a support, and watched the jungle go by. I had done this before on the Yavari River of Peru, and this time I was glad to see the well-armed soldiers also aboard.

Perhaps five miles up the river, we came to a clearing. The area was sprinkled with one-story frame buildings. A tall flagpole flying the colors of Brazil dominated the garrison. We pulled into a short wooden dock, tied up, and everybody stepped ashore.

The men on the launch moved by me and spread out into the area. Others began unloading the cargo. I pulled out my two bags and just stood there wondering which way to go. There were no stores or signs, or hotel, or restaurant. I didn't have the foggiest idea which way to turn until I was approached by a tall, very well-built, and straight as a die soldier. He was no shave-tail; there was gray in his hair. He came directly to me, and in a most military and businesslike manner inquired what I was doing there. Or, at least, that's what I suspected he asked.

"*Habla Español?*" I hopefully asked.

"No," he answered. And he then barked orders to soldiers who had gathered around. They quickly picked up my bags. He gently took me by the elbow and directed me into the military compound. We walked to where a young man in uniform was speaking to several soldiers, lecturing them, I thought.

I liked the way my man stood at attention and waited for the young man to turn and face him. With military snap, he saluted the young officer, and rattled off a string of Portuguese. The young man, dressed in neatly pressed khakis, listened and looked me over. I don't think he liked what he saw. Then, in broken Spanish—about as good as mine—he asked me what I was doing.

Once again I went illegal and said what I really should not have said. Harking back to the time I worked my way through the Colombian border, I stood as tall as I could, nearly clicked my boot heels, and responded, "*El Coronel de los estados unidos*, Romain Wilhelmsen," and however I messed up the language of Spain—which I'm sure I did and which I'm sure he wouldn't have known—I attempted to tell him that I was here to go up the river to the old Portuguese fort of Principe da Beira, that the United States Military School at West Pointe was making an historical survey of such ancient citadels; and that I was here to film this unspoiled antiquity of Brazil's magnificent heritage. I tapped my tripod to give a little authenticity to the yarn. And I finished by requesting, "an escort of not less than seven soldiers to take me up the river." I shut up then.

He didn't respond as quickly and as deferentially as did the young Colombian lieutenant six years ago, but he did stiffen up a bit and look me over. I certainly didn't look like a colonel, but how was he to know?

"Coronel," he quietly said, and put out his hand, "*Bienvenida.*" I could feel that he did not want a problem here and that he would like me to vanish. But, as I was to find out soon, he was a career soldier working his way up the chain of command. He didn't want any bad marks against him, certainly not international bad marks from the Goliath United States up north. He played along with me.

There were no accommodations in the garrison, no spare rooms, no hotel. Graciously, the young officer escorted me to his own quarters. He had a neat and clean room with two cots in it, a toilet setup, and a water basin. He apologized by saying that these were his quarters, and that he could do no better. He indicated the mosquito nets hanging over the cots. I was told to use one. Especially now that he was suffering from malaria.

After seeing that my bags were stowed beneath my cot, the Brazilian officer led me down a dirt path or street of sorts to a group of thatched roofed bungalows all perched upon four-foot stilts. We went up the steps of one of them, and into a house where I was pleased, for some reason, to see the tall erect soldier who had brought me to the post. We were in a room that had a table, several chairs, a shabby sofa, and a cabinet.

Language flowed between the young officer and—as I was soon to realize—his sergeant. This man now called out to a back room. I was startled to see a natural blond woman come in from behind a curtain. She had about as perfect a female figure as any woman would ever want. She was graceful; she had the right moves; she was proud of her looks as evinced by the makeup that she used in this remote place, and she was very cordial.

The young officer commented, "*Habla Español*," and the young lady quickly spoke Spanish.

I almost imagined that she might say, "I am Tandaleyo" (from the provocative play and movie *White Cargo*), and she darn near did. "*Soy Terezinha* (Teresa)."

She was wearing an off-the-shoulder crisp white blouse, and it took very little imagination to evoke what was beneath it. I have more than a little imagination, but as startling as this young woman's entry was to me, the fact that she spoke Spanish was at the moment even more welcome. I was back in business. I went into my hesitant attempt in that language, and she picked up on it. She was no better at it than I was, and she laughed unashamedly as she acknowledged it. Nevertheless, the two of us communicated immediately.

"*Siénta te*," she said in familiar Spanish, and actually took my hand and led me to a chair. The two soldiers settled into the other two chairs. When I realized there was no place for the young lady, I gallantly stood up and gestured to my chair. (I have thought back on that gesture and have come to the conclusion that that moment, undoubtedly made my whole adventure in Brazil the success that it would be.) "*Señor*," she almost whispered, "*gracias*."

Then in a strident tone, almost fretful, she said something in Portuguese to the sergeant. He leaped up, went through the curtain and brought back another chair. He put it down, but again she corrected him. He brought it over to her, and she patted the seat and again said to me, "*Sienta te*." I sat down beside her. From then on I could do no wrong in the eyes of Terezinha Carvalho. She actually doted on me. And what a person to have dote on one!

"You will take your meals here with me and my mother and the sergeant." She indicated the tall straight soldier, "and I will help you if I can."

Brazilian coffee—the strongest—was served in big heavy crock cups. An elderly lady carried them to us. She belonged to the household, but I never found out in what capacity, perhaps a mother or aunt or grandmother.

The officer, who I detected might have felt somewhat left out by the lady's rather casual indifference to him, spoke up. I'm sure he asked, "What does he want here?"

Again, I requested seven soldiers to take me up river to the fort of Principe da Beira.

This was translated to him, and I noted a glint of satisfaction in his demeanor when he stuck out his chin of adolescent whiskers and told us all that "he could not allow any of his soldiers to travel up river into an area that the government does not want us to agitate." He sat back rather smugly and continued, "The military plane will be here within a week or so, and our guest will be welcome until then. But, he must be on that plane when it leaves." He stood up, tapped his thigh with a little riding crop that he carried, and strode out. Then he stopped at the doorway and said pleasantly, "The Colonel is welcome to stay in my billet until he leaves for Guajara Mirim."

The lady translated this all to me as well as she could, and in doing so we both had a couple of laughs. So did the sergeant. I liked him more and more. But not as much as I liked Terezinha Carvalho. She was hard not to like.

She had seen the concern in my face at the prospect of not being able to accomplish my goal, and with a tender and a warm hand, she took mine and told me, "I'll get you up the river. I will go myself with you to the fort. I have friends who will take us there in their boat."

"*Indios!*" the sergeant interjected. He had caught the gist of her last sentence. "*Indios?*" He looked at her in an almost fatherly attitude.

"My friends know the Indians," she answered him, and translated it to me. "They will get us through."

"Are you sure?" the big man asked with a tenderness that was touching.

"I am sure," she answered. And then she wavered, "I think so, Paul."

"I hope so," he responded. "I hope so."

The sergeant stood up and held his hand out to the lady. She took it and spoke affectionately to him. He gave me a little salute and marched out of the house. I stood up but she restrained me. She asked me to stay for lunch.

All sorts of vegetables were served. I don't know the names of most of them, but they were good. Especially, I remember the avocadoes. This wasn't a freebee. I was informed that, while at the post, I would be boarding here. I had expected that. My hostess then took me for a tour of the facility. I managed with her help some very interesting films of life on an Indian army frontier garrison. One man said that he would bring a *jacoré* or alligator for me to film, but I never saw him again.

My dinner at Terezinha's place consisted of chunks of some sort of meat in a bed of farina covered with sauce; and at that dinner, I learned a little about this fascinating young lady. She was engaged to a young man who was soon to be an attorney in Guajara Mirim. His studies took him to centers of higher learning in Brazil so he wasn't around as much as she would like him to be. It appeared as though he was destined for better things than this frontier life and Terezinha was hanging her star on him. I don't blame her.

That second night we had an occasion. It was, as they say, a dark and stormy night, and the word was out that a Brazilian aircraft was in trouble and almost lost in the turbulent skies. Radio messages had been picked up and our young officer was on the spot. He handled the situation well. I discretely followed him from our cots in his room after he had been awakened by his batman. We went to the small radio shack, and he took over. A military plane was in trouble up there somewhere and needed to land. Now! The pilots dared not stretch their luck any further. Puerto Velho and Guajara Mirim were out. They were desperate: alone in the black night over even darker jungle.

I give great credit to my roommate. He talked them down out of the sky and to the little runway four miles away. We could all see the shadow of the big L-47 as it passed above us, and we could hear the sputtering motors as it glided into the strip. It had been a close call.

Better yet, once down, the plane's main cargo consisted of a troupe of U.S.O.-type army entertainers destined for distant *manaus*. They all shortly showed up at our army post. They had been gladly ferried over by whatever river craft were available at this time of night. It was easy to see why. They were a typical group of Brazilian show people. The dancing girls were short of dress and long in talent. They were so relieved to get out of that faltering plane that they soon setup their act and gave a performance for the outcasts of our little post.

This was 1957, and I was amazed at the display of flesh, abandonment, and interracial camaraderie that these performers displayed. The drums were beat in a sensuous manner, the guitars were strummed to a provocative beat, and the young dancers swirled and bumped and leaped about in a rhythm that's totally Brazilian. We were all, including Terezinha and me, swaying to the beat of the drums and encouraging the company to even more frenetic moves. This went on until close to dawn, and then one group of soldiers gallantly gave up its barracks to the tired assembly and pitched a couple of tents for themselves. Another one of those nights to be remembered.

The next morning the flight engineer, who had remained with his plane, and thus missed the fun, announced that the broken gas line that had caused the problem had been repaired. Not looking quite as exotic as they did the previous night, the tired troupe of singers and dancers dragged themselves back to the river launches and waved us a farewell.

The young officer, I know, got little rest that night. He shook with malaria the few hours he was in bed. I felt very sorry for him.

I made a quick shave and joined the sergeant as we and a couple of boarders went to Terezinha's breakfast table. You can't go wrong with bacon and eggs (unless you're on the *Omega*), and she did right well by us.

Terezinha asked me to stay after the others had left, and then led me down to the Guaporé River and its little makeshift wharf. Tied to it was one of those typical jungle straw-covered river launches. Six quite swarthy and rough-looking men came out to meet her. They had obviously talked before. Now they turned toward me. She spoke for them.

They would take me up stream to the old fort for the equivalent of $38. "It is an honest and fair price," she explained. "It is more than they usually charge to charter their boat, but in this case, we are going into the Indian country, not away from it." I could see that they wanted to make the deal—Cash was scarce where we were: I was happy that I had had converted traveler's checks into *cruzieros* while still in Cochabamba.

"*Bom. Bom*," I said (Good. Good.) and stuck out my hand. They all brightened up, stepped forward, and shook it. It was agreed.

I then turned to Terezinha and asked, "Would it be possible to take the sergeant with us?"

She quickly, and almost conspiratorially whispered to me. "No. No. Do not tell him. He will not let me go. He protects me . . . too much."

"Are you going?" I asked expectantly.

"Of course," she defiantly said. "Nobody has ever asked me to go to that place. I will go with you, and I will protect you."

I would have liked to have the big sergeant, but I would much rather have the young lady. "When do we leave?"

"*Mañana por la mañana.* Early in the morning before the bugles blow. We will go. They will not see us leave. And if we go early, we can be back here before nightfall."

I couldn't have asked for a better plan. "Five in the morning. I will be here at the wharf."

"No," she firmly said, "Three o'clock. You will be at my place for coffee and food. We will leave at 4:00. We will go into the Pacas Novas country before they are awake. We will fool them. Do you have a weapon?"

I didn't want to admit to that little international illegality, but in her case, I was sure it would be all right. "I do. I have a little .32 caliber revolver."

"Good," she answered. "I will have my Winchester and my friends, who are used to this country, will also be armed." Then she changed the tone of her voice. "But do not be afraid," she comforted me and placed her hand on mine. "Let's hope that the *bravos* (Indian warriors) are off on a raid somewhere."

"Tomorrow," she said and repeated it to the boatmen. They slipped back into the vessel, and we walked back to the army outpost hand in hand like a couple of conspirators.

As Terezinha coached me, that afternoon I spoke to the young officer and told him that she and her friends would be taking me out on an alligator hunt early the next morning. "I'll be leaving here before you get up. So, don't be concerned." He was not feeling well, and I don't believe gave a hoot one way or the other. I also placated him by adding, "I'll be on the plane when it leaves here."

The rest of that day I continued to film the drills and the marches of the soldiers. I pretty well kept to the sergeant and used him as a protagonist. He was a robust born soldier and leader of men. I would have liked to have known him better.

Early to bed that night and very early to rise. There was no light in our room, so I just slipped on my clothes and left. My tripod was at the door as was my bag of film, cameras, and pistol. I stumbled over to my lady friend's house and found my way up the steps to her dimly lit room.

"Ah, you are here," she exuded and gave me an *abrazo*. "I was afraid that they might stop you. But you are here so now eat."

She filled a plate with scrambled eggs and ham and the ever present farina. I ate little. I wasn't hungry.

We then walked down to the river. I felt like a fugitive making his escape. Yet, Terezinha was exuberant and chatted all the way.

The little vessel was there, and we could make out the light of a candle in the straw hut on it that served as a cabin. Their leader came out, looked around, and greeted the lady. We were quickly ushered into the little hut and out of sight of the fort.

At this early hour, the smell of the jungle was more than ever all around us. Not the clean odors that many say the "rain forest" offers, but the decay, the putrification, and the rot of centuries of dying and dead vegetation. At times it was sickenly sweet and other times the effluvium was rancid and moldy. One wanted to move away from it to be elsewhere.

I was surprised at the quietness of the outboard motor that was being used. It barely purred as we glided into the sluggish current of the Guaporé River and began our journey. The motor was German. The few lights of the garrison faded away behind us, and I no longer tried to see them. Terezinha took my hand in hers, and we both sat down together on a bench and stared ahead into the darkness.

The river was not silent. It had an accent of its own: fish, insects, and birds of prey made little 'plopping' sounds as they searched for food on the surface of the water. And from the tangled brush, vines, trees, and foliage along the banks of the stream, the noises of the night sounded in our ears. Occasionally, a dreadful shriek was heard: The call of the jaguar. This was always followed by the yelping of monkeys.

The crew was professional river men. Even in the darkness, they seemed to know where to steer their vessel. Like the legendary pilots of the Mississippi River, they could sense, feel, hear, and smell the direction of the water should it contain an obstacle, a tree trunk, or otherwise. They spoke in hushed voices. We said nothing. Once one of the men turned and made his way back to us. He whispered to Terezinha and pointed to the right of our boat. We looked and saw several reflections, little points of light in pairs.

"*Jacoré*," he said to me, and resumed his place in the bow with the others. The *jacoré* is the alligator of the Amazon River System. They have been hunted ever since man had a weapon that could be used against their formidable armor, great strength, vicious tail, and their deadly jaws full of teeth. Their skin sells at a premium. In Brazil in 1957, there was a law that limited the size of alligators that could be taken. Those we saw this night and later would have been fair game for our men. But my money was fairer game; we passed them by. We came close to the brush along side of the river occasionally, and I thought of Father Ambi and his encounter with the anaconda. I asked my companion about the flesh eating piranha fish, but she assured me that they do not gather in large rivers. There is another creature out here that Hermann Becker had told me to avoid. It is the canero. A deadly little aquatic being that looks like a king-sized cigarette, which has a nasty habit of swimming into any human or animal orifice that it can sense or smell. It then works its way into the body of its prey. The canero has one bone or cartilage in its body and when secure in its host, it pops out that one large barb. Like a fishhook, it is extremely hard to remove. In men, the penis is the target. In women, the vagina. Or the rectum. Once in the urinary track, it will die and pollute the body. The advice I had been given was, "Don't go into the waters of those rivers."

Soon, things began to lighten up. The sun made an appearance. Most noises along the riverbanks quieted down. The night creatures slithered back into their safe holes and the hum and the buzz of insects was intensified. In front of the army post I had seen very little river traffic. Now I saw none. We had the river to ourselves. The men in the bow came back to us and gestured and told us to stay where we were, beneath the shelter of the grass roof. I got the idea that if one of those Pacas Novas Indians got it into his head to let fly an arrow, he would have very little target.

Nine o'clock a.m. Terezinha squeezed my arm and pointed to a log in the river. "*Mira*," she said, and I saw a huge turtle sunning itself on a dead tree stump. "*Tartaruga*," she identified it. "*Pelegrosa*," she added. Dangerous.

Ten o'clock a.m.—or there abouts. Our men all gathered their rifles and looked intently at movement on the banks of the river. Then they relaxed as a large tapir, the size of a pony, lumbered out from beneath the trees, and slipped into the water. It disappeared from sight, and we never saw it again.

The river narrowed, and then quickly widened almost to the size of a small lake. In the distance there were big boulders, and we could see white water where the stream continued on its way. I was startled when our motorist abruptly cut the engine to almost an idle. He and his men hunched over and peered into the jungle. One of them spoke to Terezinha, and she said to me, "*Cerca de aquí. Muy cerca. La Fortaleza.*"

It was not yet high noon. Our vessel was allowed to drift quietly and slowly to the northern shore of the Guaporé. The water backed up against the shoreline. There was very little current here. The life seemed to have gone out of the river. It had taken on a saffron hue and seemed to palpitate with an uneasy motion. We approached the shore, and angry water creatures surfaced, trying to avoid us. I took my hand away from Terezinha's and put it on the handle of my little revolver. I just didn't like the feel of the place. I looked at the young lady, and sensed that she, too, was not at all at ease. She had the Winchester carbine close by. For a moment I wanted the big sergeant here.

"Shussish," the motorist hissed.

"Quiet. We are approaching the fort," Terezinha whispered. "They are not sure if any Indians are here in it." We all tensed as the little vessel bumped the shore. For a moment nothing happened, and then one of the men leaped ashore, and carried our anchor, a fifty-pound stone, to the land.

The young lady directed my gaze upward, and I made out the dark form of a wall. To me it seemed to rise to an unusual height. The wall was made of smoothly dressed red stone blocks. The neatness of the wall was broken by the barrel of a dark and fat cannon that protruded from it. All else was obscured by vines and vegetation that seemed to bind the place together.

"We are here," Terezinha said. "You must now do your work quickly. Two hours; no more. My friends do not want to alert the Indians. Make your pictures and then we will go. *Dos horas, no más*."

The boat was secured, and I hustled ashore with my bag of film and my movie camera and its tripod.

One of the men led me around the wall until I came to the entrance of the fort. A ditch had been dug at the foot of the walls, and, I was to find, completely surrounded them. This had been a moat and still here and there we saw water in it that was fed from the stream. A sturdy wooden drawbridge, held together with rusty iron studs and spikes, spanned the trench and led us to the impressive open doorway. Carved above the stone archway in Latin were these words: "*Anno Christi MDCCLXXVI*," and beneath that "*Dei Mensis Juni*." I looked back and made sure that my people were coming along. Leading them was my fair companion. "*Vámanos*," she hastened me on. "Let's go." She went ahead of me, and I hand held a movie shot of her entering the fort. I followed her.

The walls were at least six feet thick and thirty feet tall. They were huge. It is still an enigma to me why they were built so high and so thick. Whatever the reason, there they were and there they still are. They were built to last. We all stepped into a large area completely paved with well laid out stones. This was all surrounded by the walls. The interior of the fort was rectangular. I counted twenty-four cannons set in place in geometrically positioned parapets. The majority faced the river. I speculate to fire on any Spanish vessels coming up the stream. Much of the fort was overgrown with jungle vegetation.

The boat people fanned around this area and poked into any spot that looked interesting. They kept their weapons handy, but it appeared that the Indians were not in the area . . . or so we hoped.

I had my hands full setting up that awkward wooden tripod and taking my films. I had little time to use the still camera.

Bishop Armond, the Franciscan in Guajara Marim, had shown me a sheaf of old documents pertaining to the area. Some facts had been translated to me. Ground had been broken for Fort Principe da Beira on June 20, 1776, by SR. Luis Albuquerque Melo Pereira

E Caceres. Fifteen years were needed to build it. Thirty-two hundred blacks from the West Indies and 844 Indians from Bolivia were pressed into service. The trapezoidal walls of the fort had been surrounded by a moat that opened into the Guaporé River. This moat was filled with alligators that the soldiers fed by throwing dead animals into the waters to encourage their presence. Somewhere in the fort is the opening of a tunnel leading to the foothills of the Serra Dos Parecis. The tunnel could be used as an emergency exit. Bishop Armond had asked me to look in the dungeon where a Spanish missionary had been imprisoned and had died. There would be an inscription on the wall of his cell. The Bishop somehow had heard this—perhaps passed down by word of mouth. He asked me to ascertain its truth, and to bring him a photograph of the inscription.

We located several low doorways with stone steps that went down about six feet below the floor pavement. There we saw rows of lightless room. By the bolts on the outer side of those doors we were sure that these were the dungeon cells. The wooden doors were now in a state of rot, and we had no problem breaking into them. With the help of one of the boatmen, who had had the foresight to bring along a flashlight, we could examine the rooms. Sure enough, on a wall of one of the eight cells, we found the message that Bishop Armond had mentioned. Having no flash equipment with me, I could not get him his picture, but I did copy the script. It is written in Spanish, not Portuguese. The text read: "Mato Grosso has caught me. The fort holds me captive. I am a victim of one who hates me greatly. I shall have great satisfaction when I am set at liberty, and I shall thank the kindness of some who showed me great favors in adversity. I am very grateful for the time that Captain Cunha has given me. His name is engraved in my heart, and there it shall be preserved." Such is a literal translation of the Spanish on the wall; it had been scratched there perhaps by use of a nail on the plaster that covered the stone wall.

Another of the stories that had been passed down about the fort was that along side of the little church within the fortress walls was a cemetery where officers had been buried. Somewhere in or near this graveyard, a quantity of gold, which had been taken from the river, was buried in a sealed crock pot. Possibly gold dust.

The little church was there all right. The roof had collapsed, but a stone altar was still firmly in place, and there were niches in the walls on either side of the altar that undoubtedly held statues of various saints. None of us had the inclination or the time to dig into the several marked gravesites that we saw.

One of the persistent stories about Fort Principe da Beira is that the Portuguese used it as a holding place for West Indies black slaves who had been brought down the rivers in flat-bottom scows and then sold to the Spaniards across the river.

And one story—that seems to be substantiated—is that at one time in history, the indentured slaves, who were held there, managed to escape. They set upon the commandant and his men and killed them. The Africans then slipped off into the forest and joined the Indians. Several years later, the Portuguese recaptured the fort, but the place got the reputation of being haunted by tortured slaves. Officers turned down well-paying invitations to go there for a tour of duty. And when Brazil became independent in 1888, the fort was abandoned.

The whole place looked pretty well picked clean of any artifacts, but the sure-sighted boatmen came across a few things: here a metal decoration, there a button, and better yet twelve silver coins. They were the typical piece of eight of the eighteenth and early nineteenth century. The coins weren't in good condition, but they were mementos of a time in history that has gone forever. I negotiated with the men and bought them all for $7. Numismatics have appraised them, and they really are not worth more than I paid. I was informed they are quite common on the market. These coins, however, were marvelous souvenirs for me to take home.

I had my films, the coins, and the story. Time to go. We walked out of the rough main archway and over the once dangerous moat of alligators, and to our launch. Without seeing an Indian, hostile or otherwise, we returned to the Brazilian garrison.

Two days later, the loud and unnatural rumble of a plane boomed over the post. The military shuttle had made its weekly call. I said goodbye to my host, and he grinned as he held out his hand and took mine. I really think he liked me, but was afraid or uncertain about my Army rank. For a Brazilian, he had an odd name, Lieutenant Hamilton.

Terezinha walked with me to the wharf and launch that would take me to the landing strip. "Goodbye," she said in English, and extended her hand. "Please remember me." (I mailed her copies of all the still photos that we had taken.) The sergeant was there also. He gave me an *abrazo*.

✧✧✧

Although the Brazilian plane stopped at Guajara Mirim, I stayed on it until we landed at Puerto Velho on the Madeira River. I had read of the little railroad that had been pushed through the jungles a century before to transport the rubber. It was said that a man lost his life to Indians, snakes, disease or gun battles for every railroad tie that was laid down. The Madeira-Mamoré Railroad is still making its run. It was an experience making that two-day run in antique coaches pulled by a 1918 locomotive.

The end of the line was back to Guatjara Mirim. There I gave the very grateful Bishop Armond his Principe da Beira inscription copy. Next were Cochabamba, La Paz, Lima, and the final plane to California.

Author in the "Cave of the Giant."

Author digging up 16th century armor.

16th century Spanish armor found in a cave in the Sierra Madre Mountains of Mexico.

they hid spanish armor

in the

cave of the rock mouth

by russ leadabrand

Today... Sunday, July 6, 1958

PASADENA EXPLORER DISCOVERS FABULOUS LOST CITY IN MEXICO

An exclusive adventure account
...today in SCENE Magazine

Newspaper coverage.

Author with Tarahumara Indians.

Newspaper coverage.

Franciscan Bishop Armond of the Matto Grosso jungle state of Brazil.

Newspaper coverage of the 'Legend' of the Haunted Fort.

Author and jungle expedition in the Haunted Fort in Brazil.

Author in the fort.

Author and enigmatic Chulpa of
Siustani in Bolivia.

Newspaper coverage and
photo of the author in the
dead city of Baroyeca in
the Mexican desert.

A.P. coverage of the Indian war in Peru.

Newspaper coverage of the 'shoot out' in Colombia.

15 — SHOOT OUT

The story I took home from Bolivia and Brazil caused a stir. I presented the films at the Los Angeles Adventurers' Club, and the newspapers picked them up. My man, Mr. Olds of the CIA was pleased with the information I gave him regarding the presidents of Peru and Bolivia. My accounts would be compared with other private evaluations of these nations by agents, and assessments would be made. The global Cold War was a very real war for different people around the world. I was very pleased when the CIA asked for a print of my Mexican travelogue film to show to agents who were being sent in that country.

The *L.A.Times* and the *Pasadena Star-News* ran with the story and this publicity generated interest in my lectures.

A result of the good press was that, when a lecture booking took me to Baton Rouge, Louisiana, I was invited to the governor's office. Governor Earl Long was not of unsound mind as many of his detractors claimed. The Kiwanis Club of Baton Rouge had sponsored the lecture. One of its members was the publisher of the local newspaper, which gave me full coverage. Another member owned the local TV station, and I was given a big play there. Another owned the bank. Ever the politician with an eye out for publicity, old "foxy" Earl Long invited me and the press to his tower and executive offices, and presented me with a document written in beautiful calligraphy and handsomely framed. He officially commissioned me a "Colonel in the Militia of Louisiana." Long got his publicity, and I would no longer have to fake the title of 'colonel.'

The travelogue business was developing nicely, but more and more photographers— good ones—were entering this so-called glamorous profession. They were edging out the older adventurers, explorers, and odd characters who had originally attracted the public's eye. Television was becoming more and more selective and technically demanding. Nevertheless, the Jack Douglas Productions were more than glad to accept two of my films from the last trip. *The Haunted Fort* was particularly well received. Jack gave me the nickname, "The Legend Hunter" on that show. I liked it at once. The sobriquet seemed appropriate, and also appealed to my sense of drama. These programs from my trip to Bolivia and Brazil eventually ended up in Douglas' *Bold Journey* syndicated series.

My family and I had moved to the lovely beach community of Corona Del Mar, just north of Laguna Beach, California. The town overlooked the Pacific Ocean and was a quite desirable spot before the Interstate Highway bisected it and made room for the new city of Irvine and its extension of the University of California. Dana and Ginger Lamb lived in Corona Del Mar. They were the main draw for me. This couple had inspired me as a young-ster; we had eventually become colleagues and friends. We shared a lot in common.

I kept going over my journals, photos, and files, and a nostalgia for where I had been began to pervade my thoughts. I longed to go back especially to Peru. I was jolted into action when the Christmas of 1959, I received a letter from Santiago Jimmy Flynn. "I am now working for the Anaconda Corporation in the capacity of a manager of mines in the Cuzco region. I have visited and am quite friendly with the manager of an hacienda—a charming lady—who tells me that there is a rather large Inca ruin in her area that is not listed in the official book of Peruvian archaeological sites. She claims they are extensive. Come on down and let's take a look. Bring the detector. This is gold country."

Here was an invitation I couldn't resist. And then, right after his letter, there came one from Hermann Becker in Iquitos, Peru: "A new tribe of Indians has been 'discovered' in the headwaters of the Amazon. I can get a military sea plane to take us there. Wire me if you are interested."

I answered both in the affirmative.

Julie, quite correctly, cautioned me, "You will be duplicating your first film. Will the lecture circuit accept a repeat?"

I realized the wisdom of her forethought, but I, indeed, did want to go. Flynn had mentioned "gold." I admitted to her and to myself, "It will be difficult, but I am sure that I can come up with a different approach and story."

Indeed, I did!

❖❖❖

To flavor up this new adventure, I chose to travel to South America in another tramp steamer. I had not yet used, in any lecture film, the little footage that I had taken while on the *Grammerstorf*, so that now such a steamer trip would be a new twist. My good travel agent booked me on the *Mormacisle* of the Moore McCormick Lines. In 1960, the tramp steamers were still accepting passengers who could put up with their erratic and confusing time schedules. This ship was set to sail out of Long Beach California, not very far from my home. I waited at the phone until the call came telling me to be on Pier 232 on the morning of May 20. (This was the anniversary of the day in 1953 I boarded the *Grammerstorf* in New York for my first adventure.) Julie drove me to the docks, and came aboard to see what my billet might be. She and I were quite pleased. A large room with bed and sofa, table, desk, chairs, and a bathroom all to myself. The price was $270, California through the Panama Canal, to Cartagena, Colombia. The voyage would last ten days.

Julie continued to have a bad feeling about this particular trip.

She always respected my work, but down deep in her psyche or her woman's intuition, she sensed something wrong. Perhaps it was the recent newspaper stories of increased violence in Colombia that bothered her. We both realized that anything could happen . . . here or there. As a result, I had taken out a $1,000,000 life insurance policy payable to her should I not return. It did not assuage her apprehension.

The very corpulent steward tapped on my cabin door and literally called "All's ashore whose going ashore." Julie debarked in a sad state. She walked down the gangplank, turned, and looked at me, waved, and walked across the wharf to the old 1948 Cadillac that we maintained. I watched her. We waved, and she drove off for home.

I was not alone for very long. A thirtyish fellow approached me and introduced himself. "I am Ricardo Peña, and am a passenger on this ship. I believe you, and I, and my wife, Juli, are the only passengers." He was correct. We introduced ourselves and soon became friends. Ricardo was a Colombian who had gone to the United States to learn the new technology of computers. In 1960, he was a pioneer. He had done well with IBM and was on his way to big things. However, his wife was unable to get over her longing for Bogotá. She wanted to go home. Ricardo was a good husband, and he put her desires before his career. They were returning to Bogotá, furniture and all. We three hit it off very well. Especially when, after a day, he said, "Please be a guest in my home when we get there." I had lucked in again . . . despite all the misgivings.

The Peñas were fine companions. We enjoyed our meals with Captain Mulvag who was a traditional Norwegian sailor. On our second day out, after the captain had called the Peñas and me to see some whales cavorting off of the coast of Baja, California, I brought out the picture that I had taken seven years earlier. It showed the *Mormicile* cutting closely in front of the *Grammerstorf*. I had taken the measure of the captain and was confident he wouldn't be offended. On the contrary, he was delighted. "I was not on the *Mormicile* at that time," he announced. "A colleague was. Please give me this photo so that I can hurrah him." I had brought it along for that very purpose—my travel agent had suggested it— Captain Mulvag was quite pleased. I'm sure that picture has made the rounds of his peers.

Having cruised both ways I now say, "Never knock the cruise ships of today. On these new and stable floating hotels there are so many things to do. On our tramp we had nothing more than a shuffleboard, that worked for several days and then shut down after we had shuffled all the pucks overboard, and a ten by ten foot swimming pool. I caught up on my reading.

On our seventh day we arrived at the Panama Canal and dropped our anchor. The Peñas and I hired a car to take us into old Panama City. That bastion of Spanish might is now all in ruins and partly covered by the jungle. Its vulnerability to English pirates in the seventeenth and eighteenth centuries, and its sack by the pirate Henry Morgan, caused it to be moved across the isthmus to the Caribbean side where the Spanish fleets of gunboats could better protect it. So now, old Panama lives in the tropical sun, picking up a mantle of green vegetation. It was a very interesting sight.

The next day we went through the Canal, and that is an experience. The locks are engineering marvels. The captain was pleased to point out the slovenliness of a couple of English ships coming from the opposite direction. He contrasted them with a Maru or Japanese ship that looked like a bandbox, neat and clean as could be. I reminded him the English didn't do too bad in World War II battling these neat Nipponese ships. "We must forget the war," he ended the conversation.

Soon our ship moved on toward Cartagena, Colombia. We arrived at 9:00 a.m., May 30, 1960. I was back in South America.

We were taxied to the rich Boca Grande residential section of the city, and selected rooms in the Boca Grande Hotel, which was on a sandy beach of the Caribbean. The whole setup was right out of a travel poster, $3.50 a day.

Again, it was my plan to take one of those Mississippi-like paddleboats up the Magdalena River and duplicate my 1953 route. Fortunately, in 1960, those grand floating palaces were still in business. Unfortunately, my best offer was one that was leaving the very next evening. I had wanted more time in this colonial city, but I didn't want to lay over a week waiting for another such ship. I made my arrangements while Ricardo saw to the shipment of his furniture to Bogotá. He and his wife were taking the plane.

The three of us then took an excursion by small boat to the island of Boca Chica on which is situated one of Cartagena's massive stone Spanish forts. Massive is the word. The whole city is surrounded by these towering fortifications. A tall thick wall still encircles the city proper. Spain had suffered so many pirate attacks and invasions by the English and the French that the king ordered his best army engineers to come here and fortify the place. It took decades of work, but that work has stood the battles of not only several English armadas, but also the battle against time. The walls and the castles are just as strong today as they were four hundred years ago. In the mid eighteenth century, the English Lord Admiral Vernon with a huge fleet sailed up to the gates of this "Pearl of the Indies," as Cartagena has always been called, and challenged the Spaniards. He made his move and was then roundly defeated. One of the officers of that fleet was the brother of George Washington. As a result, Washington's home was named Mt. Vernon, after the name of the defeated British Admiral.

The Peñas and I spent that day and much of the next one exploring this very histori- cal and romantic city. In time, I would return to the "Pearl of the Indies" with my own Julie and do full justice to its charm. But, now the time had come to pack and get on with my adventure. We all took a taxi to the wharves on the Dique Canal that leads into the Magdalena. Ricardo and Juli were appalled at my little cabin, although it was actually much larger and more commodious than the one I had had on the *Jesucita* seven years before.

With the very hospitable words, "Send us a wire and tell us your arrival time in Bogotá and we will meet you," my friends left me.

My ship, the "*Monseratte*" was twice the size of the old "*Jesucita.*" It had three decks and a large calliope that would keep us awake most of the trip. I noticed a paucity of passengers. The river trade was being superceded by the airlines, and it is still considered a dangerous adventure to go up or down the river. The military had a grip on things, but bandits, in the guise of righteous revolutionaries—a'la Fidel Castro—were roaming the mountains and jungles at will.

The one passenger who I took up with was Jorge Valencia, a young twenty-ish Co- lombian artist. He was very full of himself, very wealthy, very educated, very handsome, very well dressed, and very much afraid of flying. His fear of the air had driven him to passage on this "scow." Despite his flaws and my flaws, we seemed to hit it off. Jorge was admittedly a coward. When the other passengers and I would always take the leap ashore from the deck of the "*Monseratte*" while docking, he would wait for the gangplank to be lowered. "I must protect my hands," he excused himself. Where he didn't excuse himself was his active libido. At every little town that we stopped, for more than an hour, he would go looking for the local house of prostitution. Because they all had such establishments he had one fine time for himself all the way to Dorado. I went along with him one night in Puerto Berrio and sat in the parlor of the bordello while he was entertained in one of the private rooms. The ladies there seemed to respect me when I pointed to my wedding ring. We had a lively conversation.

The river cruise duplicated the one I had taken seven years before except that we encountered no bandits. The captain did tell me that in 1953 his ship had been boarded by thirty brigands, everyone had been robbed, but not injured.

Our voyage ended safely after ten days on the river.

A ten-hour railroad ride from La Dorado put us in the station at Bogotá. A stretch limo was waiting to pick up Jorge, and I'll be darned if he didn't ask me to be his houseguest. I thanked him just as Ricardo and Juli walked up.

We had a problem. As easily as Ricardo had gotten me through customs, he was having a difficult time getting his American furniture through to his house in Bogotá. The place was totally devoid of any furnishings. The couple was bunking in with an uncle. Always with an eye on my budget, I agreed to stay in the empty house. I had my sleeping bag.

Cabs are inexpensive in Bogotá and during my six-day stay the Peñas taxied me wherever I wanted to go. I had hopes for Lake Guatavita and its mysterious gold peddler, but we were cautioned not to try it. Again, the old story of Colombian bandits. They were everywhere: in the mountains, in the forests, and even in the cities. "There can be no guarantees at Guatavita" the museum's security people told me. "Its proximity to the capital city makes Guatavita all the more chancy. Motorists and busses have been followed from here until they are a distance away, and then they are waylaid. Your embassy will advise you the same."

I did visit all of the important museums and saw them at my leisure. I met Jorge Gómez at the *Gold Museum*. He pointed out the priceless little golden raft that had been found near Guatavita.

I reluctantly pulled myself away from my two Colombian friends. They had entertained me all through my stay, dined and wined me at their family's homes, and done all in their power to make my visit a pleasant one. But, now I turned south once again. Santiago Flynn and Hermann Becker had legends for me to follow. I said 'goodbye' to the Peñas in the Bogotá Railroad Station, and I was again on my way.

Straight south to Neiva with the ever-present plump Indian lady and brood chatting alongside me all the way south to the big new Hotel Plaza that had opened since my bout with the spider and the moth at the Atlántico. I was glad to book into it for $6 a day including meals. I put in two days there filming this flower-like subtropical city, the hotel swimming pool, with the many stunning Colombian girls in their very abbreviated swimwear, and the elegantly turned out dancing couples as they did the cha-cha-cha in the ballroom on top of the hotel.

It was a quick and quite romantic little interlude that ended abruptly at 5:00 a.m. two days later when I boarded a bus for the town of Garzón and then the valley of the stone giants, San Agustín.

Colombia, despite its political revolutionary problems, was moving along. The road to Garzón from Neiva was just about all paved. But, the rest of it going to San Agustín was the same miserable abomination that I had experienced seven years before. The buses were somewhat better, but the San Agustín hotel, the Panama hadn't changed one bit. It smelled as vilely as before and the food was even worse.

I had come here to refilm some of the monuments that I hadn't done well with in 1953, and to attempt to reach the waterfall in the mountains that the local people had mentioned. That was described as the place where the water falls from the Heavens of the Andes, and where there are caves with marvelous things in them. The caves were just the sort of Legend I enjoyed seeking. My plans, then, were to include a visit to the underground stone grottos that contain geometrically designed galleries with colonnades and painted walls. The weather was holding well for filming. No rains were in the forecast; the sky was as blue as blue can get; and here and there snow-white puffs of clouds floated through the sky.

The jump-off place for the waterfall was a village named Plata Vieja. The police at San Agustín assured me that there would be plenty of mules and horses at Plata Vieja and the hundred or so people who lived there were friendly. However, I was given a stern warning by the military of San Agustín not to attempt that trip. "Enemies of the state operate quite openly in this port of Colombia." Soldiers did not want me going there.

I had heard this sort of pessimistic talk ever since I had began traveling off of the beaten path. I took their advice, and moved on. I had come this far and was determined to follow through on my plans.

I took the bus back to the town of Garzón, which was the most modern of all the towns in that area, and felt lucky to find transportation leaving almost immediately for Plata Vieja. This vehicle was in the same class as those miserable contraptions that I had experienced on my first trip. It was similar to a small school bus of the 1930s in the Ozarks of the United States. Except for the front and the back seats, that had cushions of a sort, all the other seats were nothing but heavy wooden boards that could easily be removed to provide space for cargo. Besides me, there was the *maestro* or driver, his assistant, and three Indian couples with their large bundles of produce, several trussed up piglets, and any number of chickens that were tied to the roof. It was a typical rural omnibus.

The dirt road led us west, and we climbed slowly into the wooded country of the Cordillera Central highlands of Colombia. It was a lonely road that curved in and out of dark shady patches of trees that brushed the open windows and forced us to keep heads and arms inside. Here and there the bus crept over steep and stony grades, and then it would travel through open spaces.

I was dozing in my 'best seat of the bunch' up front with the driver, when I awakened as we slowly squeaked to a stop. We hadn't seen any people in the three hours we had been driving, so the three men standing by the side of the road did seem a little unusual. "*Pasajeros*," the *maestro* nodded to me, and we stopped in front of them. There was no door on this bus, only a doorway. One of the men quickly stepped aboard. He reached into his pocket, as though for money, and pulled out a .32 caliber revolver. He barked out directions in a high-pitched voice. I couldn't understand his words, but I got the meaning. We were being held up. The women began screaming; the men all raised their hands above their heads.

"*Abajo*," the man pointed to the doorway, and I followed the three couples and the two busmen out of the bus. We stepped into a pleasant park-like clearing. One of the men produced a single-barrel shotgun that had been concealed behind him. He leveled it at us all and swung it back and forth. The third man had a long, wide machete hanging from his belt. That wasn't unusual in this part of the country, but he now withdrew it and eyed us with a sardonic grin. He rubbed his thumb across the blade and made a threatening gesture. The women wailed all the louder.

One of the men ripped open the bundles that the ladies still clung to. Their contents fell to the earth; mostly household items: clothes, a pan, sandals, some combs made of shell, several blankets. Nothing of value. The man spread out a blanket and yelled at us all to throw what we had in our pockets into it. He motioned to the women to take off their jewelry and to toss it in. This the frightened people did. The man pulled on his earlobe and indicated that he wanted their earrings. When one of the women had trouble undoing a pierced earring, he stepped up to her, and slapped his hand on her mouth. While she put her hand to her lips, he then grabbed her earrings and ripped them from her ears. She cried out in pain, and blood splattered her blouse.

All the while, the man with the revolver kept it pointed at us, especially towards me. I'm sure I appeared to be the most formidable of the passengers. The third man climbed to the roof of the bus. He used his machete to cut the bindings that held the luggage to the rack there. He tossed everything to the ground. Among those things was a small steamer trunk of mine.

I had obeyed the first command and had thrown my wallet into the blanket. I wore a buckskin shirt, that I had used on all of my trips, and it covered the money belt that contained my American Express traveler's checks. No one had seen it.

My trunk was locked, and the two men began hammering at the lock with a rock.

The leader with the pistol approached me and shouted a confusing command. I couldn't understand it, and said, "*Qué quiere?*" He lashed out with his gun and the short barrel caught the left side of my face. It was a wicked blow and in a moment, I felt blood flowing down my cheek and onto my lips where I could taste it.

With his left hand, he grabbed my leather shirt, bunched a bit of it into his fist and again shouted. He wanted that shirt.

I looked at him for a moment as he raised his gun for another swipe at my face and responded, "*Sí*," and again, "*Sí*." I began undoing the neck thongs.

The man working on my trunk now had it opened. It held countless treasures for such as they were, items from the States.

The man confronting me stepped back and, though keeping his gun leveled at me, he kept glancing at his accomplices as they pulled out my binoculars, my still camera, a pair of shiny boots, a travel alarm clock, a hunting knife in its leather sheath, and my clothes.

I had begun to remove my shirt when a hot wave of indignation seemed to suddenly envelop me. The cut on my cheek stung, and the physical contact had brought up a temper that I did not know I had. The stark realization of the danger in which I now was seemed to clear my mind of all unnecessary emotion. I reached around to my back with my right hand as though to pull up the shirt. I felt for the little leather holster that was secured to my money belt in the small of my back. In that holster was a black and ugly looking .380

Baretta automatic pistol. One thought now seemed to dominate me and I eyed the man confronting me. "You'll never hit me with that toy again."

Then all action was delayed as the machete man let out a whoop. "*Aquí, aquí,*" he shouted gleefully as he lifted from my trunk the graceful .22 Frontier model *Ruger* six-shooter that I had brought with me for Jimmy Flynn.

All three bandits shouted triumphantly. They had my weapon. I was no danger to them. The pistol man turned to me and laughed. He gestured with his gun for me to get a move on with the shirt.

I knew that there would be no turning back once my shirt was off and my gun was revealed. I must do it quickly.

Then I got a break.

"*Oiga,*" the machete man yelled again. "*Oiga,* look here." He lifted high in the air my passport case and with it four hundred dollars in cash. They had hit the jackpot.

The leader turned toward him. "*Cuánto suma?*" He shouted again, "*Cuánto?*"

Twenty dollar bills were being sifted through the fingers of the machete man. His partner with the shotgun moved in close; in so doing he stepped behind the terrified passengers. "He won't get a shot at me," I thought as I unfastened my holster.

All eyes were on my green American dollars as I jerked the Baretta out and slipped off the safety catch. It seemed to make an awfully loud 'click.' Yet, the pistol man still kept his attention on my money (I believe he thought he was going to be cheated.)

But, now he turned as he heard me draw back the slide of the gun and cock it.

He stared at me with what seemed to be utter hate. And before he had fully uttered, "*Qué pasa?*" I fired.

My shot went harmlessly into a grove of trees. I pulled the trigger again. And again I was wide of the mark.

The man fired back. I heard the explosion and then felt, at the same moment, his bullet smack into my left side.

My finger hadn't stopped working, and I fired again. It had all happened within a time frame of three to four seconds.

The man stared at me for a moment and almost genuflected as he went down on one knee, steadied himself with his free hand, and then rolled over onto the grass.

I stood stunned as the women screamed, and the bus driver and his helper took off for the trees. I looked toward the other two bandits. They had risen from their hunkering positions and were facing me. The shotgun man did not raise his weapon. He abruptly turned and ran for the woods. His companion followed him. In their hands went my four hundred dollars and Santiago's .22 *Ruger* six-shooter. I slowly sat down on the ground and pulled up my shirt. There wasn't much blood, but a dark blue mark was forming around the puncture wound. I put my hand on it, and nearly jumped back on my feet. It hurt like the very devil. I reached around to my back where the bullet would have exited but felt nothing. The slug was still in me.

The three Indian couples, after a short delay, now made a scramble for their goods on the blanket. I bellowed, "*Traiga me mi bolso.*" Somehow I figured that they too would now rob me. I still held that ugly automatic in my hand, and one of the Indian passengers brought me my wallet.

The man on the ground now let out an audible moan. He rolled over, and I realized he still held his gun in his hand. I leveled my Baretta at him and said in English, "No, you don't, you son of a bitch." But before I had the chance to do the murderous thing I had in mind, the *maestro* had returned and had placed his hand on my shoulder. "*No, caballero,*" he said, "*No, no. No es necesario.*" He reached down and took the revolver from the stricken man's hand. (I am eternally grateful that the driver did this.)

He asked me how I was. I told him I needed a doctor. He excitedly agreed. "*Sí, sí, ya vamos.*"

"*Mis cosas,*" I indicated my trunk. I watched as my goods were replaced in it, and it was tied shut with a rope.

The passengers now gathered about me and murmured among themselves. Finally, the driver and his aid extended their arms and I stood up. No problem at all except for a searing pain in the wound. I was helped back into the bus and taken to the padded back seat which gave me room to stretch out. Once seated, the pain subsided.

The bus was abuzz with chatter from the passengers, and I believe I detected a little anger when the driver announced that we would be returning to the town of Garzón. I understood that there was a doctor there.

Then, as we were about to leave, the people really made a protest. The driver and his man were now manhandling the man I had shot into the bus and bringing him back to my seat. I moved over and they sat him down so that he reclined on the backrest. The man was breathing. He was alive.

The bus made a 180-degree turn, and we started back.

The man along side me appeared to be in his late forties. He had a week's growth of black beard. He was dirty and he smelled. He looked at me through a glassy mist over his eyes.

I reached into a pocket of my shirt and pulled out a half-pint silver flask that my drinking Uncle Ed had given me. Before leaving San Agustín I had topped it off with rum. Now I poured some on my wound, and then took a good swallow.

The man kept staring at me so I handed the flask over to him. He barely had the strength to get it to his lips. He took a long drink and then let out a wheezing cough. I grabbed the flask as he proceeded to spit and spew blood all over everything within reach. My bullet had perforated his intestines. He gasped in a spasmodic manner and then laid his head back on the cushion. "María," he whispered. And he then died.

It is hard for me to remember the drive back to Garzón; things began to haze up on me. I do remember clutching my wallet and my automatic pistol. I believe my fellow passengers were quite leery of me; perhaps afraid is the better word. Not for a second did the pain in my side let up.

We arrived in Garzón late in the afternoon. The driver's assistant made a dash for the police department. I called after him, "*Un doctor. Favor, un doctor.*"

Within moments, two members of the civil guard were in the bus confronting me. They were decent sounding men and were genuinely concerned about my wound. They were shortly followed by several uniformed soldiers and an officer who took charge.

I was asked if I could walk. I stood up and felt that I could but the pain increased. The officer barked some orders to the bus driver. By now, all of the passengers had quickly disappeared and I was alone with the soldiers, the two bus men, and the dead man. Following the command of the officer, I was driven two city blocks to the Hotel Damascus. It was the same hotel where I had stayed in 1953. I was helped into a room and laid out on the bed. I was then gently told that there was no doctor in town.

It came to me in bits and pieces that I was not the main player in this tragedy. The man I had shot was. He had been the leader of a gang of marauders who were keeping the countryside terrorized. The impression I got was that the people in town were deathly afraid of reprisals from the small army of revolutionary bandits of which this man had been a part. The leader of the organization was Negro Dalfin. I heard his name mentioned several times.

I could see through the window of my room that a priest had been summoned and was giving the Last Rites to the deceased.

The very nice hotel proprietress brought me the ever present bowl of soup and I took a few spoonfuls. She then brought in a basin of water, pulled up my shirt, and very tenderly cleaned away the blood that had accumulated. Very little was now coming from the wound. It seemed to have shrunken into my body. She taped a big bandage over it.

The whole area of the little bungalow-like hotel was full of people who were trying to get a look at me. They all seemed to have an opinion. Shortly, the bus with its sad passenger drove off; the priest stayed with it. The lady shushed everyone out of my room. She had brought her darning needles and yarn with her and now began clicking away on some sort of project. As one of the soldiers left, he said to me, "*No problema. Hay una salucíon.*" The lady settled down in a chair beside me.

At 9:00 p.m., the soldier was back. With him was a clean-cut looking man about my age. He spoke passable English. "My name is Rolando Fierro. I fly an observation plane for the military, but I am not one of them. I have been asked to fly you to Popayán where there is a hospital and where there are proper federal investigators to take your statement. Do you have an objection to flying this very night?"

"Anything to get away from here and get this bullet out," I answered in a stronger voice than I thought I had.

He leaned in close to me and almost confidentially said in a low voice, "That's good. I think it best for you to leave this area."

Fierro had driven to the hotel in a pickup truck, and now he and the lady assisted me into it. She made me comfortable while he put my trunk and gear in the truck bed. I cannot say enough about the tenderness and the compassion that the hotel proprietress showed to me. Latin American men often boast a macho attitude, but their ladies are just the opposite. They are quite feminine, soft, and gentle.

We drove through dark streets to the outskirts of Garzón, and came to a Quonset hut-like hanger and office. By the light in the structure, I saw a Piper Apache four-place plane. With apparent caution, my man left the truck and checked out the surroundings. No one else was there. The pilot returned and helped me out of the pickup and into the back seat of the plane. We were on the clay runway in a moment and immediately thereafter into the air.

At that time, I had a pilot's license, and I was pleased to see that this fellow knew the manual of flight. He circled the area several times, climbing on each turn, until the lights of Garzón had vaporized away. I knew that we were flying over the Andes Mountains and that we were doing it at night. There would be no visual sightings. A pilot gets as high as he can, and then makes his run. When altitude had been achieved, we headed almost due west. As the plane flies, the distance was about one hundred miles. I knew that we had crossed the heights when Fierro cut back the throttle and we began the descent. Quite soon he touched my knee and pointed. I could see the lights of a good size city, Popayán. He knew the way, and we soon came in for a perfect landing. Several floodlights had gone on to illuminate the trim little airfield. It contained two runways.

We rolled to a stop, made our turn, and taxied back to a suburban type vehicle that was parked on the field. It had the markings of an official vehicle: Comisaría De Policía.

I was helped into it by three uniformed men and the pilot. They were all very considerate. Once in the van, the pilot said to me in English, "Good luck, pal," and then returned to his plane. He had kept the motor running, and before we had left the field, he was already rolling down the runway. I did not envy him his search for the dimly lit Garzón on the other side of the *cordillera*.

The policemen were courteous, asked how I felt, and informed me that I was being taken to the hospital downtown. Seeing the bright and colorful lights of a fairly large city perked up my spirits. Yet, the hospital did little to uplift them. It was all locked up and was only opened after the officer had given the main entrance door a few hefty thumps with his baton. A heavyset woman in a dirty white dress let us in and turned on several lights. I was put on a rolling cot and wheeled into a nearby room. I managed to move myself from the cot to a hospital bed. The nurse informed me, as best I could make it out, that a doctor had been summoned. The Garzón people had radioed Popayán to be ready for me.

This middle-aged gentleman soon arrived. He prided himself on his English; although he had little to be proud of. He claimed that he had attended the University of Ohio and pointed to a medical degree on the wall that did spell "University of Ohio." How he got through it with his little command of English, I cannot say.

However, he did go about his procedure with speed and dexterity. He carefully undid my bandage. Quite gingerly, and then more forcibly, he began to poke around my bullet hole. About the time he exhaled, "*Sí. Sí,*" I let out a yelp. He had found the slug. "*Está agui,*" he happily said to me. "*Aquí, muy cerca. No problema.*" He opened his black bag and pulled out a long probe and a long tweezers-like instrument. The nurse had placed a bottle of alcohol on the bed stand and he plunged the tweezers into it. He stirred it around for a moment. Then, with what seemed one coordinated movement, he placed the thumb and forefinger of his left hand around the wound, spread them apart, and with the right hand, he inserted the tweezers into the bullet hole, and in a moment pulled them out. They enclosed the bullet. It was out. I let out one big "ouch," and then felt instant relief.

The doctor waved the tweezers under my eyes. Then he dropped the .32 lead slug into a basin where it clanked around and then went silent.

"I would like that," I said and reached for it. I wasn't fast enough. The one officer who had stayed with us plucked it from the bowl and dropped it into a small cellophane bag. He turned to me, "*No, señor, es evidencia.*"

I nearly blurted out, "Evidence of who? The guy's already dead," but I held my tongue. A feeling of physical relief had come over me the moment that piece of lead was out of me. I felt stronger.

The doctor put his hands on my shoulders and gently eased me back to the bed. He then went to work cleaning out the bullet wound. He seemed elated and soon convinced me that the bullet had touched none of my vitals. It had just put a hole in what I've heard called a 'love handle.' We all relaxed.

Finally, it was done and the doctor had me bandaged up. He washed his hands in the sink in the room, reached over to me, and shook my hand. "You are lucky, my friend," he said in passable English. "But you must stay here until the inspector of crime has questioned you. He will be here tomorrow morning."

I didn't particularly care to go anywhere this evening, but I was apprehensive about my trunk. The doctor opened a metal locker door and pointed it out to me. "It will stay there," he said. "Try to sleep. Here is a pill." And, with that, he walked out.

I was leery of any Colombian pills, so I let it lay. The nurse and the policeman talked together and it was made known to me that the officer was staying for the night; right outside my door. They closed it, and I was alone. I was more alone than I ever had been.

There was a lamp on the stand next to my bed. I turned it off and relaxed. In my condition, all I could do was think.

Now that I was safe and the frightful last several hours had come to an end, I began to become bitter. "There go my underground grottos, and the mysterious cave that I knew would be one great legend. And now, what happens to me here? Alone, with only a couple hundred dollars left. And a smuggled gun to boot!"

Fortunately for me, sleeping pill or not, I quickly faded off to sleep. My body was smarter than my brain. It had suffered trauma and stress. Now it took over, banished my thoughts, and it fell asleep.

The sun was well up when I awoke from a near dead sleep.

The door to my room was open and several people were in conversation in the corridor beyond it. One of them looked up and realized that I was awake. They all trouped in. One took charge. He was dressed in a smart business suit. In good English, he addressed me, "Mr. Wilhelmsen," he had my passport in his hand, "how do you feel? Did you sleep well?"

I had slept well and, except for stiffness and the ache of my wound, I felt tolerably well. I told him so.

"Very good," he answered, "I am Inspector Angel Guttiérez of the Central Police of Popayán. We must have your story. Will you tell us how this all happened?" He was precise, yet very courteous.

I had confidence in him, and told him the story from first to last. One of the men had a wire recorder, and I saw that he was recording everything said.

"This is a very sad thing." Inspector Guttiérez sat down on my bed. "The man who you shot is one of a group of bandits who work with Negro Dalfin, a notorious revolutionist and enemy of the government. Those people all work with one Roberto González Prieto who has been trained in Cuba. Did this man that you shot mention any names to you?"

"He said one word, 'Maria'."

"No more? Is that all?"

"Nothing else."

My interrogator gave me a sheet of paper that contained the names of the above revolutionaries. There were several others listed; one of them was Ché Guevara. The investigators huddled together for a moment, then, "Why are you carrying guns with you in Colombia? I have found no permits issued to you. Why do you have a gun?" He indicated my trunk in the locker.

"To protect myself," I answered.

"From what?"

"From people like Negro Dalfin."

I had debated well and had won the debate. He smiled and in a much softer tone said, "You were lucky to have a gun up there in those hills. And so were the people in the bus lucky that you were there." He smiled briefly, stood up, and finished the discussion. "Of course, you will have to return to Bogotá where you will speak to the chiefs of Colombian Intelligence. They have questions to ask you, and of course, your United States Councilor services will guide you through the proper legal procedures. Please do not worry; it is merely a formality. I will be back here tomorrow at noon to tell you what arrangements have been made to take you to the capitol. Either Air Colombia or, better yet, a military plane. The doctor told me you will be able to travel in a couple of days." He extended his hand, and I took it.

All I could say as he and his men left was, "Thank you."

That night I hatched a plan to circumvent a return to Bogotá, and to get out of Colombia quickly.

Although I slept well despite the ache about the wound, I told the doctor that I felt terribly weak, dizzy, and disoriented. Especially when I stood up and did any walking.

This he relayed to Inspector Guttiérez when he came to see me at noon. The result of that was that any thought of moving me to the capitol city was postponed for several days. I was told that a military transport flew on the weekends and that arrangements had been made for me to be on one this coming Saturday. That gave me six days to come up with something.

I was being handled with soft gloves. Colombia was at that time promoting a large government sponsored advertising campaign hoping to lure foreign tourists and their money to come and to visit the country's many fine attractions. Tourists frown upon shootings, so my episode was being kept quite hush-hush. (Nevertheless, one wire had somehow picked up the story and a garbled version of it was broadcast in Spain. There my mother, who was visiting my brother Fritz in Avila, heard it.)

The inspector shook my hand and said that he would be traveling to Bogotá with me—I believe he had a mistress there—and that he would be looking in on me in a couple of days.

The doctor informed me that all I needed was a few days rest. He said he would be working in another hospital for a couple of days and would then check me out.

I wearily said, "*Gracias*" to both of them as they left the hospital.

I had my eye on a young teenager who had been emptying bed pans and doing such work around the facility. He and the part-time nurse seemed to be the only people there except for a couple of other patients. That afternoon, I asked the boy when the busses left for Cali. That city is quite large and sophisticated. It is some one hundred miles north of Popayán. (Today Cali is now headquarters for many of the cocaine cartels.) It is a place where one might become lost in its foreign population. There was method in my madness. I knew that the main bus terminal was near by, and I asked the youngster if he could get me and my luggage to it early the next morning. I showed him a ten dollar bill. "*No problema,*" he eagerly responded. "*Mañana a las tres.*" I made it as clear as my Spanish could make it that he was to tell no one.

I had noticed that the nurse, who was also the admitting committee, always left her station at midnight and did not return until 8:00 a.m. All was clear then at 3:00 a.m. when the young man came for me with a wheelbarrow. The wheelbarrow wasn't for me—I was not yet a basket case—but for my trunk and two bags. I was fortunate that my passport and my gun had been left in my trunk in the locker.

We stole out into the night, walked a couple of blocks, and came to the busy bus station. I followed signs to the Cali-Medellín busses, and made sure that my *mozo* was with me when I cashed a twenty-dollar traveler's check for *pesos* and bought my ticket to Cali. I then paid him off and he left.

Once he had disappeared in the crowds, I found the bus that would be traveling south to Pasto and Ipiales on the Ecuadorian border. With *pesos* I purchased a seat on that bus. My trunk was put aboard, and we were off at 4:30 a.m. I thought that I had covered my tracks rather thoroughly. Should anyone come looking for me, he would be looking north, not south. Even so, when we arrived at Pasto twelve hours later, I disembarked and hailed a *colectivo* that was ready to drive on south to Ipiales on the border. *Colectivos* are independently owned vehicles. No paper or tickets were involved. Two dollars and forty cents took me to the border at 7:30 p.m. A taxi took me across the bridge by the impressive Santuario De Nuestra Señora De Las Lajas. I placed my weapon beneath the car rug of the taxi and so arrived in Tulcán, Ecuador. This had become quite a busy border crossing; many local day workers cross it morning and night. I had none of the delays I had experienced in 1953. I flashed my U. S. passport and was waved on.

By 8:00 p.m. I was safely in a hotel enjoying a filet mignon steak.

(I have often thought of this "dash to freedom." I have come to the conclusion that Colombia at that time was very wary of any international incident. Especially with the United States. Nor did Colombia want the tourist world to know about their burgeoning bandit/revolution situation. I did us both a favor; I faded away. I have been back to Colombia several times since, and have never been questioned. My name, I suspect, was scratched from the records.)

However, now my side began to hurt like the furies. Blood and puss oozed from the bullet wound. I bought gauze, iodine, and tape from a drug store, and administered to myself.

I spent the following day in a room at the Granada Hotel, mostly in bed. I did slip out for meals and to send a wire to Ernesto Batanero in Trujillo. The little activity did me and my body good. The following day, I was ready to roll again. My wound had quieted down. I had picked up a Colombian newspaper and gone through it thoroughly. There was no mention of me or of my shoot-out.

Again, it was a *colectivo* that took me to Quito, Ecuador. During the nine and a half hour run, my wound acted up again. I would have loved to spend some time in this old and fascinating colonial city, but I was in no mood or condition to go sightseeing. I stayed in a $1.15 hotel close to the bus station, and was on my way at 7:00 the next morning for Riobamba. A night there in the familiar Hotel Metropolitano, and the next day at 6:15 I was on the train to Guayaquil. Once again, my seatmate was an Indian lady of ample proportion who juggled two babies. I was too tired to do anything about it; I slept most of the way to the waters of Guayaquil. The ferry boat there took me to the Peruvian border. The delays that Barbara Holbrook and I had experienced had been smoothed over, and mercifully, I finally found myself in the comparative luxury of the Turista Hotel of Tumbes, Peru.

Again, I lay over for a day. My wound and the left side of my body were aching, and my bandages needed constant changing. The traveling was not doing me any good. Nevertheless, with an almost manic obsession, I was determined to reach Trujillo. Without let up, I continued south on the Pan American Highway. Peru's buses were easier on me, and two nights later, I arrived at the Turista Hotel in Trujillo. It was 9:30 p.m. I hired a young boy to make a run for the Batanero house. And then I dozed in front of the big fireplace where Barbara and I once held hands.

I was asleep when I felt a tap on my shoulder and looked up in the face of a beautiful young woman. She was Maria Batanero, Nieves' oldest daughter. "*Señor* Romain," she eagerly said to me, "you are home." I began to cry.

Directly behind her was Nieves who hadn't changed one bit. Holding her hand was eight-year-old Robin. I have never—really never—been happier to see friends than I was at that moment.

"*Señor* Romain," Nieves embraced me. "*Qué pasa?*" She stood back when I didn't rise from the sofa. "What's wrong?"

Now the shock of the last week washed over me, and the tears rolled down my cheeks as I struggled up and faced my dear friend of past adventures. I steadied myself on Maria's arm but I could find no words. Not even English ones.

"*Por Dios*," Nieves suddenly cried out and stared at my leather buckskin shirt. It was saturated with fresh blood. The bandage had let go again.

I found my voice and weakly said, "I've been shot, Nieves. I've been shot."

"Don't talk," she demanded and loudly called a bellboy. He brought a taxi man over to us and, with Nieves, helped me into his car. I had gone weak, very weak. But, I was 'home.'

They drove me to the familiar Batanero house in Trujillo, and they guided me to the room and bed I had been in before. Their concern and care was a comfort and relief after a week of uncertainty.

"Where is Ernesto?" I finally asked between sips of hot chocolate. "Did he get my wire?" My mind had gone from overdrive back to a sort of normalcy. I wanted it to be as it was before all this happened.

"Ernesto is in Lima. He is to phone us tomorrow morning," Nieves answered me. Then she went to the phone—a new addition in the Batanero household—and dialed a number. "Doctor," she spoke into it, and I knew that Nieves was doing what she always did best: taking care of her men.

I had briefly explained my shoot-out to her and to Maria, and now I told the story to their friend the doctor Nieves had summoned. He cleaned up the wound. He looked into it and examined the surrounding area. I heard a frightful word that sounded like gangrene. I had caught it right, but I was assured that such had not settled into me. There was, however, a possibility. Nieves—who had the ability to converse with me in any language, in other words total rapport—now explained that I needed bed rest; no more activity for at least two or more weeks. If I continued to move about, the bullet hole could not close up properly. The wound would fester and might suffer any number of complications, even gangrene. She smiled and then laughed, "*Mi adventurero*, you must stay here with Maria and me. We will like that. Ernesto is now away so much in Lima. We need a good man in the house. You are the man."

"Not too good yet, Nieves." I tried to laugh back. Then the doctor hushed us both up. In effect, he said, "No laughing. Bad for the wound."

And so I began my convalescence. I was nursed back to health by two of the loveliest and most efficient nurses that I could have ever wanted.

Ernesto did phone the next morning, and the following day he was home. We had quite a reunion.

But, after the reunion was over, he settled back in his chair by the side of my bed and gave me the bad news: "Flynn cannot wait the two or three weeks that the doctor tells us you must remain inactive. The people who are to take you up into the mountain have only so much time. They have arranged their time for this month. They will not be available next month. Nieves told me what the doctor has said. She was adamant. You know Nieves. I have spoken to Santiago but he tells me it is out of his hands. You know he is not the manager anymore, not the big boss. We are not dealing with Uningambal anymore."

I asked him to repeat all that he had just said. He did.

All I could think was: 'Murphy's Law.' First I had lost the opportunity to visit and film the legend of the underground grotto at Tierradentro in Colombia and with it the waterfall that drops from the heavens to caves of marvelous things. And then I was banged up by bandits, and now I was being denied my adventure with Jimmy Flynn. I could only say, "Thanks, Ernesto, for trying."

"I know what you are thinking," he commented. "Your plans were made, and then changed. But, listen, there are yet things to do around here. *Señor* Flores, who loaned us the mules in 1953, tells me that while hunting in the mountains, he came across a boulder with the insignia of the Inca beautifully carved upon it. It could mean there are others, perhaps something worth looking into. We can go there. Any time. It could make you a good film. We could take Robbie along with us."

His last sentence stopped that adventure right there. Robbie was Ernesto's pride and joy eight-year-old daughter. A pretty and fine little girl. But, an adventure with her along . . . ? No way!

I still had my ace in the hole: Hermann Becker and a jungle trip. I would wait for that.

"Ernesto," I resignedly said, "I think I'll stay here if you'll have me . . . and I do doubt that Nieves will let me out of this bed for some time yet. I'll recuperate, and then go to the Amazon. In the meantime, we can play around with the metal detector that I left here. Maybe come up with something at Moche or in some old colonial house. I'm sure we can get new batteries for it."

My friend's face fell, and he made a confession. "*Señor* Romain, I do not have the detector any more. I sold it."

He looked at me as though I might lash out at him. I only shrugged and chalked it up as a by-product of Murphy's Law. Down deep I was pretty sure the contraption wasn't any good anyway.

Or was it?

"I have things for you to see. Things to give you for payment."

"You've paid me enough, Ernesto." I perked up a bit.

"I needed the money, *Señor* Romain. I needed it badly to keep my *Fábrica* going. I had befriended a group of Americans who had some sort of a clue or map where one of Atahualpa's treasures had been buried. It was in the mountains north of Trujillo, not in the Sechura where you and I went. They heard that I had a detector, and they came to me. I had hoped to become part of the group, but they only wanted the machine. I made them pay dearly for it. My business is now thriving."

He indicated that I wait a moment while he got up from his chair and went out of the room. He came back with five photographs. Each one showed a quantity of large golden cups and other treasures. "Those are things that were detected by your Goldak metal detector. I am sure they were part of the ransom that never reached Pizarro while he held the Inca Atahualpa captive."

"The gold at the end of the rainbow," I murmured to my friend as I fingered his photos. Neatly printed on the back of one of those pictures was this list of what was actually found:

"262 cups - 110 grams each
  30 cups - 3 kilos each
  20 kilos of 3/4 diameter gold balls
  60 necklaces of turquoise, gold, and pearls
   7 idols app. 1 kilo each with stones
   3 masks

19 feet below a small 15' by 20' adobe room, neatly stacked around. Ruins of solid adobe buildings in block room."

"When Francisco Pizarro captured the Inca Atahualpa on November 16, 1532, he held him in a room that was 22 feet long and 17 feet wide. He asked for a ransom of gold. The emperor reached his arm up as high as he could and proclaimed that he would fill the room with gold that high. This measured about 8 feet. Runners were sent out throughout the Empire, mainly to the capitol city Cuzco. Temples were cleaned out of their idols and golden vessels. Great slabs of gold were stripped from the Inca's private chambers. Tons of the stuff were caravanned on the backs of llamas south to the city of Cajamarca where the treasure room was located. That room began to fill up; it exceeded the conquistadors wildest dreams. Apparently, the Costillians had conquered a kingdom even richer than Hernán Cortez's fabled Aztec Empire. Unfortunately, rumors were heard by the Spaniards that the Inca was plotting his escape and was secretly preparing a huge army for the destruction of Pizarro's two hundred-odd men. Atahualpa had himself been a ruthless conqueror; and now his fate was sealed. He was garroted. In effect, Pizarro said, "If the gold can come to us, we can go to the gold." However, the old tough-as-leather conquistador had miscalculated. With Atahualpa's death, the flow of gold abruptly ceased. The gold-ladened llamas were turned away from Cajamarca. Their burdens were hid, buried, secreted, or just dumped at any convenient place. All historians of the Peruvian conquest concede that most of that treasure is still out there somewhere: in the mountains, in the jungles, in the deserts, even beneath some of the cities that were yet to be built. It is all out there waiting. And those Americans, with my metal detector had just found one of those hoards.

"They had a private plane and flew off with it all." Ernesto shook his head. (The best-selling author Harold Robbins coauthored a book about that caper.)

"With my detector," I grumbled.

"But, my friend, let up. In that room where the gold was were also some of the finest *huacas* or pottery that I have ever seen. The American men wanted no part of those things; they were only after the gold. They gave me quite a quantity of Lambayaqui earthenware. Their room had been part of a long abandoned pre-Inca temple. Please take three of those pieces as payment for the detector. They are worth much more than it was."

Several days later, when I was feeling stronger, Ernesto took me to his secret storeroom. He unlocked the door and showed me shelf after shelf of beautiful 1500-year-old perfectly preserved pieces of pottery. I took my three, and eventually got them home (Sotheby's auction house has put a price on each of them of $12,000 a piece.)

My letter to Becker in Iquitos was promptly answered. The German was extremely reliable. He informed me that a military plane was to fly to the remote Tigre River with several anthropologists to visit and to study the Zaparo Indians. They would be making contact with a very primitive tribe. My films would be a first. The trip would be highly publicized. He finished with, "I do not foresee any dangers."

I felt much better after his response. I relaxed. Three weeks later, I felt well enough to take the one-day horseback ride into the foothills of the Andes with Ernesto, Robbie, and Maria. We did locate the large boulder with a beautiful line drawing of a condor etched into it. What it meant and what it was doing there, we never did determine.

Another note from Becker suggested that I go to Lima to pick up papers from the Agency of Indian Affairs. These would grant me permission to visit the Zaparo Indians. He added, "and then come to Iquitos."

I was glad to be on the road again, to be doing something. Nieves went with me. She and I threw a blanket over us to keep the night air out, and boarded the nocturnal bus for Lima. Ernesto followed two days later. We arrived safely at 7:00 a.m., and took rooms at the Savoy Hotel. Nieves went into town to the Batanero office, and I put in a phone call to Jimmy Flynn. I was unable to contact him, and so I took care of my permit. Hermann had greased the way for me.

I then went to a bookstore that I knew. Past experience had advised me to be prepared. As exotic as those jungle river trips might be, they can also be very boring: hour after hour of the sameness. I had selected a couple of thick novels and was perusing another when I heard the lilting sound of a Gaelic accent. "No, my dear, I do believe he'll be taking that one there, the western book. From what I hear he's the fastest draw east of the Andes."

I spun around and kept spinning as Santiago Jimmy Flynn embraced me and actually picked me up. "Romain, 'tis you!" he said. "I've been calling the hotel. Nieves told me you were here."

I was overjoyed to see this very welcome face and to experience again his jovial ways. A very attractive, willowy blond woman joined us and spoke out cheerfully. "I guess it was just plain destiny that you two would meet out here in the streets of Lima."

We turned to her and Jimmy said, "Nuria, this is my good friend, Romain." To me, "This is my wife, Nuria."

I stuck out my hand, but she preferred a hug. Nieves had told me that Flynn had remarried and I now realized why she had said, "She's someone you take a second look at." I got corny, "Jimmy, you not only had the prettiest mule in the Andes, now you've got the prettiest bride in Lima."

He leaned back and let out a hearty laugh. "You remember," he laughed again.

"Mule," she said. "What's this about a mule? Am I now being compared to your stockyard, Jimmy?"

Again we all laughed and strolled down the Union Jiron Street to the nearest lounge.

Over a tall highball, Jimmy and I renewed our acquaintance. I came to know and to appreciate his wife.

She was from Chile, and spoke perfect English. "I come from way down south. My family owns the southernmost cattle ranch in South America."

Jimmy broke in, "Her father boasts the most southern working commode in the world." Nuria gave him a kick, and I knew that I was going to like her father.

The long and the short of our meeting was that two days later, we joined forces and took the Faucett plane to Cuzco and then the little train and shuttle bus through the Urubamba Valley to the famous lost city of the Incas, Machu Picchu. Once there, we were all having such good rapport that I nearly didn't get the films that I wanted. In deed, I did enjoy her father and mother.

From the little hotel at Machu Picchu, one cannot see the ruins. It was justifiably built that way. A footpath takes one from the modern world of dinner parties and cocktails to an opening in the nearby mountains. Beyond that, and out of sight of the hotel, suddenly the path ends and one is confronted by acres and acres of stone buildings. They are really not 'ruins' because they have all been restored to the appearance they had before the Spanish Conquest. There are better descriptions of Machu Picchu than I could attempt, so I will leave that to the many books relating to the tourism of Peru. Suffice it for me to say that only once in my travels have I been so impressed with such a scene of past and remote history. (That other awesome view was the sight of a dead Dogon city hanging from the cliffs of the Bandiagara Mountains in the sub Saharan Desert of Africa.)

With great *abrazos*, I left my friends on this mountaintop in Peru, and traveled alone back to Cuzco and to Lima.

A message awaited me at the Savoy to immediately call Ernesto. This I did, and there collapsed the last of my great expectations for 1960.

Ernesto insisted I meet him at his office. This I did.

"*Señor* Romain, have you seen the newspaper?"

"No, I hadn't."

He had the *Commercio* ready. The headlines on the second page read: "Zaparo Indians on a rampage. The army is prepared to move. The country there is under martial law. All travel in the region is suspended. Ecuador suspects a Peruvian takeover of its borders. Mobilization!"

Those headlines in bold letters, almost duplicating today's scandal tabloids, were in all the Peruvian papers. The words that riveted my attention were, "All Travel Suspended."

I had very little to say to my friend except, "Murphy's Law is well and thriving." My Amazon trip was out. And, sure enough, that evening, I received a radiogram from Hermann Becker. "Impossible to travel to destination. Very bad Indian trouble. Maybe next year. Regards."

I flew home to the States with little to show for my months of "Legend Hunting" except a nasty bullet hole and three very valuable pre-Inca relics.

EPILOGUE

History is often what one wants it to have been.

Upon my return home from South America in 1960, I had quite a change of heart regarding the profession that I had enjoyed for six years and that had fueled my adventures' momentum. It is said that man does not often realize the absolute danger he is experiencing until it is over. When he does, he begins to see it for what it was, and then he begins to tremble. It took several months of recuperation with Ernesto and Nieves and then the collapse of my well-made plans with Flynn and Becker, and then my return home to confront my wife and family, before the realization of how close I had come to not returning at all finally set in. As Julie changed my bandage—it was still discharging—I realized that but two inches separated the aim of my weapon and the one that was used against me. I did not want to think of that. I dearly wished I could have changed it. The still vivid memory of 1955 and the motorist Ferdie and his chopped up body seemed to tie in with this recent life-and-death experience. I began to wonder. Living close to the edge was one thing, but was I living on the edge? Would I come back the next time?

❖❖❖

Although this last trip did not produce a film, the publicity that it received put me right in the celebrity class—at least locally. The Los Angeles and the Pasadena newspapers, and others too, made much of my shoot-out. This was a time, 1960, before the random killings and school shootings of today have jaded the media and the nation. I was reluctant to go over and over the events of that fateful morning in the Cardillero Central of Colombia. I didn't feel right talking about it. Nevertheless, my adventure was thrust upon me time and time again. Especially, when I went on my lecture tour in October. If I wasn't asked to tell the story before my film presentation, I was asked to relate it afterwards at some cocktail party in my honor.

A film lecturer will use a film for at least three years, sometimes more. The season begins in October and ends in spring, usually by May. Depending on the subject, a lecturer could make about a hundred forty appearances. Fewer and fewer adventure films were produced in the early sixties. World War II was long past, and people were traveling more and more. They tended to want mainly European subjects. An adventure film had to be really exciting. The public is pretty astute, and those who attempted to stage a hazardous film sequence were most always caught up in it. Jack Douglas' *I Search For Adventure* TV series was having trouble coming up with authentic stories.

Audiences, too, were becoming discriminate. Speakers were receiving personal critiques, not only from our sponsors, but also from audiences. Good reviews got you invited back. Bad ones kept you out. I have a few of those reviews in front of me.

"An extremely interesting, entertaining, and worthwhile presentation." (The Chicago Geographical Society)

"His tuxedo was shabby." (Nothing else.) (The Chicago South Shore Country Club)

"The man has a golden voice; he doesn't need a film." (New York Town Hall)

"Mr. Wilhelmsen should take a course in public speaking; his films are fine, but he gets on my nerves when he talks." (Patterson, New Jersey)

"I've traveled the Sahara Desert for twenty years; that man tells it the way it is." (A letter from Richmond, Virginia)

"I flew over the Sahara on my recent round the world cruise. Wilhelmsen doesn't know what he's talking about." (Orlando, Florida)

"He called it a Russian plane; it was a French plane." (Kokomo, Indiana)

"He claims he was shot by a bandit. How come he doesn't have any film on that?" (Seattle)

"Makes you want to leave town with him." (Petersburg, Florida)

"Not very exciting." (Jacksonville, Florida)

"Very exciting." (Ottumwa, Minnesota)

"Don't send him again." (Burlington, Iowa)

"Would like to see other travelogues by this one." (Delphos, Ohio)

"Not enough appeal to a complete audience." (Hamilton, Ontario)

"Very favorable audience reaction." (Metropolis, Illinois)

"Talked too fast." Sedalia, Missouri)

"Narration excellent." (Pontiac, Illinois)

It was a profession that was both easy and hard on the ego. The money came in fast and went out just as quickly.

One thing for me was certain. In the aftermath of my shooting drama, nothing would do for me but to seek another adventure. An honest, straightforward, hazardous, life threatening, and daredevil enterprise. Or, at least something a bit more exciting than Colorful Colorado or Wonderful Wyoming or Sunny Spain.

I did give the strict travelogue phase of the business a try and took the family on a marvelous vacation to the State of New Mexico, one of my favorite places. Yet, my style and story telling just wasn't appropriate for the subject. The film received little favorable comment, and the word was: "We thought he was going to give us something exciting, not just a rundown on Route 66."

I continued to receive letters from Ernesto. They were loaded with ideas. Not quite as often, but occasionally, Jimmy Flynn would pen me a note. One did, and still does, intrigue me: "Romain, I have it on very good authority that there are the remains of a jungle mountain city overlooking the Lake of the Condor along the eastern Andes. That is not far from where your friend, the German, wanted to fly with you a couple years ago. It is between the Huayabamba and the Utcubamba Rivers. Indians say there are caves with buildings in them and chulpas all over the place . . . I just might be able to get away from my duties here and take a couple weeks if you are interested."

Indeed, I was interested, but I also realized one film lecture on pre-Inca ruins was all that audiences wanted out of me for some while. (Thirty-five years later, the prolific Andean explorer, Gene Savoy, led a forty-six member expedition into that region and discovered the remains of the ancient Chachapoya civilization that had been conquered by the rapacious Incas. Shortly thereafter, the National Geographical Society jumped on his story.)

The testosterone or macho in me, plus a big dose of curiosity, was stimulated by these letters. I began to reread the notes that I had been keeping for all of my adult life. With a much more mature and practiced eye, I sifted the fancy from the fact. There were a lot of places to see, and perhaps a discovery for me yet to make without the attendant threat of finality. I consulted Dana Lamb, the old and very successful adventurer. We began to make plans. I informed my lecture people that I was preparing a trip that would have audiences sitting on the edge of their seats. The 1960s saw an older, wiser, but still impressionable teller of tales on the United States lecture circuit.

In 1961, Dana Lamb and I decided to do a film on the Amazon River. Not a travelogue, but a real adventure. We went down the Amazon on a raft.

In 1963, my wife Julie and I discovered a grotto in a deep cave close to Oxkutzcab, Yucatan. It contained a six-hundred-year-old Mayan altar with invaluable relics.

Two years later, my old friend, Truman Smith—of the *Haunted Fort* source—and I flew a 1939 antique monoplane over the Arizona and old Mexico border seeking the 'Lost Peg Leg Smith' gold mine. With but seconds to spare, we skedaddled out of Mexico with the Mexican border police right behind us. The following year, I stood with revolver in hand while some thirty-eight angry Yaqui Indians charged their horses toward me and my family. I had been filming one of their ancient ceremonies.

In 1968, there was the return to the San Agustín statues in cocaine war-torn Colombia. Julie and Dana Lamb were with me. With the help and protection of the Colombian Cavalry, we rode far enough into the mountains to see that "Waterfall that drops from the Heavens."

Shortly after that, in 1969, I was to meet with and to dance with the most exquisitely beautiful woman I have ever seen in person or in picture: A Falani African princess on the Niger River of the Dark Continent. And then to follow that river to the city of Timbuktu and beyond it to the most spectacular site of all, the deserted Dogon city hanging from the cliffs of the Bandiagara Mountains of Mali in Africa.

A return to Lake Titicaca in 1972 with my wife for a more in-depth study of the enigmatic city of Tiahuanaco, and a visit to the Islands of the Sun and the Moon on that highest of all lakes, took me back to Bolivia.

South of the Atlas Mountains of Algeria in the burning sands of the Sahara is the lost tomb of Mulai Reshed the sultan who conquered Morocco in 1668. His treasures were buried with him in the once prosperous capitol of North Africa, the city of Sijilmassa. That city boasted a population of a quarter of a million. It was once the crossroads of the caravan routes coming up from tropical Africa through the trackless sands of the Sahara. When we finally came to it in 1975, there was little more than acres of crumbling ruins stretching for two miles along the banks of the River Ziz. How close to the tomb we were, I'll never know.

In that region, we were stranded in 130-degree heat when our vehicle refused to move on towards the 200-year-old Roman City the Bedouins had told us of. That was an adventure the audiences savored.

And I have returned to the source of it all, and to my old illegal ways when I joined up with that master *hucero*—who else but Ernesto Batanero—and went to digging in the world's largest pyramid, the Huaca De Sol not far from Trujillo. Julie was with me on that one in 1982.

These and other adventures came about after my hesitation following the shoot-out in Colombia's Cordilleron.

I have a document and map that Jimmy Flynn sent me a while back. It is the approximate location of some prehistoric city east of the Andes Mountains. It is not the cave ruins mentioned earlier, but it could be the mysterious city that the grand old English explorer Col. Percy Harrison Fawcett was seeking before he disappeared in the Mato Grosso of Brazil in 1924. I'd like to have a crack at that before I call it quits. Just like I'd like to return to the Mexican Sierra Madres for a look-see for the lost Jesuit Mission of Santa Isohel. I think I still have time.

Regrets? I do have a few. The cave with the circles of mummies in it "four more days" from Huasachuga. I would liked to have followed up on that one. And, I would like someday to return to the Mochica City in the Sechura Desert where Ernesto and I dug into the tomb of the twenty-four skulls. He can't make that trek anymore; he went on his final adventure at age 84. He waited too long to somehow circumvent the laws and the regulations of the Peruvian archaeological society. I keep the map that we made to that location in a safe place. Occasionally, I take it out and relive that adventure. The valley and the cave of armor: I have regretted not going farther into the mountains. There must be more there than Sergio and I brought out. And what became of the bag of gold dust that the Spaniards had collected? The Tarahumara and Apache had no interest in it. It might be there yet. I wonder, too, what caused Father Trampas' metal detector to "go into orbit" when he passed it over the ruins of the Jesuit way station of San José Huacaibo? Unfinished business!

One other regret: I am sorry that I never followed through on my brief encounter with Barbara Holbrook. She would have been worth it. That I can guarantee.

Photograph by Dr. Alexandra Wilhelmsen

Romain Wilhelmsen supported himself on these and other solo expeditions to Mexico, South and Central America, and Africa by filming documentaries and adventure travelogues...and by reporting to the CIA. He was often referred to as the "Indiana Jones of the Travelogue-Lecture Circuit." He is a past director of the Los Angeles Adventurers Club, and has been the recipient of the prestigious I Search for Adventure, Golden Voyage, and Bold Journey television awards. Jack Douglas, the producer of these films, gave him the title of "The Legend Hunter." Romain makes his home in East Lansing, Michigan in the shade of Michigan State University where he has lectured in the past. He writes historical novels, and lives with the memories of his late wife and with the momentos of his incredible adventures. Occasionally he will point to a map, and say, "I just might go back there." He is the author of two other Sunstone Press books: *BUCKSKIN AND SATIN* and *CURSE OF DESTINY.*

www.ingramcontent.com/pod-product-compliance
Lightning Source LLC
Chambersburg PA
CBHW032036080426
42733CB00006B/100